Paradox of Freedom:

A History of Black Slaveholders in America

By

Larry Allen McCluney, Jr.

The Paradox of Freedom

Paradox of Freedom:
A History of Black Slaveholders in America

by Larry Allen McCluney, Jr.

Copyright © 2025 Larry Allen McCluney, Jr.

All Rights Reserved

First Printing

The Scuppernong Press
PO Box 1724
Wake Forest, NC 27587
www.scuppernongpress.com

Printed in the United States of America

No part of this book may be reproduced or transmitted in any form or by any means, electronic or mechanical, including photocopying, recording, or by any information and storage and retrieval system, without written permission from the editor and/or publisher.

International Standard Book Number
 Hardback ISBN 978-1-942806-78-3
 Paperback ISBN 978-1-942806-77-6

Library of Congress Control Number:
2025919718

Table of Contents

Dedication iv

Acknowledgment v

Preface ix

Chapter 1: The Shadows of Freedom: Introducing Black Slaveholding in America 1

Chapter 2: Free Black Slaveholders in Colonial America, 1526 – 1787 28

Chapter 3: Black Masters in the Early American Republic, 1780-1830 70

Chapter 4: The Rise of the Free Black Elite, 1830 – 1850 91

Chapter 5: Social and Economic Motivations 115

Chapter 6: Legal and Moral Issues: Navigating the Laws and Jurisprudence of Slave Holding 140

Chapter 7: The Emancipation Echo: The War Between the States and Aftermath 163

Chapter 8: Conclusion: An Author's View 193

Appendices 198

Endnotes 247

Bibliography 285

Index 305

About the Author 311

Dedication

This book is dedicated to the memory of all Free Black slaveholders, whose lives and experiences have been largely overlooked in the historical narrative. Their stories, though often hidden or obscured, offer a glimpse into the complexities of race, power, and freedom in antebellum America. Their choices, their struggles, and their legacies deserve to be remembered and understood. This work is a small attempt to honor their memory and to shed light on their lives and present their historical place in America's story, with insight, respect, and understanding.

Acknowledgments

I am indebted to several people for providing invaluable assistance in the completion of this project. First a great friend from Australia, Gerry Lefurgy. Gerry has given me non-biased advice and insight that I will never forget. His viewpoints as a historian are invaluable which are refreshing and inspiring.

I would like to thank Dr. Curt Fields (a.k.a. General Ulysses S. Grant) for his support as a fellow living historian, his sustaining encouragement to add to the body of knowledge, and, above all, his insight and sense of perspective regarding this project, and others in the past. To quote Dr. Fields, *"We as living historians are to remember, respect, and revere the deeds of these men who fought because they gave their all for a cause they believed was worth dying for. I am pleased."* It was Dr. Fields who encouraged me to take on the persona of General P.G.T. Beauregard at living history events. During those events, we have shared many conversations about Grant and Beauregard while in first-person character as well as out of character. Dr. Fields has also been a huge supporter of my writing, an inspiration, and I feel fortunate enough to call him my friend. Just remember to watch out for the flanking maneuver I always have up my sleeve general, you never know where I will "roll up" that Federal army of yours.

I also want to give a special thanks to Gerry Lefurgy, my good friend from Australia. Gerry and I have not met in person but we communicate by the internet and facetime on many occasions. He has become a fan of Dr. Fields and I for our living history programs and our writings. Gerry has been instrumental to this work for his selfless volunteering to edit this project and give great insight from a nonbiased viewpoint. He has a keen holistic viewpoint on this work and I thank him from the bottom of my heart.

The Paradox of Freedom

I want to express my appreciation to the Department of History at Mississippi State University for allowing me to realize my full potential as a historian. Special thanks goes to Dr. William Parrish (My wife thinks he looks like Mark Twain) for believing in me all those years ago and encouraging me to write history with passion. Without your encouragement, I would not be in the position I am at this moment in my life as an educator and a historian. Thank you for your guidance, encouragement, and insight.

I would like to express my gratitude to the McCabe family for allowing Henry to be my inspiration for writing. Henry was a local Civil War historian in Greenwood, Mississippi, a fellow reenactor, and my friend. His humorous stories, research (that he was kind enough to share with me in my first two books), and his inspirational personality will never be forgotten. Henry died on May 9, 2018, and I miss him still.

Thanks also goes to a very close friend and considered family, George Conor Bond, for his honest opinions and insight as this project proceeded in the beginning stages.

Finally, an incredibly special expression of appreciation goes to three important people who have shaped my life and made me the person I am today; my parents, Mary, and Larry McCluney Sr., and my loving wife, Julia "Annette" McCluney. First my father who has always been there for me, supporting me and encouraging me throughout my life. I remember the pictures he took of me as a baby being held by my mother while I sat on a cannon on Ruggles' line at Shiloh National Military Park and the pictures of him posing in front of the monuments. It was through him that I inherited my interest and passion for history. I always remembered growing up listening to him telling stories he had heard from older relatives about the past that has fueled this passion I have developed about history. As a result, it has defined me as the person I have become. He passed away on August 16, 2020, the day after my birthday and I miss him very much. I still find myself today wanting to call him up and ask for advice and opinions. I will always remember your love, encouragement, and support.

Second, my mother, Mary, passed away on April 14, 2022. My mother gave me the support and encouragement that any mother gives to their children, but most of all, I want to thank her for her inspiration to make my dreams a reality. (Even though she was a transplanted Yankee. That's all right mom, we know where your heart is.) She was always proud of me and my various accomplishments throughout life and always bragged about me to other people. It was her way of showing how proud she was of me. I miss you to this day mom.

My parents and I as a child in 1966 at Shiloh National Military Park. *Courtesy of Larry McCluney, Sr.*

To my wife Annette, who has always supported all my projects (as if she had a choice with all my crazy ideas), giving me encouragement, motivation, and the support to see it through. If not for you and your mom, Barbra Nell, encouraging me to go back to school to get my Masters' degree, I would not be the educator, writer, and historian I am today. Oh, and my dog Delta, who kept me company in my office while I was doing research and writing. She was great to have near when I got writer's block and just needed a distraction so I could refocus.

(Delta, please quit squeaking your ball while I am writing. I cannot concentrate.)

There are others that helped as well with advice and inspiration too numerous to list here. Thank you for your love and support.

Preface

The American South, a region steeped in the history of slavery, is often associated with a rigid social hierarchy defined by race and power. White slaveholders, at the apex of this hierarchy, exerted absolute control over the lives of enslaved Africans. But within this seemingly monolithic system, a complex and often overlooked phenomenon existed: Free Black slaveholders. These individuals, free by birth or through emancipation, owned and controlled enslaved people, defying the seemingly simple categorization of the South as a society divided solely between White masters and enslaved Africans.

The existence of free Black slaveholders challenges our conventional understandings of the antebellum South. It prompts us to question the rigidity of the racial hierarchy, to consider the multifaceted nature of freedom, and to recognize the complexities of power dynamics within a system built on the foundation of forced labor.

This book delves into the little-known history of Free Black slaveholders, exploring the social, economic, and legal factors that shaped their lives and experiences. It examines their motivations, their relationships with both the White slaveholding class and the enslaved population, and the impact of their status as slaveholders on their lives, their acceptance within the community, and their place in the social hierarchy after the Civil War.

Drawing on archival research and primary sources, the book sheds light on a nuanced and often overlooked aspect of American history, challenging conventional narratives and providing a more complete understanding of the complexities of race, power, and freedom in the United States. It aims to tell the story of these individuals, their choices,

The Paradox of Freedom

their struggles, and their legacies, in order to provide a richer, and more accurate, understanding of the American past.

Chapter 1:
The Shadows of Freedom:
Introducing Black Slaveholding in America

"The aim of this report on the free Negro is to facilitate the further study of this neglected group. Most of these people have been forgotten, for persons supposedly well-informed in history are surprised to learn today that about a half million, almost one-seventh of the Negroes of this country, were free prior to the emancipation in 1865. It is hardly believed that a considerable number of Negroes were owners of slaves themselves, and in some cases controlled large plantations."

- Carter G. Woodson, April 1, 1924[1]

It is difficult to digest the concept of free Blacks owning slaves in America, but numerous records indicate that thousands of Free People of Color in the United States before 1865 did in fact own slaves. Not only did they own slaves but, in some instances, they harshly disciplined and sold their slaves. In other instances, Black slave owners treated their slaves benevolently, and ultimately freed them. How and why, they acted as they did was bound with the reasons why they became *"Black Masters"* in the first place.

This *"peculiar institution"* as it has been widely referred to, encompasses many different facets that make it particularly *"peculiar."* Among these is the existence of a third class within the black slave-free white Antebellum society of free Black American slaveholders. Though their origins varied, this group managed to clearly distinguish themselves from the slave class and live among the affluent White class creating a prosperous social class made up of Free People of Color, who owned sizable property, including slaves. This very idea challenges ingrained narratives about slavery in the United States, forcing us to confront a complex and often uncomfortable realizations about our nation's past. This phenomenon, though rarely discussed in historical accounts, played a significant role in shaping the social and economic landscape of early America and the antebellum South. How and why they acted demands a careful examination, not just to understand the motivations and experiences of these individuals, but also to unravel the complex relationship between race, power, and freedom in a society deeply divided by the institution of slavery.[2]

This story about a large number of free Negro slaveholders in America has become a lost chapter and almost forgotten. The full data for this long lost chapter has never been collected, and probably never will be in an exhaustive way. Much material on this subject has perished through the ravages of time and the generations that were familiar with this condition have long gone. The facts have not only their own kind of interest, but they throw light upon the economic and industrial condition of the free negroes before Abraham Lincoln's Emancipation Proclamation.

When President Lincoln signed that paper he by the same pen reduced to comparative poverty many Black people who thus lost possession of their bondsmen. Some of these were pure blacks; some were mulattoes; while still others had in them only enough African to classify themselves with that race, according to social decree that a drop of African blood makes a negro, or as Booker T. Washington phrases it, *"makes him fall to their pile."* [3] According to Calvin D. Wilson, author of *Creating Black Masters, A Side-Light on Slavery* (1904), many of these Black slave masters owned from one to a dozen slaves, while others had in servitude from sixty to a hundred or two hundred men, women and children. These were to be found at one period or another, in nearly all, if not quite all, the colonies or states where slaves were held. In some counties they were numerous, while in others they were unknown. In certain states this condition was at times forbidden by law, but often continued in spite of the law, tolerated or ignored; the laws upon the subject also varied from time to time. In other states, free

Negroes were given the privilege of being masters by special statute or this liberty was covered by general laws.[4]

Wilson reported in his research that B. F. Jonas, of New Orleans, wrote to him and stated:

A great many slaves were owned by free Blacks before the war, not only in this State, but throughout the South. In this State, there were quite a large number of colored slave-owners, most of whom were of the class known as 'quadroons' but some of them were mulattoes and full-blood negroes, who, as a rule, inherited property and afterward added to it, probably by purchase. Free Colored People had a right to the ownership and possession of slave property, as well as movable property and other real estate, slave property having been considered real estate under our laws at that period. I have never heard of a case where a free Black owner of slaves voluntarily manumitted his slaves. On the contrary, they were as a rule considered hard task masters, who got out of their slave property all that they could. I suppose that proof of this and the names of slave-owners could be obtained from an examination of the assessment rolls of the City of New Orleans and the parishes, previous to the war; but this is so long ago that the information could probably not be obtained without a great deal of labor and investigation.[5]

A certain number of these slaveholders became such by inheritance through White relatives; others by gift; and still others by purchase after the manner of their Caucasian neighbors. In some instances they owned members of their families, as husbands their wives and children, and in other cases the wives owned husbands and children, and again children owned their parents, in order to protect them or ultimately to set them free; the complicated legislation in regard to free Negroes at various times and in various places often made it difficult for a free member of a family to manumit the others; sometimes when so liberated they had to be sent out of their state. A large number were owners of slaves without regard to relationships and held them for service and bought and sold them just as did the White people.

For many years, historians have virtually given little attention to how Blacks had reached the upper crust of the economic level in the pre-War South. Most had completely ignored the records of free Black landowners and prosperous Black businesspeople. In 2003, Pulitzer Prize winning author Edward P. Jones released his popular, yet controversial novel, *The Known World,* about Black slaveholders. The novel stirred interest among historians and other scholars on this peculiar subject leading to the discovery of records of slaveholding among Blacks dating from the colonial period through the antebellum era. Such records include wills in which Black slave owners left slave property to family members or friends; deeds of emancipation required when slave owners manumitted their slaves; bills of sale recording the purchase and sale of slaves; court records detailing suits disputing ownership of slave property; and personal papers referring to slave ownership. Some early historians saw free Black slave ownership in semi- positive terms, because it meant that free Blacks had the economic and legal ability to own slaves while others attacked these findings with racist assumptions.[6]

Much of our nation's history that is taught today in classrooms is contextualized when it comes to sensitive topics like the system of slavery that was imposed on African Americans for 250 years. What we know, what we do not know, and what we choose to remember, erase, or forget, has become a common practice in American schools today. Thus, when it comes to such controversial questions in American history many students and historians are surprised when they learn that some free Blacks actually owned slaves. Because of this, many are skeptical about the number of free Black slave owners that existed and the number of slaves they actually owned.

The Paradox of Freedom

The legal institution of human chattel slavery, comprising the enslavement primarily of Africans and African Americans, was prevalent in the United States of America from its colonial period until 1865, predominantly in the South. From 1526, during the early colonial period, it was practiced in the European colonies in America and what became Britain's Thirteen Colonies that formed the United States. The institution would carry on even after the American Revolution and existed in every state in the United States until the early 19th Century, as some states gradually abolished the practice. Under the law, an enslaved person was treated as property that could be bought, sold, or given away. Slavery, as an active day to day practice, lasted in about half of the United States until its abolition in 1865 with the 13th Amendment to the Constitution.[7]

By the time of the American Revolutionary War (1775–1783), the status of enslaved people had been institutionalized as a racial caste associated with African ancestry. Alongside this *"peculiar institution"*, slavery as we know it, encompassed a third caste within White Antebellum society. Though its origins vary, they clearly distinguish themselves as an affluent group made up of free people of color, who owned sizable property and slaves. Because of this hidden fact about slavery, many believed it was an institution exclusively utilized by White slaveowners. In fact, by 1830 this third caste of wealthy free African Americans numbered just over 3,000 and owned over 12,000 slaves, along with hundreds of thousands of land acreage. In St. John the Baptist Parish, Louisiana, three free Black plantation owners held an average of forty-six slaves each; likewise, in Pointe Coupee Parish, Louisiana, eight planters had about thirty-seven slaves each. These numbers alone directly challenge the commonly held belief that slave owning was based strictly on racial distinctions: That Whites owned slaves and Blacks were slaves.[8]

The fact that free Black people owned slaves has been essentially lost in the annals of history surprises many when evidence is uncovered.

The Paradox of Freedom

Historians like Carter G. Woodson, Abram Harris, Merah Stuart, Luther Porter Jackson, John Hope Franklin, and Vernon Lane Wharton to name a few, briefly mention free Blacks who had acquired property.[9] This lack of focus may have been a result of the 1960s and 1970s focus on the Black experience such as *"racial exploitation, black culture and black consciousness, and the political activities of Blacks during Reconstruction than with those who achieved financial success."*[10]

Dr. Carter G. Woodson' "Father of Black History Month", *Image comes from the Public Domain*

The comparatively lack of scholarly attention, in the face of a large amount of historical evidence, begs numerous questions, *"How many black "masters" were involved, how many slaves did they own, and why did they own them?"* Historians have been arguing for some time over whether free blacks purchased family members as slaves in order to protect them, motivated by benevolence and philanthropy, as historian Carter G. Woodson put it, or whether they purchased other black people primarily to exploit their free labor for profit, just as white slave owners did. The evidence shows that, unfortunately, both reasons are true.[11] African-American historian John Hope Franklin stated this position clearly when he said, *"The majority of Negro owners of slaves had some personal interest in their property."* But, he admits, *"there were instances . . . in which free Negroes had a real economic interest in the institution of slavery and held slaves in order to improve their status."*[12]

Larry Koger in his groundbreaking text *Black Slaveowners: Free Black Masters in South Carolina, 1790–1860* also disputes the dominant narrative propagated by Woodson and his disciples:

The Paradox of Freedom

When Carter G. Woodson asserted that free blacks purchased slave relatives and friends, he was quite correct. However, free blacks who held loved ones bought other slaves to be exploited for profit. To classify these transactions as benevolent would be a mistake. Even though these slaveowners usually demonstrated benevolent behavior towards their slave relations and friends, a commercial and materialistic exchange existed between them and their slaves purchased as investments. In fact, the free blacks who maintained a dual relationship with their slaves had no universal commitment against slavery. To them, slavery was an oppressive institution when it affected a beloved relative or a trusted friend, but beyond that realm, slavery was viewed as a profit-making institution to be exploited.[13]

Other historians are just now uncovering more research and asks us not to be shocked that Blacks in America expressed an interest in owning slaves, as summarized by Calvin Wilson:

The Negroes brought with them from their native land African ideas and customs. Many of those who brought thence to America had been slaves in their own lands. Others had been owners of slaves in Africa. In both cases, they were used to slavery. It did not, therefore, seemed unnatural for a Negro in America to hold his brethren in bondage when he had become free and able to buy his fellows.[14]

Ronald E. Hall's publication, *An Historical Analysis of Skin Colour Discrimination: Victimism among Victim Group Populations,* points out that like White slave owners, some Black slave owners were notorious for their brutality. This challenges the belief that black owners were always humane using the example of William Ellison:

William Ellison is prominent for both his wealth and the cruelty toward his black slaves, for which he was known among Southern blacks and whites. Historians for whatever reasons have attempted to justify his version of victim-group discrimination perhaps as a matter of political correctness.[15]

If one assumes that Hall's commentary on Ellison is an anomalous case, then maybe this condemnation of black slave owners by a Louisiana slave featured in Frederick Law Olmstead's *Journeys and Explorations in the Cotton Kingdom* will change your perspective and clearly show how untenable Woodson's view is indefensible:

You might think, master, dat dey would be good to dar own nation; but dey is not. I will tell you de truth, massa; I know I'se got to answer; and it's a fact, dey is very bad masters, sar. I'd rather be a servant to any man in de world, dan to a brack man. If I was sold to a brack man, I'd drown myself. I would dat—I'd drown myself! Dough I shouldn't like to do dat nudder; but I wouldn't be sold to a coloured master for anything.[16]

As a result, the position that black slaveholders were mainly motivated by humanitarian concerns is discredited. Records suggest that many Black slaveowners owned slaves for the same reasons as Whites, for profit. As historian Joseph Holloway points out on the website, *The Slave Rebellion:*

In 1860 there were at least six African Americans in Louisiana who owned 65 or more slaves. The largest number, 152 slaves, were owned by the widow C. Richards and her son P.C. Richards, who owned a large sugar cane plantation. Another Black slave magnate in Louisiana with over 100 slaves was Antoine Dubuclet, a sugar planter whose estate was valued at $264, 000. In North Carolina 69 free Blacks were slave owners.[17]

So how was a class of free Blacks created? Historian R. Halliburton, Jr. wrote in his essay, *Free Black Owners of Slaves: A Reprisal of the Woodson Thesis*, that:

Some had never been slaves. They had been indentured servants who had become free. Some had purchased their freedom. Others were born of free parents while some were born free by miscegenation. Slaves were emancipated for meritorious military duty, for faithful service, by last will and testament, saving a life, advanced age or infirmity and other reasons. Moreover, runaway slaves constantly swelled the ranks of freedmen. As a result, free Blacks were slave owners for more than two hundred years.[18]

A previously stated, the origins of the free Black population in America is multifaceted. The legal framework that allowed for the existence of free Blacks was fraught with contradictions and discriminatory measures. Some individuals gained their freedom through acts of manumission, granted by their enslavers or through legal means. Others were born free to parents who had achieved emancipation, often through complex legal battles or through the gradual process of emancipation laws. While they were technically free, they often faced significant legal and social limitations, including restrictions on their right to vote, own property, the type of work they could do, and even travel freely.[19]

For some Black slaveholders, owning slaves offered a means to advance economic standing. In a society where opportunities for advancement were limited for African Americans, owning slaves provided a path to landownership, access to labor, and the potential for profit. For others, it was a way to secure their family's legacy and build a secure future for their descendants. They saw the acquisition of slaves as a means of gaining power and influence within the community, navigating the complex racial hierarchies of the time.

Despite these challenges, some free Blacks were able to carve out a space for themselves in these economic and social spheres by establishing businesses, acquiring property, and even participating in the slaveholding system. The motivations behind this seemingly contradictory practice were varied, complex, and influenced by a combination of economic factors, social pressures, and personal circumstances.

At one time or another, free Black people in this country lived in every Southern state that embraced the practice of slavery, and in Northern states as well. They bought and sold other Black people, and did so at least since 1654 and continued to do so right through the Civil War. As an educator, in our schools today I find it interesting how such a topic is left out in many curriculums or is not revealed to students thus creating the perception that the institution of slavery was only practiced by Whites and only in the southern United States. Most Black slave owners obtained their slaves through inheritance from White and Black relatives and in some cases, purchasing them as well. *"It did not therefore seem to them unnatural for a Negro in America to hold his brethren in bondage, when he had become free and able to buy his fellows,"* as historian John Russell wrote.[20]

Many people do not want to acknowledge, that slavery in the United States is predated by the inhabitants of the African and Middle Eastern continent who have practiced various forms of slavery since Antiquity and still do today. Slavery in historical Africa was practiced in many different forms: Debt slavery, enslavement of war captives, military slavery, slavery for prostitution, and enslavement of criminals were all practiced in various parts of Africa. Accordingly, Black slave owners were uncommon compared to the *"two and a half million African Americans living in the United States in 1850, the vast majority [were] enslaved,"* but they did exist. The most fascinating questions about Black slave-owning this study will focus on includes: What are the origins of Black slave ownership and the historical development revolving around the third caste? What defined a Free Person of Color, and how was such a status obtained? What was the rationale behind becoming a free Black slaveholder? Did they own slaves for benevolent reasons or *"as an act of exploitation,"* of their free labor for profit, just as white slave owners did? Finally, how significant was Black slave ownership and seeks to examine more fully how the lives of free Black slaveholders was impacted, socially, financially, etc., with slavery's end after the War Between the States. Historians have been arguing for many years over these questions.[21]

The rights of free Blacks to own slaves has always been a matter of contention and depended upon time and place. In some instances, being unable to manumit their loved ones, some Black masters were forced to hold their kinsmen and friends as nominal slaves. In 1833, the Supreme Court decision, *North Carolina v. Edmund, a Slave*, settled the matter regarding the rights of free Blacks to own slaves. Judge Daniel speaking for the Court rendered the following decision, *"By the laws of this State [North Carolina] a free man of color may own land and hold land and personal property including slaves...."*[22] As a result, a good number of Black slave owners obtained the capital to buy slaves through their own industry and their work as artisans, entrepreneurs, and even as unskilled laborers. With the absence of large-scale European immigration as compared to the North and West, slave states and a long-standing reliance on Black slave labor. As a result of selective manumission, a highly skilled free Black population that enjoyed a higher economic standing , was produced allowing them to purchase slaves and elevate themselves into the planter class of society.[23]

The laws governing Black slaveholders often reflected the inconsistent and contradictory nature of the system. In some states, free Blacks were granted limited rights of property ownership, including the right to own slaves. This was largely due to the efforts of individual free Blacks who challenged legal boundaries, leveraging the system to achieve a small quantity of agency and control over their lives. For example, in states like Virginia and Maryland, where a substantial free Black population existed, laws allowed for free Blacks to inherit enslaved people from their White relatives. However, these laws were often subject to interpretation and manipulation by local officials, resulting in an uneven and often discriminatory application. In other states, laws governing the inheritance of slaves by free Black people often stipulated that enslaved individuals would be emancipated upon the death of their owner, but only if they were White. This reflects the complex and often discriminatory nature of the legal system that governed the lives of both free Black people and enslaved people in the antebellum South.

Miscegenation was another way for slaves to obtain freedom. According to Larry Koger, *"from the early eighteen century until the prohibition of private manumission in 1820, the pattern of interracial intimacy appears to have been the most common means of gaining liberty in South Carolina."*[24] The freed slave women and their children often received not only their freedom but also slaves. In many instances, the female slaves and their children received their freedom by deeds of manumission. Still in other instances, they had to wait until the death of their owners. Once emancipated, some females continued to live in the household of their former masters, exercising not servant-master roles, but those of a husband and wife.[25]

However, not every freed woman agreed to live with the former master. According to Steven J. Niven in an article he wrote, "A Cane River Tale: From Slave to Free Woman to Slave Owner," for *The Root,* (March 10, 2015). Niven writes about a freed Black woman who established plantation and expanded their economic assets by purchasing slaves. a smaller number of African Americans took part in the domestic slave trade for financial advantage, as well as family protection. Notable among these, Niven wrote:

. . . the antebellum businesswomen Eufrosina Hinard, who owned a brickworks and 13 slaves in Florida, and Maria Weston, who purchased 20 slaves on behalf of her millwright husband (who was legally still enslaved) in Charleston. Another, and perhaps the best

known, was Marie-Thérèse Coincoin, who lived for eight decades in Natchitoches Parish, La. She would help to found a family dynasty of Free, Colored planters, the Metoyers, who by 1830 owned over 200 slaves—8 percent of all enslaved people in the parish.[26]

Benevolent slave ownership among African Americans is characterized by the purchase of relatives or friends. For instance, a free African American woman might purchase her husband to remove him from the threat of a cruel master, or a parent might purchase his or her children for the same reason. Because some state legislatures, such as the 1806 Virginia legislature, required emancipated slaves to leave the state, a woman's continued ownership of her spouse, or a parent's continued ownership of his or her children, was often the only way for a family unit to remain intact within the state. As Woodson put it:

The census records show that the majority of the Negro owners of slaves were such from the point of view of philanthropy. In many instances the husband purchased the wife or vice versa . . . Slaves of Negroes were in some cases the children of a free father who had purchased his wife. If he did not thereafter emancipate the mother, as so many such husbands failed to do, his own children were born his slaves and were thus reported by the enumerators.[27]

Some free African Americans purchased slaves with the understanding that the enslaved person would then purchase his or her freedom over time in installments. Or a slave might accumulate his or her purchase price through the practice of hiring out and approach a free Black person to buy him or her with that money with the understanding that the slave would live as a free person, understood as "de facto manumission." Thus, in some particular situations, these African American owners were not necessarily enslaving people for their labor, but purchasing relatives or friends to keep families together or to help people move out of slavery.[28]

This idea has been perpetuated by scholars like Carter G. Woodson's major study in 1924 of black slave owners entitled, *"Free Negro Owners of Slaves in the United States in 1830."* According to Colton Adams in a paper he wrote at Southern Adventist University in 2014, he states:

Woodson established the popular conclusion that the majority of black slaveholders simply acquired slaves to preserve family ties or protect other loved ones." Adams continues to say, *"Later scholars such as John Hope Franklin in his 1967 edition of From Slavery to Freedom echoed the same thought,"* and argued that *"the majority of black slave owners had some personal interest in their property. Frequently the husband purchased his wife, or vice versa; or the slaves were the children of a free father who had purchased a wife; or they were other relatives of friends who had been rescued from the worst features of the institution by some affluent free black.*[29]

Some scholars of African American history argue about whether commercial slaveholding was more common than benevolent slaveholding among Blacks as Adams points out. As a result, scholars have researched further about the role of Black slave owners such as historian, R. Halliburton Jr., who challenges Woodson's study in his 1976 research article, *"Free Black Owners of Slaves: A Reappraisal of the Woodson Thesis."* Halliburton concluded, after examining the evidence, that *"it would be a serious mistake to automatically assume that free blacks owned their spouse or children only for benevolent purposes"*. Halliburton also points out that Woodson's thesis *"does not give a fair representation of black slaveholders and skewed statistics in his study."*[30]

Other historians John Hope Franklin noted that in North Carolina, *"without doubt, there were those who possessed slaves for the purpose of advancing their [own] well-being . . . these Negro slaveholders were more interested in making their farms or carpenter-shops 'pay' than they were in treating their slaves humanely."* These Black slaveholders, he concluded, made *"some effort to conform to the pattern established by the dominant slaveholding group within the State in the effort to elevate themselves to a position of respect and privilege."*[31]

Adams also mentions Larry Koger's 1985 book, *Black Slaveowners: Free Black Slave Masters in South Carolina, 1790-1860*, about a prominent mulatto by the name of William Ellison, a cotton gin maker from South Carolina. Ellison did not consider himself a Black man but a Free Man of Color, a mulatto. At a time when the vast majority of blacks in the South were slaves and almost all free Blacks were poor; Ellison was one of the wealthiest Free Persons of Color in the South and wealthier than most Whites. Ellison owned a large cotton plantation and more slaves than any other Free Person of Color in the South outside of Louisiana, even more than all but the richest White planters. In 1840 Ellison owned thirty slaves. By 1847 Ellison's property grew to 350 acres and thirty-six slaves. And on the eve of the Civil War, he owned sixty-three slaves. His slaves toiled in fields and were trained to make and repair cotton gins.[32]

With the appearance of David Rankin's article "*The Impact of the Civil War on the Free Colored Community of New Orleans*" and Gary B. Mills's book *The Forgotten People: Cane River's Creoles of Color* in 1977, a renewed interest in the subject of free Blacks who owned slaves was ignited. This led to studies examining how Blacks, despite slavery, racism, and White oppression, acquired substantial amounts of wealth. In his study of Andrew Durnford, a Plaquemines Parish sugar planter, David Whitten uncovered rare documents about one of the wealthiest free black planters in the slave holding states. They did not indicate Durnford as a benevolent owner, as in his Will, as his son Albert, born to an enslaved woman, was freed.[33]

Another great work that Adams reveals is David L. Lightner's and Alexander M. Ragan's 2005 study entitled "*Were African American*

Slaveholders Benevolent or Exploitative? A Quantitative Approach." Lightner and Ragan focus on the way Black slaveholders treated their slaves and identified the problems with quantifying it. Adams opined that, *"these works represent a shift in scholarship on this topic, yet in recent years there have been few contributions to the question."*[34]

Larry Kroger continues to point out in his research of cross referencing tax records, bills of sale, mortgages, wills, and census records, a different picture emerges of Black slaveholding and it argues that Black slaveholding was linked to a kind of *"pigmentocracy"* (darker skin complexion of obvious mixed racial heritage). He affirms that a survey of local documents and the Census of 1850 indicates that 83.1 percent of Black slave masters were mulattoes and 90 percent of their slaves were of darker skin. Kroger believes that this pattern does not support the belief that Black slave ownership was based upon benevolence. Kroger also points out that because mulattoes mainly married other mulattoes, the Black slaves that were owned by light-skinned Black slave owners were rarely kin and were instead held as laborers in most cases. He also argues that a great many freemen became slave masters for the same reasons as Whites, the need for labor to exploit for profits. He writes, *"by and large, Negro slave owners were darker copies of their white counterparts."* This led him to conclude, *"clearly the dominate pattern of commercial use of slaves recorded in the documents indicates that black slaveholding was primarily and institution based upon exploitation of slaves rather than a benevolent system centered upon kinship or humanitarianism."*[35]

John Hope Franklin supports Kroger's views when he points out that some colored masters used slaves as collateral to secure loans. For many black slaveholders, slaves were merely property to be purchased, sold, or exchanged. The fact that freed black men and women owned slaves for benevolent reasons demonstrates that for some blacks, just as for whites, greed has no boundaries. *"There may not have been much objection to the ownership of one's own family by a free Negro; [but] .*

. . when one undertook to acquire slaves to improve his economic status, there were those who looked upon it as a dangerous trend, the legality of which was seriously questioned," as Franklin indicates and concludes that free Blacks had rights as long as Whites allowed them those rights. Those rights could be taken away at any time. For example, at the beginning of hostilities during the War Between the States, a law was passed in North Carolina *"to prevent Negroes from having the control of slaves."*[36]

Despite these studies, there is still only a vague understanding of Blacks who climbed to the upper economic levels. We know little about how much land and other property they accumulated, how their wealth changed from one generation to the next, and how their holdings compared with those of other Blacks and Whites. We know even less about the group's socio-demographic profile, mulatto and black, male and female, rural and urban, and how those demographics changed over time in various parts of the South.

The fact is many free Black people owned slaves regardless of their reasons. According to Irvin S. Cohen and Raford Logan in their study titled, *The American Negro; Old World Background and New World Experience (1970)*, that the 1860 U.S. Census report reveals, *"only a small minority of whites owned slaves. The census reported there were 27 million whites in the United States with an estimate of eight million living in slave holding states. The census also determined that fewer than 385,000 individuals owned slaves. Thus, if all slaveholders were white, that would only be 1.4 percent of all whites in the country, or 4.8 percent of slave holding whites in the South."*[37]

The 1860 federal census also reports that there were 4.5 million African Americans in the United States, with fewer than four million living in the slave holding states. Of those Black people living in the South, 261,988 were not slaves with 10,689 of those reported [free] lived in New Orleans. John Hope Franklin recorded that, *"those free Blacks in*

New Orleans, over 3,000 owned slaves, or 28 percent of the free Black people in that city. The census reveals a staggering number when compared to the less than 1.4 percent of all white Americans and less than 4.8 percent of southern whites. One could assume that based on those statistics, once free, Black people became slave owners themselves. Most slaveholders, both black and white, owned on average only one to five slaves." [38]

Contrary to the widespread image of slave chattel, Black slaves and White masters worked and ate beside their charges in the fields, the house, or in the workshop. Contrary to widespread images of Southern slavery, wherein Black slaves engaged in endless., and excruciating physical labor and their White masters lived wholly separate lives of complete ease, it was common for the latter to toil and eat alongside the former amidst the fields, structures, and workshops, forming an interracial familiarity. Those individuals who owned 50 or more slaves made up the top one percent and were considered slave owning magnates. In 1860, there were at least six free Blacks who owned 65 or more slaves. The largest number, 152 slaves, was owned by sugar cane planters, the widow C. Richards and her son P.C. Richards. Another slave magnate from Louisiana was Antoine Dubuclet, who owned over 100 slaves. He had an estate worth $264,000 in 1860 dollar value. This was in comparison with the wealth of White men of that time averaging $3,978.

Black slaveholders were not just men. The wealthiest Black person in Charleston in 1860 was Maria Weston, who owned fourteen slaves and property valued at more than $40,000, at a time when the average White man earned about one hundred dollars a year. The historian Larry Koger tells that, at least for a time, *"in Charleston City, [South Carolina,] the female heads of black families dominated the black slaveholding community. In 1850, the number of black women who owned slaves was reported at 123 by the federal census."* As one can see, greed is gender blind. These people were among the largest free

Negro slaveholders, and their motivations were neither benevolent nor philanthropic. A large majority of these profit-oriented free Black slaveholders resided in the Lower South. For the most part, they were persons of mixed racial origin, often women who cohabited or were mistresses of White men, or mulatto men. Provided land and slaves by Whites, they owned farms and plantations, worked their hands in the rice, cotton, and sugar fields, and like their White contemporaries were troubled with runaways.[39]

In the Halliburton essay, it is revealed that free Black people have owned slaves *"in each of the thirteen original states and later in every state that countenanced slavery,"* at least since Anthony Johnson and his wife Mary went to court in Virginia in 1654 to obtain the services of their indentured servant, a black man, John Castor, for life. Haliburton also points out, *"free Black people could even own the services of white indentured servants in Virginia as well."* Free Black people owned slaves in Boston by 1724 and in Connecticut by 1783; by 1790, 48 Black people in Maryland owned 143 slaves. One particularly notorious Black Maryland farmer named Nat Butler *"regularly purchased and sold Negroes for the Southern trade,"* Halliburton wrote.[40]

For some Black slaveholders, owning slaves offered a means to advance their economic standing. In a society where opportunities for advancement were limited for African Americans, owning slaves provided a path to landownership, access to labor, and the potential for profit. For others, it was a way to secure their family's legacy and build a secure future for their descendants. They saw the acquisition of slaves as a means of gaining power and influence within the community, navigating the complex racial hierarchies of the time.

However, it's crucial to recognize that the practice of free Black slaveholding was not solely motivated by economic gain or social advancement. Some individuals, particularly those who had experienced the horrors of slavery themselves, may have been driven by a desire to create a semblance of control over their own lives and destinies. They may have seen owning slaves as a means of mitigating the power dynamics that often put them at the mercy of White slaveholders, allowing them to influence the lives and experiences of those they enslaved.

The geographic distribution of free Black slaveholding further illuminates the complexities of this historical phenomenon. While it existed throughout the South, certain regions witnessed a more concentrated prevalence of free Black slaveholders. These regions were often characterized by a combination of factors that created both opportunities and challenges for free Black populations. By the 1830s, the decade that marks a peak in the percentage of free Blacks within the social caste that held slaves, free Blacks in 1830 in the combined territories of Alabama, Arkansas, Florida, Georgia, Louisiana, Mississippi, the Carolinas, Tennessee, and Virginia owned about 10,653 slaves. In South Carolina, where forty-three percent of the free Black families owned slaves, the average number of slaves held per owner was about six. Similarly, in Louisiana forty percent of free Black families owned slaves, twenty-six percent of those in Mississippi held slaves, twenty-five percent of those in Alabama, and this was also true for twenty percent of those in Georgia. On average, around sixteen percent of free Black families in the states that would eventually make up the Confederacy (except Texas) owned slaves in 1830.[41]

The presence of a large free Black population, often associated with areas like Virginia and Maryland, provided a context for the emergence of these free Black slaveholders. These regions also witnessed a more diversified economy, offering opportunities for skilled labor and entrepreneurial ventures. However, these regions were also marked by the presence of a powerful White slaveholding class, creating a dynamic of both cooperation and conflict between free Black slaveholders and their White counterparts.

The Paradox of Freedom

Their enterprise and property have convinced some observers that opportunities did exist for free "People of Color" to prosper and not just to survive in these areas. Their possession of fellow Afro-Americans as human chattel, however, has persuaded others to accuse them of being no better than White slaveowners. In fact, the existence of free Negro slaveowners only made clearer the conditions of life in a society dominated by slaveholders and dependent on slave labor and ultimately, a social indicator of the reality and fabric of overall American life itself in the era. Later recognized as *"slaves without masters"* who were *"neither slave nor free,"* free Negroes lived perilously close to what sociologist Orlando Patterson has called *"social death."* Their ownership of slaves consequently was exceptional and anomalous, allowed only at the sufferance of White slaveowners and mostly intended to reduce the risks of living free and Black in a slave society. The 1830s was probably the peak of such ownership, no more than one thousand of the more than fifty-five thousand free Negroes in Virginia held human property for any reason. Although the number of free Black Virginians would grow to more than fifty-eight thousand by 1860, the number of those who were slaveowners dramatically declined after 1830.[42]

Free Black slaveholding was not a singular, homogenous practice. It encompassed a diverse range of individuals with varying motivations, experiences, and perspectives. For one to truly understand this complex phenomenon, we must delve into the lives and stories of these individuals, recognizing the nuances and contradictions inherent in their experiences. Through these personal narratives, drawn from archival research and primary sources, we can begin to appreciate the multifaceted nature of this historical phenomenon and its profound impact on the lives of those who lived through it.

The legacy of slavery casts a long shadow over the lives of free Black individuals in America, shaping their opportunities, their social standing, and their relationships with both the White slaveholding class and the enslaved population. Historian Ira Berlin wrote, *"In slave societies, nearly everyone, free and slave, aspired to enter the slaveholding class, and upon occasion some former slaves rose into slaveholders' ranks. Their acceptance was grudging, as they carried the stigma of bondage in their lineage and, in the case of American slavery, color in their skin."* While the institution of slavery was inherently brutal, it paradoxically created opportunities for some free Blacks, particularly in the context of skilled trades and small businesses. The ability to acquire land and establish enterprises, though often limited by racial prejudice and legal restrictions, allowed some free Blacks to accumulate wealth and social status.[43]

Free Black slaveholders faced a complex social reality that while their ownership of enslaved people gave them a degree of economic power and social standing, it also made them outsiders in a society deeply divided by race and power. Their motivations behind slaveholding were multifaceted. Economic factors certainly played a significant role. The ability to own land and acquire enslaved labor provided opportunities to establish businesses, accumulate wealth, and improve their social standing. This was especially true in the agricultural South, where land ownership and access to labor were essential for economic success. However, it is crucial to avoid oversimplifying these motivations. Their status as slaveholders, while seemingly contradictory, was not simply a matter of economic opportunity but a reflection of the legal and social complexities of the time. They were simultaneously recognized as property owners and subject to racial discrimination and legal limitations.[44]

Manumission was one of those difficult limitations. Should free Blacks have obtained freedom, *"freedom"* was not always advantageous, especially to one of low economic standing. By 1830 there were only three areas which allowed a master to manumit a slave without any significant legal constraints, the States of Maryland & Missouri, and the Arkansas Territory. Other States such as Delaware and Kentucky called for the master to issue a bond in order to assure the freed slave was of good character. Tennessee and North Carolina allowed manumissions only as a reward for good standing and meritorious service, which discretion was left to the courts. Nevertheless, most other States allowed manumissions only through acts of their legislatures (South Carolina, Georgia, Alabama, Mississippi, and Louisiana allowed slaves to be emancipated in 1830, only by special resolutions).[45]

As the total Black population expanded, both free and slave, more regulations and restrictions were placed on free individuals. In most States, they could not vote nor move and meet freely; neither could they own guns. Until the 1835 Constitution of Tennessee, most privileges for free blacks were retained legally, but restricted socially in many situations. Therefore, Article I, Section XXVI read, *"That the free white men of this State have a right to keep and to bear arms for their common defense;"* and Article IV, Section I, *"Every free white man . . . shall be entitled to vote."*[46]

The lives of free Black slaveholders were marked by both privilege and limitation. They enjoyed the benefits of property ownership and the power that came with it, but they also faced the weight of the institution of slavery and the contradictions inherent in their position. Their stories offer a unique perspective on the complexities of race, power, and freedom in antebellum America, challenging conventional narratives and revealing a more nuanced understanding of this historical period. Owning enslaved people, regardless of one's race, meant participating in a system built on exploitation and oppression. While recognizing the complexities of the motivations behind this practice, it is crucial to understand that free Black slaveholders were not simply victims of circumstance. They were active participants in a system that deprived others of their fundamental human rights. Their actions must be examined within the historical context of slavery, acknowledging the immense suffering it inflicted on those who were held in bondage.

The Paradox of Freedom

This study is not meant to glorify the actions of Free Black slaveholders or paint them as heroes, but to serve as a reminder of the complexities of history. By exploring the stories of these people, we can gain a deeper understanding of the past and the enduring legacy of slavery in shaping the American experience. While these individuals navigated the system of slavery in a way that allowed for some degree of upward mobility, they also participated in an institution that was inherently unjust and dehumanizing. The ownership of slaves, regardless of motivations, contributed to the perpetuation of a system that stripped individuals of their basic human rights and denied them the opportunity for freedom and self-determination.

Moreover, free Black slaveholders often found themselves caught in a precarious position. Their ownership of slaves could complicate their relationships with both white slaveholders and enslaved people. They might face suspicion and hostility from White communities, who often viewed them as a threat to the racial and social order of the time. At the same time, they might experience tension and distrust from the enslaved population, who recognized their status as both members of the Black community and participants in the system that oppressed them. The experience of Free Black slaveholding highlights the complex and often contradictory ways in which racial identity, social status, and economic opportunity intersected within the antebellum South. It underscores the difficult choices that individuals faced in a system that offered limited opportunities and demanded difficult compromises.

The historical context of the practice of Free Black slaveholding is crucial to understanding its complexities. The free Black population in colonial America emerged from various sources: some were born free, while others gained their freedom through purchase, manumission, or through legal challenges. The legal status of free Black people varied significantly across the colonies, with some granting them limited rights and others denying them basic freedoms. In some cases, free

The Paradox of Freedom

Black people could own property, conduct business, and even vote. However, they were often subject to discriminatory laws and social restrictions, and their lives were constantly shaped by the pervasive fear of re-enslavement.

The concentration of free Black slaveholding in the Upper South can be attributed to various factors. First, the relatively early development of free Black communities in these states, coupled with the presence of a more diversified economy, allowed for greater economic mobility and opportunities for wealth accumulation. The presence of a vibrant urban sector, with skilled trades and small businesses, facilitated the financial success of some individuals.

Virginia, for example, witnessed the emergence of a significant free Black population early on due to a combination of factors. During the colonial era, the influx of indentured servants, many of whom were Black, led to a gradual increase in the free Black population. The gradual emancipation of slaves, often as a reward for service or due to the owner's will, also contributed to the growth of this group. In Virginia, the presence of a robust agricultural economy, based heavily on slave labor, facilitated the economic opportunities that allowed some free Blacks to accumulate wealth, including the ownership of slaves, as exemplified by the movement, post-Nat Turner, which saw Virginia come close to abolishing slavery in 1831-32, there was present in that state, a moderate, but clearly present, emancipationist element among the White American population.[47]

Maryland, a border state with a significant slaveholding population, also witnessed a notable concentration of free Black slaveholders. Maryland's location, straddling the Mason-Dixon Line, placed it at the center of the tumultuous debate over slavery, and its complex legal landscape allowed for the emergence of free Black communities. These communities thrived in various sectors, from agriculture to skilled trades, and some individuals managed to accumulate enough wealth to purchase enslaved people. The economic opportunities, coupled with the state's laws, provided the fertile ground for free Black slaveholding.[48]

Moving southward, free Black slaveholding became less common in the Deep South, states like Georgia, Alabama, and Mississippi. The Deep South was characterized by a highly concentrated plantation economy, reliant on a vast enslaved workforce. While free Black populations did exist in these states, their numbers were limited and their opportunities for advancement were more restricted. The dominant plantation system, based on a large-scale, forced labor system, offered limited avenues for free Blacks to amass wealth and acquire slaves.[49]

The aftermath of the Civil War marked a turning point for free Black slaveholders. The emancipation of enslaved people fundamentally altered the legal landscape, abolishing the practice of slaveholding entirely and leaving many free Black slaveholders facing economic, social challenges, and other uncertainties. Free Black slaveholders were left to grapple with the legacy of their past, navigating a new era of freedom and equality in a society still deeply marked by racial prejudice and discrimination.

Their stories offer a nuanced and complex understanding of the realities of race, power, and freedom in antebellum America. They remind us that history is not always a simple tale of heroes and villains, but a multifaceted and often contradictory tapestry of human experience. By exploring the lives of these individuals and the broader social, legal, and economic contexts that shaped their lives, we gain a richer understanding of the complexities both of their motivations. As we delve into the stories of these individuals, we must strive to understand the historical context that shaped their choices while never losing sight of the enduring impact of slavery on the lives of those who were enslaved.

Their stories challenge us to grapple with the complexities of historical narratives and to understand the nuanced ways in which individuals navigate the often conflicting realities of freedom and control and recognize both the potential benefits and the profound costs associated with their participation in the system of slavery. By exploring the spectrum of experiences within free Black slaveholding, we gain a deeper appreciation for the complexities of American history.

Chapter 2:
Free Black Slaveholders in Colonial America, 1526 - 1787

"As all the negroes introduced into America were brought as slaves, the black color of the race raises the presumption of slavery, contrary to the principles of common law, which would presume freedom .... This presumption is extended, in most of the States, to mulattoes or persons of mixed blood, casting upon them the onus of proving a free maternal ancestor."

– Thomas R. R. Cobb, *An Inquiry into the Law of Negro Slavery in the United States of America*[50]

The story of free Black slaveholding in colonial America is a tangled web of freedom and bondage where individuals who themselves had escaped the shackles of slavery found themselves intertwined in the same system. To comprehend this complex phenomenon, we must explore the historical context of slavery in colonial America and the legal and social frameworks that defined the lives of Black people, both enslaved and free.

It is traditionally held that all Africans coming to the Americas in the seventeenth century were involuntary slaves differing from Whites who came as indentured servants, or contract workers. Though untrue, widespread acceptance of this theory increased dramatically between 1830 and 1860 as tensions over the issue of slavery amplified. Many within the White pro-slave class argued vehemently that slavery had been the God-ordained, intended state of all Africans upon their arrival in the Americas. One pro-slavery pamphlet shared this view, stating, *"Every negro in this country, or his ancestors, came in as a slave. Every negro, legally free, has reached that condition by his ancestors or himself having been emancipated by a former master."* Thus, this concept left the class of Free Persons of Color as nothing but a by-product of slavery, or as historian John H. Russell put it, a class *"dependent in its origin and existence upon the disintegration of slavery."* Yet one must wonder why a pamphlet like this was published, unless there was already a clear and significant distinction between two different classes of African-Americans, slave and free.[51]

The origins of slavery in colonial America predates the period of English colonization. Spain, the dominate colonial power in America in the early years, introduced African slavery to the New World but its practices were different from other European nations. Spanish slave laws granted enslaved people certain rights and protections. Those laws derived from ancient Roman traditions and had been incorporated into the Castilian code of law known as the *Siete Partidas* in the thirteenth century. These laws were not based on race,

Francisco Menendez, free Black soldier in Spanish West Florida and former slave. *Courtesy of the Florida Museum.*

and Africans joined slaves of other races and ethnicities who had been captured in *"just wars,"* been condemned, or had sold themselves into slavery. The *Siete Partidas* held that slavery was an unnatural condition, for God had created man free, and it established ways in which enslaved people could eventually become free. This practice of African enslavement in colonial Florida by the Spanish dated as early as 1526, 93 years before the first African slaves were brought to Jamestown in 1619. Florida was also the site of the first emancipation of escaping slaves in 1687 and the first settlement of free Blacks in 1735. The Roman Catholic faith, which, at least initially, discouraged the enslavement of anyone who had accepted Christianity, contributed to the relatively liberal attitude of the Spanish and Portuguese toward free people of color.[52]

In some ways, the French had a similar outlook, imagining a society where class was more important than race and in which everyone was entitled to fair treatment, provided they had been baptized into the Catholic Church. For all its harshness, the French Code Noir, adopted in 1685, included articles protecting the rights of freed slaves, which were essentially the same as those of Whites, with the exception that they could not vote, hold public office, or marry a White person. While generally, the French, Spanish, and Portuguese codes treated slaves and free blacks less harshly and offered greater legal protection than did Protestant nations, in practice, local conditions such as slave revolts and the distance of the colonies from central administrative control probably more directly affected their experiences. The French were also more tolerant of racial mixing, especially in sparsely settled frontier societies like Louisiana, where there were significantly fewer White women than men. At the same time, they developed elaborate color categories to define the results of that mixing.[53]

The introduction of African slaves in the North American English colonies started at the settlement of Jamestown, in the Virginia colony. The exact date is not definitively known (a letter from the time identified the ship's arrival coming in *"the latter part of August")*, but August 20, 1619, has been chosen by many to mark the arrival of the enslaved Africans in the English colonies. Colonist John Rolfe wrote to Sir Edwin Sandys, one of the founders of the Virginia Company and its then-treasurer, of the arrival of the first Africans on Virginia's shores in 1619. According to Rolfe, the first enslaved Africans to arrive in Virginia from the privateer ship the *White Lion*, owned by Robert Rich, 2nd Earl of Warwick but flying a Dutch flag, docked at what is now Old Point Comfort (located in modern-day Hampton) with approximately 20 Africans. They were captives from the area of present-day Angola and had been seized by the privateer's crew from a Portuguese slave ship, the *"São João Bautista"*. To obtain the Africans, the Jamestown colony traded provisions with the ship. Some of these individuals appear to have been treated like indentured servants, since slave laws were not passed until later, in 1641 in Massachusetts and in 1661 in Virginia. But from the beginning, in accordance with the custom of the Atlantic slave trade, most of this relatively small group, appear to have been treated as slaves, with *"African"* or *"negro"* becoming synonymous with *"slave"*. Virginia enacted laws concerning runaway slaves and 'negroes' in 1672.[54]

Some number of the colony's early Africans earned freedom by fulfilling a work contract or for converting to Christianity. Historians such as Edmund Morgan say this evidence suggests that racial attitudes were much more flexible in early 17th Century Virginia than they would later become. A 1625 census recorded 23 Africans in Virginia. In 1649 there were 300, and in 1690 there were 950. Over this period, legal distinctions between white indentured servants and *"Negros"* widened into lifelong and inheritable chattel-slavery for Africans and people of African descent.

Between 1670 and 1700, Virginia's economy grew to become increasingly dominated by the tobacco plantation. Tobacco required labor which was cheap and tireless rather than skilled. As the demand for labor grew, the system of indentured servitude proved inadequate, especially in the colonies of Virginia and Maryland. The need for a permanent and readily available labor force led to the gradual shift towards institutionalized slavery, where individuals were considered property and their lives were entirely controlled by their owners. This need for labor played more directly upon the settler's views about freedom and bondage.[55]

Initially, slavery was not an established institution in the colonies; rather, it emerged gradually over the course of several decades. Early colonists relied heavily on indentured servitude, a system where individuals contracted to work for a set period of time in exchange for passage to America and a chance at a better life. Until slave codes began to appear in the late seventeenth century, the system in the North American English Colonies was a system of contract servitude. Those early colonists in Virginia would not have been familiar with a system of slavery or a slave code, since there had been no such thing in England.

Thus, the question arises, if there was no such thing as a system of slavery in England, how did it emerge in the North American English Colonies? To answer this question, one must look at how slavery emerged in the future United States from the beginning with the Spanish, French, Dutch, and English as they gradually established colonies in North America from the 16th century onward, they began to enslave indigenous people, using them as forced labor to help develop colonial economies. As indigenous peoples suffered massive population losses due to imported diseases, Europeans quickly turned to importing slaves from Africa, primarily to work on slave plantations that produced cash crops. The enslavement of indigenous people in North America was later replaced during the 18th century by the enslavement of Black African people. Concurrent with the development of slavery, racist ideology was developed among Europeans, the rights of free people of color in European colonies were curtailed, slaves were legally defined as chattel property, and the condition of slavery held as hereditary.

The Thirteen Colonies of British North America, which would become the thirteen states of the United States of America, were for much or all of the period less dependent on slavery than the Caribbean colonies, or those of New Spain, or Brazil, and slavery did not develop significantly until later in the colonial era. Nonetheless, slavery was legal in every colony prior to the American Revolutionary War (1775-1783), and was most prominent in the Southern Colonies (as well as, the southern Mississippi River and Florida colonies of France, Spain, and Britain), which by then developed large slave-based plantation systems. Slavery in Europe's North American colonies which did not have warm climates and ideal conditions for plantations to exist primarily took the form of domestic labor or doing other forms of unpaid work alongside non-enslaved counterparts.[56]

Before 1619, the importation of African people into the Americas was already well established by the Portuguese, Spanish, and Dutch. The English officially joined in 1672 when labor, between 1619 and the late 1700s, in the British colonies transitioned from mainly White European indentured servants to enslaved Black people. England's Royal African Company transported about 5% of the total transatlantic slave trade forcing the migration of about 500,000 people into its own colonies. Because the southern colonies were so close to the well-established Caribbean slave trade, the majority of these enslaved people were brought from the West Indies to what would become the southern United States.[57]

Although slavery in the United States is typically associated with the Caribbean and the Antebellum American South, enslaved people existed to a lesser extent in all of the Thirteen English colonies: historians estimate that between 1755 and 1764, the Massachusetts enslaved population was approximately 2.2 percent of the total population; the slave population was generally concentrated in the industrial and coastal towns.[58]

The fact that slavery was more common in the South should not obscure the fact that Africans were enslaved in both the mid-Atlantic and New England colonies as well. Slaves were brought into these Northern Colonies throughout the colonial period performing a variety of types of labor including working on the docks and working as artisans. The exact number of slaves being brought into these colonies are difficult to obtain for census taking in the colonies was imperfect. It was not until 1715, when the first general census was made in the New England Colonies by race which recorded there were approximately 158,000 Whites and 4,150 Blacks.

Unlike in the American South, enslaved people in Massachusetts had legal rights, including the ability to file legal suits in court. Massachusetts had the largest black population with 2,000; followed by Connecticut with 1,500; and Rhode Island and New Hampshire with 500 and 150 respectively (See Table 1).[59]

Table 1
APPROXIMATE NUMBER of BLACKS AND WHITES IN NEW ENGLAND BEFORE THE REVOLUTION[60]

Year	Colony	Total Population	Whites	Negros
1771	Vermont	4,669	4,650	19
1775	New Hampshire	48,129	47,588	34
1776	Massachusetts	349,094	343,845	5,249
1774	Rhode Island	50,678	54,435	3,761
1774	Connecticut	197,856	191,392	6,464
		650,446	641,910	16,034

As the slave trade developed, so did its wealth and population increase in the late 18th Century, the number of slaves increased as well in New

The Paradox of Freedom

England. On the eve of the American Revolution in 1775 in New England, out of a total population there were 659, 446 Whites and 16,034 Blacks. This was the largest proportion ever reported in that section of the colonies.

Northern slavery grew out of the paradox the new continent presented to its European masters. So much land was available, so cheaply, that no one was willing to come to America and sign on to work as a laborer. The dream that drew Europeans across the Atlantic was owning acres of land or making a fortune in a trade or a craft. It was an attainable dream. In the 1680s a landless Welsh peasant from the mountains of Montgomeryshire could bring his whole family to Pennsylvania for £10 and acquire 250 acres for another £5; placing just one son in a trade in Britain would have cost the family £7.

Yet workers were needed in the new continent to clear the land, work the soil, build the towns. Because of this labor shortage, all the American colonies turned to compulsory labor. In New Netherland, in the 1640s, a free European worker could be hired for 280 guilders a year, plus food and lodging. In the same time and place, experienced African slaves from the West Indies could be bought outright, for life, for 300 guilders.

"To claim that the colonies would not have survived without slaves would be a distortion," historian Edgar McManus writes, *"but there can be no doubt that the development was significantly speeded by their labor. They provided the basic working force that transformed shaky outposts of empire into areas of permanent settlement."* Or, to consider the situation from a broad view of the entire New World, *"... export agriculture and effective colonization would not have occurred on the scale it did if enslaved Africans had not been brought to the New World. Except for precious metals, almost all major American exports to Europe were produced by Africans."*[61]

The Paradox of Freedom

Early in the 17th century, Black slave status in the British Americas was not quite absolute bondage. It was a nebulous condition similar to that of indentured servants. Some Africans brought to America were regarded as *"servants"* eligible for freedom in a certain number of years. Slavery had been in a decline in most of Europe since the Middle Ages. That may be why the legal definition of slavery as perpetual servitude for blacks and their children was not immediately established in the New World colonies. Slavery in the colonies is divided into two distinct regions, North and South. For this reason, this study should separate those two regions and look at how slavery developed differently in those areas and how Free Black slave masters established a foothold in those regions as well.

The Northern Colonies

The first official legal recognition of chattel slavery as a legal institution in British Colonial North America was in the Massachusetts Bay Colony. The first slaves were brought to the colony in the early 17th century. Since New England's climate was not suitable for large-scale farming, most slaves in Massachusetts were laborers for merchants and tradesmen or domestic servants for wealthy families, although some did work as farmhands. As most slave owners did not have enough slaves to justify building separate living quarters for them, their slaves often lived with them in their homes.

Many famous buildings and structures in New England were built with money from Massachusetts' slave trade, such as Faneuil Hall in Boston, which was constructed by wealthy slave trader and merchant Peter Faneuil, whose family regularly sold slaves in public auctions on nearby Merchants Row.

Harvard Law School was built with money made off the sale of land donated by a wealthy plantation owner, Isaac Royall Jr., and the House of Seven Gables in Salem was built with money from Captain John Turner's small role in the Triangle Trade of selling fish to Caribbean plantation owners to feed their slaves while importing the sugar they harvested on the plantations (although he didn't actually ship or sell slaves himself).[62]

The exact date slaves first entered Massachusetts is unknown, but many sources suggest Samuel Maverick was the first slaveholder in the colony after he arrived in early Boston in 1624 with two slaves. According to the book *Bound for America: The Forced Migration of Africans to the New World*, the first slaves brought directly from Africa to Massachusetts arrived in 1634.

A few years later, in December of 1638, a slave ship named *Desire* brought Boston's first shipment of slaves from Barbados, who had been exchanged for enslaved Pequot Indians from New England. In 1641, Governor John Winthrop, a slave owner himself, helped write the first law legalizing slavery in North America, the Massachusetts *Bodies of Liberty*, which the General Court passed on December 10, 1641:

There shall never be any bond slaverie, villinage or captivitie amongst us unless it be lawfull captives taken in just warres, and such strangers as willingly selle themselves or are sold to us. And these shall have all the liberties and Christian usages which the law of God established in Israel concerning such persons doeth morally require. This exempts none from servitude who shall be judged thereto by Authoritie.[63]

According to the Massachusetts Historical Society website, it wasn't long before Massachusetts became engaged in what was called the Triangle Trade:

In 1644 Boston merchants began importing slaves directly from Africa, selling them in the West Indies, and bringing home sugar to make rum, initiating the so-called triangular trade. From 1672-1696 the British Parliament granted the Royal African Company a monopoly in the slave trade. Yankee slavers avoided the monopoly by smuggling slaves

The Paradox of Freedom

in through small coastal harbors. In 1681, John Saffin and other Boston merchants wrote to the shipmaster William Welstead, warning him that the authorities planned to seize a slave ship heading for Rhode Island, and that he should intercept the vessel and direct it to Nantasket to offload its human cargo. In 1696 the British Parliament revoked the monopoly held by the Royal African Company, enabling Massachusetts merchants and shipmasters to engage freely in the slave trade.[64]

Slavery was legalized in New Plymouth and Connecticut when it was incorporated into the Articles of the New England Confederation (1643). Rhode Island enacted a similar law in 1652. That means New England had formal, legal slavery a full generation before it was established in the South. Not until 1664 did Maryland declare that all Blacks held in the colony, and all those imported in the future, would serve for life, as would their offspring. New York and New Jersey acquired legal slavery when they passed to English control in the 1660s. Pennsylvania, founded only in 1682, followed in 1700, with a law for regulation of servants and slaves.

Even slavery in the North can be broken down in two areas, New England and the Mid-Atlantic Colonies. New England slaves numbered only about 1,000 in 1708, but that rose to more than 5,000 in 1730 and about 13,000 by 1750. New England also was the center of the slave trade in the colonies, supplying captive Africans to the South and the Caribbean island. Black slaves were a valuable shipping commodity that soon proved useful at home, both in large-scale agriculture and in ship-building. The Mid-Atlantic colonies (New York, New Jersey, Pennsylvania) had been under Dutch rule before the British conquered them in 1664.

The systematic use of Black slaves in New Netherland began in 1626, when the first cargo of eleven Africans was unloaded by the Dutch West India Company. The company had been founded in 1621, and it *"operated both as a commercial company and as a military institution with quasi-state like powers."* The company had tried its colonial experiment of New Netherland at first with agricultural laborers from Holland, but this plan went nowhere. Most of the Dutch who came to America sought to pile up money in the lucrative fur trade and then hurry back to the comforts of Holland to enjoy their wealth. So the company increasingly turned to slaves, which it already was importing in vast numbers to its Caribbean colonies.[65]

From the 1630s to the 1650s, the West India Company *"was unquestionably the dominant European slave trader in Africa."* In 1644 alone, it bought 6,900 captives on the African coast. Most of these went to the company's colonies in the West Indies, but from its stations in Angola, the company imported slaves to New Netherland to clear the forests, lay roads, build houses and public buildings, and grow food. It was company-owned slave labor that laid the foundations of modern New York, built its fortifications, and made agriculture flourish in the colony so that later White immigrants had an incentive to turn from fur trapping to farming.[66]

But private settlers still faced an acute shortage of agricultural labor that was retarding the colony. A company audit report noted that, *"New Netherland would by slave labor be more extensively cultivated than it has hitherto been, because the agricultural laborers, who are conveyed thither at great expense to the colonists sooner or later apply themselves to trade, and neglect agriculture altogether."*[67]

As a result, the West India Company relaxed its monopoly and allowed New Netherlanders to trade their produce to Angola and *"to convey Negroes back home to be employed in the cultivation of their lands."* The company was willing to forego profit for the sake of spreading slavery in New Netherlands and getting the colony settled. It even allowed private owners to exchange slaves they were dissatisfied with for company slaves.

But only a trickle of slaves flowed into New Netherland from Angola; the colonists found the Africans *"proud and treacherous,"* and preferred to seek *"seasoned"* slaves from the West Indies, specifically Curaçao. In addition to those they bought from the West Indies, Dutch settlers bought slaves seized by privateers from Spanish ships. The steady flow from various sources allowed the colony to stabilize and, by 1640, to expand its agricultural output. *"Slavery helped to prepare the way for this transition by providing the labor which made farming attractive and profitable to the settlers. Slave labor was especially important in the agricultural development of the Hudson Valley, where an acute scarcity of free workers prevailed."*[68]

Between 1636 and 1646 the price of able-bodied men in New Netherland rose about 300 percent. By 1660, slaves from Angola were selling for 300 guilders and those from Curaçao for about 100 guilders more. By the time the British took over the colony in 1664, slaves sold in New Amsterdam for up to 600 guilders. This was still a discount of roughly 10 percent over what they would have brought in the plantation colonies, but the West India Company had been subsidizing slavery in New Netherland to promote its economic progress. The Hudson Valley, where the land was monopolized in huge patroon estates that discouraged free immigration, especially relied on slaves.

The purely economic status of slaves in New Netherland contrasted with the malignant and sometimes bizarre racism of the religious British citizens who followed the Dutch into the north Atlantic colonies. Free Blacks in New Netherland were trusted to serve in the militias, and slaves, given arms, helped to defend the settlement during the desperate Indian war of 1641-44. They were even used to put down the *Rensselaerswyck Revolt* of White tenants. Blacks and Whites had coequal standing in the colonial courts, and free Blacks were allowed to own property. They intermarried freely with Whites and in some cases owned White indentured servants.

The Paradox of Freedom

Slaves who had worked diligently for the company for a certain length of time were granted a "half-freedom" that allowed them liberty in exchange for an annual tribute to the company and a promise to work at certain times on company projects such as fortifications or public works. Individual slaveowners, such as Director General Peter Stuyvesant, adopted this system as well, and it enabled them to be free of the cost and nuisance of owning slaves year-round that they could only use in certain seasons. For the slaves, half-freedom was better than none at all.

The British took over in 1664, and control of the colony passed to the Duke of York, who, with his cronies, held controlling interest in the Royal African Company. The change of name from New Netherland to New York brought a crucial shift in policy. Whereas the Dutch had used slavery as part of their colonial policy, the British used the colony as a market for slaves. *"The Duke's representatives in New York -- governors, councilors, and customs officials -- were instructed to promote the importation of slaves by every possible means."*[69]

Both the Dutch and English colonists in the North would prefer to get their slaves from other New World colonies rather than directly from Africa. *"These slaves were familiar with Western customs and habits of work, qualities highly prized in a region where masters and slaves worked and lived in close proximity."* Having survived one climate change already, they also adjusted better to Northern winters, which incapacitated or killed those direct from Africa.[70]

By the late colonial period, the average slave-owning household in New England and the Mid-Atlantic seems to have had about 2 slaves. Estates of 50 or 60 slaves were rare, though they did exist in the Hudson Valley, eastern Connecticut, and the Narragansett region of Rhode Island. But the Northern climate set some barriers to large-scale agricultural slavery. The long winters, which brought no income on Northern farms, made slaves a burden for many months of the year unless they could be hired out to chop wood or tend livestock. In contrast to Southern plantation slavery, Northern slavery tended to be urban.

Slaveholding reflected social as well as economic standing, for in colonial times servants and retainers were visible symbols of rank and distinction. The leading families of Massachusetts and Connecticut used slaves as domestic servants, and in Rhode Island, no prominent household was complete without a large staff of Black retainers. New York's rural gentry regarded the possession of black coachmen and footmen as an unmistakable sign of social standing. In Boston, Philadelphia, and New York the mercantile elite kept retinues of household slaves. Their example was followed by tradesmen and small retailers until most houses of substance had at least one or two domestics.[71]

There is argument among historians about the economic role of Northern slaves. Some maintain that New England slaves generally were held in situations where they did not do real work, such as might be done by a White laborer, and that many, if not most, of the New England slaves were held without economic justification, working as house servants or valets. Even in Pennsylvania, the mounting Pennsylvania Quaker testimony against slavery in the 1750s and '60s was in large part aimed against the luxuriousness and extravagance of the Friends who had domestic slaves. But other historians who have studied the matter in some depth (Lorenzo Greene and Edgar McManus) make a forceful case for slave labor being an integral part of the New England economy. And even those slaves who did the arduous work required in a colonial household freed their White owners to pursue careers in law, religion, medicine or civil service.

In the North, slavery was most prominent in major port cities such as New York and Philadelphia. Slaves were auctioned openly in the Market House of Philadelphia; in the shadow of Congregational churches in Rhode Island; in Boston taverns and warehouses; and weekly, sometimes daily, in Merchant's Coffee House of New York. Such Northern heroes of the American Revolution as John Hancock and Benjamin Franklin bought, sold, and owned Black people. William Henry Seward, Lincoln's anti-slavery Secretary of State during the Civil War, born in 1801, grew up in Orange County, New York, in a slave-owning family and amid neighbors who owned slaves if they could afford them. The family of Abraham Lincoln himself, when it lived in Pennsylvania in colonial times, owned slaves.[72]

African bondage in the colonies north of the Mason-Dixon Line has left a legacy in the economics of modern America and in the racial attitudes of the U.S. working class. Yet comparatively little is written about the 200-year history of Northern slavery. Robert Steinfeld's book, *The Invention of Free Labor,* 1991, states, "By 1804 slavery had been abolished throughout New England," ignoring the 1800 census, which shows 1,488 slaves in New England. Recent archaeological discoveries of slave quarters or cemeteries in Philadelphia and New York City sometimes are written up in newspaper headlines as though they were exhibits of evidence in a case not yet settled.[73]

Slaves were mentioned in Hartford, Connecticut from 1639 and in New Haven from 1644. As in the rest of New England, they were few until about 1700. Connecticut citizens did not participate directly in the slave trade in the late 17th century, at least that's what the colonial governor assured the British Committee for Trade and Foreign Plantations, but the governor's report in 1680 implied that Massachusetts merchants were bringing in three or four Black slaves a year from Barbados. Since the average price of a Black slave in Connecticut was £22 that year and the rate in Massachusetts was £10 to £20, this was a worthwhile venture for a Boston slaver.

Even in the early 1700s, however, direct slave imports to Connecticut were considered too few to be worth the trouble of taxing. The governor reported only 110 White and Black servants in Connecticut in 1709. In 1730, the colony had a Black population of 700, out of a total enumeration of 38,000.

Yet on the eve of the Revolution, Connecticut had the largest number of slaves, 6,464, in New England. Jackson Turner Main, surveying Connecticut estate inventories, found that in 1700 one in 10 inventories included slaves, rising to one in 4 on the eve of the Revolution. Between 1756 and 1774, the proportion of slave to free in Connecticut increased by 40 percent. All the principal families of Norwich, Hartford, and New Haven were said to have one or two slaves. By 1774, half of all the ministers, lawyers, and public officials owned slaves, and a third of all the doctors. But Connecticut's large slave population apparently was based in the middle class. More people had the opportunity to own slaves than in Massachusetts or Rhode Island, so more did so. As historian Lorenzo Johnston Greene pointed out in his book, *The Negro in Colonial New England, 1620-1776,* "*The greater prosperity of Connecticut's inhabitants and their frugal and industrious habits were responsible for this situation. The wealth of the colony was also more equally distributed, with few extremes of riches or poverty.*"[74]

The largest increase came in the period 1749-1774. By the latter year, New London County had become the greatest slaveholding section of New England, with almost twice as many slaves as the most populous slave county in Massachusetts. New London was both an industrial center and the site of large slave-worked farms; with 2,036 slaves, it accounted for almost one-third of all the Blacks in Connecticut. New London town itself, with 522 blacks and a white population of 5,366, led the state in number of slaves and percentage of Black inhabitants.

In the northern colonies, slave-owning households may have only owned two or three slaves, while the enslaved population accounted for less than 5% of the total population of New England (though in larger cities like Newport, Rhode Island, slaves accounted for closer to 20%

The Paradox of Freedom

of the population of the city). In the mid-Atlantic colonies like Virginia, enslaved people made up closer to 50% of the population by the mid-18th century. This number increased to roughly 60% in colonies like South Carolina, where much of the enslaved population lived and worked on vast plantations together with 50, 100, or more slaves.

It is in this context of the evolution of slavery in colonial America that in 1688 Quakers in Germantown, Pennsylvania presented the first petition against the institution of slavery. The petition argued that slavery violated basic human rights-based upon the Biblical Golden Rule, *"do unto others as you would have done unto you."* The petition was neither adopted nor rejected, and largely forgotten until the 19th century.

The 1677 work *The Doings and Sufferings of the Christian Indians* documented how hundreds of raying Indians, who were allied with the New England Colonies, were enslaved and sent to the West Indies in the aftermath of King Philip's War by the colonists. Captive indigenous opponents, including women and children, were also sold into slavery at a substantial profit, to be transported to West Indies colonies.

African and Native American slaves made up a smaller part of the New England economy, which was based on yeoman farming and trades, than in the South, and a smaller fraction of the population, but they were present. Most were house servants, but some worked at farm labor. The Puritans codified slavery in 1641 when the Massachusetts Bay royal colony passed the *Body of Liberties*, which prohibited slavery in some instances, but did allow three legal bases of slavery. Slaves could be held if they were captives of war, if they sold themselves into slavery, were purchased from elsewhere, or if they were sentenced to slavery by the governing authority. The *Body of Liberties* used the word *"strangers"* to refer to people bought and sold as slaves, as they were generally not native born English subjects.

Colonists came to equate this term with Native Americans and Africans.[75]

The New Hampshire General Court passed *"An Act To Prevent Disorders In The Night"* in 1714, prefiguring the development of sundown towns in the United States: *Whereas great disorders, insolencies and burglaries are oft times raised and committed in the nighttime by Indian, Negro, and Molatto Servants and Slaves to the Disquiet and hurt of her Majesty's subjects, No Indian, Negro, or Molatto is to be from Home after 9 o'clock.* Notices emphasizing and re-affirming the curfew were published in *The New Hampshire Gazette* in 1764 and 1771.[76]

The legal approach to slavery was also different between Northern and Southern colonies. Massachusetts, a colony with a strong Puritan tradition, initially did not have a comprehensive set of slave codes. This can be attributed to the influence of Puritan beliefs, which emphasized the inherent equality of all humans in the eyes of God. However, as economic pressures and the demand for enslaved labor grew, by 1641, Massachusetts would have the dubious distinction of becoming the first colony to recognize slavery as a legal institution. With the establishment of slavery in Massachusetts, the legal framework surrounding it was less formalized and more contested. Early laws in Massachusetts addressed slavery in a less explicit manner, "life-long servitude" as it was presented, allowing them to focus more on regulating the treatment of enslaved individuals rather than defining their legal status as property. Regardless of how it was defined, New York and New Jersey followed Massachusetts example by 1664. The colonies also adopted laws prohibiting non-Whites from owning firearms, and established laws that negated a person's conversion to Christianity from affecting their status as a slave.[77]

The Southern Colonies

As previously stated, the first African slaves, or indentured servants as they were called and treated, did not arrive until 1619. It was not until 1662 that Virginia's law established that children born to an enslaved mother would also be enslaved further codified race-based and hereditary enslavement in that colony. North Carolina and South Carolina followed suit in 1663.

Beginning in the 1650s, in response to demographic and economic change, the Virginia legislature passed race-based laws limiting the rights of black people regardless of free or unfree status. The legislature codified two of the key elements of American slavery: a black servant was enslaved for life, and any child born of an enslaved woman was automatically enslaved. These laws took hold across the colonies and developed in tandem with market capitalism, creating "chattel" slavery, the treatment of human beings as commodities; products to be bought, sold, given, inherited.

Between 1670 and 1700, as Virginia's economy grew even more dependent upon the tobacco plantation. Tobacco required labor which was cheap and tireless rather than skilled. As labor demands grew, the system of indentured servitude proved inadequate, especially in the colonies of Virginia and Maryland. The need for a permanent and readily available labor force led to the gradual shift towards institutionalized slavery.[78]

Enslaved people were regarded and treated as property with little to no rights. In many colonies, enslaved people could not testify in a court of law, own guns, gather in large groups, or go out at night. Especially on southern farms, enslaved people were expected to work from sunup to sundown, though they may have been given Sundays off to tend to their own small gardens, repair allotted clothing, or tend to other needs that might supplement their meager allotments of clothing and food. As property, slaves were frequently bought and sold, and sometimes family groups were divided across plantations or even colonies, though some slave owners sought to keep families together as a safeguard against slaves running away. Slaves of small households often lived in the kitchen or a small outbuilding, while slaves on larger plantations often lived together in a quarter, or a group of quarters, with an overseer. Religion, storytelling, music, and dancing were important parts of an enslaved person's life, and could help share and preserve African cultural traditions across generations. Increasingly in the 18th century, slaves responded to the Great Awakening and began converting to Christianity, worshiping both alone and together with Whites in Baptist and Methodist congregations.

Georgia was the last of the English Thirteen Colonies to be established and the furthest south. Founded in the 1730s, Georgia's powerful backers did not object to slavery as an institution, but their business model was to rely on labor from Britain (primarily England's poor) and they were also concerned with security, given the closeness of then Spanish Florida, and Spain's regular offers to enemy-slaves to revolt or escape. Despite agitation for slavery, it was not until a defeat of the Spanish by Georgia colonials in the 1740s that arguments for opening the colony to slavery intensified. To staff the rice plantations and settlements, Georgia's proprietors relented in 1751, and African slavery grew quickly. After becoming a royal colony, in the 1760s Georgia began importing slaves directly from Africa.[79]

Utilizing evidence from court records, statute declarations and wills, one can recognize that the enforcement of slavery was not written into statue law in the American colonies until around 1660s. It is believed that Anthony Johnson, a former indentured servant, was one of the first to establish this concept of slavery. The unusual twist about this was that Anthony Johnson was Black.[80]

Anthony Johnson
In the early 1620s, African Portuguese slave traders kidnapped the man who would later be known as Anthony Johnson in Portuguese Angola.

He was renamed António and was sold into the Atlantic slave trade. He would sail to Virginia in 1621 aboard the *James*. The Virginia Muster (census) of 1624 lists his name as *"Antonio not given,"* recorded as *"a Negro"* in the *"notes"* column. Johnson was sold as an indentured servant to a White planter named Richard Bennet to work on his Virginia tobacco farm (Slave laws were not passed until 1661 in Virginia; before that date, Africans were not officially considered to be enslaved) in what was then known as *"Warresquioake County,"* on the south side of the James River near present day Isle of Wright.[81] In 1623, a Black woman named Mary arrived aboard the ship *Margaret*. She was brought to work on the same plantation as António, where she was the only woman present. António and Mary would eventually marry and live together for more than forty years and had at least four children. Sometime after 1635, António and Mary both concluded the terms of their indentured servitude after which António changed his name to Anthony Johnson. He first entered the legal record as an unindentured man when he purchased a calf in 1647.[82]

Anthony Johnson, *Courtesy of the Public Domain*

When Anthony Johnson was released from his servitude, he was legally recognized as a *"free Negro."* The colonial government granted Johnson a large plot of farmland after he paid off his indentured contract by his labor. On July 24, 1651, he acquired 250 acres of land under the headright system by buying the contracts of five indentured servants, one of whom was his son, Richard Johnson. The headright system worked so that if a man were to bring indentured servants over to the colonies (in this particular case, Johnson brought the five servants, four White and one Black), he was owed 50 acres a *"head",*

The Paradox of Freedom

or servant. The land was located on the Great Naswattock Creek, which flowed into the Pungoteague River in Northampton County, Virginia.[83]

In 1653, John Casor, a Black indentured servant whose contract Johnson appeared to have bought in the early 1640s, approached Captain Goldsmith, claiming his indenture had expired seven years earlier and that he was being held illegally by Johnson. A neighbor, Robert Parker, intervened and persuaded Johnson to free Casor.

Parker offered Casor work, and he signed a term of indenture to the planter. Johnson filed a Freedom suit against Parker in the Northampton Court in 1654 for the return of Casor. The court initially found in favor of Parker, but Johnson appealed. It was argued that Johnson's Black indentured servant ran away and began working for Parker before his contract with Johnson had been completed, and thus should be his servant for life. Concluding the case, the Court ruled in the following:

Whereas complaint was made on this made to ye court by ye humble peticion of Anth. Johnson Negro agt Mr. Robert Parker that hee detayneth one John Casor a Negro the plaintiffs Servt under pretense yt the sd Jno. Casor is a freeman the court seriously considering & maturely weighing ye premises doe fynd that ye sd Mr. Robert Parker most unrightly keepeth ye sd Negro John Casor from his rt mayster Anth. Johnson as it appeareth by ye Deposition of Capt. Small Gold smith & many probable circumstances. Be it therefore ye Judgement of ye court & ordered that ye sd Jno. Casor negro, shall forthwith bee turned into ye service of his sd. Master Anthony Johnson and that the sd Mr. Robert Parker make payment of all charges in the suite and execution.[84]

In 1655, the court ruled that Anthony Johnson still *"owned"* John Casor and ordered that he be returned with the court dues paid by Robert Parker. This becomes the first instance of a judicial determination in the Thirteen Colonies holding that a person who had committed no crime could be held in servitude for life.[85]

Though Casor was the first person who was declared a slave in a civil case, there were both Black and White indentured servants sentenced to lifetime servitude before him. Many historians describe indentured servant John Punch as the first documented slave (or slave for life) in America, as punishment for escaping his captors

Handwritten court order given to Anthony Johnson condemning John Casor as a "servant for life,"
Courtesy of the Public Domain

in 1640. Punch was required to "serve his said master or his assigns for the time of his natural Life here or elsewhere". The Punch case was significant because it established the disparity between his sentence as a negro and that of the two European indentured servants who escaped with him (one described as Dutch and one as a Scotsman). It is the first documented case in Virginia of an African sentenced to lifetime servitude. It is considered one of the first legal cases to make a racial distinction between Black and White indentured servants.[86]

Several things can be concluded from the Casor court case. Firstly, this case infers the notion that free Blacks initially held and practiced their rights as normal citizens, similar to those held by Whites during the Colonial Period. It is also one of the first in which the right to own a person indefinitely was affirmed, thus being part of the early legitimization of the institution of slavery which plagued the United States. Consequently, between the legal legitimization of slavery and the explosion of the Atlantic Slave Trade, within one hundred and fifty years the slave population of the United States grew to 694,207. Shortly after the Johnson case, others also found their way into the third caste of free slaveholding African-Americans.[87]

The legal landscape of slavery in colonial America was a complex and ever-evolving web of laws and regulations that varied significantly from colony to colony. In most cases the institution existed before being specifically authorized or protected by law. The northern colonies also allowed slavery although in a much milder form than in the south. Even the western regions in which slavery was illegal, discriminated against people of African descent and tried to prohibit their entry.

While the institution of slavery was deeply entrenched in the fabric of colonial society, the legal framework surrounding it was far from uniform, leading to a patchwork of regulations and interpretations. This subsection delves into the legal justifications for slavery, exploring the distinctions drawn between enslaved and free Black individuals. It will examine the laws and regulations governing slavery in different colonies, shedding light on the legal complexities surrounding Black ownership of slaves, a phenomenon often overlooked in traditional historical narratives.[88]

One of the most fundamental legal distinctions in colonial America was the clear separation between enslaved and free individuals, particularly when it came to Black people. The legal definition of slavery was rooted in the concept of chattel, meaning that enslaved people were considered property, with no legal rights or protections. This legal concept served as the foundation for the brutal system of exploitation that characterized slavery in the colonies. Even though most colonies defined enslaved people as property, the laws surrounding their ownership and treatment were often ambiguous and subject to interpretation. This ambiguity arose, in part, from the fact that the colonies were grappling with conflicting ideologies regarding slavery. On one hand, the economic and political power of slaveholders pushed for the perpetuation of slavery and the protection of their *"property rights."* [89]

Paul Heinegg, a genealogist who has searched for over forty years through the state archives of Virginia, North Carolina, Maryland, and Delaware, looking for records about the lives of free African Americans during colonial times. Heinegg's work reveals that:

. . . most free African American families that originated in colonial Virginia and Maryland descended from White servant women who had children by slaves or free African Americans, and many descended from slaves who were freed before the 1723 Virginia law requiring legislative approval for manumissions. Perhaps most intriguingly, Heinegg has found that very few families that were free during the colonial period descended from White slave owners who had children by their slaves, perhaps as few as one percent of the total. [90]

Heinegg's principal sources for Virginia, North Carolina, and Maryland were all the surviving colonial county court order and minute books on microfilm–nearly a thousand manuscript volumes. Also important were the colonial and early national tax lists, deeds, wills and estate accounts, late-eighteenth to early nineteenth-century free Negro Registers, marriage bonds, colonial parish registers, census records, newspapers, and Revolutionary pension files. The sources encompass virtually every surviving public document relating to these families. The county court records give us a glimpse of the daily life of the ordinary people in the county. They include apprentice indentures (which usually contain the name, age, and parent[s] of the apprentice), suits for debt, and charges for various offenses. Many families appear in colonial deeds and wills without racial designation. Their African ancestry, and often their origin, is revealed only in their conviction by the court for the violation of a race-based law.[91]

The legal framework surrounding slavery varied significantly across the different colonies. Initially there were few specific laws regarding slavery, as the practice became more widespread, colonies began to codify its parameters. Some colonies, such as South Carolina, had more codified and stringent slave codes, while others, like Massachusetts, had less comprehensive legal frameworks governing slavery. These differences in legal structure reflected the varying economic and social contexts of each colony and the shifting political legal tides surrounding the institution of slavery.[92]

Laws were passed to define the status of enslaved individuals that outlined their rights and responsibilities. These laws often denied enslaved people basic human rights, such as freedom of movement, assembly, and the right to own property. In Virginia, the legal framework for slavery was deeply ingrained in the colony's economic and social structure. From the early colonial period, laws were enacted to define the status of enslaved individuals, limiting their rights and freedoms. The Virginia Slave Codes, codified in the 17th century, established the legal basis for the ownership and control of enslaved Africans. These codes outlined the rules governing the treatment of slaves, including their ability to marry, gather in groups, learn to read, or even own property. They also defined the harsh penalties for disobedience and escape, including imprisonment, flogging, and even death.[93]

In contrast, Massachusetts, a colony with a strong Puritan tradition, initially did not have a comprehensive set of slave codes. While slavery existed in Massachusetts, the legal framework surrounding it was less formalized and more legally contested. Early laws in Massachusetts addressed slavery in a less explicit manner, focusing more on regulating the treatment of enslaved individuals rather than defining their legal status as property.[94]

One of the most significant legal developments was the emergence of the *"one-drop rule,"* which declared that anyone with even a single drop of African blood was considered Black and subject to enslavement. This rule was not only a legal construct but also a social reality, shaping the racial hierarchy of colonial society. It effectively solidified the notion of Blackness as a permanent state of inferiority, defining the social and legal standing of Black people, regardless of their individual circumstances.[95]

However, the legal and social landscape of slavery was not monolithic. Within this system, a small but significant number of Black people were able to attain their freedom. Some gained their freedom through manumission, a process by which their owners granted them freedom. Others were born free, having parents who had been emancipated, or were born into families that had achieved legal freedom through various means like indentured servitude. These free Black individuals faced a complex reality, navigating a society that was deeply divided by race and where they often faced discrimination and prejudice.[96]

An explanation of how free Blacks were assimilated into Virginia society and eventually owned slaves would be beneficial. When Africans arrived in Virginia, they became a part of a society that was divided between master and White indentured servant, a society with such contempt for White servants that masters were not punished for beating them to death. They joined the same households with White servants, working, eating, sleeping, getting drunk, and running away together. Some of these first African slaves became free. John Geaween (Gowen), *"a negro servant,"* was free by 1641. Francis Payne of Northampton County paid for his freedom about 1650 by purchasing three White servants for his master's use. Emanuell Cambow (Cumbo), *"Negro,"* was granted fifty acres in James City County in 1667. John

Harris, *"negro,"* was free by 1668 when he purchased fifty acres in York County.[97]

A number of people of African descent living on the Eastern Shore gained their freedom in the seventeenth century. There were at least thirty-three people of African descent in Northampton County, representing one-third of the taxable African Americans in the county in the 1670s, who were free, later became free, or had free children. By the mid-seventeenth century, some free Blacks were beginning to be assimilated into colonial Virginia society. Many were the result of mixed-race marriages such as Francis Payne who was married to a White woman named Amy in 1656 when he gave her a mare by deed of jointure. Elizabeth Key, a *"Mulatto"* woman whose father had been free, successfully sued for her freedom in Northumberland County in 1656 and married her White attorney, William Greensted. Francis Skiper was married to Ann, an African American woman, before 1668(?) when they sold land in Norfolk County. Peter Beckett, a *"Negro"* slave taxable from 1671 to 1677 in Northampton County, married Sarah Dawson, a white servant. Hester Tate, an English woman servant in Westmoreland County, had several children by her husband James Tate, *"a Negro slave to Mr. Patrick Spence,"* before 1690.[98]

As the percentage of people of African descent in the population increased, so did tension between free Blacks and slaveholders. As more and more slaves replaced White servants, the colonial legislatures passed a series of laws between 1670 and 1723 designating slavery as the appropriate condition for people of African descent. Also in 1670, free Blacks and Indians were forbidden to own White servants. In 1691 the manumission of slaves was prohibited unless they were transported out of the colony. In addition, interracial marriage was prohibited and the illegitimate, mixed-race children of White women were to be bound out for thirty years. In 1705 church wardens were allowed to seize and sell the farm stock of slaves to support the poor of the parish. And in

1723 the manumission of slaves was prohibited unless they had rendered some public service.[99]

Despite the efforts of these legislatures, White servant women continued to bear children by Black fathers through the late seventeenth century and well into the eighteenth century. It appears that they were the primary source of the increase in the free Black population for this period. Over two hundred mixed-race families in Virginia descended from White women. Many of these women may have been the common-law wives of slaves since they had several mixed-race children. Forty-six families descended from freed slaves, twenty-nine from Indians, and sixteen from white men who married or had children by free Black women. It is likely that the majority of the remaining families descended from White women since they first appear in court records in the mid-eighteenth century when slaves could not be freed without legislative approval, and there is no record of legislative approval for their emancipations.

Racial contempt for Blacks did not fully develop in the manner which would be more well known to history, as in the 9th and 20th Centuries, as long as there were White servants in similar circumstances. It was during this period, as late as the end of the eighteenth century, that free Blacks were accepted in some White communities. Since so many free Blacks were light skinned, many observers assume that they were the offspring of White slave owners who took advantage of their female slaves. Only three of the approximately 570 families in Virginia and the Carolinas were proven to descend from a White slave owner. They were the children of South Carolina planters, and like their fathers, they were wealthy slave owners who were accepted in White society.

In 1782 Virginia relaxed its restrictions on manumission, but the descendants of families which had been free during the colonial period continued to comprise a major part of the free Black population due to its natural increase. In 1810 the Gowen family, free since the mid-seventeenth century, headed forty *"other free"* households with 105 persons in Virginia, sixty-two persons in North Carolina, eleven in South Carolina, and ten in Louisiana. The Chavis family, free since the seventeenth century, headed forty-one households containing forty-six persons in Virginia, 159 in North Carolina, and twelve in South Carolina.[100]

By the 1790s free Blacks were concentrated on the Eastern Shore of Virginia, the counties below the James River, and the northeastern part of North Carolina. This was the pattern of settlement similar to that of newly freed White servants because land was available in Southside Virginia and in the northeastern part of North Carolina at prices former servants could afford. Despite their freedom, free Black individuals often found themselves operating within a system that was designed to limit their opportunities and control their lives. They faced limitations on their access to education, employment, and even the right to vote. They were subject to racial prejudice and discrimination, and often faced violence and threats to their safety.

The presence of free Black individuals in colonial America challenged the prevailing notion that Blackness was synonymous with enslavement. They demonstrated that it was possible to achieve freedom, even within a system designed to suppress them. However, their experiences also highlighted the pervasive and insidious nature of racism and the enduring power of slavery as a system of social control.[101]

The existence of free Black slaveholders adds another layer of complexity to this intricate social and legal landscape of colonial America. The very notion of a free Black individual owning enslaved people seems contradictory. While slavery was often viewed as a system that denied Black people agency and control, the historical record reveals that free Black individuals, who had been born free or had attained their freedom through emancipation, owned slaves in various colonies. This phenomenon raises profound questions about the nature of freedom, power, and race in colonial America and forces us to confront the complexities of race, power, and freedom in colonial America, and to challenge our assumptions about the nature of slavery.[102]

Freedom appeared to come to Africans and African Americans during the colonial period with the expectation that they would become full members of their communities which suggests that *"free Blacks attempted to transform themselves into black Englishmen."* This would entitle them to the same privileges as White Englishmen such as the right to own property.[103]

The legal framework surrounding Black ownership of slaves was often fraught with contradictions and ambiguities. Many colonial acts governing free Black slaveholders often mirrored the laws governing white slaveholders allowing free Black individuals to inherit slaves from their White masters, deceased spouses, or purchase enslaved individuals to provide labor for their businesses or farms, but these laws for the justifications for Black ownership of slaves varied from colony to colony. While the legal system generally recognized the rights of free Black individuals to own slaves, societal biases and prejudices often resulted in challenges and limitations for Black slaveholders. The legality of Black slaveholders in colonial America was a dynamic and complex phenomenon, reflecting the shifting tides of power and the ongoing struggles for freedom and equality which created both opportunities and constraints for Black individuals.

The legal framework surrounding slavery provides invaluable insight into the realities of colonial life. By examining the laws and regulations that governed slavery in different colonies, we can gain a deeper understanding of the complex social, economic, and political forces that shaped the institution of slavery and its impact on the lives of both enslaved and free individuals. The legal landscape serves as a reminder that the history of slavery was not a monolithic narrative but a complex and multifaceted story that requires careful examination and critical analysis.[104]

In Virginia, the ultimate property right of free Blacks was the right to acquire, own, and alienate slaves. For more than twenty years from the time that free Blacks first appeared in court there was no legal restriction upon their right to own white indentured servants. Such a reversal of the usual order may have been in a few cases actually attempted, for in 1670 a law was enacted that *"noe negro or Indian though baptized and enjoyned their freedome shall be capable of any purchase of Christians, but not yet debarred from buying any of their owne nation."*[105] (See Appendix I)

Equally intrusive is the following *"Deed of sale of slaves to a freeman"* based on colonial Virginia laws passed in 1752:

Know all men of these presence that I David A. Jones of Amelia County (Virginia) of the one part have and in consideration of the sum of five hundred dollars grant unto Frank Gromes a black man of the other part a negro woman named Patience and two children by name Phil & Betsy to have and to hold & to hold the above-named negroes to the only proper use and benefits of him and his heirs forever.[106]

Free Black slave ownership was less complicated when it began in the 1650s, but when it threatened to grow, legislators took quick action to limit it. The number of free Negro slaveholders would start to rise again only after legislation in 1782 allowed emancipation, by deed or will rather than by action of the state assembly, which had proven to be rare. From 1782 to 1806, most ownership of Blacks by Blacks was temporary, having as its object the manumission of that *"species of property."*[107]

The Paradox of Freedom

Yet, the economic realities of colonial America played a significant role in shaping the decisions of free Black slaveholders. While often overlooked in historical narratives, the desire for economic advancement and the potential for wealth accumulation drove some free Black individuals to own slaves. Many free black entrepreneurs, who were the children of White slaveowners, were provided with slaves or the means to acquire slaves. In 1735, Joseph Pendarvis, a white planter of Colleton County, South Carolina, wrote a will, which provided his children by a Negro woman named Parthena with the means to become one of the largest free black slaveowners in South Carolina. They had seven mulatto children (James, Brand, William, John, Thomas, Mary, and Elizabeth Pendarvis). James Pendarvis (b. 1718) was the oldest child and appears to have inherited most of his father's estate. Between 1785 and 1787, he owned taxable property, which consisted of 3,500 acres of land and 113 slaves in St Paul's Parish, Colleton County in Charleston District. By 1792, Pendarvis owned 4,710 acres of land and 123 slaves. When he died about 1797, his estate comprised 4,709 acres of land and 151 slaves. With such wealth and status, the Pendarvis family married into the White planter class and merged into the White community.[108]

Other free Black colonial entrepreneurs followed James Pendarvis' example. During the 1760s, Elizabeth Cleveland Hardcastle, the mixed blood daughter of William Cleveland, a slave trader from the coast of West Africa and his African mistress, arrived in Charleston, South Carolina not as a slave but a Free Woman of Color born in what is now Sierra Leone. She came to America with a dream and money to acquire a plantation for her brother, John Cleveland, who was also a mixed blood slave trader. By 1790, she owned an estate, which consisted of 26 slaves and plantations in St John & Berkeley Parish and St. Stephen's Parish in Charleston District. When Catherine died in December 1808, she owned two plantations, Raccoon Hill which consisted of 700 acres and Tucker Plantation, which had about 700 - 900 acres of land. In her inventory, she reportedly owned 33 slaves. Like the Pendarvis family, Catherine married into the White aristocratic class but she conceived no children to blend into white society.[109]

The experiences of the Pendarvis and Hardcastle families were not limited to the rural communities in the low country of South Carolina where only 23 of 59 or 39 percent of free black slaveholders lived in 1790. The first federal census reported that the majority (36 of 59 or 61 percent) of the Black slaveholding families lived in Charleston City. In that year Lydia Watson was the head of a free black family, which consisted of 5 slaves. Even though Lydia held a small number of slaves, she was not a benevolent slave master who held family members. Lydia Watson was part of the Black elite who held slaves to exploit their labor. According to her will, recorded in 1829, she was the owner of a slave woman named Lucy. Her slave was recorded in Lydia's will and inventory and given to her freeborn daughter Abigail Webley Beale as chattel.[110]

Ana Gallum

Ana Gallum, sometimes known as Nansi Wiggins, a Senegalese lady, had been abducted from her own country and forced to serve as a bondswoman in the Americas and rose to become a plantation owner. She lived from around 1755 to 1840.[111]

From the beginning, her experience mirrors that of millions of other Africans who were sold into slavery during the Transatlantic Slave Trade and endured the Middle Passage. But Gallum's life was not like theirs in any significant way. She served as a bondswoman for a brief time, and then married her former master, Joseph "Job" Wiggins, a white plantation owner from England,

The Paradox of Freedom

Artist's rendering of Ana Gallum,
Courtesy of Kids Encyclopedia Facts

and was eventually set free. She would have six children with him, four daughters and two sons. The two remained together for another 18 years until Wiggins died in 1797, leaving his entire estate and all property to Gallum as the rightful inheritor on the behalf of their children. She retained ownership of the estate, the rights of her children, a furnished plantation house, and any bondspeople who worked the property. Thereafter, Gallum continued to run her newly acquired estate as her husband had, the only difference being that she was now the head of household, with the assistance of her eldest son Benjamin. After the death of her husband, Gallum worked the plantation and actively participated in the trading of both cattle and enslaved people while doing so.[112]

Due to Gallum living in Florida during the period of Spanish colonial rule, the conditions of her enslavement were different than those faced by other enslaved Africans living elsewhere in Colonial America. Where an enslaved individual was sold into bondage for generations in the Americas, enslavement was seen as a legal condition. It came with some rights under the Spanish *Siete Partidas*. Under these guidelines, enslaved people were afforded certain rights, and enslaved women were placed into the same protected class as children and other "invalids" who were believed to require "*supervision*" but were deemed deserving of some certain amount of privilege. Women were protected from physical and sexual assault under Spanish law, and enslaved women were no exception. Spaniards were typically accustomed to African communities, and miscegenation was common in the Spanish colonies. According to historian Dr. Jane Landers, *"the courts in Spanish Florida regularly supported the inheritance rights of women and children of African descent if their relationship to the deceased had been publicly acknowledged, even when the mothers were not legally married to the fathers of their children."*[113]

George Gardiner, who was reported on the 1790 census, was a bricklayer by trade and a commercial slave. When he died in 1797, George was listed as the former owner of the following slaves: Frank, a laborer; Jack, a laborer; Paul, a laborer; Bob, a bricklayer; Betty, a house servant; Clarissa and her child, Mary. Those slaves were given to his daughter, Elizabeth Gardiner. During the late 1790s, many, if not the majority of free black slaveholding families held slaves to exploit their labor.[114]

One crucial factor in the economic decisions of free Black slaveholders was access to land. Owning land was a central pillar of economic stability and independence in colonial America. It provided a means of subsistence, a platform for agricultural production, and a tangible asset that could be passed down through generations. However, for free

The Paradox of Freedom

Black people, acquiring land was an uphill battle. Laws and social norms often hindered their ability to purchase or inherit property.

Despite these obstacles, some free Black individuals managed to acquire land through various means. Some purchased property, often through laborious saving and financial assistance from benevolent whites or other free Black individuals. Others inherited land from family members or acquired it through legal claims. In some cases, they were granted land by the government, particularly through land grants awarded to those who served in the Revolutionary War or who were deemed valuable members of society.[115]

The acquisition of land provided free Black slaveholders with a crucial economic foundation. It not only gave them a source of livelihood but also created the possibility for economic expansion. With land, they could cultivate crops, raise livestock, or engage in other agricultural activities that could generate income and build wealth. However, land ownership alone did not guarantee economic success. Labor was the other critical ingredient in the equation. The lack of access to skilled labor, limited by societal prejudices, further restricted opportunities for free Black individuals. Owning slaves provided a way to overcome these limitations, offering access to a dependable workforce.

It is crucial to note that the motivations of free Black slaveholders were not monolithic. Some were driven by a genuine desire for economic security and social mobility, seeking to create a better life for themselves and their families. Others may have viewed slavery as a necessary means to overcome the systemic inequalities and economic hardships they faced. They viewed slaves as a consistent and exploitable source of labor that could be utilized in various economic endeavors such as the cultivation of crops, the production of goods, the operation of small businesses, or even as skilled craftsmen. The potential for increased production and profits through slave labor held significant allure for free Black individuals seeking to advance their economic standing.

The economic benefits of owning slaves varied significantly, depending on factors such as the size of the slaveholding, the nature of the work performed, and the prevailing market conditions. They sought to gain access to land, labor, and resources, hoping to establish their own economic independence and a measure of security in a society that often denied them equal opportunities. In a world where opportunities were scarce, owning slaves could provide a form of self-sufficiency, a way to build wealth, and a path towards achieving social mobility.

For some, slave ownership provided modest gains, while others were able to achieve significant wealth accumulation. Keep in mind, the economic motivations of free Black slaveholders must be understood within the larger historical context of colonial America. They operated within a system of slavery that was deeply ingrained in society, impacting all facets of life, from the economy and law to social relationships and cultural norms. While some sought to navigate this system and achieve economic success through ownership, their decisions reflected the difficult and complex choices that faced individuals living in a society built upon the foundation of enslaved labor. This was seen throughout all thirteen colonies. As a result, the phenomenon of Black slave owning goes beyond the issue of benevolent versus commercial. The very idea of free Black individuals owning enslaved people highlights the complex and often contradictory nature of the colonial society.

In a society where social standing was often tied to the ownership of property and the ability to command labor, owning slaves could elevate a free Black person's standing within the community. It could be a way to establish a sense of power and authority in a system that consistently sought to marginalize them. This was particularly true for free Black individuals who might be denied access to other forms of social and economic capital, such as education or professional opportunities.

Let's focus on the ownership of slaves and how it reflected upon the complexities of familial ties and inheritance. Free Black individuals might inherit slaves from family members, often as a way to preserve family property and maintain kinship networks. In some cases, this inheritance was seen as a burden, a reminder of the system that had enslaved their ancestors, while in other cases, it was accepted as a part of the existing social order.

Marie Thérèse Metoyer

One such person was Marie Thérèse Metoyer, a free Black who lived in colonial French and Spanish rule of Louisiana. As a free woman, Coincoin, as she was so often called, exploited a variety of economic enterprises. She manufactured medicine, planted tobacco, and trapped wild bears and turkeys, which were sent to the local market and shipping peltry and oil along with indigo that she sourced from the bear skins to New Orleans along with her cured tobacco. Saving her money, over time, she became a landowner and a taxpayer. Like many other freed slaves in colonial Louisiana, she eventually acquired slaves in order to protect them from others in the parish purchasing them. Most were related to Marie Theresa or close friends, she labored alongside of them until her own health began to fail.[116]

Maire Carmelite Antey is the granddaughter of Marie Thérèse "Coincoin" Metoyer owned 12,000 acres of land and a hundred slaves in what is today Natchitoches, Louisiana. *Courtesy of Public Domain*

The Paradox of Freedom

By taking advantage of the liberal land-grant policies of the Spanish Crown, Marie Theresa established her first farmstead on the Grand Coast of Red River, known today as Cane River, about ten miles below Natchitoches. That small tract of 67 acres, alluvial river-bottom land adjacent to Metoyer's plantation, was conceded by the local commandant in January 1787 and patented by the Crown in May 1794.[117]

On the heels of that patent, Marie Theresa applied for a significantly larger concession, about 670 acres of piney woods on Old River to the west of her farm, where she established a *vacherie*, or cattle range, and hired a Spaniard to operate it for her. She eventually bought in 1807 a third tract of already developed farmland north of her property rounding out 1,000 acres under her control.[118]

That third holding, adjacent to her homestead, provided a stake for a younger son who had come of age after the Louisiana Purchase, too late to benefit from the more-liberal land policies of the Spanish regime. Marie Theresa has been credited with the founding of Cane River's fabled Melrose Plantation. However, this land has been documented as a grant to her son, Louis Metoyer, who built most of the surviving plantation buildings prior to his death.[119]

Marie Theresa tried for nine years to free all of her children from slavery and in 1815 when Metoyer died all her children were freed. In 1816 written Church documents show that she had twelve slaves, but local tradition credits her with many more. Marie Theresa now had three plots of land estimated at 11,000 acres by the time she was in her late sixties. She eventually completely turned over the plantation to her children. She died sometime in the spring of 1816.[120]

The experiences of Free Black slaveholders within the colonial landscape were as diverse as the individuals themselves. While some strived to provide their enslaved individuals with a degree of autonomy

The Paradox of Freedom

and humane treatment, others perpetuated the harsh realities of the system, driven by factors of economic ambition or a desire to maintain a perceived social standing. Understanding these divergent experiences necessitates delving further into the complexities of their motivations, the social and economic circumstances that shaped their choices, and the impact of their actions on those under their control. Their actions were not without controversy. The very act of owning slaves, even by a free Black person, raised questions about the nature of freedom and the implications of participating in this system that enslaved others. It challenged the notion that *"freedom"* was a universally recognized right.

Chapter 3:
Black Masters in the Early American Republic, 1780-1830

"He said, in answer to further inquiries, that there were many free Negroes all about this region. Some were very rich. He pointed out to me three plantations, within twenty miles, owned by coloured men. They bought black folks, he said, and had servants of their own. They were very bad masters, very hard and cruel . . . If he had got to be sold, he would like best to have an American master buy him. The French [black Creole] masters were very severe, and 'dey whip dar niggers most to deff—dey whipe de flesh off of 'em.'"
  – Unknown Former Slave[121]

With the establishment of United States of America, the phenomenon of free Black slaveholding continued as a result of a confluence of factors, including family ties and inheritance, economic opportunity, and social status. These factors played a significant role in the decision-making process of free Black slaveholders. While some free Black individuals may have been motivated by a desire for wealth and power, others may have been driven by a desire to protect their families, or to maintain the bonds of kinship. In many instances free Black husbands purchased their wives, or vice versa. Slaves belonging to such families were few compared with the large numbers of slaves found among the Whites on well-developed plantations. Slaves of Negroes were in some cases the children of a free father who had purchased his wife. If he did not thereafter emancipate the mother, as so many such husbands failed to do, his own children were born his slaves and were thus reported to the enumerators. Benevolent Negroes often purchased slaves to make their lot easier by granting them their freedom for a nominal sum, or by permitting them to work it out on liberal terms.[122]

The Paradox of Freedom

For those moved by a desire to maintain familial connections, inheritances influenced their slaveholding decisions to ensure the well-being of their loved ones extended beyond their immediate household. In a society where free Blacks; freedom and social mobility was often restricted; the ownership of slaves also offered a means to build a secure future for their descendants. In many instances, slaves were passed down through generations, becoming part of a family legacy. Free Black slaveholders often inherited enslaved people from relatives, creating a complex web of family dynamics and ownership. The desire to maintain those familial connections could outweigh any ethical considerations, leading to a continuation of slavery within Black families. This paradox of freedom and control in the lives of free Black slaveholders was a deep personal and societal struggle. Their experiences expose the complexities of agency and autonomy within a system designed to strip Black people of their freedoms. It also serves as a reminder that historical narratives are often multifaceted and can challenge easy categorization, and revealing crucial insights of unique individuals larger themes in the social and psychological landscape of the early Republic.

Inheriting slaves from a parent or other family members was a common occurrence, and the act of passing down slaves through generations served as a tangible expression of familial bonds and financial security. It may come as a surprise to some but General Ulysses S. Grant inherited a slave named William Jones, Abraham Lincoln inherited slaves from his wife's father who was the largest slave holder in Kentucky, and a free Black woman named Ann Deas Jones inherited slaves from her father using them to create one of Charleston, South Carolinas' finest hotels, the *Mansion House Hotel*.[123]

In a society that often denied Black individuals equal opportunities to accumulate wealth and property, the ownership of slaves provided a means of establishing financial stability and passing on a legacy to future generations. This was particularly significant for free Black women, who faced even greater limitations in acquiring property and economic independence. The ownership of slaves by free Black individuals often transcended the desire for personal economic gain and encompassed a broader vision of securing the future of their families.

Jehu Jones, Sr.
The story of Jehu Jones, a prominent free Black hotel owner in Charleston, South Carolina, is one of those stories. Born into slavery in 1769, Jones was enslaved by Christopher Rogers, a successful tailor. Under Rogers, he learned the skills of tailoring and running a business from Rogers while developing his own knowledge through personal experiences. When Rogers manumitted him in 1798 for £100 sterling, Jones set up his own business. Jones succeeded and expanded the business with his oldest son, also named Jehu.[124]

Because he lived in Charleston, a thriving urban center, Jones utilized and capitalized upon urban modifications of slavery. Although not much is known about Jones's younger years, it is believed that he took advantage of the "hiring out" system that characterized urban iterations of slavery. This system involved an enslaved person, an enslaver, a hirer, and a contract that specified pay, length of labor, and any other stipulations. Enslavers used the hiring out system because they usually took some, if not all, the pay earned by enslaved people. Hirers saw an opportunity to take advantage of enslaved labor without making the costly investment of purchasing enslaved workers. At the same time, enslaved people exploited the hiring out system to gain and increase autonomy and agency over their lives.

In Charleston, enslaved people were hired out to perform various tasks, including municipal jobs, domestic work, and, in Jones's case, tailoring services. While the details of Jones's involvement with the hiring out system are not known, the historic record reveals that Jones purchased his freedom in 1798 for $140, most likely with money he earned by using the hiring out system. By the early 1800s, Jones not only expanded his tailoring business but also delved into real estate ventures, purchasing property downtown and on Sullivan's Island in 1802.

Jones' combined real estate investments and expanding tailoring business proved so successful, he gained enough wealth and prestige to join the Brown Fellowship Society, one of the oldest benevolent societies for African Americans in South Carolina. The Brown Fellowship Society was founded in 1790 by Black and mulatto members of St. Philips Episcopal Church who were restricted from using the church's all white graveyard. The Brown Fellowship Society began as a way to support African American members, and their widows and children, but came to represent classism and elitism among African Americans in Charleston. Usually, only lighter-skinned free African Americans were allowed to join the Brown Fellowship Society. All members had to be relatively wealthy as initiation fees were $50 in addition to annual membership dues. In fact, some members of the Brown Fellowship Society, including Jehu Jones, were wealthy enough to purchase enslaved people. At the end of the Antebellum era in Charleston, 131 free African Americans enslaved a total of 338 people. This fact, combined with the elite Black community's attempts to separate themselves from enslaved communities, created an environment of tension among Black Charlestonians.[125]

His endeavors flourished and in 1807 he began to buy slaves to assist him in his business ventures. In the 1810s, Jones made a series of real estate transactions that included purchasing from William Johnson a lot and house on Broad Street behind St. Michael's Church. In 1815 Jones bought the adjoining property at 33 Broad Street, known as the Burrows-Hall House, with adjacent outbuildings for $13,000. The following year he sold the Johnson House to St. Michael's Church. Jones then left the occupation of *"tailoring"* to his son, Jehu, Jr., and turned his efforts to innkeeping, a venture in which he had already achieved some success. By 1816, Jones and his wife Abigail turned 33 Broad Street into a popular hotel known as the Jones Hotel which catered to elite Whites only, such as the portrait artist Samuel F. B. Morse. Jones used enslaved labor to create an exclusive and luxurious inn. Elite White society patronized the establishment and praised it highly for its comfort and fine food.[126]

The events following the Denmark Vesey Conspiracy of 1822 (a slave revolt led by a free Black in Charleston that was uncovered before it could be carried out) affected the Jones family. Free African Americans, whether they were part of the elite Black society or not, were closely scrutinized and subjected to stricter regulations. Adult African American men were supposed to be supervised by a White guardian. After the conspiracy, free Black South Carolinians were not allowed to travel in or out of the state unless they sought and obtained expressed permission from the state government. After 1823, this law prevented Abigail Jones from returning to South Carolina after taking her children and grandchildren to New York for a visit prior to the Vesey Rebellion. Jones, along with his guardian, Governor John Lide Wilson, petitioned the Assembly for a leave of absence from the state so that Jones could visit his own family because Abagail Jones had been traveling with her children and grandchildren in New York before 1822 and faced difficulty returning home.[127]

The petition was granted and Jones saw his family, but, he could not return to the state. In 1827 he requested permission to visit his family in St. Augustine, Florida, but the records are unclear as to whether he made the trip or not. There was a rumor circulating that Jones moved to New York and walked the streets disguised as a woman. Abigail never returned to South Carolina and stayed in New York as an innkeeper where she died before her husband.[128]

Jehu Jones, Sr. passed away in 1833. His estate, which included enslaved people but not Jones's real estate properties, was valued at $40,000 and was split between his three sons and his stepdaughter, Ann Deas, who had been traveling with Abigail Jones in the 1820s. Deas petitioned South Carolina's governor for a pardon and returned to Charleston to obtain her inheritance that included the Jones Hotel. Ann Deas took over the hotel of her stepfather in 1834. She managed it with great success and it continued to be one of the most elite hotels in Charleston. She renamed it the *Mansion House Hotel*.[129]

Jones Hotel and later Mansion House Hotel as it appeared in 1928, *Courtesy of the South Carolina Historical Society*

The origin of these elite free Black slaveholders can be traced to the late 18th and early 19th Centuries, when the Republic was young. Some White men in the Lower South took Black women as their sexual partners and bequeathed them, or their mulatto children, land and slaves. Of course, these practices were frowned upon by the English who had established themselves along the Atlantic seaboard. Thus in the American English colonies only a few Black families acquired property in such a way, but along the Gulf Coast and Louisiana, where Spanish and French customs prevailed, interracial unions were encouraged, especially with the lack of White females in these regions. Here, several hundred Black families received or inherited property from Whites. What is unusual about this is that marriages between Whites and Blacks, whether they be free or slave, were illegal in every state. Such laws did not prevent mixed race couples from becoming so common in Louisiana that an institution called "*placage*" was developed. This required White men contracting to live with Black women to provide them with financial support. In Louisiana, this became a social norm. In addition, during the early 1800s, White (and free colored) immigrants from the Caribbean, often of French background, arrived in the United States with Black spouses or, upon arrival, took free Women of Color or slaves as their partners.[130]

Placage was a recognized extralegal system in French and Spanish slave colonies of North America, including the Caribbean, by which ethnic European men entered into civil unions with non-Europeans of African, Native American and mixed-race descent. The term comes from the French *placer* meaning "to place with". The women were not legally recognized as wives but were known as *placées*; their relationships were recognized among the Free People of Color as *marriages de la main gauche* or left-handed marriages. They became institutionalized with contracts or negotiations that settled property on the woman and her children and, in some cases, gave them freedom if they were enslaved. The system flourished throughout the French and Spanish colonial periods, reaching its zenith during the latter, between 1769 and 1803. In addition, during the early 1800s, White and Free Colored immigrants from the Caribbean, many of French background, arrived in the United States with Black spouses or took Free Women of Color, or slaves, as their partners. These were the social norms that were inherited by the United States after the acquisition of the Louisiana Purchase territories.[131]

Upon the death of her protector, the *placée* and her family could, on legal challenge, expect up to a third of the man's property. Some White lovers made their mixed-race children primary heirs over other White descendants or relatives. A notable inheritance case was the daughters of Nicolás María Vidal, a former high official in Spanish Louisiana, who, with their mother, Eufrosina Hinard, successfully petitioned the US government in the 1830s to intercede on their behalf to secure a portion of Vidal's estate.[132]

The women in those relationships often worked to develop assets: acquiring property, running a legitimate rooming-house, or a small business as a hairdresser, *marchande* (female street or country merchant/vendor), or a seamstress. She could also become a *placée* to another White Creole. She sometimes taught her daughters to become *placées*, by education and informal schooling in dress, comportment, and ways to behave. A mother negotiated with a young man for the dowry or property settlement, sometimes by contract, for her daughter if a white Creole were interested in her. A former *placée* could also marry or cohabit with a Creole Man of Color and have more children.[133]

Whatever the circumstances, and despite the various traditions across the Lower South, the vast majority of Free People of Color who reached the upper economic levels during these early years was of mixed racial ancestry. Most were children or grandchildren of White planters or merchants and slave women. They had inherited land, slaves, and other property from their White relatives. One such small group of prosperous free Black artisans in Charleston during the 1790s was virtually all directly related to Whites, as well as those who in later years, established successful businesses or became rice planters. The wealthiest free Black in South Carolina, James Pendarvis, owned 3,250 acres of land, was the son of a White planter and a slave woman. Other prosperous Free People of Color, including John Holman, Jr., Elias Collins, Jehu Jones, William Penceel, William Ellison, and Margaret Noisette, were descendants of White men and slave or free Black women. In Georgia, Anthony Odingsells was one of the largest Black property owners in the state. He received his land and nine slaves from Charles Odingsells, an officer in the American Revolution. The most prominent "colored Creole family" in Florida, the Pons family, claimed they were the descendants of two Spanish officers. In Alabama, the two largest Black landholders, Zeno and Basile Chastang, were the children of Dr. John Chastang, a prominent surgeon who had served as a medical consultant at the Spanish fort of San Esteban de Tombecbe. Similarly, in Mississippi and Louisiana. Such examples indicated that many prosperous Free People of Color were of mixed racial heritage.[134]

The Paradox of Freedom

Acquiring slaves through inheritance served as a way to preserve family unity and prevent separation in a world where Black families were constantly under the threat of being broken apart by the forces of slavery. By maintaining the ownership of enslaved individuals within the family, free Black individuals could limit the risk of their loved ones being sold away or separated from their kin. Furthermore, the ownership of slaves could be viewed as a means of ensuring the continuation of family traditions and cultural practices. By passing down enslaved individuals to their descendants, free Black individuals could ensure that certain skills and knowledge were preserved and passed on to future generations. This was especially important in the context of the slave trade, where families were frequently broken apart and the transmission of traditional knowledge was disrupted. Through the ownership of family members, free Black slaveowners offered a measure of control and stability for their families. Their desire to maintain family ties also ensured financial security and navigate the complexities of racial power that were intricately woven into the decision-making processes of free Black slaveholders. This dynamic highlighted their multifaceted experiences that started during colonial times making them both victims and perpetrators of the institution of slavery. The ownership of slaves by free Black individuals was a testament to their resilience, their desire for agency, and their efforts to create a sense of stability and security within a system that sought to undermine them at times, but mostly their desire to protect family was deeply ingrained in their experiences. Historian James Oakes once stated in 1982 that, *"[t]he evidence is overwhelming that the vast majority of black slaveholders were free men who purchased members of their families or who acted out of benevolence"*. After 1810, Southern states made it increasingly difficult for any slaveholders to free slaves to curtail the manumission of slaves by Black slaveholders and limit the future growth of free Blacks as Oaks points out, *"there were increasing efforts to restrict the right to hold bondsmen on the grounds that slaves should be kept 'as far as possible under the control of white men only.'"*[135]

Even with the advantage of inheritance, it took a lot of effort on these peoples part to maintain their holdings. In towns and cities across the South, Free Men and Women of Color took advantage of the demand for service businesses, the small number of skilled White and immigrant skilled workers, and the general appreciation of property values in the areas allowed them to expand their estates. In the rural areas, they took advantage of the economic opportunities in the West. The rising prices for slaves, and the ever increasing value of real estate. Some free Blacks speculated in city property or farmlands, while others watched as the value of their holdings increased. In Louisiana, farm acreage increased in value, especially if it was near a river or bayou, went from $2.00 an acre at the time of statehood in 1812, as high as $50.00 or more by the 1830s. They also saw a rise in the value of their livestock, wagons, tools, machinery, and especially slaves. As the value increased of their holdings, this gave them the capital needed to expand their businesses or farm acreage increasing their wealth substantially.[136]

Therefore, one can surmise that the decision to own slaves was not simply a matter of practical necessity or familial obligation but often for economic advancement as well. The desire to maintain family ties often intersected with the complexities of racial power dynamics and the desire for social mobility which made free Black individuals aware of their limitations imposed upon them by a society that viewed them as inherently inferior. The ownership of slaves offered them a means of asserting agency and challenging the dominant racial hierarchy, albeit, on that hierarchy's own terms.

Carter G. Woodson wrote in 1924 that when he outlined the "sphere of defacto freedom", *"most black slave owners acquired their slave property to preserve family ties. For example, a husband who was born or had managed to become free might buy his wife from the white person who owned her. The husband would thereafter possess his spouse as a slave, not because he wished to keep her in bondage but because the laws of the slave states often made manumission difficult or impossible. Thus African Americans held other African Americans in a kind of pseudo-slavery rather than in genuine servitude, and the owners' motivation for possessing their slave property was benevolent rather than exploitative."* Woodson did acknowledge that, *"some black slaveholders bought slaves for the same reason that whites did, to gain economic advantage from their forced labor."*[137]

For many free Black individuals, the ownership of slaves created a distinct social space where they could exercise a degree of autonomy and control. Owning slaves could elevate a free Black person's standing within the community. It could be a way to establish a sense of power and authority in a system that consistently sought to marginalize them. This was particularly true for free Black individuals who might be denied access to other forms of social and economic capital, such as education or professional opportunities. This power was not without its contradictions and ethical dilemmas, as it meant wielding power over other Black people. Some free Black slaveholders may have seen their ownership of slaves as a way to improve their social standing and gain respect within the community by establishing a sense of power and authority in a system that consistently sought to marginalize them. This was particularly true for free Black individuals who might be denied access to other forms of social and economic capital, such as education or professional opportunities.

This paradox of freedom and control within the system of slavery was a lived experience for free Black slaveholders. The very act of owning slaves, while holding the status of freedom themselves, introduced complex and often conflicting dynamics into their lives. It raised profound questions about power, agency, and the meaning of freedom within a society built on racial hierarchy. On the surface, it seemed odd, Black individuals who were themselves free, yet holding power over other Black people who were enslaved. This contradictory position forced free Blacks into a web of contradictions. They were enjoying the economic security and social status of the system of slavery, while also subject to its oppressive realities and influence.

The psychological implications had to be profound. Free Black slaveholders had to reconcile their personal experiences of discrimination and oppression with their participation in a system composed of the very structures that had denied them full rights and liberties. They were often faced with the moral and ethical dilemmas of reconciling their own pursuit of freedom with the reality of owning other human beings. This internal conflict could manifest in varying degrees of compassion and cruelty towards their enslaved individuals, revealing the complexities of agency and autonomy within a system that recognized humanity, contingent upon racial background.

The motivations for owning slaves, the treatment of enslaved individuals, and the overall impact on Black communities were all influenced by a multitude of factors, making it essential to avoid generalizations and to acknowledge the diversity of experiences within this historical phenomenon. The reality is though that ownership of slaves by free Black individuals did happen and was a reality that challenged the simplistic notions of *"slave"* and *"free"*. It highlighted the ways in which race, freedom, and economic opportunity were interwoven, creating a system of both privilege and oppression in American society at that time.

This moral and ethical struggle caused free Blacks to become aware of their own vulnerabilities and the precariousness of their freedom, while simultaneously exerting control over the lives of other Black people. As previously stated, their presence within White communities challenged racial hierarchy that demonstrating that "slave" and "free" did not always align racially. This blurring of lines challenged the very foundation of slavery, where racial identity was inextricably linked to one's status making free Black slaveholders a testament to the fluidity of racial boundaries, a reminder that Black people could be both oppressors and oppressed. The ownership of slaves by free Black individuals also carried significant risks and limitations. While owning slaves might have provided economic and social advantages, it did not erase the fundamental reality of racial prejudice and discrimination that permeated society. This created a social landscape rife with internal contradictions and tensions.

Some free Black individuals, particularly those who had attained a degree of economic and social status, as with Jehu Jones, saw themselves as part of a distinct group, separate from the enslaved African population. They might have sought to maintain their own social standing by distancing themselves from the plight of enslaved individuals. This, in turn, created a tension between those who had achieved freedom and those who remained enslaved, highlighting the internal divisions within Black communities shaped by the very system of slavery.

Marianne Celeste Dragon
Another was Marianne Celeste Dragon a prominent Creole born on March 1, 1777, in New Orleans, Spanish Louisiana. Her father was American Revolutionary War hero Michel Dragon was Greek and he migrated to New Orleans during the 1760s. Her mother was a former slave named Marie Françoise Chauvin Beaulieu de Montplaisir. She belonged to Mr. Charles Daprémont de La Lande. Records indicate that Marianne's parents were married, which was legally prohibitive for an interracial couple since she was of African descent.[138]

There are over 36 documented slave records clarifying that Michel Dragon and his wife Françoise Chauvin Beaulieu de Monplaisir were planters. There are also many documented slave trades organized among individuals with the last name Monplaisir. Some are listed

The Paradox of Freedom

as *nègres* (in French *"of Black African heritage"*) which is indicative of black slave ownership. Some if not all may have been related to Marie Françoise.[139]

In 1795, a portrait was painted of the young creole Marianne by famous Mexican painter José Francisco Xavier de Salazar y Mendoza, documenting her appearance and physical characteristics. In marriage records, her mother was listed as a quadroon which is considered highly unlikely due to Marianne's complexion. Older baptismal records documented her mother's race as mulatto. Around the same period, Marianne met a Greek man named Andrea Dimitry and wanted to marry him which was against the law for interracial marriages at that time. Documents indicate that the priest Père Antoine read the law prohibiting interracial marriages out loud at the ceremony and knowingly married the couple. Marianne was listed as White in marriage records to make it possible for her to legally marry Andrea. They were married in 1799 and had ten children.[140]

Marianne Celeste Dragon, 1795 portrait.
Courtesy of the Public Domain

The territory became part of the United States in 1803 with the Louisiana Purchase, and the family became American. They are one of the oldest Creole families in New Orleans history. The family identified with their Greek heritage. Andrea was one hundred percent Greek, and Marianne was fifty percent Greek, so their offspring were seventy-five percent Greek. The family mostly identified as European, reinforcing the stereotype of creole society.[141]

The Paradox of Freedom

By 1811, the area experienced the largest slave revolt in American history occurring just thirty miles outside of New Orleans. Slave owners began to dislike the Louisiana free Black people and forced the local government to issue special restrictions for them. William C. C. Claiborne decreased the number of Free Men of Color in the local militia and set special curfews for People of Color. He made Free People of Color carry special passes. Slave owners of Color were also under attack. By the 1830s, White slave owners in Louisiana demanded race distinction. This created a segregation system that was more about the legal status of People of Color. Marianne's family worked hard to conceal their racial identity and made sure that her children were well educated. Her son, Alexander Dimitry, spoke eleven languages and would eventually be the first U.S. Ambassador who was colored. The family established a strong Greek community in New Orleans, and by the 1860s, there was a Greek Orthodox Church and a Greek consulate.[142]

Andrew Dunford

Then there was Andrew Dunford of Louisiana. As well as being a physician, Durnford was also a plantation owner. From the 1820s onwards, he grew his sugar business across the state of Louisiana, ultimately becoming the owner of not just large amounts of land but of dozens of slaves too. Furthermore, the history books show that he regarded the system of slavery as just.[143]

Andrew Dunford,
Courtesy of the Abbeville Institute

Born in 1800 in New Orleans, Durnford was the son of an Englishman, Thomas Durnford, and a free woman of color named Rosaline Mercer. Thanks to the Louisiana Purchase, Andrew automatically became a citizen of the United States and earned a fine education, being fluent in both French and English. While Durnford was still a young man, his father died in 1826. After that, he became first friends, and then business partners, with one of his father's old friends, a white New Orleans merchant and plantation owner by the name of John McDonogh. Durnford turned to McDonogh for advice and credit in order to enter the plantation business. His friend agreed, they struck favorable terms and the young man was able to purchase a small piece of land just south of the city that became St. Rosalie Plantation named after his mother.[144]

Over the years, Durnford's plantation grew, and the man himself climbed steadily through Louisiana society. In the late 1820s, the historian David O. Whitten revealed that Durnford paid $7,000 for seven male slaves, five female slaves and two children. What's more, soon after that he traveled to Virginia to acquire 24 more slaves to work his land. In all, it's estimated that Durnford owned more than 80 slaves at the peak of his operations, earning a small fortune off their hard work. It seems that Durnford was a kindly master, but he appears to have had no illusions about his property. When slaves escaped, Durnford sent his overseer to track them down. Of one disobedient slave he wrote, *"I ordered five round [lashes] to be given him yesterday . . . He is a wicked fellow."*[145]

According to some accounts of the time, Durnford might have been able to free his slaves. His friend, John McDonogh, had sent his former slaves to be free in Liberia, Africa, asked Durnford if he would consider doing the same. Though John McDonogh freed 85 of his Blacks and set them up with jobs in Liberia, Durnford thought it was foolish to free slaves, since he thought they could not care for themselves: *"There is not one in a hundred that could save money. They do not have the moral courage to deprive themselves of luxuries."* During his life he freed only four slaves, a laborer in his 50s and three mulatto children. McDonogh freed all but a few slaves in his will, but Andrew Durnford freed only one at his death, an illegitimate child. In 1859, Durnford died on his own St. Rosalie Plantation, the land still tended by slaves, including slave children.[146]

John Carruthers Stanly

Like many slave children born on plantations, John Carruthers Stanly's parentage was questionable. According to most accounts, he was born in March of 1795, the son of John Wright, a prominent merchant from New Bern, North Carolina. His mother was an enslaved Africa woman working on a nearby plantation. As such, the child their affair produced was also born enslaved. Fortunately for him, however, the owners of the plantation, a couple called Alexander and Lydia Stewart, were far kinder to their slaves than the majority of their peers.[147]

John Carruthers Stanly,
Courtesy of facetofaceAfrica.com

It was due to this benevolence that Stanly was able to learn a trade while still being enslaved. Alongside a standard education (itself quite rare for slave children), young John learned to become a barber. What's more, he was able to work part-time cutting hair while not busy on the plantation. After a few years, he had saved up a sum of money and earned himself a reputation in the local community as an

Home of John Carruthers Stanly in New Bern, North Carolina.
Courtesy of New Bern Magazine

honest and diligent young man. So, in 1798, when he turned 21, he was able to buy his own freedom, backed by the support of the Stewarts.[148]

In 1801, Stanly not only purchased his wife, Kitty, but two slave children as well. This meant he and Kitty could be legally married according to the State of North Carolina. Then, with his brother's freedom purchased, he focused his attention on moving out of cutting hair and into making some serious money. With two of his own slaves taking care of his barber shop, Stanly bought some land just outside of New Bern. Over time, he expanded his operations significantly and, at his peak, he had an estimated 163 slaves under his control.[149]

At some point in the 1820s, Stanly's wife died. He was also forced to cope with some serious financial troubles. At one point, Stanly was even forced to sell some of his land and his slaves in order to cover a debt run up by his own brother. By the 1840s, he had lost much of his fortune. Indeed, at the time of his death in 1843, at the age of 71, Stanly had just 160 acres and seven slaves to his name. His children inherited all his property, slaves included.[150]

The Pendarvis Family

For a white plantation owner to take a female slave as a mistress was hardly unique in eighteenth-century America. So, few people would have been so shocked to see the wealthy Joseph Pendarvis become involved with a Lady of Color. However, Parthena was more than just a slave lover for Joseph. The pair were so close that they had seven children together. And so, when Joseph died, he remembered all of them in his last will and testament. The children, along with their mother, not only inherited a large expanse of arable land, but they also took on dozens of slaves. Indeed, in 1830s Carolina, few families owned more slaves than the Pendarvis clan.

In fact, James Pendarvis, the eldest son of Joseph, inherited 1,009 acres of land close to Green Savanna. He was also bequeathed on a plantation in nearby Charleston Creek. Moreover, according to the record books of the time, James inherited 113 slaves to work this land, making him the largest non-while slaveholder in all of South Carolina. James carried on growing his business interests and so, by the time of his death in 1798, the Pendarvis family owned 155 slaves, the majority of them picking cotton or rice. James himself left his property as well as his slaves to the next generation. Well into the nineteenth century, then, his heirs were among the most prominent individuals in all of not just their native Collerton County (modern-day Charleston) but of all of South Carolina.[151]

William Ellison

The Antebellum era of American history saw a number of people of color achieve marked success in business. Indeed, from the end of the 18th century right through to the start of the Civil War in 1861, several former slaves became entrepreneurs, none more so than William Ellison Junior. Born April Ellison, William was an American cotton gin maker and blacksmith in South Carolina, and former African-American slave who achieved considerable success as a slaveowner before the American Civil War. He eventually became a major planter and one of the wealthiest property owners in the state. According to the 1860 census (in which his surname was listed as "Ellerson"), throughout his life he owned up to 171 Black slaves in

William Ellison Jr. was a Black slave owner in South Carolina, who achieved considerable success before the Civil War. He was a major planter and one of the wealthiest property owners in the state. According to the 1860 census, throughout his life he owned up to 171 black slaves making him the largest slave owner in the area.

South Carolina and Georgia making him the largest slave owner in the area. He held 63 slaves at his death and more than 900 acres of land. From 1830 to 1865 he and his sons were the only free Blacks in Sumter County, South Carolina to own slaves. The county was largely devoted to cotton plantations, and the majority population were slaves. So how did a slave get to become such a prominent figure in Southern society?[152]

He was born into slavery on a plantation close to Winnsboro, South Carolina, though there was some confusion over his parentage: either Robert Ellison, the plantation owner, or his son, William Ellison, who was listed as April's 'owner', could have fathered the child. This status gave William some relative privilege on the plantation. Significantly, the Ellison men decided that young April should learn a skill. And so, at the age of 10, he became an apprentice cotton gin maker. Six years later, he finished his apprenticeship and was armed with a skill that was much in demand across the Deep South. He immediately got to work.

Since he was still technically a slave, albeit one who was 'hired out', April's master kept most of what the young man earned in a nearby workshop. April was, however, allowed to keep a small portion of his earnings, including wages for work done on a Sunday, and he was ultimately able to buy his freedom from Ellison. The date was June 8, 1816, and April was just 26 years old. Perhaps as a sign of gratitude, he changed his name to William Ellison Jr and immediately bought his wife's freedom and, as soon as he was able, that of his children. In 1817, he moved to Sumter County, South Carolina and set up shop as a cotton gin maker. Very soon, he had purchased four slaves to help him with his growing business. Then, by 1850, he had bought 156 hectares of land, with 32 slaves to work it.

Ellison and his sons were among a number of successful Free People of Color in the antebellum years, but Ellison's master had passed on social capital by apprenticing him to learn a valuable artisan trade

The Paradox of Freedom

as a cotton-gin maker, at which Ellison made a success. He took a wife at the age of 21. After buying his own freedom when he was 26, a few years later Ellison purchased his wife and their children, to protect them from sales as slaves. The Act of 1820 made it more difficult for slaveholders to make personal manumissions, but Ellison gained freedom for his sons and a quasi-freedom for his surviving daughter. During the American Civil War, Ellison and his sons supported the Confederate States of America and gave the government substantial donations and aid. A grandson fought in the regular Confederate Army and survived the war.

A decade before the start of the Civil War, Ellison managed to acquire more land, so that by 1860, he had 53 slaves. His children also had slaves of their own. Once war erupted, he not only sided with the Confederacy, but he also offered the army 53 of his slaves. Ellison also bought war bonds for the cause but with the defeat of the Confederacy, these became worthless. Like many others in the South, Ellison lost almost all his wealth. Nevertheless, when he died in 1861, Ellison was able to leave a will dividing more than 60 slaves up between his one surviving daughter and two sons.[153]

As a result, free Black slaveholders existed within this intricate network of power structures, their motivations for owning slaves multifaceted and rooted in a combination of economic opportunity, social status, and family ties. While their freedom allowed them to own property, including slaves, they were still bound by limitations and constraints. They were caught between the desire for economic independence and the inherent contradictions of owning enslaved people. They were, in essence, trying to *"play the game"* of the system, seeking to secure their own place within it, even if it meant participating in the very system that had originally oppressed them. The existence of free Black slaveholders is a reminder that even within a system of oppression, Black people were not monolithic.

Chapter 4:
The Rise of the Free Black Elite, 1830 – 1850

"... *rascally Negroes, I have to threaten them severely to get them to do their dutys* ... " – Andrew Dunford, free Black slaveholder[154]

By 1830, there were 3,775 Black slaveholders in the South who owned a total of 12,760 slaves; around 2 million in the south. 80% of the Black slaveholders were located in Louisiana, South Carolina, Virginia, and Maryland. There were economic and ethnic differences between free Blacks of the Upper South and the Deep South, with the latter fewer in number, but wealthier and typically of mixed race. Half of the Black slaveholders lived in cities rather than the countryside, with most living in New Orleans and Charleston. In particular, New Orleans had a large, relatively wealthy free Black population composed of people of mixed race, who had become a third social class between Whites and enslaved Blacks, under French and Spanish colonial rule. Relatively few non-White slaveholders were substantial planters; of those who were, most were of mixed race, often endowed by White fathers with some property and social capital.[155]

By the 1830s, free Blacks had about reached their highest mark as a distinct class per the census records of the time. This census reports the names of a larger number of free Blacks than any other census from the South. The reaction which began earlier in the century restricted their freedom and in many cases expelled them from this area. Most of the free Blacks in the North in 1830, had been there for some years. As a result, we see the rise of the free Black elite establishing themselves in the South during this time period and prospering through the 1850s. The census records also shows that the majority of free Black slaveowners were from the point of view of philanthropy. In many instances the husband purchased the wife, or vice versa. The slaves belonging to such families were few compared with the large numbers found among the Whites on the well-developed plantations. Slaves of free Blacks were in some cases the children of a free father who had purchased his wife. If the mothers of these were never manumitted, as so many such husbands failed to do, his own children were born his slaves and were thus reported by the enumerators.[156]

Carter G. Woodson wrote an article in 1924 where he reported:

Some of these husbands were not anxious to liberate their wives immediately. They considered it advisable to put them on probation for a few years, and if they did not find them satisfactory they would sell their wives as other slave holders disposed of slaves. For example, a Black shoemaker in Charleston, South Carolina, purchased his wife for $700; but, on finding her hard to please, he sold her a few months thereafter for $750, gaining $50 by the transaction. The writer personally knew a man in Cumberland County, Virginia, whose mother was purchased by his father who had first bought himself. Becoming enamored of a man slave, she gave him her husband's manumission papers that they might escape together to free soil. Upon detecting this plot, the officers of the law got the impression that her husband had turned over the papers to the slave and arrested the freedman for the supposed offense. He had such difficulty in extricating himself from this complication that his attorney's fees amounted to $500. To pay them he disposed of his faithless wife for that amount.[157]

The story of the development of free Black communities in the antebellum South is marked by both resilience and struggle. These communities, though living in a society deeply divided by race and power, built unique social structures, engaged in diverse economic activities, and nurtured rich cultural institutions. Their experiences highlight the multifaceted nature of freedom and the challenges of navigating a world of rigid racial boundaries.

The Paradox of Freedom

Woodson's article also went on to state, *"Benevolent free Blacks often purchased slaves to make their lot easier by granting them their freedom for a nominal sum, or by permitting them to work it out on liberal terms. John Barry Meachum, a free Black Baptist minister in St. Louis was such a man who came into possession of as many as 20 slaves by 1836. The exploitation of slaveholder sometimes left the sting of conscience and liberated his slaves. Samuel Gibson, a free Black of Mississippi was an example. In 1844, he brought his six slaves to Cincinnati, Ohio, and settled them on free territory."*[158]

A chart created by Woodson's 1924 article also indicates:

Practically all of these Black slaveholders were in the South. The chart also shows that all states in the United States, North and South, had free Black slaveholders who owned at least one slave. Slavery, at that time had not been exterminated altogether in the North, and even there free Black slaveholders were following in the footsteps of Whites, as the report shows. (See Appendix II for the chart)

In the South where almost all of the Black slaveholders were found, moreover, we find some of them competing with the large planters in the number of slaves they owned. Most of such Black proprietors lived in Louisiana, South Carolina, Maryland and Virginia, as did the majority of such slave owners. There are, moreover, a few instances of confusing absentee ownership with Black ownership. Sometimes a free Black had charge of a plantation, but did not own the slaves himself, and the enumerator returned him as the owner of the slaves.

Excepting those of Louisiana, one may say that most of the Negro owners of slaves lived in urban communities. In those parts of the South where the influence of the kind planter near the coast was not felt the Negro owner of slaves did not frequently appear. The free Negroes themselves, moreover, encountered such difficulties in the lower South and Southwest that they had to seek more hospitable communities in free States.

By 1840 the trend toward degrading the free Negro to a lower status had become evident even in the apparently benevolent slaveholding States. Just before the outbreak of the Civil War the free Negro was receiving practically no consideration in the South and very little in the North. History here repeats itself, then, in showing the varying attitude of the whites toward the blacks in the cycles of national development.[159]

Chapter 2 revealed the earliest days of colonial America's free Black populations and how it began to emerge, primarily due to the gradual emancipation of enslaved people, often as a result of individual acts of generosity, legal proceedings, or gradual changing of societal attitudes. As these free Black communities grew, churches, schools, and fraternal organizations were established creating spaces of community and empowerment.

Some free Black individuals were able to achieve economic success, acquiring property, building businesses, and even becoming slaveholders, representing accumulation of wealth and power in a society that simultaneously denied them equal rights and opportunities, highlighting the paradoxical nature of their existence. The rise of free Black elites, with some individuals owning slaves, introduced a new layer of complexity to the racial and social dynamics of the antebellum South.

Beyond their economic pursuits, free Black communities fostered vibrant cultural traditions. They celebrated their heritage through music, dance, and storytelling, preserving their African roots in the face of constant pressure to assimilate. They also developed unique forms of religious expression, often drawing upon African traditions and incorporating them into Christian practice such as hand clapping and stomping to replace drum beating that was outlawed by slaveholders.

Another example is Gospel congregational singing which reflects oral traditions in African American society by embodying the communal and participatory nature of worship through musical expression. This relies on the transmission of lyrics and melodies through spoken word, allowing for the preservation of cultural heritage. These cultural expressions served as important sources of strength and identity, creating a sense of community and reaffirming their shared cultural heritage by creating stories of both hardship and triumph, a testament to their enduring power and resilience.[160]

The reality of free Black slaveholding in the antebellum South is complex and nuanced, far removed from the simplistic narratives often presented in textbooks. The act of owning slaves, even for free Black individuals, served as a microcosm of the contradictions that defined their lives in a society deeply divided by race and power. As a result, they found themselves navigating a precarious path between the White slaveholding elite and the enslaved population. While their legal status granted them certain rights, they were often relegated to a liminal position within the Southern hierarchy. On one hand, they were recognized as free individuals, capable of owning property and engaging in economic activities. On the other hand, they were still considered to be "Black," subject to the prevailing ideologies and social structures that relegated them to the margins of society. As a result, they faced discrimination and exclusion from the White community, and they struggled to find acceptance within the Black community, where their ownership of slaves could often be seen as a betrayal of their own racial identity.

Free Black slaveholders often sought to justify their ownership of slaves by arguing that they provided better treatment and more opportunities for their enslaved people than White slaveholders. They believed that their ownership of slaves was a means of protecting their families and achieving economic security. They were acutely aware of the inherent injustices of slavery, yet they also recognized the economic

The Paradox of Freedom

benefits and social status that could be derived from owning slaves. This internal conflict led many free Black slaveholders to adopt a range of strategies to navigate the complexities of their situation.

The geographic distribution of free Black slaveholding in the United States was not uniform. Instead, it reflected a complex interplay of factors, including the size of the free Black population, the economic opportunities available to them, and the specific laws governing slavery in each state. Free Blacks in America were generally not prevented from owning slaves, however, their ability to do so was often restricted by legal and social barriers. In the North, free Blacks could own land and businesses, and some owned anywhere from 1 to 3 slaves, but they faced discrimination and restrictions that limited their economic opportunities. In the South, free Blacks could own slaves, but they were also subject to racial prejudice and social restrictions. The presence of free Blacks in the South was significant, as they played a crucial role in the economy and society, despite the challenges they faced. (Refer to Appendices II to review table of average number of slaves that some free Blacks owned in Northern states.)

Free Black slaveholding was most prevalent in the Upper South, particularly in Virginia, Maryland, and the Carolinas. This concentration was due to several factors. Firstly, the Upper South had a larger population of free Blacks than the Deep South. Many of these free Blacks had descended from enslaved people who had been emancipated by their owners, or who had purchased their freedom. Secondly, the Upper South had a more diversified economy than the Deep South, which was heavily reliant on large-scale plantation agriculture. This diversification provided opportunities for free Blacks to engage in skilled trades, commerce, and small-scale farming, which allowed them to accumulate wealth and purchase slaves. Finally, the laws governing slavery in the Upper South were less restrictive than those in the Deep South. For instance, in Virginia, free Blacks were allowed to own slaves, but they were subject to various limitations, such as restrictions on the type of slaves they could own and the number of slaves they could hold. The Deep South, allowed free Blacks to own slaves as well but they were subject to harsher laws than in the Upper South. These laws divested free Blacks of their rights, such as the right to testify against Whites in court or the right to seek employment where they pleased. The difference in treatment between free blacks in the Deep South and those in the Upper South, historians have surmised, came down to economics. In the Deep South, slavery as an institution was strong and profitable because of cotton. In the Upper South, the opposite was true the institution was slowly waning because of the agricultural differences. The anxiety of this economic uncertainty manifested in the form of harsh laws that targeted free blacks.

In Virginia, the cradle of free Black slaveholding, a unique set of circumstances fostered its development. The colony's history of indentured servitude and its relatively large population of free Blacks laid the foundation for this practice. Moreover, the Virginia Assembly passed laws that allowed free Blacks to own slaves, albeit with certain restrictions. This legal framework, coupled with the economic opportunities available in the colony, made it possible for a small number of free Blacks to acquire slaves and build wealth. Notable examples include William Ellison, a free Black man who owned a large plantation in Virginia and amassed significant wealth through his tobacco business. He owned more than 50 slaves and played a significant role in the state's economy. His story is a testament to the complexities of free Black slaveholding in Virginia, showcasing both its opportunities and its limitations.

Maryland, a border state straddling the line between freedom and slavery, presented a different context for free Black slaveholding. While the state had a significant population of free Blacks, it also had a strong tradition of slavery. Maryland's economy was a mixture of large-scale plantations and smaller farms, which created opportunities for free Blacks to engage in a variety of economic activities. However, the state's laws governing slavery were more restrictive than those in Virginia. Free Blacks were often required to obtain special licenses to own slaves, and they were subject to stricter regulations regarding their property rights. Despite these challenges, some free Blacks in Maryland managed to accumulate wealth and own slaves. Anne Bailey, a free Black woman who owned a small farm in Maryland, provides an example of a free Black individual navigating the complexities of slavery in a border state. Her story underscores the resilience and adaptability of free Blacks who managed to carve out a space for themselves in a society where civil liberties were often tied to racial background.

The Carolinas, like Virginia, had a larger population of free Blacks compared to the Deep South, and this demographic factor contributed to the emergence of free Black slaveholding. However, the Carolinas also had a strong plantation economy, which presented both opportunities and challenges to this same population. They could potentially acquire slaves through inheritance, purchase, or other means, but they also faced the challenges of competing with larger White landowners for access to land and resources. Moreover, the Carolinas' laws governing slavery were more restrictive than those in Virginia, making their ownership of slaves more difficult. Despite these obstacles, some free Blacks in the Carolinas did manage to acquire slaves and establish themselves as owners. The Johnson family, a multi-generational family of free Black slaveholders in the Carolinas, exemplifies this phenomenon. Their story highlights the struggles and triumphs of free Blacks who managed to navigate the complexities of slavery and ownership in a landscape, on both the local and national levels, committed to uphold slavery.

The Deep South, with its highly centralized plantation economy and its rigid social hierarchy, posed the greatest challenges to free Black slaveholding. Take for example, the laws in Mississippi. As early as 1820 Mississippi presumed every "negro," or Person of Color, to be a slave. To prove otherwise, free Black individuals were required to secure certification for their free status. (See endnote for further explanation)[161]

The Deep South's economy was heavily reliant on slave labor, which created competition, fraught with possible risk between free Blacks and White slaveholders for access to land and resources. These factors made it significantly more difficult for free Blacks to acquire slaves and establish themselves as owners in the Deep South. The Williamses of Louisiana, a family of free Black slaveholders who lived and worked in the heart of the Deep South, offer a poignant example of the challenges they faced. Their story illustrates the tenacity and resilience of free Blacks who dared to venture into the deeply entrenched slaveholding society of the Deep South.

The stories from Virginia's thriving tobacco plantations to the Deep South's challenging slave-driven economies, provide a unique perspective on the complexities of slavery and freedom in the antebellum South. Their experiences reveal the interconnectedness of race, power, and economics in shaping the lives of free Blacks and the broader Southern landscape.

Virginia, the cradle of the American republic, also held a unique distinction in the history of free Black slaveholding. While the practice existed across the South, Virginia stood out as a hub for this complex and often overlooked phenomenon. This was due to a confluence of factors, including a relatively large population of free Black people, a robust economy, and a legal system that, while ultimately upholding the institution of slavery, permitted some degree of freedom for Black people.

The roots of free Black slaveholding in Virginia can be traced back to the colonial era. The colony's early laws regarding slavery were ambiguous, and in some instances, allowed for the existence of free Black populations. This was further influenced by a social dynamic where Black individuals, whether born free or emancipated, could amass wealth and property, including slaves, through skilled trades, business ventures, and inheritance. The practice of manumission, whereby enslaved individuals were granted their freedom, also contributed to the growth of the free Black population in Virginia. Many slaveholders, particularly those in urban areas, released their slaves, often with the stipulation that they would continue to work for a specific period or become indentured servants. This, however, did not ensure that free Black individuals would be treated as equals.

The social and economic landscape of Virginia fostered the development of a distinct free Black elite, many of whom owned slaves. Prominent individuals such as William Ellison, a successful planter and businessman, and Anthony Johnson, a renowned tobacco farmer, became influential figures within their communities. These individuals navigated the complex legal and social frameworks of the state, securing their rights and carving out spaces for themselves within the predominantly White slaveholding society. The story of William Ellison, a free Black man who inherited a plantation and owned over 50 slaves, exemplifies the paradoxical nature of Free Black slaveholding. His ownership of slaves gave him a degree of economic power and social standing, yet his status as a Black man still subjected him to the limitations and prejudices of the racist society in which he lived.

The existence of free Black slaveholders within Virginia created a complex social dynamic. While some members of the White elite saw free Black slaveholders as a potential threat to the existing social order, others engaged in business relationships with them or even accepted them into their social circles. The relationships between free Black slaveholders and the White community were complex and often contradictory. They could find themselves accepted in some circles, while ostracized in others. This dynamic was further complicated by the relationships between free Black slaveholders and the enslaved population.

The Paradox of Freedom

The experiences of enslaved people under the ownership of free Black slaveholders differed in some ways from those of enslaved people owned by White slaveholders. While many enslaved people were still subjected to harsh labor conditions and the limitations of slavery, there were instances where they found greater opportunities for skill development, education, and even emancipation. The narratives of enslaved people under free Black ownership paint a nuanced picture, reflecting both the cruelty and the kindness that could be found within the system.

The story of free Black slaveholding in Virginia is a testament to the complexities of race, power, and freedom in the antebellum South. It reveals a nuanced and often overlooked aspect of American history, challenging conventional narratives about slavery and race relations. The experiences of these individuals highlight the contradictions and complexities of a society divided by race and bound by the institution of slavery, and their story serves as a reminder of the enduring legacy of slavery in American history and the complexities of navigating freedom within a system that sought to deny it.

Maryland, a border state perched between the deeply entrenched slaveholding South and the burgeoning abolitionist North, presented a unique and complex landscape for free Black slaveholders. It was a state where the lines between freedom and slavery blurred, where the echoes of the institution reverberated even in the lives of those who had tasted freedom.

For free Black individuals in Maryland, the path to slaveholding was often intertwined with family legacies, economic opportunities, and the desire to secure their place within a society still deeply divided by race and power. Many free Black families in Maryland had long histories in the state, some having been freed through manumission or having descended from generations of Free People of Color. This history, however, did not erase the realities of racial discrimination and the limitations imposed by White supremacy.

The Paradox of Freedom

The presence of free Black slaveholders in Maryland was often met with a mixture of bewilderment and unease. Some viewed it as a contradiction in terms, an anomaly that challenged the prevailing assumptions about race and power. Others, however, saw it as a testament to the resilience and agency of free Black people in a society that sought to deny them both.

One prominent example is the story of Anne Bailey, a free Black woman who owned slaves in Maryland. Bailey's story, chronicled in historical records and family accounts, provides a glimpse into the multifaceted lives of free Black slaveholders in this state. Born into a free Black family in Baltimore, Bailey inherited a sizable estate, including enslaved people, from her father. She used her wealth and her position as a landowner to build a successful business, operating a tavern and a store in the city.

As a free Black woman, she faced discrimination, prejudice, and the constant threat of being stripped of her freedom and possibly sold back into bondage as Solomon Northup had experienced. Her ownership of slaves, while a reflection of her resilience and her ability to navigate the complexities of the slaveholding system, also placed her in a precarious position, blurring the lines between freedom and oppression.[162]

The legal landscape surrounding free Black slaveholding in Maryland was similarly fraught with contradictions. While the state technically allowed free Blacks to own slaves, the laws governing their rights and responsibilities were often vague, ambiguous, and open to interpretation. The legal framework was designed to maintain White supremacy and to ensure that free Black people remained subservient to their power.

Free Black slaveholders in Maryland often found themselves caught in a legal labyrinth, navigating a system that could shift at any moment, leaving them vulnerable to exploitation and legal challenges. Their ownership of slaves, a mark of their agency and their ability to

The Paradox of Freedom

accumulate wealth, was also a constant reminder of the limitations placed on them by White power and the precariousness of their position within society.

The economic realities of free Black slaveholding in Maryland were also complex. While some free Black individuals were able to accumulate wealth through landownership and the use of slave labor, others struggled to make ends meet, caught in a system that limited their economic opportunities and their ability to compete with White slaveholders.

The state's economy, heavily reliant on slave labor, provided limited opportunities for free Black individuals, especially those who did not own slaves. The scarcity of landownership and the competition for scarce resources often made it difficult for free Black individuals to build economic independence and to challenge the power structures that had long held them down.

Maryland, as a border state, embodied the conflicting forces at play in the antebellum South. It was a place where slavery was deeply entrenched, yet where the winds of abolitionism were also beginning to blow. This unique context shaped the experiences of free Black slaveholders, who were caught in a constant tug-of-war between the forces of oppression and the yearning for freedom.

The stories of free Black slaveholders in Maryland, while complex and sometimes contradictory, offer valuable insights into the history of race and power in America. They remind us that the fight for freedom was not a simple binary, but rather a nuanced and multifaceted struggle, even for those who had tasted the fruits of liberation. Their stories invite us to look beyond the simplistic narratives of the past and to grapple with the complexities of a history that still shapes our present.

The Carolinas, a region known for its strong ties to the institution of slavery like other Southern states, held a significant population of free Black people. These individuals, though officially free, navigated a

The Paradox of Freedom

complex social and economic landscape marked by the ever-present shadow of racial prejudice. Their lives, including the choice to own slaves, were a testament to the contradictions and complexities of freedom in the antebellum South. This led the Carolinas to developed a unique legal framework that governed the status of free Black people. While they were not considered legally equal to white citizens, they could own property, conduct business, and even own slaves. This legal framework, however, was constantly evolving and subject to interpretation, leaving free Black slaveholders in a precarious position.

Economic realities played a significant role in shaping the experiences of free Black slaveholders in the Carolinas. The region's economy, heavily reliant on agricultural production, often required a significant amount of labor. For some free Black individuals, owning slaves presented an opportunity to acquire land, to establish a viable business, and to gain a measure of economic independence. These factors, coupled with the lack of access to White-owned labor, made slaveholding an attractive option for those seeking to secure their livelihoods.

However, free Black slaveholding in the Carolinas was not without its challenges. Social prejudice against Black people, regardless of their legal status, permeated all aspects of life in the region. Free Black slaveholders often faced discrimination and hostility from the white population, limiting their access to opportunities and creating barriers to social advancement. Their ownership of slaves did little to mitigate the deep-seated racism that pervaded Southern society.

Furthermore, the relationships between free Black slaveholders and the enslaved population in the Carolinas were complex and nuanced. Some slaveholders, driven by a desire for economic gain, treated enslaved people as mere commodities, subjecting them to harsh conditions and limited opportunities. However, others, motivated by a desire to improve the lives of enslaved people or by family ties, sought to provide their slaves with better treatment and access to education. The stories of these individuals, though often overlooked in the grand narratives of slavery, highlight the diverse experiences and motivations of those who owned slaves in the Carolinas.

The lives of free Black slaveholders in the Carolinas were also shaped by the broader context of the abolitionist movement. Many free Black individuals, even those who owned slaves, were deeply involved in the fight against slavery, contributing to anti-slavery societies, advocating for the rights of enslaved people, and challenging the racial hierarchies of the time. Their involvement in the antislavery movement further underscores the complexities of their experiences and the contradictions they navigated.

The Carolinas were a region where the realities of freedom and slavery intertwined in intricate ways. Free Black slaveholders in this region faced both opportunities and challenges, as elsewhere. Their stories, often forgotten or obscured in the grand narratives of slavery, offer a unique perspective on the complexities of race, power, and freedom in the antebellum South.

Regardless of their motivations, free Black slaveholders were often caught in a precarious balance between their desire for economic security and social acceptance and their moral objections to the institution of slavery. They were forced to make difficult decisions, balancing their own ambitions and the needs of their families with the ethical implications of owning slaves. Their lives were a testament to the complexities of race, power, and freedom in the antebellum South, where the lines between oppressor and oppressed were often blurred and the pursuit of individual advancement could come at a significant moral cost.

Expanding on specific examples in the Carolinas:
Ann Deas of Charleston, South Carolina: As mentioned in Chapter Three, Ann Deas was the daughter of Abigail Deas Jones and the stepdaughter of Jehu Jones, Sr. (1769-1833). She was a member of the

class of Free Colored in Charleston, South Carolina: Both her mother and her stepfather had been slaves, but were manumitted in 1798. Ann was the half-sister of Jehu Jones, Jr. who became the first Black Lutheran Pastor. Her stepfather bought the Burrows-Hall House hotel in 1815, and developed it into the famous *Jones Inn*, one of the most successful hotels in Charleston, frequented by the rich White elite.[163]

After the *Denmark Vesey Conspiracy of 1822*, the South Carolina General Assembly to pass laws to closely monitor free Blacks. One of the laws passed in 1823 prevented free Blacks from returning if they left the state, a law that prevented Abigail Jones from returning to South Carolina after taking her children and grandchildren to New York for a visit prior to the Vesey Rebellion. Jehu Jones, Sr., along with his guardian, Governor John Lide Wilson, petitioned the Assembly for a leave of absence from the state so that Jones could visit his own family.[164]

The petition was granted and Jones saw his family, but could not return to the state. In 1827 he requested permission to visit his family in St. Augustine, Florida, but the historical record is unclear as to whether he made the trip or not. Abigail never returned to South Carolina and stayed in New York as an innkeeper where she died before her husband.[165]

His estate, which included enslaved people but not Jones's real estate properties, was valued at $40,000 and was split between his three sons and his stepdaughter after his death. Deas petitioned South Carolina's governor for a pardon and returned to Charleston where she and another free Black Charlestonian, Eliza Seymore Lee, purchased the Jones Hotel in 1834, renaming it *Mansion House Hotel,* and operated the inn until 1847 when Ann retired and left the hotel to her former business associate Eliza Seymore Lee.[166]

The Paradox of Freedom

Like her step-father, Ann Deas used slave labor to maintain high standards of the inn. In 1840 she owned five female slaves between the ages of 10 and 36, all worked in the hotel. Ann's hotel was so successful it was looked upon as a training school for cooks where apprenticed slaves were taught the art of fine Southern cuisine. Ann attributed the success of her hotel to the slaves who cooked as well as those who attended to the needs of the clientele who were always treated as royalty at the hotel.[167]

Justus Angel of South Carolina was a wealthy Black master who lived in Colleton District, South Carolina in 1830. Angel was a plantation owner who owned 84 slaves, a staggering number even for a Black master. He was a man of great wealth and influence which allowed him to amass such a large number of enslaved individuals under his control. As a Black master in a time when slavery was rampant, Justus Angel's position was unique and undoubtedly faced many challenges and complexities.

Born into slavery himself, Justus Angel had managed to gain his freedom through unclear means, perhaps purchasing his own freedom or being emancipated by his previous owners. With his newfound freedom, he became a successful businessman and acquired a significant amount of wealth through his plantation operations.

Being a Black master in the antebellum South presented its own set of contradictions and challenges. On one hand, Justus Angel had the ability to own slaves and exercise control over their lives, just like White masters. However, his race also subjected him to discrimination and prejudice from both White slave owners and other free Black individuals who disapproved of his ownership of slaves.[168]

Further exploration of the Carolinas:
The Legal Framework: Further exploration of the legal framework surrounding free Black slaveholding in the Carolinas would delve into

the specific statutes governing ownership, inheritance, and emancipation. It would also analyze the legal challenges faced by free Black slaveholders, such as disputes over ownership rights, challenges to their right to vote, and the ongoing threat of being re-enslaved.

The Anti-Slavery Movement: A deeper examination of the growth of the anti-slavery movement in the Carolinas would explore the role of free Black communities, including those who owned slaves, in advocating for the end of slavery. It would analyze the arguments they presented, the strategies they employed, and the challenges they faced in challenging the prevailing social and political order.

The Experiences of the Enslaved: A more in-depth investigation into the experiences of enslaved people owned by free Black slaveholders in the Carolinas would consider the conditions of their lives, their interactions with their owners, and their opportunities for resistance and self-emancipation. It would also explore how their experiences differed or mirrored those of enslaved people owned by white slaveholders.

The Carolinas, with their unique blend of freedom and slavery, offer a compelling lens through which to examine the lives of free Black slaveholders of this region. By uncovering their stories, we gain a more complete understanding of the American past and the challenges that continue to shape our present.

The Deep South presented a different landscape for free Black slaveholders, a terrain carved by a unique blend of opportunity and profound challenge. Unlike the more established free Black communities in states like Virginia, where access to land and skilled trades could facilitate ownership, the Deep South was a region built on the foundation of vast plantations, a system driven by the relentless force of enslaved labor. Here, the desire for landownership and the potential for profit often intertwined with the brutal realities of a slave-driven economy, forcing free Black slaveholders to navigate a complex and often contradictory existence.

The Paradox of Freedom

For free Black populations in the Deep South, the idea of acquiring slaves was a far cry from the economic strategies employed in the Upper South. In states like Virginia and Maryland, free Black communities had built a degree of economic independence through skilled trades, small businesses, and even landownership. However, the Deep South presented a different picture. Here, the plantation system held sway, shaping the social and economic realities of the region. Land was often concentrated in the hands of a wealthy planter class, leaving little room for aspiring Black landowners. The availability of skilled trades was also limited, as the demand for labor was dominated by the needs of large-scale agriculture.

This economic reality meant that the motivations for free Black slaveholding in the Deep South often took on a different character. In the Upper South, ownership could be seen as a pathway to upward mobility, a means of establishing economic security, and even a form of social advancement. However, in the Deep South, the desire for landownership often became a driving force. The scarcity of available land, coupled with the inherent power dynamics of the region, made land acquisition a formidable goal. Acquiring slaves, particularly in regions where the plantation system held sway, could offer a path to achieving landownership, as slaves could provide the necessary labor to cultivate and maintain plantations.

The experience of free Black slaveholders in the Deep South was therefore shaped by a complex interplay of factors. They navigated a landscape where the pursuit of economic security often intersected with the brutal realities of a slave-driven economy. They faced the challenge of owning slaves within a society deeply divided by race and power, a system that condemned them to a life of social marginalization even as they held legal ownership over others. Their story is a testament to the resilience of the human spirit, its ability to find pathways to agency and aspiration even in the face of profound adversity.

The limited records that survive from this era paint a picture of free Black slaveholders in the Deep South who faced challenges and made choices within a system not designed for their advancement. Their stories are often fragmented, hidden within the larger narrative of slavery. However, even these fragments reveal a complex and nuanced reality, one that challenges conventional narratives and offers a glimpse into the lives of individuals who defied the limitations imposed upon them.

Expanding on specific examples in the Deep South:

William Johnson of Mississippi known as *"the Barber of Natchez,"* William Johnson was born into slavery, the son of his mother, Amy, and presumed father and owner, William Johnson Sr. When William T. Johnson was born in 1809, his mother was a slave of mixed race. His father freed William's mother in 1814 and their daughter Adelia in 1818. His mother, Amy Johnson, is listed in the 1816 Natchez census as the Head of household of a Free Negro family, set up a retail business and *"by 1838 the Tax rolls listed her slave property as three women and two children, valued at $1650,"* In 1820 he freed William when he was 11 years old, setting him on a path that few Black men in the antebellum South could travel. His father made sure that William had a basic education that prepared him for the future. This was unusual for Laws in Mississippi as early as 1820 presumed every "Negro," or Person of Color, to be a slave and anti-literacy laws had been adopted by the state.[169]

William Johnson, the *"Barber of Natchez"*, Courtesy of BlackPast.org

After working as an apprentice to his brother–in-law James Miller, Johnson bought the barber shop in 1830 for three hundred dollars and taught the trade to free Black boys. His Main Street shop became more than a place for haircuts and shaves, it was a hub of conversation, news, and community. The barbershop sat near bustling hotels, banks, and the courthouse, ma king it a prime location to serve the town's businessmen, planters, and travelers. It was shortly after he established a barber shop in downtown Natchez that he began to keep a diary. The diary was a mainstay in Johnson's life until his death in 1851.[170]

William Johnson's Home in Natchez, Mississippi controlled by the National Park Service today, *Courtesy of Natchez Trace Travel*

As a young prominent citizen in the free Black community of Natchez, Johnson's interest in marriage and s tarting a family was strengthened by his thriving business. By 1835, his initial investment of three hundred dollars had grown to almost three thousand. His dress was impeccable and he was confident in his future. So confident that he caught the eye of twenty year old Ann Battles. Battles, also a free Black, married Johnson in 1835. Their eleventh child was born in 1851 at the time of Johnson's death.[171]

Education was an essential value that Johnson's wife, Ann, inculcated within her family. Although her mother appears to have been illiterate, Ann Johnson obtained the ability to read and write at some point in her early life. She and William recognized that literacy was key to their placement within the community and afforded that opportunity to their children by personally teaching them, hiring private tutors, and sending some of the children to private schools in New Orleans. The Johnson children studied reading, writing, mathematics, geography, and literature. Additionally, the boys learned the barbering trade from their father and Ann instructed her daughters in music as well as domestic skills like sewing. Ann's daughters Anna and Catharine utilized this education by eventually becoming schoolteachers.[172]

William Johnson chose friends carefully, both Black and White, free and slave. He avoided "White trash" and "Black trash" as diseases against his own social health and the welfare of the Natchez community. He did business and socialized with people who took care of their lives and approached society with the same care he did. Race and status were not barriers to him except as Mississippi's laws denied his civil liberties. He engaged both races and made close, intimate friends across the social and economic barriers. For example, William Thompson Martin, a White attorney and later a Confederate general during the Civil War, first caught Johnson's eye in 1843 when he impressed him giving a speech on a "Bond Question." From that evening on Johnson commented often in his diary on the young attorney's progress. They were personal and business friends. In 1851, Martin represented Johnson winning the real estate tussle against Baylor Winn, a free mixed-race Black man, who several days later murdered Johnson and his son, Byron. Johnson lived long enough to name Winn as the guilty party but, through strange circumstances, Winn was never convicted of the killing. Winn and his defense argued that he was actually White and not a Free Person of Color because of his Indian ancestry in Virginia. Therefore, the "mulatto" boy who accompanied Johnson on that fateful day could not testify against

Winn. Mississippi law allowed for Blacks to testify against Whites in civil cases, but not in criminal cases. Two hung juries could not decide if he was White or Black, so Johnson's killer walked free.[173]

Census records show that in 1850, 12% of the population of 773 free Blacks in Mississippi owned slaves. William Johnson was one of them. The ownership of slaves guaranteed the family's hierarchical position within the free Black community. During his lifetime, William enslaved at least thirty men, women, and children. These enslaved people performed a variety of tasks within the household: cooking, cleaning, working at the family's cotton plantation, and being hired out to others. Although the family engaged in slave ownership for economic reasons, there were other compelling reasons to enslave a few members of the household. In 1840, Ann purchased her cousin, Julia, and her two daughters, Laura and Margaret, with the future plan to free them, which was difficult due to Mississippi's restrictive policy of manumission. When William died in 1851, Johnson's property was valued at $25,000, making him the wealthiest African American in Mississippi. He wrote openly in his diary about his slaves and his trial and tribulations of being a slave owner. For example, this entry from his diary:

March 19, 1838, Buisness not very good. Steven got drunk Last night and went of[f] and remained all night and was not Here this morning to go to Market. I sent Bill Nix to the Jail to see if He was there and He was not there. I sent Him out to Dr Ogdons and in going there He found Him and brought Him Down and Left Him in the gate and he Jumped over the Fence and went threw in Judge Montgomerys yard. Bill He ran around the Corner and found him and brought Him in, I Kept him [in] the shop a Little while and then sent him to Help Mrs Lieper to move from the old House Down to the House belonging to Bill Hazard He ran off 4 times in about three hours and Bill Nix Caught Him Every time, so He Brought Him Home after a while and I went to the stable and gave him a pretty sef[v]eere thrashing with the Cow hide — then he *was perfectly Calm and Quite and could then do his work. Tis singular how much good it does some people to get whiped. Mr. Kenney paid me $40.00 for One month's House rent due today, the 19th inst I then told him here after He could have the Room for $35 per month.*[174]

William Johnson's diary encapsulates sixteen years of his life, between 1835-1851, filling fourteen leather bound volumes with diary entries. Today, his diary is an important resource for the study of free blacks, African –American History and American History in general. It is also an important part of his legacy and what sets William Johnson apart from other free Blacks during the time period. Today, through an act of Congress in 1990, the home of William Johnson, Jr. became part of the Natchez National Historical Park and has been restored for people to visit to get an insight on the life of this important figure in Natchez history.

After 1840, there is a decline in the number of new free Blacks establishing themselves as slaveholders as events occur and laws are changed to suppress free Blacks or to discourage them from living in the states that they were emancipated. Times were changing by 1850 as the political realm was changing and the fears of a coming national crisis approached. Regardless of this ever approaching crisis, those that had established themselves before 1840 had prospered and became the elite among their social class.

Chapter 5:
Social and Economic Motivations

"For many years, historians paid only slight attention to Blacks who reached the upper economic levels in the nineteenth-century South. In 1905, amateur historian Calvin Dill Wilson wrote a ten-page essay in the North American Review called "Black Masters: A Side-Light on Slavery," and a decade later John Russell added a brief article in the 'Journal of Negro History' on the same subject. The "scientific historians" of the William A. Dunning school such as Walter Lynwood Fleming, Mildred Thompson, James G. De Roulhac Hamilton, James W. Garner, among others-almost completely ignored Black landholders and prosperous Black businesspeople, but to some extent this was also true for a later group of historians who attacked the racist assumptions of the Dunning school. The books and articles of Carter G. Woodson, Abram Harris, Merah Stuart, Luther Porter Jackson, John Hope Franklin, Vernon Lane Wharton, and other revisionist authors included only brief notations of blacks who had acquired substantial amounts of property. Even with the explosion of research on various aspects of the Black experience during the late 1960s and 1970s, historians seemed more interested in racial exploitation, black culture and black consciousness, and the political activities of blacks during Reconstruction than with those who achieved financial success."

Loren Schweninger[175]

The social and economic dynamics of race and power in the antebellum South were a complex tapestry of contradictions and tensions, with the institution of slavery serving as the bedrock of the South's social and economic order. Within this intricate web of power, the presence of free Black slaveholders presented a profound challenge to the established hierarchies and assumptions about race and freedom.

The Paradox of Freedom

The role of class and "tatus played a significant role in shaping the social experiences of free Black slaveholders. Wealthy and influential free Black slaveholders, often those who had acquired land, education, or other forms of social capital, might have enjoyed greater acceptance within the White community, forging alliances with White elites and gaining access to social circles they would otherwise be excluded from. However, this acceptance often came with the price of upholding the racial hierarchy and sometimes even defending the institution of slavery to maintain their own social standing.

As a result, Mulattos became the apex of free Black society. Mulatto elites distanced themselves from the Black masses both monetarily and racially. They used their money and power to create a brand new class across the south that was similar to, but distinct from, both Black and White communities. This new class used its wealth and power as a way to insure its own survival through its members, relationships, and the societies they formed. Mulattos were common in South Carolina and Louisiana as they were often products of the relationships between masters and their slaves whether they be forced or consensual. These relationships led to many Mulattos to receive their freedom from their master's and at times with some financial earnings as well. The use of slaves for sexual relationships may have been common within the White community but was fairly absent from those who were Mulatto slaveowners. In some rare cases, such as Elias Collins, a Mulatto planter from Georgetown County, South Carolina would use his power as a master to sexually exploit his female slaves which resulted in two children; Jonathan and Elizabeth, with his mistress.[176]

For many of these Mulatto slaveowners, the blackness of one's skin had a direct connection to slavery, and many felt it would be a dilution of their blood to have children with a Black slave. Most mixed owners refused to purchase any slave with visible mixed blood, opting instead to use those with darker skin for their business. One example was William Ellison who never reported to have owned a Mulatto slave.

The Paradox of Freedom

This was confirmed by the census taken in 1850 and 1860, none of Ellison's 50-60 slaves were listed as Mulatto.[177]

Conversely, free Black slaveholders who lacked wealth or social connections might have faced more discrimination. The complexities of their social position meant they could be ostracized by both the White and Black communities, catching them between the competing pressures of race and class. Their lives would often illustrate the struggle for acceptance and recognition within a society deeply divided by race and power.

Thus, within the free Black community, Mulatto elites took measures to distance themselves. Those who sought profits closely mimicked White elites. This included many of the White superiority ideas held by the White community. For those who were Mulattos, the ability to pass as White was a gift which allowed them to openly express a physical superiority to Blacks. When the Liberian colonization effort was in full swing, many of the wealthy Mulattos expressed disdain for the idea of living in Africa. Some, such as William Kellogg, a Mulatto planter from North Carolina, even wrote to the American Colonization Society requesting a separate location for Mulattos due to their relationship to the White community. Using skin color and wealth, the Mulatto elite kept the Black community at arms distance, often spending on extravagant items to insure their distance.[178]

To further the distance between themselves from darker skinned Blacks, many of these Mulatto slaveowners began arranging the marriages of their families. All interactions between the families of the Mulatto elite was done to further their families' statuses. Arranged marriage in particular held great importance for these elite families. It was expected a certain criteria to be met before any marriage was carried out such as cultural status, economic position, and presence of free, mixed- blood were all factors that had to be met. In so doing, many of the elite Black families would become intertwined. Take for example the Holman and Collins families. They were both rice planters and would marry together several times in the first half of the nineteenth century. The marriages between important families allowed them to retain wealth, power, and social position within their community but also expanding it. The mixing of families ensured that new wealth could be made using the opposing family for support. People such as William Ellison used the families his children married into as new clients and the spouses as new employees for his businesses. This consideration of family status extended to every important aspect of the person's life. Sponsors of baptisms and executors of wills all had to meet a strict standard of familial prestige as well.[179]

Because of their position, Black slaveowners did have a place in the system. For both those who owned slaves for profits and those who owned their family, their ownership helped maintain the slavery system. In the case of those who owned slaves for profits, they often chose to fully side with the White ruling class to solidify their own position in the community. These individuals often took steps to associate with the White elite, viewing themselves as an extension of this class. In doing so, the Black slaveowners were able to carve out a place for themselves within the ruling class. With this position, many Black slaveowners used their mixed blood and lighter complexion began to form social clubs. In the same way that Whites would form social clubs of the time to separate themselves, these Mulatto elite would form social clubs to provide a location where the Mulatto elite could interact with other elites.[180]

The most well-known of these social clubs was Brown Fellowship Society, founded in 1790 by five free non-Whites at St. Philip's Episcopal Church in Charleston, South Carolina, to separate from other free Blacks. These societies were able to provide a valuable service for Blacks especially when city officials targeted Black churches. In addition to the initial reasons for the society's creation, many of these societies would go on to create additional help programs for its members. The Brown Fellowship Society and Humane Brotherhood Society, both had programs that focused on the welfare and education of the children, widows, and orphans of their members while refusing to allow entry to those who were seen as too dark skinned.[181]

Determined not to upset the White community, the Society did nothing to help slaves because some of its members were slave-owners themselves. The Society was very careful about whom they admitted to their ranks, which consisted of no more than fifty men at a time. Those who joined the club considered themselves "brown", mulattoes, an important distinction at the time when society in Charleston recognized three races: White, Mulatto, and Negro, including octoroons and quadroons. According to E. Horace Fitchett, the Brown Society was an example of *"mulattoes"* separating themselves from other free African Americans thus creating a caste system as he explained that *"they came to occupy a position to separate the masses of Negroes on the one hand and the White inhabitants on the other hand. Their accommodation to such a position seemed to protect them from some of the most oppressive techniques of control. Hence, this technique tended to give this group a superior conception of itself."* Typically only free lighter skinned African Americans were allowed to join, but sometimes darker-skinned individuals who had naturally straight hair were permitted as well. Prospective members were voted on at three meetings before they were allowed to join, and had to pay a hefty, for the time, $50 initiation fee plus regular dues. Many of the members of the Brown Fellowship Society had their own businesses and some were prosperous, but were still subject to prejudice from the white community.[182]

The Brown Fellowship Society did not intervene in the status of slaves at the time instead it focused on creating a cemetery for "brown" Black people and forbid its members from talking about political or religious matters. The organization also cared for widows of members, provided a primary school, supported its members' businesses, and lobbied towards the White society.[183]

Free Black slaveholders also faced challenges and complexities in their relationships with the enslaved population. Their status as slaveholders placed them in a position of power over enslaved individuals, creating a unique dynamic of power and resistance. Some free Black slaveholders, driven by personal beliefs or societal pressures, may have treated their enslaved people more humanely than their White counterparts. Others, however, faced the same challenges and pressures as White slaveholders, often struggling to maintain control and order within their slaveholding operations.

Those free Blacks who owned slaves realized though that they were not totally free, their skin color was a prescriptive hinderance for them to be accepted into the White community. Those who owned slaves for economic gain were often the most likely to attempt to join with the White community. Even for these individuals, however, they understood the barriers that still existed between the races, which rarely broke. The relationships that formed between Black slave owners and the White Community often defined and formed the actions of these Black slaveowners. The relationship between these two groups was never set in stone, creating both friendly and hostile actions that resulted from this relationship. However both the positive and negative aspects of the relationship created a stark difference between the official stance of the state and the feelings of the people. As with the typical free Black, the relationship between Black slaveowners and the White community was based on the actions of the Black person. Those who were viewed with a good reputation were treated kindly while those who were viewed just the opposite were treated harshly. For Black slaveowners, this was more extreme. Those who owned slaves not only had to ensure the quality of their morals but also the treatment of their slaves as well. Those who treated their slaves too kindly could be stigmatized as sympathetic. This could be especially dangerous for those who wished to merge with and associate with the White planter elite. To rectify this, many would attempt to mimic the White versions of slavery including the cruelty sometimes associated with the White plantation system. On the other hand, Black slaveowners could not treat their slaves too harshly as the years leading up to the Civil War was changing the nature of master-slave relationship. From the initial ownership and property relationship that defined the slave system, a belief of paternalism had begun to take hold that had extended from providing basic care to making sure families remained together. This fine line could lead to many punishments for the Black slaveowner who did not follow this including mobs or having their property confiscated.[184]

To avoid such consequences, many free Blacks who owned slaves took to assimilating into the culture of the White planter class. For those who were able to assimilate, they enjoyed the benefits of trust from the White community. This trust would even go so far as White people publicly supporting the continuing ownership of slaves by Black people. One such case revealed in the *Charleston Courier* stated that a Black person owning slaves gave them a stake in the institution and therefore it is their interest to uphold the system. This respectability and dispersal of trust often came with what the White Southern community perceived as *"hard work and a balancing effort"* on the part of the Black slave owners.[185]

The acceptance and rejection of free Black slaveholders varied depending on factors like wealth, social connections, and the specific community they resided in. Some communities, particularly in urban areas where free Black communities were more established, might have accepted free Black slaveholders. Others, particularly in rural areas where racial tensions ran high, might have viewed them with suspicion or hostility such as poor Southern Whites who had not attained cultural and materialistic success.

The Paradox of Freedom

The good name and wealth of a free Black kept their freedom and the freedom of their family. On the other side, having too much wealth could cause jealousy among their White neighbors. For example **William Ellison**, for whom this balance was critical for his life, used his businesses to steadily increase his wealth, and thus preserving his freedom. As a difference from White elites, Ellison refused to splurge or decorate himself as a grand person, despite his incredible wealth. Ellison made all efforts to present his family as wealthy and respectable but refused to appear he was wealthier or better than his White neighbors. This restraint was deliberate and presented some manner of subjugation despite his wealth being greater than 90 percent of the population of Sumpter. This even extended to how Ellison labeled himself. Despite owning a very successful and large plantation, Ellison labeled himself as his original trade of gin maker. This was a common practice among the Black elite as it showed that the person was wealthy but only in the service of Whites. Had Ellison labeled himself as a planter, he may have caused others to see him as presenting himself equal to White planters or better in some ways, thus, render himself, his family and property vulnerable to White societal aggression.[186]

As once can see, the presence of free Black slaveholders at times complicated the narratives of race, power, and freedom in the antebellum South. It challenged the assumptions that only White people could be slaveholders, revealing the complexities and contradictions within the institution of slavery itself. Their experiences illuminate the ways in which racial categories and power dynamics were fluid and contested, constantly were evolving and redefining by the social and political realities of the time.

For some Black slaveowners, the acceptance they received from the community gave them their greatest reward. In some cases, wealthy Blacks were offered the chance to join White churches in the lower pews. For some churches, having Black people in the building was nothing new as many allowed free Blacks and some slaves to sit in the upper sections. For some special Black slaveowners, after proving their character, their family would be allowed to sit in the pews on the bottom floor with the White members. Black slaveowners such as William Ellison were allowed to sit on the same level as the wealthy Whites. For many this was one of the goals upon achieving wealth from their slaves even though Ellison and his family sat in the back of the church. This was almost symbolic in social standings with those his wealthy White counterparts.[187]

When it came to commerce, free Blacks took extra measures to be successful because their business may not be the only one of its kind in the area. In some cases, shops owned by Blacks or Whites would be present in the same area causing competition. In order to compete and even receive business, Black owners and planters would have to be more accommodating than Whites including selling their goods at a lower price than market value or selling items on credit. Sometimes selling on credit and collecting could be difficult for free Blacks when the time came. William Ellison, even with his upstanding position in the community, struggled at times to collect from those he did business with. In a letter to his son Henry, William Ellison describes the attempt of his grandson John W. Buckner to collect debts that were owed:

Dear Henry,

Your letter of 23rd instant was duly received and I perceived by it that you had not received mine of the 22d. John went over the river yesterday. He saw Mr. [John] Ledinham [of Columbia, S.C.]. He said that he had not sold but half of his crop of cotton and had not the money but when he got the money and was working on this side of the river that he would send his son with it and rake up his account. He also saw Mr. Van Buren and he was ready to pay but before he did so he wished his overseer to certify to it but John could not find him and as it became late he had to leave for home but left the account with Mrs. Mitchel, his wife. You will find enclosed Mrs. Mathew Singleton's account. She will be found at No. 4 Akins range. Mr. Turner said that it was his fault that the account was not paid before. He thinks that she will get another gin. There is one of the saws in the new gin that is worn half in two. He says that he will send the gin over to be repair[ed] and also another old gin providing Mrs. Singleton don't get a new gin. As you did not get my letter in due time and for fear that you may not [have] as yet received it, I will mention a few items of importance that I wish attended to at one if you have not done so. Leave three hundred dollars in Messrs. Adams and Frost hands subject to my order. And also the money that I have borrowed from William. Mr. Benbow wrote to me and I sent you a copy in the letter that I wrote you. Mr. E. Murray's account and order was presented to him last Friday and he was to send his note when he sent to the post office but he failed to do so. I want you to get me a half doz. Weeding hoes. No. 2 get two hand saws from Mr. Adger for the shop. I want you to get me 8 bags of guano. The above articles and instruction was states in the other letter. I mention the same in case you should not have received my other letter. We are all well as usual. Give my respect to all my friends.

Your father,
William Ellison[188]

The case of William Ellison exemplifies the complex social landscape inhabited by free Black slaveholders. They were simultaneously seen as outliers, challenging the established norms of the era, yet also as individuals who could exploit the very system that oppressed them, seeking to improve their own social standing and economic security. Their existence posed a profound challenge to the prevailing notions of race, power, and freedom, forcing both White and Black communities to confront the contradictions and complexities of a system built upon the brutal reality of slavery. Ellison's status as a free Black man with slaves always remained a point of contention, and he was often subjected to prejudice and discrimination, reminding him that his success could not fully erase the prejudices that then-American society prescribed, based on the color of his skin.

The concept of class and status was deeply intertwined with the social experiences of free Black slaveholders in the antebellum South. This was a society where racial lines were rigidly enforced, and social standing was determined by a complex interplay of factors, including wealth, education, and social connections. Free Black slaveholders, while technically enjoying a degree of freedom, found themselves navigating this precarious landscape where their race and their ownership of enslaved people created both opportunities and limitations.

As stated earlier, wealth and position played a significant role in shaping the social status of free Black slaveholders but education also played a crucial role in defining this social standing. While access to education for Black people, was severely limited, those who could afford it often pursued literacy, which opened doors to higher-paying jobs and greater social mobility. An educated free Black slaveholder could command greater respect and influence within the community, demonstrating intellectual prowess and a level of sophistication that challenged the prevailing stereotypes about Black people. Therefore, the pursuit of an education was a testament to their abilities to overcome and reinforce their positions in society. However, education alone could not erase the stigma attached to their racial identity and their ownership of enslaved people. Despite the societal conditions or restrictions imposed upon them to appreciate an education, Free Blacks maintained a strong reverence for literacy and schools, which epitomized their legacy of education and self-improvement.[189]

The acceptance or rejection of free Black slaveholders within the Black community was equally nuanced. While some Black communities might view these individuals with suspicion, recognizing the inherent extra contradiction of a Person of Color holding another in bondage, others might see them as figures of influence and potential allies in the fight for racial equality. Free Black slaveholders, with their access to resources and their position within the larger society, could potentially advocate for the rights of enslaved people, offering a platform for change from within the system.

Free Black slaveholders, like their White counterparts, were not a monolithic group. Some actively engaged in anti-slavery activities, advocating for the end of slavery through public speeches, writings, and participation in abolitionist societies. Others, while not openly supporting abolition, practiced a form of "benevolent" slavery, offering their enslaved individuals better living conditions and opportunities than those found on other plantations. Still, others remained staunchly opposed to anti-slavery notions, clinging to the economic and social advantages associated with owning enslaved people.

Advocates for Freedom:
A number of Free Black slaveholders became prominent figures in the abolitionist movement. One such individual was James Forten, a successful sailmaker in Philadelphia who was born free to a family of formerly enslaved people. Forten was a vocal critic of slavery and a staunch supporter of the American Colonization Society. He financially supported the movement, donated his time and resources to abolitionist causes, and used his influence to advocate for the end of slavery.[190]

Another notable example is the story of William Lloyd Garrison, a prominent White abolitionist who, while never owning slaves himself, recognized the critical role of Free Black slaveholders in the fight for freedom. Garrison, known for his radical approach to abolitionism, acknowledged that Free Black slaveholders were often caught in a difficult position, compelled by circumstance to own slaves while holding strong convictions against the institution itself. He argued that their unique perspective could be valuable in exposing the hypocrisy of slavery and galvanizing public opinion against it.

The Internal Conflict:
For many Free Black slaveholders, the issue of slavery presented a complex moral dilemma. They often found themselves in a contradictory position, holding the legal right to own slaves while simultaneously advocating for the freedom of their fellow Black people. This internal conflict is evident in the lives and choices of individuals like John Russworm, a Free Black man who owned a printing press and newspaper in New York City. Russworm initially supported the colonization movement, believing that the only path to true freedom for Black people lay in a separate society. However, he later became a critic of colonization, recognizing its inherent limitations and the value of fighting for racial equality within the United States.

The experience of William C. Nell, a prominent abolitionist and journalist born free in Boston, also reflects this internal struggle. Nell, who was actively involved in the abolitionist movement, acknowledged the complicated realities of free Black slaveholding. He argued that the ownership of slaves by free Black individuals was often a product of necessity and survival rather than a choice driven by cruelty or indifference. He recognized that some Free Black slaveholders, while grappling with the ethical implications of owning slaves, sought to provide better conditions and opportunities for their enslaved individuals compared to the brutal conditions on larger plantations.

The Legacy of Conflict:
The role of Free Black slaveholders in the fight against slavery will always remain a subject of debate and scrutiny. Some scholars argue that their participation, even with its complexities, contributed significantly to the broader anti-slavery movement. They highlight the role of individuals like Forten, Russworm, and Nell in advocating for freedom, contributing financially, and raising awareness about the evils of slavery. Others contend that their ownership of slaves, regardless of

their personal beliefs or intentions, served to perpetuate the system of slavery and undermine the fight for racial equality.

Ultimately, the story of Free Black slaveholders within the context of the anti-slavery movement is a nuanced and multifaceted one. Their experiences highlight the intricate web of social, economic, and political factors that shaped the lives of Black individuals.

To comprehend the phenomenon of free Black slaveholders, we must examine not just the social but the financial motivations and practices that fueled the institution of slavery as well. Mostly based on an agrarian economy, the South's five major commodities were cotton, grain, tobacco, sugar, and rice, with cotton the leading cash crop. During the early 19th century, the South saw large expansions in agriculture spurred on by increased demands for cotton for the new textile factories of the industrial North. Over time, the South's economy became heavily reliant on the cultivation of cotton, which became the backbone of its economy by the 1850s, accounting for two-thirds of U.S. exports and linking the South to Britain's textile industry. The warm, humid climate and fertile land facilitated year-round agricultural production, causing the demand for cotton to become insatiable, driving the need for more land, more slaves, and more production. In light of the successful cotton industry, anti-industrial and anti-urban attitudes resulting from a belief that the agrarian life would continue to be the best way forward, as a result, the Southern economy experienced little industrialization or other manufacturing development.

The Southern economy was also characterized by a low level of capital accumulation, largely slave-labor-based, and a shortage of liquid capital, which led to a South dependent on export trade. This was in contrast to the North and West, which relied on their own domestic markets. Since the Southern domestic market consisted primarily of plantations focused on a few specific crops Southern states imported sustenance commodities from the West and manufactured goods from England and the North.

The South's population growth was primarily internal, with little immigration due to the lack of non-agricultural jobs. Because of that lack of immigration, the South developed a biracial society characterized by stark power and status differences between Whites and Blacks. Slave labor provided the backbone of the Southern economy causing plantation owners to rely on the labor of enslaved men, women, and children to cultivate, harvest, and process vast quantities of cotton. This relentless pursuit of profit created a dynamic where slaves were seen as both a source of labor and a form of capital, their value fluctuating with the market price of cotton and the demand for their labor.[191]

The economic incentives for owning slaves were substantial. The value of a slave was determined by factors such as age, health, skill, and gender. Skilled slaves, such as blacksmiths, carpenters, or those proficient in domestic work, commanded higher prices. Slaves were often considered a reliable and long-term investment, their labor generating profit for years to come that could be reinvested, allowing slaveholders to purchase more land, acquire additional slaves, and expand their operations. As a result, the profitability of slavery and the financial incentives it offered drew many free Blacks into the system of slaveholding. While seemingly paradoxical, this complex phenomenon was driven by a confluence of economic factors, social pressures, and individual circumstances. For many free Blacks, slave ownership represented an avenue to economic security in a society that often limited their opportunities.

The economic motivations for free Black slaveholding were various. In a society where racial discrimination and prejudice limited their access to land and capital, owning slaves provided a means to secure economic independence and build wealth. The purchase of slaves allowed free Blacks to acquire land, establish businesses, and access the labor needed to expand their operations.

Whatever the circumstances, the economic realities of free Black slaveholding were intertwined with their social and political experiences. In a society where they faced constant discrimination and limitations, their status as slaveholders could offer a degree of protection and influence. As stated in previous chapters, the vast majority of free Blacks who reached the upper economic levels was of mixed racial ancestry. Most were descendants of White planters or merchants and slave women who received land, slaves, and other property from their White relatives or through inheritance.

Even with this advantage, it took energy, industry, and good business sense for these people to maintain their property holdings and expand their wealth and holdings. In urban settings, free Men and Women of Color took advantage of the demand for service businesses. Because of the small numbers of skilled Whites and immigrants, service skills allowed them to establish successful businesses especially with the appreciation in city property values which allowed them to expand their estates. **William Johnson** of Mississippi, probably the best known free Black in that state, became a successful entrepreneur with a barbershop, bath house, bookstore, and land holdings. Though a former slave, in 1834 he would own three slaves and about 3,000 acres of property and would eventually own sixteen slaves before his death. He even hired out his slaves to haul coal and sand. Throughout his life, the white community in Natchez and Adams County held Johnson in high regard. He associated with and was close to many of Adams County's most prominent white families. Following Johnson's untimely death at the hands of a "free black, Baylor Winn, the *Natchez Courier* was moved to comment that Johnson held a *"respected position [in the community] on account of his character, intelligence and deportment."*[192]

The Paradox of Freedom

Johnson obituary in the Natchez Concordian Intelligencier, Dreadful Murder in Natchez

On Monday evening last, just at dusk, as Mr. William Johnson, an esteemed citizen, and long known as the proprietor of the fashionable barber's shop on Main Street, when returning from his plantation, a few miles from the city, was fired upon and killed from the roadside. He was accompanied by two or three young persons, one of them being his son. The oldest boy with him, named Hoggatt, was desperately wounded by the same shot; as well as two of the horses with the party. Johnson was seen to fall, as if killed instantly and the rest of the party, the wounded boy with them, made as rapid flight as they could to Natchez, and gave the alarm. Dr. Blackburn, in his carriage, instantly repaired to the spot and found Johnson lying on his face apparently insensible. On turning him over, he groaned; and when the Doctor gave him some cordial, he revived sufficiently to speak. The first words announced the name of his murderer, as also did his last, as he died, in great distress, at his family residence at two o'clock the following morning.

About an hour after Johnson's death, Mr. Baylor Winn, a planter, living some seven miles below Natchez, was arrested by officers Dillon and Benbrook, and brought to the city jail. The officers were accompanied by Messrs. W. Rotrammel, John Munce, N. Strickland and B. Massey; but no resistance to the process was made, and the prisoner surrendered himself without any remark, or appearance either of fear or surprise. The boy Hoggatt still lingers in a most precarious condition, with but little hope of his life. Johnson was shot through the left lobe of the lungs, and the boy in the abdomen.

The court of examination before the Justices will commence this morning at the Natchez Court House, and will no doubt be attended by many hundreds. Both parties being in good pecuniary circumstances, the best lawyers of the Natchez bar have been arrayed, either for the prosecution or the defence.

The funeral of Mr. Johnson was attended by a numerous procession on Wednesday morning, the Rev. Mr. Watkins of the Methodist Church performing the religious services. This event has made a deep and painful impression upon our community.[193]

In rural areas, free Blacks took advantage of the expanding economy in the West causing the price of slaves and real estate values to increase. Some free Blacks speculated in city property or expanded their farm acreage, while others simply watched as the value of the land they had acquired years before appreciate in value. For example, improved farm acreage in Louisiana went from $2 an acre at the time of statehood in 1812 to as high as $50 or more during the 1820s and 1830s. Free Blacks also witnessed a rise in the value of their personal holdings, including wagons, livestock, tools, machinery, and slaves. Those who astutely managed their businesses or expanded their farm acreage were able to increase their wealth substantially.[194]

Real Estate Holdings among Prosperous Free People of Color in the Lower South, 1850 and 1860 (those with at least $2,000)

	Owners		Average Real Estate Holdings	
State	1850	1860	1850	1860
Alabama	12	32	$3,817	$ 3,691
Arkansas	4	**	2,500	**
Florida	2	8	4,000	3,825
Georgia	5	13	5,200	3,585
Louisiana	504	472	7,922	10,311
Mississippi	6	13	4,033	4,685
South Carolina	47*	162	4,411	4,723
Texas	3	6	5,667	5,133
Total	583	706	$7,428	$ 8,384

* = probable census undercount
** = none
SOURCE: Computed from the U.S. Manuscript Population Census, 1850, 1860.

To sustain their wealth, Free People of Color acquired increasing numbers of slaves with skills. Urban artisans, carpenters, bricklayers, stonemasons, and mechanics purchased Black apprentices and helpers; merchants and businesspeople bought haulers, carters, and stock boys;

plantation owners purchased house servants, cooks, mechanics, and field hands. As a result, these Black apprentices and helpers learned a trade or skill that increased their value. Take for example **William Raper**, a free Black and a bricklayer of Charleston. He was provided the skills and the economic tools which helped to establish one of the largest slave owning families in St. Paul's Parish in Colleton County. Raper was born in the mid-1700s either freeborn or an emancipated slave. By 1787, he was the owner of 10 slaves who were acquired as laborers. Three of his slaves were trained as bricklayers while the others were laborers or domestics. Raper requested that his daughter Ruth Gardiner should have the slave, John (the son of his slave, Tamer) after the death of his wife. He also provided his granddaughter Susan Elizabeth Gardiner with Tom, a skilled bricklayer, Tamer, and Bella. As mentioned earlier, Ann Deas used slave labor to maintain high standards for her well established hotel and restaurant in Charleston, South Carolina. In 1840 she owned five female slaves between the ages of 10 and 36, all worked in the hotel. Ann attributed the success of her hotel to the slaves who cooked as well as those who attended to the needs of her White clientele.[195]

Ann Deas would eventually sell her hotel to her business partner **Elizabeth Seymour Lee**, the daughter of the emancipated slave Sally Martin alias Sarah Seymour, was born after her mother was freed from slavery. Elizabeth never knew what it was to be a slave. Yet she benefited from the institution of bondage. In March 1823, her mother, Sarah Seymour, gave Elizabeth two slaves (Flora and her child George). Elizabeth was trained as a pastry cook by her mother and used her slaves in that line of business. In 1823, Elizabeth married John Lee and established a profitable business catering to the white aristocrats of Charleston. They not only acquired slaves for their business but trained slaves in the art of cooking. In 1841, Nathaniel Heyward provided John and Elizabeth Lee with a slave boy named Robert, to be trained in the art of cooking. In 1847, they acquired the Jones Inn, one of the renowned eateries and boarding houses in Charleston City. With the use of slave labor, they established a profitable business which allowed them to acquire 17 slaves and real estate valued at $15,000.[196]

In her essay that was published in The American Historical Review (February 1990) titled, *"Prosperous Blacks in the South, 1790-1880,"* Loren Schweninger pointed out that:

By 1830, approximately 1,556 free black masters in the Deep South owned a total of 7,188 slaves. Representing about 42 percent of the black owners in the South, they owned 60 percent of the black-owned slaves. In the Charleston District, 407 owners held a total of 2,195 slaves. In New Orleans, there were 753 free black owners, including 25 who owned at least 10 bondsmen and women and another 116 who owned between 5 and 9 slaves. Although some of these slaveholders owned members of their own families, or loved ones, unable to free them by law, in 8 rural Louisiana sugar and cotton parishes, 43 Creoles of color (1.2 percent of the black slaveholders in the South) owned a total of 1,327 blacks, or 1out of 9 slaves owned by blacks. In St. John the Baptist Parish, 3 plantation owners held 139 blacks in bondage-an average of 46 slaves each; in Pointe Coupee Parish, 8 planters held 297 slaves, an average of 37 slaves each. In 1830, approximately a 1out of 4 free black families in the region was a slaveholder.[197]

Schweninger also explains further, *"Because not all free Blacks who had slaves listed in the same household were owners of those slaves, several of Woodson's listings are incorrect. The forty-three Creoles of Color in Louisiana cited above have been checked in parish records. I have used Koger's findings for South Carolina and the compilations of Halliburton, excluding the Arkansas Territory, for the other states in the Lower South. The debate concerning the extent of "benevolent" versus "commercial" ownership has generally focused on the entire South and thus minimized the diversity among Black slaveowners in different regions during different time periods."*[198]

The Paradox of Freedom

One of the most significant challenges faced by free Black slaveholders was access to capital. They were often denied loans from White-owned banks, making it difficult to acquire land and establish businesses. This forced many to rely on informal credit networks within their own communities, or to partner with White individuals, which could come with its own set of limitations and risks. This is how William Dunford was able to expand into the plantation system. While Durnford was still a young man, his father died in 1826. After that, he became first friends, and then business partners, with one of his father's old friends, a White New Orleans merchant and plantation owner by the name of John McDonogh. Durnford turned to McDonogh for advice and credit in order to enter the plantation business.[199]

To manage enslaved labor, free Black slaveholders employed a range of strategies. Some sought to create a system of mutual respect and cooperation, recognizing the inherent humanity of their enslaved workers. They may have allowed for some degree of autonomy in daily tasks, provided opportunities for skill development, or even allowed for the possibility of emancipation. However, the realities of a slaveholding society meant that these approaches were often limited by the constraints of the system and the prevailing power dynamics.

Other free Black slaveholders mirrored the practices of their White counterparts, employing harsh punishments, limiting the autonomy of their enslaved workers, and seeking to maximize their profits through the exploitation of labor. The extent to which individual free Black slaveholders deviated from or aligned with prevailing practices is difficult to determine, as the historical record is often incomplete and biased.

Free Black slaveholders also participated in the complex world of the slave market. **John and Samuel Holeman** were free Black slaveowners and African slave traders. They bought and sold enslaved people, often within their own communities or through established networks of brokers.

In 1790, John Holman, Sr. (White), arrived in South Carolina but the political climate had changed in regard to the importation of African slaves. The state assembly had prohibited the importation of African slaves and barred Holman from entering the state. He was forced to travel to Georgia and establish a temporary residence while his business associates petitioned the state legislature to grant them the right to settle in South Carolina with a cargo of African-born slaves. The legislation that allowed him to enter the state was not passed until February 19, 1792. By July, he was living on his plantation called Blessing in St. Thomas & St. Dennis Parish.[200]

On July 24, 1792, John Holman, Sr., died with an estate consisting of the Blessing Plantation and about 70 slaves. After the death of the elder Holman, his two sons, John and Samuel (mulatto), as well as Henry Laurens, Jr. (White), son of the elder Laurens who was a United States founding father and slave trader, managed the estate of the deceased slave trader. In fact, John and Samuel Holman had been groomed by their father to succeed him. While in Africa, John, Jr., and Samuel were trained as slave traders and brought their own slaves with them when they arrived in South Carolina. The brothers had 62 slaves separate from the estate of their father.[201]

Between January 1798 and August 1803, John Holman, Jr., rented a plantation in Georgetown County from George Parker and cultivated rice with the slaves of his father's estate and his own. After the lease expired on August 3, 1803, he signed a contract to purchase the rented plantation and used his slaves as collateral to ensure the payments would be made. The payment plan between Holman and Parker called for the first installment of $10,000 payable on August 16, 1804, and the final payment of $5,000 on August 16, 1806. With the agreement established John Holman, Jr., gave George Parker power of attorney and boarded a vessel in Charleston bound for Rio Pongo, West Africa and established a "factory" on the Rio Pong River, north of Sierra Leone, and for nearly a quarter-century, reaping huge profits buying and selling fellow Africans. He did not return to Charleston until January 1805 and four months later Holman revisited his homeland and never came back to South Carolina.[202]

Before his voyage to Africa, he placed his brother Samuel Holman in charge of his estate and returned to Africa to resume slave trading that his father had taught him. John Holman, Jr., was probably the first and only African-born entrepreneur who resided in Africa as an absentee planter in the United States.[203]

John Holeman, Jr. realized that the slave market itself posed significant financial risks. Fluctuations in the price of enslaved people, influenced by factors like age, health, and skill, could result in substantial losses. Additionally, the legal framework surrounding the ownership and sale of enslaved people was riddled with complexities and uncertainties. The constant threat of legal challenges or disputes over ownership could significantly impact the financial well-being of free Black slaveholders. Therefore, he diversified his investments by allowing his younger brother to manage his plantation in America thus insuring his wealth.

As one can see, the economic impact of free Black slaveholding was very complex, yet for some individuals it offered a pathway to wealth and social mobility. They were able to acquire land, build businesses, and accumulate capital, contributing to the development of free Black communities. However, the economic activities of free Black slaveholders had implications for the broader community. By competing with White slaveholders for land and labor, this contributed to tensions and power struggles that characterized the antebellum South. They also challenged the prevailing racial order, demonstrating that Black individuals could participate in the economic system that was built upon the foundation of slavery.

Despite these complexities and contradictions inherent in their economic practices, free Black slaveholders played a significant role in the economic landscape of the antebellum South. As stated in a previous chapter, the story of William Ellison, a prominent free Black slaveholder in Virginia, illustrates the complex economic realities of this practice. Ellison, through shrewd business ventures and the ownership of enslaved labor, amassed a considerable fortune, owning a large plantation and engaging in various commercial enterprises. His success challenged the racial hierarchy of the time and demonstrated the economic potential of free Black individuals. However, his story highlights the social pressures for which slave-owning Black Americans had thrust upon them, or chose to expose themselves by their involvement with the institution.[204]

Free Black slaveholders, by their very existence, exposed the fluidity and inconsistency of racial boundaries within the social landscape. They were, in a sense, living embodiments of the paradoxical nature of freedom and bondage. They had achieved a degree of personal freedom, yet they still participated in the institution of slavery. Their ownership of slaves poses a direct challenge to the prevailing ideology that only Whites owned slaves in the United States. The fact that free Black individuals could legally own slaves, engage in economic transactions, and even possess a degree of social influence within their communities force challenging questions to the widespread, contemporary assumptions of Southern society and the wider American culture. Their presence demonstrated that the concept of "Blackness" was necessarily definitive, and that some Black people could, in fact, navigate and even benefit from the system of slavery, albeit in a limited and often precarious way. As a result, the ownership of slaves also presented a significant ethical and moral dilemma for free Black individuals. They were often faced with the difficult task of reconciling their own aspirations for freedom with the reality of owning and controlling the lives of other Black people.

It's important to emphasize that Free Black slaveholders were not monolithic. They were individuals with diverse motivations, experiences, and perspectives, operating within a system that offered them limited opportunities for self-determination. While some may have participated in the institution of slavery with a sense of moral justification, others may have felt constrained by circumstances beyond their control.

Ultimately, the existence of Free Black slaveholders serves as a reminder of the complexities and contradictions that existed challenging us to move beyond simplistic narratives and appreciate the nuanced realities of the past. Their story is a testament to the resilience, agency, and often-overlooked complexities of Black life in a time marked by oppression and a constant struggle for freedom. By examining their experiences, we can gain a deeper understanding of the multifaceted nature of slavery and its enduring legacy in shaping American society.

The Paradox of Freedom

Chapter 6:
Legal and Moral Issues: Navigating the Laws and Jurisprudence of Slave Holding

The legal and moral jurisprudence of slave holding in America was complex and reactive. Unlike many other slave societies, the United States never developed a systematic law of slavery. In his paper, *Free to Enslave: The Foundations of Colonial American Slave Law*, historian Jonathan A. Bush, writes:

To nineteenth-century Southern judges as well as Northern abolitionists, it was a commonplace that slavery, in legal contemplation, had never been created. Historians today agree that slavery had instead simply evolved in practice, as a custom, and then received statutory recognition involving no legislative debates. For the first few decades of English colonization, there was likely no slavery in practice and no legal mention of slavery. Suddenly, legal documents began to appear in reference to slaves. A Maryland act of 1638, noted that 'all Christians-except slaves' shall have the full rights of Englishmen at home, and a Rhode Island statute of 1652 cited 'the common course practised among English men to buy negars, to that end that they may have them for service or slaves forever.' The famous <u>Fundamental Constitutions</u>, drawn up by John Locke in 1669 for the South Carolina colony, guaranteed freedom of religion to black slaves provided that they remained slaves, and then added that 'Every Free man of Carolina, shall have absolute power and authority over Negro Slaves, of whatever upbringing or Religion soever.' Almost from the outset, slavery was assumed in this way, ex nihilo (out of nothing), but it was nowhere justified, explained, or systematically described.[205]

Legal Issues
In legal terms, the lasting legacy of free Black slaveholders is multifaceted and far-reaching. The mere fact of their existence disrupts

the simplistic binary of "White slaveholders" and "Black slaves," forcing a reckoning of nuance in how power and privilege were distributed within a society deeply intertwined with slavery. Therefore, understanding the historical context of free Black slaveholding is essential. For instance, the legal landscape surrounding slavery was far from uniform across the United States during Colonial times through to the Antebellum period. While some states like Massachusetts saw a gradual shift toward abolition, others, like South Carolina, fiercely defended the institution of slavery. This divergence in legal frameworks created opportunities for free Black individuals in certain regions to own slaves, as the laws commonly did not prohibit them from doing so.

The legal framework governing slavery in the United States from about 1776 to 1865 was contradictory itself woven from state and federal laws, judicial decisions, and the prevailing social norms of the time. While slavery was explicitly sanctioned by the Constitution, its legal parameters varied significantly across different states, creating a patchwork of regulations that shaped the institution's reality at the grassroots level. The fact is, there were no separate laws specifically regulating Black slave owners. Instead, Black slaveholders were subject to the same slave codes that governed White Americans, as common slaveholders. These codes were designed to: (1) Define enslaved people as property, (2) Restrict their movement, education, and assembly, and (3) Protect the interests of slaveholders, regardless of race. However, Black slaveholders often faced additional scrutiny and social hostility, especially in the South. Their legal rights were limited compared to White citizens in many ways, such being unable to vote or hold public office in many states, give testimony against White Americans in court, and often fewer legal means to manumit their slaves. Some examples of restrictions include: (1) In Maryland, free Black people were prohibited from immigrating into the state until 1865, (2) In Virginia, laws banned Black people from owning weapons and restricted their movement, and, (3) In South Carolina, free Black people were denied business licenses.[206]

In addition to the legal complexities surrounding ownership, free Black slaveholders also faced challenges in managing their slaves. While they were subject to the same laws as White slaveholders, their ability to enforce those laws was often limited. This was due in part to the fear of White slaveholders, who viewed free Black slaveholders as a threat to their own power and authority.

At the heart of this legal labyrinth lay the concept of chattel slavery, which defined enslaved people as property, stripping them of their fundamental human rights and subjecting them to the absolute control of their owners. This legal framework was codified in various state laws and codes that governed every aspect of enslaved people's lives, from their movement and work to their interactions with Free People of Colour. These codes served to reinforce the rigid racial hierarchy that defined antebellum American society.

For instance, laws governing the movement of enslaved people restricted their ability to travel without their owner's permission, while "vagrancy" laws were used to capture runaway slaves and return them to bondage. Enslaved people were veritably denied the right to own property, to testify against their owners, or even to learn to read or write. These restrictions aimed to maintain the absolute control of slaveholders, ensuring that enslaved people remained subservient and powerless within the legal framework of the system.

Many Black masters were emancipated slaves. They knew what it was to be a slave of another man or woman. Yet often their desire to excel and prosper overrode the moral dilemma of slavery. Lamb Stevens, an emancipated slave, was not of mixed racial heritage. He was a man described as "coal black" in complexion. Without the patronage of White or Black family members of wealth, he amassed a 500-acre plantation called Cherry Hill and 35 slaves in 1850. Several of his slaves were family members but most were acquired as labourers used to till the soil of his plantation. In Charleston City, Bersheba Cattle, the former slave of J.H. Stevens, invested in chattel property. In 1818, she purchased a servant woman named Nanny, who was about 38 years old, for $550. Cattle hired out her slave to prospective users. In her will, she requested that her executors should receive the wages of Nanny. During the antebellum period, many Afro-Americans of free status acquired slaves as commercial assets to be used in their businesses, to be hired out, or to be purchased as investments to be sold at a higher price.[207]

Beyond state laws, federal legislation played a significant role in defining the legal landscape of slavery. *The Fugitive Slave Act* of 1793, for example, was enacted by the United States Congress to require states to return fugitive slaves to their owners. It authorized local governments to seize and return escapees and imposed penalties on anyone who aided in their flight. This act was a response to disputes between states, particularly between Pennsylvania and Virginia, regarding the return of escaped slaves. The act established a legal framework of means for slaveholders to recover runaway slaves, reinforcing the national and constitutional nature and status of the institution of slavery in the United States. This law fuelled tensions between North and South, further entrenching the divide that would lead to the War Between the States.

The *Compromise of 1850*, a series of measures aimed at easing tensions between the two sides, included a strengthened *Fugitive Slave Act* that imposed harsher penalties on those who aided runaway slaves and placed the burden of proof on the accused. This legislation further cemented the legal buttress of slavery, making it more difficult for enslaved people to escape and securing the institution's grip on the nation.

The legal framework surrounding slavery also extended to the complex issue of manumission, the process of freeing enslaved people. While some states allowed for individual manumission, others imposed stringent restrictions, making it difficult, if not impossible, for enslaved

The Paradox of Freedom

people to gain their freedom. In many cases, the legal process of manumission required the owner to petition the legislature or a court, often subject to strict conditions and scrutiny.

Furthermore, legalities played a significant role in determining the fate of enslaved people who were caught attempting to escape. Runaway slaves could be subjected to severe punishments, including imprisonment, whipping, and even death. The legal system was not only a tool for enforcing the institution of slavery but also for deterring any attempt to challenge its boundaries and dominion.

It is important to note that this legal framework of slavery was not static. It evolved over time, reflecting the shifting political landscape, slave revolts and risings such as Nat Turner in Southampton County, Virginia, in 1831. During the rebellion, the Virginia General Assembly targeted free Blacks with an African relocation bill, and a police bill denying them trials by jury and criminal punishment by slavery and relocation. The General Assembly received petitions from at least seven slave owners asking to be compensated for slaves lost without trial because of the insurrection; they were all rejected.[208]

John Brown's raid on Harper's Ferry arsenal in 1859 is another example. After his trial and execution, Southerners had a mixed attitude towards their slaves. Many slaveholders, both Black and White, lived in constant fear of another slave insurrection; paradoxically, Slaveholders also claimed that slaves were content in bondage, blaming slave unrest on Northern abolitionists. After the raid Southerners initially lived in fear of slave uprisings and invasion by armed abolitionists. The South's reaction entered the second phase at around the time of Brown's execution. Southerners were relieved that no slaves had volunteered to help Brown, as they were incorrectly told by Governor Wise and others, and felt vindicated in their claims that slaves were content. In the North, the rise of abolitionist movements, and rising voices regarding the institution's inherent injustices intensified with more debates surrounding slavery, with escalating demands to end the practice in the years leading up to the Civil War causing Southern opinion to evolve into what James M. McPherson called *"unreasoning fury"*.[209]

However, despite both change and challenges, slavery, and its enabling constitutional/legal framework, remained deeply embedded in the fabric of American society, shaping the lives and destinies of millions of enslaved people and the rest of the nation. It was a system built on the denial of basic human rights, the assertion of absolute power, and the reinforcement of a racial hierarchy that deemed enslaved people as property rather than human beings. This legal framework was a cornerstone of the antebellum South, a powerful engine that drove the institution of slavery, and a testament to the deeply ingrained racism and oppression that marked this period in American history.

The legislation, litigation, common law, conventions, and traditions governing free Black ownership of slaves were a tangled web of contradictions and ambiguities, reflecting the complex and often hypocritical nature of American society in the Antebellum period. While free Black people were recognized as citizens and entitled to certain rights, their ownership of slaves was often met with suspicion, discrimination, and legal challenges by the wider White American society. Thereby, Black American slave ownership varied significantly from state to state, with some states offering more lenient regulations than others. In most cases, free Black slaveholders were subject to the same laws as White slaveholders, but with some important exceptions. For example, free Black people in colonial Maryland were subject to unique taxation, these taxes used to dissuade free Black immigration and limit their opportunities within the state's borders. In South Carolina, free Black people were required to pay an annual "head" or "capitation" tax. In contrast, White slaveholders paid less in taxes in these same states. This was often seen to discourage free Black people from acquiring slaves and to maintain the dominance of the White slaveholding class.[210]

Moreover, the legal status of free Black slaveholders was frequently challenged in court. In some cases, white slaveholders attempted to use the courts to strip free Black slaveholders of their rights and property, claiming that they were not truly free or that they were unfit to own slaves. These legal battles often went to the Supreme Court, with mixed results. In some cases, the courts upheld the rights of free Black slaveholders, while in others, they sided with the White slaveholding class.[211]

The most significant legal challenge faced by free Black slaveholders was the inherent contradiction between their legal status as citizens and their ownership of slaves. This contradiction was deeply rooted in the racial ideology of the time, which viewed Blacks as inferior and unfit for freedom, let alone the power and responsibility of owning slaves. While the laws technically allowed for free Black slaveholders, the prevailing social and political climate often made it difficult for them to exercise their rights and to navigate the legal system without facing discrimination and prejudice.

To protect their property, Free People of Color began to link their families through intermarriage. For example, in South Carolina, the Holman and Collins families were related by ties of kinship and marriage, as were the Ellison, Weston, Holloway, Johnson, and Bonneau families. In Charleston, the same was true for the Cole-Seymour, Garden-Mitchell, Inglis-Glover, Lee-Seymour, and McKinlay-Huger families. Free Blacks of "status" often chose marital partners based upon three important points economic well-being, social status, and free, mixed-blood ancestry. In Mississippi, **John Barland**, a wealthy planter, married Mary Fitzgerald, the daughter of a prosperous free mulatto in Natchez. Among prosperous Creoles of color in Louisiana, endogamous marriages were very common. **Antoine Decuir** and **Antoine Dubuclet**, the richest blacks in Pointe Coupee Parish, signed formal contracts concerning their children. In the case of Decuir's son, **Antoine, Jr.**, and Dubuclet's daughter,

The Paradox of Freedom

Josephine, a four-page document, written in French, specified the size of the dowry and arrangements for the distribution of property in their marriage contract. Similar contracts, or verbal agreements, followed this example in St. Landry Parrish by the following free Black families; the Donatto, Meullion, Simien [Simon], Guillory, and Lemmelle families; the Conant, Metoyer, Rogues, and Llorens in Natchitoches; the Reggio, Oliver, and Leonard families in Plaquemines; and the Bienville, Ricard, and Turpin families in East Baton Rouge. One local court judgment described the Decuir, Deslondes, Honore, and Dubucelet families in West Baton Rouge and Pointe Coupee parishes as being *"all free persons of color, Relations & friends."*[212]

Antoine Dubuclet Jr. was considered one of the wealthiest African Americans in the nation before the Civil War. After the war, he was the first person of African descent to hold the office of Louisiana treasurer. *Courtesy of the Public Domain*

Furthermore, the laws governing free Black slaveholding were constantly evolving, with new laws and legal interpretations emerging as society grappled with the complexities of race, freedom, and slavery. In some cases, these changes were driven by the growing abolitionist movement, which sought to eliminate slavery altogether. In other cases, they were motivated by a desire to maintain White dominance and to restrict the rights of free Black populations.

Mississippi's consistently low, free Black American population between 1810 and 1860 was a direct result of a network of controls, backed by laws and race prejudice. Most apparent were those laws that controlled, discouraged, and prevented free Black people from moving into Mississippi. Of those very few who did arrive, their lives were governed by an ever-widening range of laws specific to free Black people. Mississippi laws as early as 1820 presumed every "negro," or Person of Colour, to be a slave. To prove otherwise, free Black individuals were required to secure onerous certification for their free status.

Mississippi's laws required every person of free status to appear before the local court to give evidence of his or her freedom. When the court was provided satisfactory proof, the applicants received certificates of free status, ("freedom papers", as the certificates became commonly known). The certificate indicated the bearer's name, color hue, physical stature, and any distinguishing features, such as scars. Every three years the certificate had to be renewed at a fee of $1, the equivalent of $25 today. In 1831 the fee was increased to $3.[213]

Free Black people in Mississippi placed themselves at significant risk if they failed a certificate of registration in their possession, at risk of seizure and even imprisonment. If Black people were unable to establish their free status within a specified period, state laws permitted them to be sold into slavery at public auction. Thus, these certificates of registration were the single most important articles for Free Persons of Colour to possess.

Excerpt from Charles Griffin's free papers
Note: This excerpt is from the original records on microfilm at the Mississippi Department of Archives and History. Because of extensive use by researchers, the microfilm is heavily scratched, making it impossible to get a copy with all words legible for reproduction. Therefore, this excerpt was taken from *Mississippi Now*:

From the **Deed Record,** *Volume S, Year 1830 Adams County Court House, Natchez, Mississippi*
Charles Griffin's free papers
Commonwealth of Kentucky, Gallaton County to wit:

The Paradox of Freedom

I, Perceval Butler clerk of the court of the county do hereby certify that at a court held for said county at the courthouse thereof on Monday the 13th of December 1813, an instrument of writing under the hands and seals of Nelly Love and James Love emancipating Charles Griffin a negro man slave, aged twenty seven years and acknowledging the receipt of four hundred and fifty dollars as a full consideration therefor and containing a general guarantee of the freedom of the said Charles Griffin was presented into court and proved by the oath of Joseph Hardy and Mary Hardy subscribing witnesses thereto and ordered to be recorded and certified. And it was further ordered that the clerk of the said court shall give to the said Charles Griffin a certificate of his freedom, in the manner prescribed by law, which is hereby done accordingly.

In testimony whereof I have hereunto set my hand and affixes the seal of said county this 11th day of August 1814 and in the 23rd year of the Commonwealth.

P. Butler[214]

The evolution of legal frameworks surrounding Free Black slaveholding was a dynamic and complex process, stemming from shifting tides of social attitudes, political landscapes, and judicial interpretations. From the early days of colonial America, when the concept of a "free" Black population was itself an anomaly, to the end of the Civil War, when the legal foundation of slavery crumbled, the laws governing free Black ownership of slaves underwent constant transformation.

The legal landscape surrounding free Black slaveholding was constantly evolving, shaped by this very confluence of factors. As Abolitionism gained momentum, the legal status of free Black slaveholders became increasingly scrutinized. Some states, driven opposition to Abolitionism, ended the legal right of Black Americans to own slaves. However, the legal framework surrounding this practice remained fragmented and inconsistent across different states.

The Paradox of Freedom

Early laws, often rooted in the colonial context, tended to be ambiguous and contradictory. While some colonies explicitly barred free Black people from owning slaves, others adopted a more laissez-faire approach, leaving the matter to local authorities or relying on common law precedents. This ambiguity, fuelled by a desire to control Black populations and maintain the racial hierarchy, often created legally 'gray' areas that free Black slaveholders navigated with caution and strategic finesse. By the early 19th century, a surge of legal codifications regarding slavery, reflecting the growing political and economic power of the institution in the South, began to emerge. This drive of legal codification was often driven by anxieties about the growing free Black population. For instance, Virginia, the state with the largest concentration of free Black slaveholders, passed laws that made it increasingly difficult for free Black people to purchase slaves and imposed upon them more stringent requirements on landownership, financial stability, and social standing. These laws reflected a growing fear among White slaveholders that free Black slaveholders might challenge the established power structures and erode the foundation of White supremacy.

The courtroom, with its imposing architecture and formal proceedings, often served as the battleground where the legal complexities of free Black slaveholding were played out. Here, the laws governing this peculiar institution were scrutinized, debated, and interpreted, shaping the legal landscape and the fate of those caught in its intricate web.

The courts, however, were not immune to the pervasive prejudices and biases that permeated Antebellum society. While the law might have recognized the legal right of free Black individuals to own slaves, the actual application of these laws was often colored by racial prejudice. Judges and juries, steeped in the prevailing social norms and beliefs of the time, frequently interpreted the law in a manner that favored White interests, upholding the existing power dynamics and reinforcing a racial hierarchy.

These legal issues illustrate the inconsistencies and biases inherent in the legal system of the Antebellum South. As noted, the courts, despite their supposed role as impartial arbiters of justice, were often influenced by the prevailing societal norms and prejudices, representing the legal battles fought in them as symbolic of the larger struggle for racial equality and the challenge of reconciling the legal recognition of slave ownership by Free Persons of Colour, themselves facing unique systemic discrimination.

Furthermore, the interpretation of the law surrounding Free Black slaveholding often had significant implications for the lives of enslaved people and themselves through a combination of legal and social means. The question of legal protections for enslaved people under the ownership of free Black people posed, and would remain, a contentious issue. They were denied the right to own property, travel without a pass, bear arms without special permission, assembly in groups of more than five, preach without supervision, and be taught to read. These restrictions were part of a broader system of control and exploitation that enslaved people experienced. The legal system was often used to enforce these restrictions, with the courts and laws serving as tools to maintain the status quo and prevent any form of resistance or challenge to the system. While some scholars have argued that enslaved people held by free Blacks could take comfort in a presumed greater degree of security (due to notions of empathy or kinship), others pointed out that the legal framework surrounding slavery, regardless of the owner's race, ultimately deprived enslaved people of basic human rights, regardless of any other factors. Take for example the manumission laws and how they changed over years from state to state and in some states, manumission was forbidden such as South Carolina in 1820, Mississippi in 1822, Arkansas in 1858, and Maryland and Alabama in 1860.[215]

The pre-Civil War period witnessed growing tensions between the reality of slave ownership by Free Black Americans and the rising tide of Abolitionism (a phenomenon that has escaped widespread scholastic examination). While laws continued to be enacted that restricted free Black ownership, the moral and ethical questions surrounding the practice simultaneously intensified, due in no small part to the Abolitionist movement gaining momentum. Abolitionist writings and public discourse increasingly challenged the legitimacy of any form of slaveholding, regardless the owner's race. This mounting pressure placed Free Black slaveholders in an ever more difficult position, forcing them to navigate their legal right to ownership amidst acute pressures they could not ignore with regards in the rising tide of moral condemnation.

The Civil War and its aftermath marked a watershed moment in the legal landscape of Free Black slaveholding. The Emancipation Proclamation, followed by the passage of the 13th Amendment, effectively abolished slavery and rendered the legal foundation of Free Black slaveholding obsolete. However, the complexities of the post-war era, particularly during Reconstruction, raised new legal challenges for those who had previously owned slaves. Issues such as the fate of formerly enslaved people, the legal recognition of property rights, and the struggle for economic and social equality, all shaped the legal realities of Free Black slaveholders in the years following the war in particular ways.

One of the most significant legal developments surrounding free Black slaveholding was the gradual emancipation of slaves in some states, particularly in the North. While this movement did not initially target free Black slaveholders, it ultimately led to the decline of free Black slaveholding as slaves were gradually set free. This development raised further legal complexities, as it forced free Black slaveholders to grapple with the moral implications of owning slaves in a society that was increasingly supported ending the institution of slavery.

The evolution of legal frameworks surrounding Free Black slaveholding was not a linear progression toward abolition. It was a complex interplay of social pressures, political shifts, and evolving legal interpretations that reflected the deep-seated anxieties about race and power in American society. From the ambiguity of early colonial laws to the explicit restrictions of the 19th century, and ultimately to the complete abolition of slavery in the wake of the Civil War, and the legal landscape surrounding Free Black slaveholding mirrored the shifting tides of American history. It stands as a testament to the enduring struggle for equality and the complex history of race and power in the United States.

Moral Issues
The existence of free Black slaveholders in Antebellum America presents a stark and often uncomfortable contradiction, a moral dilemma that challenged the very foundation of this "peculiar institution." To comprehend this perplexing phenomenon, we must delve into the intricate complications of ownership and its inherent ethical implications within American society of the time.

For many, the image of a Black person holding another Black person in bondage clashes with the very notion of freedom. The concept of a "free" person, especially one who had endured the brutal reality of chattel slavery, participating in a system that perpetuated such suffering seems absurd. It compels us to question the nature of freedom itself, its limitations, and its malleability in a society where racial boundaries were rigorously enforced and the concept of personal liberty was intrinsically tied to one's race.

Free Black slaveholders were, in many ways, caught between two worlds; one of the worlds of the White slaveholding class, where they were denied full citizenship and subjected to racial prejudice, the other being the world of enslaved people, where they were viewed with a mixture of suspicion, fear, and even resentment. Their status as slaveholders placed them in a position of power that, ironically, mirrored the very power dynamics they themselves had endured.

However, it is crucial to avoid simplifying the motivations of free Black slaveholders by reducing them to such mere scopes as economic opportunists. The practice was also rooted in a complex interplay of social dynamics and personal beliefs. For many, owning slaves was a way of approximating social standing with the White American community, wherein Black people were near universally marginalized and ostracized. In a system where wealth and social standing were inextricably linked to the ownership of enslaved people, acquiring slaves could be seen as a degree to achieve acceptance and belonging.

Furthermore, the motivations of Free Black slaveholders were also shaped by social and cultural context. This further compounded the moral complexities of free Black slaveholding by the relationships that developed between themselves and the enslaved population. These relationships were not monolithic but existed on a spectrum ranging from acts of kindness and compassion to instances of cruelty and exploitation. Some free Black slaveholders genuinely sought to improve the lives of the people they owned, offering opportunities for education, skill development, and even emancipation. Others, however, perpetuated the same practices of the White slaveholding class, treating their enslaved people as mere commodities, subject to the same conditions.

The moral ambiguity surrounding free Black slaveholding lies in the intersection of individual choices and the constraints of a deeply flawed system. While some free Black slaveholders may have chosen to own slaves out of economic necessity or a desire for social acceptance, their actions perpetuated a system that denied the fundamental rights and dignity of others. Their participation in the institution of slavery, even with the intent of offering a semblance of better treatment, ultimately contributed to the perpetuation of a system built upon racial inequality and the denial of basic human rights.

Free Black slaveholders were not immune to the same biases and prejudices that permeated the society around them. Their own experiences of racial discrimination and marginalization, their struggles for social and economic recognition, and their desire for acceptance within a White-dominated society often contributed to their embrace of a system that ultimately perpetuated the oppression of persons of their own race. These views can be often found amongst free Blacks slaveholders such as William Johnson in his diary entry of March 19, 1838, where he recorded his whipping of a slave named Steven. Andrew Dunford recorded how he had to handle disobedient slaves, *". . . rascally Negroes, I have to threaten them severely to get them to do their dutys . . ."*[216]

Even slaves reported they did not wish to be owned by Black masters because of their cruelty as recorded by Frederick Law Olmsted in his travels throughout the South:

He said, in answer to further inquiries, that there were many free Negroes all about this region. Some were very rich. He pointed out to me three plantations, within twenty miles, owned by coloured men. They bought black folks, he said, and had servants of their own. They were very bad masters, very hard and cruel . . . If he had got to be sold, he would like best to have an American master buy him. The French [black Creole] masters were very severe, and 'dey whip dar niggers most to deff—dey whipe de flesh off of 'em.'[217]

However, it is as essential to avoid unrestrained judgement of these individuals by a lens of contemporary moral frameworks as much as any others. The historical context of free Black slaveholding must be acknowledged, understood, and grappled with in its entirety. Their actions were shaped by the deeply entrenched ideology of their time, by the limited options available to them, and by the powerful social and economic pressures they faced. A holistic historical examination obliges both objectivity and empathy towards their position on the one hand, with the willingness to offer a measure of fair and balanced criticism on the other.

The Paradox of Freedom

The exploration of free Black slaveholding inevitably leads us to confront the complex interplay between religious beliefs and moral justifications. How did their faith, their understanding of morality, and their lived realities shape their actions and their rationalizations for holding enslaved people?

The religious landscape of the Antebellum South held a deep intertwinement with the institution of slavery. Many White Christian slaveholders, and if asked, most slaveholders of the time would have defined themselves as Christians, justified their actions through biblical interpretations that portrayed slavery as a Divinely ordained system. They pointed to passages in the Bible that spoke of servitude and obedience, conveniently overlooking the passages that preached against oppression and advocated for the liberation of the oppressed. The two most favorites texts, one from the beginning of the *Old Testament* and the other from the end of the *New Testament*. In the words of the *King James Bible*, which was the version then current, these were, first, *Genesis IX*, 18–27:

And the sons of Noah that went forth from the ark were Shem, Ham, and Japheth: and Ham is the father of Canaan. These are the three sons of Noah: and of them was the whole world overspread. And Noah began to be a husbandman, and he planted a vineyard: and he drank of the wine, and was drunken; and he was uncovered within his tent. And Ham, the father of Canaan, saw the nakedness of his father, and told his two brethren without. And Shem and Japheth took a garment, and laid it upon both their shoulders, and went backward, and covered the nakedness of their father; and their faces were backward, and they saw not their father's nakedness. And Noah awoke from his wine, and knew what his younger son had done unto him. And he said, Cursed be Canaan; a servant of servants shall he be unto his brethren. And he said, Blessed be the Lord God of Shem; and Canaan shall be his servant. God shall enlarge Japheth, and he shall dwell in the tents of

Shem; and Canaan shall be his servant. And Noah lived after the flood three hundred and fifty years.[218]

The other favorite came from the Apostle Paul's Epistle to the *Ephesians, VI*, 5-7:

Servants, be obedient to them that are your masters according to the flesh, with fear and trembling, in singleness of your heart, as unto Christ; not with eye-service, as men-pleasers; but as the servants of Christ, doing the will of God from the heart; with good will doing service, as to the Lord, and not to men: knowing that whatsoever good thing any man doeth, the same shall he receive of the Lord, whether he be bond or free.[219]

Paul repeated himself, almost word for word, in the third chapter of his *Epistle to the Colossians*; *"Servants, obey in all things your masters according to the flesh; not with eyeservice, as menpleasers; but in singleness of heart, fearing God."*[220]

Free Black people, however, often experienced religion in a quite unique way. The African American churches that emerged in the South provided spaces for Black communities to find solace, build solidarity, and develop their own interpretations of religious texts. Many free Black preachers and leaders condemned slavery as a sin against God and a violation of human dignity. They drew inspiration from religious texts that championed equality and freedom, using their sermons and teachings to inspire resistance against the oppressive system. Biblical teachings served as a powerful source of strength and resilience for the free Black community during challenging times. Through scripture, they found messages of hope, dignity, and divine worth that countered the degrading narratives of slavery and discrimination. The Bible's stories of liberation, particularly the Exodus narrative of Moses leading the Israelites to freedom, resonated deeply and provided a framework for understanding their own struggles and aspirations. They also preached passages that emphasized equality before God, such as Galatians 3:28; *"There is neither Jew nor Greek, slave nor free, male nor female, for you are all one in Christ Jesus,"* offered spiritual validation of their inherent human dignity. [221]

Thus, the experiences of free Black slaveholders, were often marked by a profound internal conflict. They were caught between the moral teachings of their faith and the social and economic realities of the world they inhabited. On the one hand, they may well have believed in the inherent dignity and worth of all human beings, a principle that directly contradicted the practice of slavery. On the other hand, they were often confronted with the limitations of their freedom, the economic pressures of survival, and the social pressures of maintaining a place in a racially segregated society.

One way to understand this moral dilemma is to consider the case of **William Ellison**, a prominent free Black slaveholder in Virginia introduced in earlier chapters. Ellison, a successful farmer and businessman, owned a significant amount of land and a substantial number of enslaved people. He was also a devout Christian, attending church regularly and actively participating in religious services. His personal journals offer a glimpse into the complexities of his moral landscape. He wrote about his belief in the equality of all people before God, but he also acknowledged the challenges of navigating the social and economic realities of slavery. His writings reveal a deep struggle to reconcile his faith with his actions, demonstrating the profound internal conflict that many free Black slaveholders grappled with.[222]

In some cases, free Black slaveholders attempted to justify their ownership by portraying themselves as benevolent masters, providing better treatment for their enslaved people than they would have received under white ownership. They might argue that they were offering a measure of protection, education, or skill development that was denied to enslaved people under the control of white slaveholders.

However, this rationale is deeply problematic for several reasons. Firstly, it perpetuates the notion that the ownership of another human being, regardless of the level of treatment, is inherently ethical. The very act of owning another person, even if done with benevolent intentions, constitutes a fundamental violation of human rights. Secondly, the argument for benevolent ownership often relies on the assumption that White slaveholders were inherently cruel and abusive, inaccurately denies that Black slaveholders could be cruel and abusive to their human property, thus perpetuating harmful stereotypes and obscuring the complexity of power dynamics within the slaveholding system. The moral justification for Free Black slaveholding remained deeply contested. Some individuals, like William Ellison, wrestled with the contradictions, trying to reconcile their faith with their actions.

It is essential to remember that the perspective of free Black slaveholders is only one part of the story. To fully understand the complexities of this historical phenomenon, we must also consider the perspectives of those held in bondage.

The narratives of enslaved people provide a critical lens through which to examine the realities of life under the ownership of free Black slaveholders. While some enslaved individuals may have experienced kindness and a degree of autonomy under the ownership of free Black people, others faced brutal conditions, harsh treatment, and the constant threat of being sold or separated from their families. These stories remind us that the experience of slavery, regardless of the identity of the enslaver, was a deeply traumatic and dehumanizing one.

The early 19th century saw a growing awareness of the inherent contradictions of Free Black slaveholding. While some saw it as a testament to the progress of free Black people, others viewed it as a troubling inconsistency, a moral stain on the aspirations for racial equality. This debate was fuelled by the rise of the anti-slavery movement (both Abolitionists and Emancipationists), which challenged the very foundation of slavery, regardless of the enslaver's racial background.

The voices of prominent Abolitionists like Frederick Douglass, who himself had escaped slavery, further intensified this moral scrutiny.

The Paradox of Freedom

Douglass argued that owning slaves, even for a free Black person, was inherently incompatible with the pursuit of freedom and justice. He saw it as a betrayal of the cause of emancipation and a perpetuation of the very system that oppressed his people. In his autobiography, Douglass illustrates the first instance of dehumanization of slaves to the reader by describing the separation of children from their mother at an early age. He writes: *"Frequently, before the child has reached its twelfth month, its mother is taken from it, and hired out on some farm a considerable distance off, and the child is placed under the care of an old woman, too old for field labor. For what this separation is done, I do not know, unless it be to hinder the development of the child's affection toward its mother, and to blunt and destroy the natural affection of the mother for the child. This is the inevitable result."* Just as people often separate animals from their parents at certain ages, the slave owners of the Pre-Civil War Era South separated small children from their parents, without putting much more thought into it than when separating cattle from their mothers.[223]

As the country moved closer to the Civil War, the issue of free Black slaveholding became intertwined with the broader debates about slavery's role in American society. Abolitionists, both White and Black, intensified their calls for an end to the institution, no matter the enslaver's race. The *Fugitive Slave Act* of 1850, which required free states to return runaway slaves, further galvanized the Abolitionist movement, including many free Black people who had once held slaves.

The story of free Black slaveholding, therefore, remains a powerful testament to the complexities of American history, challenging us to grapple with the contradictions of the past and to strive for a more just and equitable future. It is a story that demands our attention, prompting us to ask tough questions and to engage in a deeper understanding of the history of slavery and free Black slaveholders. These stories of free Black slaveholders are not simply historical curiosities. They are reminders that we must continue to grapple with the complexities of this history and understand the motivations and experiences of individuals who lived through these times. It is a history that continues to challenge our understanding of the nation's past.

Chapter 7:
The Emancipation Echo:
The War Between the States and Aftermath

"On the much-disputed question as to whether the South ever enlisted negro [sic.] soldiers, General Shelby writes to a friend denying that it was ever done. He himself, he says, solicited General Kirby Smith to allow him to enlist 10,000 negroes and move into Kansas, but General Smith's reply was, "No; we will win or go to the grave before we enlist the negro." "I thought it was a mistake," says General Shelby, "in our leaders not placing blacks in the field, nor have I changed my opinion."
- *St. Louis Republic*, August 16, 1891[224]

"A few colored men, it is said, were actually enrolled and enlisted as soldiers in the Confederate army, fighting for their own continued enslavement." - Booker T Washington, *The Negro in the South* [225]

"One may get the idea, from what I have said, that there was bitter feeling toward the White people on the part of my race, because of the fact that most of the White population was away fighting in a war which would result in keeping the Negro in slavery if the South was successful. In the case of the slaves on our place this was not true, and it was not true of any large portion of the slave population in the South where the Negro was treated with anything like decency."
          - Booker T Washington, *Up From Slavery*, 1901[226]

Sectional disputes dominated debate during the period between 1820 and 1860 as the United States went through its expansionistic period. The centre of these debates was the expansion of slavery into the newly acquired territories. As a result, compromises were made to quell these arguments, namely, the **Missouri Compromise of 1820** and the **Compromise of 1850**. It is during this *"Golden Age for the Senate,"* that a group of talented legislators and powerful orators in the U.S. Senate, (where the Constitution established an equality of states), rose

The Paradox of Freedom

to the front of the nation's attention to achieve a delicate balance between North and South, slave and free states.

During this period, senators busied themselves to craft legislation designed to resolve sectional conflicts and avoid secession and domestic hostilities. In the 1850s, however, efforts at compromise began to fail. The Senate endured a violent and turbulent decade that brought an end to its Golden Age and propelled the nation to the brink of war. The rapid expansion of the nation, as settlers moved west and new territories applied for statehood, repeatedly raised the issue of slavery being expanded by these new and potential states as permitted within their borders. The Constitution allowed slavery to exist in the states but left Congress to decide its status in the territories. The Northern states, having abolished slavery as an active practice within their state borders, sought to prevent its spread, while the Southern states, having grown more dependent on slave labour, asserted the rights of Southerners to transport their way of life into the new territories, by way of the free movement of their property. In 1820 the Missouri Compromise drew a line across the nation at the 36th parallel, above which slavery would be prohibited, and below which it could expand.

The **Mexican-American War** of 1846-48 resulted in vast new territories in the southwest, the debate over expansion of American slavery intensified. In 1850 Senator Henry Clay of Kentucky introduced a package of compromise measures to relieve the sectional tensions created by the potential expansion of the institution (combined with other fiercely competitive issues amidst the American people, such as the nature of their nation's federalism and interpretation/enactment of its Constitution, tariffs/economics and regionalism/culture). Aware of the controversial nature of his proposals, Clay urged his colleagues to "beware, to pause, to reflect before they lend themselves to any purposes which shall destroy that Union." On March 7, 1850, Senator Daniel Webster of Massachusetts rose from his Senate seat and declared: "I wish to speak today, not as a Massachusetts man, nor as a Northern man, but as an American . . . I speak today for the preservation of the Union." Other senators, most notably John Calhoun of South Carolina, opposed Clay's plan. With Webster's support, and with the assistance of Senator Stephen Douglas of Illinois, Congress passed revised versions of Clay's bills, which became law known as the **Compromise of 1850**. The compromise admitted California as a free state, left open the possibility of slavery in the territories of New Mexico and Utah, abolished the slave trade in the District of Columbia, and created a stronger federal fugitive slave law. [227]

Anxious to build a transcontinental railroad from Chicago to the West Coast, Senator Douglas introduced the **Kansas Nebraska Act of 1854** to organize those territories for statehood. To meet the objections of Southerners who were promoting a southern route for the railroad, the act opened the territories for settlement, but provided that the settlers, through "popular sovereignty" (voting processes at the grassroots level), could allow or prohibit slavery. This undermined the 1820 Missouri Compromise and further inflamed the passions in the North and the South. Both slaveholders and anti-slavery groups flooded into these areas to influence voting outcomes on state constitutions, erupting communities into violence in what became known as "*Bleeding Kansas.*" Intended to settle sectional disputes, the **Kansas Nebraska Act** instead brought the nation closer to civil war. In May 1856 Senator Charles Sumner, a fiery abolitionist from Massachusetts, delivered a five-hour oration in the Senate Chamber entitled "*The Crime Against Kansas.*" Sumner's inflammatory speech was a harsh indictment of those who supported the spread of slavery and attacked several senators by name, including Andrew Butler of South Carolina. On May 22, 1856, Preston Brooks, a member of the House of Representatives and Senator Butler's relative, retaliated. After the Senate had adjourned for the day, Brooks approached Sumner at his desk in the Senate Chamber and repeatedly struck him on the head with his heavy walking stick, breaking the wooden cane into pieces. Badly injured by the attack, Sumner was able to appear in the Senate only intermittently over the next three years, as he slowly recovered. His empty desk became visible evidence that legislative compromise could no longer settle the emotional and divisive issue of slavery in the territories. An era in Senate history ended when the Senate held its last session in its venerable old chamber, the addition of states entering the Union had doubled the number of senators and prompted construction of a new, larger chamber. On January 4, 1859, U.S. Senators marched in procession from the old chamber, so associated with the Great Triumvirate of Henry Clay, Daniel Webster, and John Calhoun, to the new chamber in the Capitol's north wing. In that procession walked men who would soon be leaders of the Union and the Confederacy. [228]

On November 6, 1860, in an election that brought the new Republican Party to the forefront, Abraham Lincoln was elected President by a strictly northern vote. Four days later, on November 10, Senator James Chesnut resigned his Senate seat and returned home to South Carolina to draft an ordinance of secession. One day later, South Carolina's James Hammond also pledged to support the Confederacy. This started a chain of events which eventually led to the secession of six more states from the deep South.[229]

In the wake of these dramatic events, the United States Senate convened the 2nd session of the 36th Congress on December 3, 1860. Vice President John Breckinridge presided as the Senate chaplain, Phineas Densmore Gurley, offered a benediction. *"Hear our petitions, and send us an answer of peace,"* he prayed. *"May all bitterness and wrath" be put away, and may senators "deliberate . . . not as partisans, but as brethren and patriots, seeking the highest welfare . . . of the whole country . . . . Hear us . . . , and heal our land."* The clerk then called the roll. Ten southern senators failed to answer.[230]

The secession crisis grew with each passing week, forcing the Senate to deal with vacant seats and diminishing quorums. Mississippi voted to secede on January 9, and by January 21, Senator Jefferson Davis gave his farewell speech to the Senate: *"I rise, Mr. President, for the purpose of announcing to the Senate that ... the state of Mississippi ... has declared her separation from the United States."* Davis explained his actions were compelled due to the secession of his home state, which in turn had occurred because, *"...we [Mississippians] are about to be deprived in the Union of the rights which our fathers bequeathed to us."* Davis implored his Senate colleagues to work for the achievement of peaceful relations between the Union and departing states. Otherwise, he predicted, interference with his or any other state's decision to secede, would *"bring disaster on every portion of the country."* A further six more senators were gone by the end of January, and three further left in February. Eventually, 25 of the Senate's 66 members left to support the Confederate cause. Even Vice-President Breckinridge walked out, although his state of Kentucky remained loyal to the Union. [231]

In the months between the election of Abraham Lincoln to the Presidency and his swearing the oath of office, the Senate faced its own civil war, yet it managed to fulfill its constitutional duties. During these months, it confirmed five cabinet secretaries and a Supreme Court justice and passed important legislation, such as the 1861 **Tariff Bill** that provided desperately needed revenue. It established a **Committee of Thirteen** to consider peace proposals, including Senator John Crittenden's plan to extend the Missouri Compromise line to the Pacific Ocean, dividing free from slave states. Crittenden hoped for another peaceful solution, but Radical Republicans like Charles Sumner dismissed such efforts. Secession was not *"merely political,"* Sumner argued, it was *"a revolution."* The era of compromise was gone, and the bitter battle lines of American were drawn. Crittenden's proposal had failed, though had it passed, it would have become the **13th Amendment** to the US Constitution.[232]

The Paradox of Freedom

By the time Lincoln took office on March 4, 1861, rumors were circulating of a threatened Confederate attack at Fort Sumter in Charleston Harbor, South Carolia. Northern Republicans, backed by an Abolitionist press, demanded military action. *"Reinforce Fort Sumter at all hazards!"* became the Northerners' cry. Lincoln agreed to re-supply the fort, but with food rather than weapons. At 4:30 a.m. on April 12, 1861, Confederate troops fired on Fort Sumter. Less than 34 hours later, Federal forces inside had surrendered. Hostilities had begun and in the words of Lincoln's old rival from the 1858 Debates, Stephen Douglas, *"Every man must be for the United States or against it. There can be no neutrals in this war."* [233]

Questions now arise; how did Black slaveowners view the coming of the war? Did they support the Northern or Southern Cause? In what ways did they express this support?

The views of Black slave owners on the eve of the Civil War were complex, often shaped by their semi-unique mix of personal survival, economic interest, and social positioning within the Southern society. The Civil War would become a cataclysmic event that tore the nation apart, but in that it profoundly impacted the lives of free Black slaveholders is an almost un-studied historical theme. Between the years 1830 to 1860, there were approximately 3,775 Black slaveholders in the South, owning around 12,760 enslaved people. 80% of the Black slaveholders were in Louisiana, South Carolina, Virginia, and Maryland, often in urban centres like New Orleans and Charleston. Many were of mixed racial ancestry and had acquired wealth, land, and social status, sometimes through relationships with White patrons or family inheritance.[234]

The conflict's reverberations shook their world, altering the very foundation of their existence. As the war raged, their status as both Free People of Colour and slaveholders became increasingly tenuous. While they had enjoyed a degree of social and economic mobility in the Antebellum South, the war's eruption cast a dark shadow over their carefully constructed lives. Many feared that upheaval could lead to loss of property, re-enslavement, or violence from both Federal and Confederate forces. For those who had achieved wealth and status, the war posed a threat to their hard-won social position. Some may have viewed secession and war as destabilizing forces that could upend the racial and economic order, even if that order had benefited them in contradictory ways.

Many will question whether or not there were "Black Confederates" and it has become one of the most controversial issues in the study of Civil War history but it is interesting to say that observers of the time reported:

- *"There are at the present moment, many colored men in the Confederate Army doing duty not only as cooks, servants and laborers, but as real soldiers, having muskets on their shoulders and bullets in their pockets, ready to shoot down ... and do all that soldiers may do to destroy the Federal government."* – Frederick Douglas[235]

- *"For more than two years, negroes had been extensively employed in belligerent operations by the Confederacy. They had been embodied and drilled as Rebel soldiers, and had paraded with White troops at a time when this would not have been tolerated in the armies of the Union."* – Horace Greeley[236]

- *"Over 3,000 negroes must be included in this number (of Confederate troops). These were clad in all kinds of uniforms, not only in cast-off or captured United States uniforms, but in coats with Southern buttons, State buttons, etc. These were shabby, but not shabbier or seedier than those worn by white men in rebel ranks. Most of the negroes had arms, rifles, muskets, sabres, bowie-knives, dirks, etc. They were supplied, in many instances, with knapsacks, haversacks, canteens, etc., and were manifestly an integral portion of the Southern Confederacy Army. They were seen riding on horses and mules, driving wagons, riding on caissons, in ambulances, with the staff of Generals, and promiscuously mixed up with all the rebel horde"* - Dr. Lewis H. Steiner, chief inspector of the U.S. Sanitary Commission[237]

Yet, a disagreement arises in part from rival ideological positions, but also traces on whether Blacks served in the Confederate military.

Those naysayers will argue that there is no question that tens of thousands of enslaved and free African Americans served *with* Confederate armies as body servants, laborers, teamsters, hospital workers, and cooks. But were these men "soldiers" in any real sense of the word? Partisans of the "Black Confederate" viewpoint answer in the affirmative, comparing the roles black men played in the Confederate army with analogous job descriptions of modern American soldiers, the labor battalions in the World Wars (especially those who were drafted and thus "forced" into service), and even the menial labor that U.S. Colored Troops units performed during the Civil War.

They will go on to question if African American laborers in the Confederate army formally enlisted in the army, equipped with uniforms, arms, and accoutrements, and paid for their own work, as were African Americans in the U.S. Army? No. Their status was that of enslaved or marginally free laborers serving in capacities in a military setting analogous to their roles in civilian life. Referring to such men as "soldiers" ignores a fundamental distinction between forced labor and military service.[238]

Regardless of one's view on whether the central cause of the War for Southern Independence was fought to preserve slavery, it cannot be overlooked that a number of African Americans actually supported the Confederates during this conflict. Jeb Smith of *History Now* looks at a wide range of ways that African Americans supported the Confederacy from financial support to the military:

"I define a soldier as one who willingly took up arms for the Confederacy or fought under a Confederate general regardless of federal recognition. In other words, state militia and individuals are actual soldiers. The Confederacy left it up to the states to decide if slaves were to fight as soldiers. If the South objected to the federal government's involvement with slave property in the old Union, why would they allow the confederate government to do the same in the South? So slaves' involvement was up to the state and, more importantly, the slave and master. Free blacks were also left to local control."[239]

"*These African Americans were real fighting men whose combat performances should not be silenced out of respect for these brave men and their sacrifices, despite the vigorous organized effort of today's politically driven historians and other black confederate deniers,"* writes Phillip Thomas Tucker author of *Blacks in Grey Uniforms A New Look at the South's Most Forgotten Combat Troops 1861-1865*.[240]

The existence of Black Confederates is a debated and controversial subject. A search of the internet will show no shortage of articles, blogs, and videos of pro-North author's claiming Black Confederates are a "myth." They ask why a Southern African American would defend the Confederacy when Blacks were treated horribly; rather they desired to run into the arms of the first white Yankee savior they saw. After all, the war was over slavery with the North fighting to liberate the slaves and the South to preserve the institution so Southern Blacks would jump at the chance to help the North and overthrow their racist masters. Regardless of one's belief on this issue, it cannot be denied that there were many Blacks who fought with and supported the Confederacy. Maybe not as organized units, as the segregated units of the North, but alongside White Confederate soldiers and not segregated.

The Paradox of Freedom

"Battle Hymers," authors who support the Union cause that the war was all about slavery, such as Eric Foner and Kevin Levin will argue that it is a myth that hundreds of thousands of Blacks served in the Confederate army as armed soldiers. As Jeb Smith puts it, *"These authors have set up a straw man to knockdown since it is easy to show hundreds of thousands of blacks were not soldiers."* This allows them to ridicule *"Lost Causers,"* authors who support the Southern cause and groups like the Sons of Confederate Veterans, for claims of hundreds of thousands of Black Confederates in an attempt to disqualify any other new documentation of Black Confederates. Yet, even those who claim Black Confederates are a myth will at the same time admit Blacks did serve in the Southern armies. In the live stream conversation *Fighting for Freedom the Civil War and its Legacies*, Eric Foner said, "There is no question that some small number of African Americans did volunteer and serve in Confederate armies."[241]

Just as John Brown's prediction that slaves would join him in a revolt against the South was not born out by actual events, Abolitionists in the North predicted massive slave revolts would occur in the South during the war. It can be argued, based on an objective and holistic scrutiny of relevant evidence, events and themes, there is an indication of a larger than-expected amount of support for the Confederate war effort from Black Americans in the South. In *Black Confederates and Afro-Yankees*, African American historian Ervin Jordan wrote that *"Black Confederate loyalty was more widespread than American historians have acknowledged."* And while Blacks who volunteered for the Union often had to be protected from Whites, Southern Blacks needed no such protection. Southerners were excited to have Black volunteers join their ranks.[242]

Frank Edward Deserino wrote a thesis for his Doctoral Degree submitted in 2001 to the University of London Department of History on the subject of Black support for the Confederacy. He writes, "*Even before the opening of the conflict, Southerners began to enroll free*

Blacks for service with the state militias, sometimes by state law or by purely local action. The use of free Blacks in the military was varied, as they saw service as laborers, support staff or in rare instances as soldiers." [243]

Regardless of whether or not organized Black Confederate units existed, some Black slaveholders, free Blacks, and slaves did serve in some capacity even though they were barred from serving as soldiers officially by the Confederate government.. The 1st Louisiana Native Guard was the first official Black regiment in the Confederacy. The Guard was formed when Louisiana Governor Thomas Overton Moore accepted into the state militia a regiment of approximately 1,100 free African American men. When Governor Moore called for troops to defend Louisiana on April 17, 1861, a committee of ten prominent New Orleans free Blacks called a meeting at the city's Catholic Institute on April 22 to pledge their loyalty to the Confederate cause. About 2,000 people attended the meeting including 1,500 free Blacks who signed a militia muster roll.

Governor Moore accepted their services and formed the 1st Louisiana Native Guard unit on May 2, 1861. All of the initial members of the Native Guard were French Speaking Creoles. Among those who joined the militia were successful arch itects, brick masons, dentists, doctors and carpenters. The Governor appointed three white officers as regimental commanders but company commanders were Creoles chosen from the ranks of the unit. Among these Creole officers was Lieutenant Andre Cailloux and Lieutenant Morris W. Morris who also served in the 1st Louisiana Native Guard. Lt. Morris had the distinction of being the only black Jewish officer in the Confederate Army.[244]

Others supported the Confederacy through financial means. An example comes from the *Richmond Daily Dispatch, April 19, 1861:*

About sixty free negroes volunteered and went down to Fort Macon to do battle for their country, while another gave twenty-five dollars cash to help support the war; and still another, who is a poor man, having just arrived at our wharf with a load of wood for sale, delivered it up to the town auctioneer, with a request to sell it and appropriate it in the same way.[245]

The 1ˢᵗ Louisiana Native Guard, *Courtesy of frenchcreoles.com*

In an essay written by Ervin Jordan, titled, *Different Drummers: Black Virginians As Confederate Loyalists,"* Jordan writes, *"Black Confederate patriotism took many forms: slaves devoted to their owners, free blacks who donated money and labor, blacks who joined the Confederate army and slaves who loyally supervised plantations of absentee-owners."* He continues by citing three examples:

- *James T. Ayer, a black farmer in Suffolk, sold so much food to Southern quartermasters that Union officers accused him of being an employee of the Confederate commissary department.*[246]
- *There are numerous but forgotten examples of Afro-Virginian civilians who were Confederate patriots. "Uncle Billy," owned by*

The Paradox of Freedom

Bedford County customs collector Micajah Davis, buried Davis's official records during the Union raid in 1864 and proudly returned them to a surprised Davis after the war. Lewis, a Mecklenburg County slave who served with the Boydton Cavalry as its bugler during antebellum times, was denied permission by the Confederate War Department to enlist when it became the 3rd Virginia Cavalry. He donated his forty-dollar bugle plus an additional twenty dollars to the regiment.[247]

- *A Winchester newspaper gleefully reported the outcome when Union raiders carried off nine slaves belonging to a local slaveowner. In Maryland, the slaves were offered a choice of freedom or return to their owners; they unanimously stated a preference for the Old Dominion, their wives and children and claimed devotion to their masters.*[248]

Many Blacks, regardless of their station, also supported the Confederacy in a non-military capacity, and *"enthusiasm with which many blacks endorsed secession"* was widespread. Prominent Black slaveholder Wiiliam Ellison, after the outbreak of war in 1861, offered labor from his 53 slaves to the Confederate Army. He converted his cotton plantation to mixed crops to supply food to the cause. His sons also supported the Confederacy and tried to enlist, but were refused at the time. This did not deter their support.[249]

In the summer of 1861, The Winston Salem NC newspaper, People's Press, reported that *"fifteen free men of color volunteered for state service"* and that they were in fine spirits and wore a *"We will die for the South emblem."* In New Bern, *"fifteen to twenty free Negros came forward to volunteer their service to defend the city."* A newspaper in Lynchburg, Virginia, reported on the 70 free blacks who enlisted to defend Virginia, *"Three cheers for the patriotic Negros of Lynchburg."*[250]

The Paradox of Freedom

From *The Daily Dispatch*, April 25, 1861:

About fifty free negroes in Amelia county have offered themselves to the Government for any service. In our neighboring city of Petersburg, two hundred free negroes offered for any work that might be assigned to them, either to fight under white officers, dig ditches, or anything that could show their desire to serve Old Virginia. In the same city, a negro hackman came to his master, and insisted, with tears in his eyes, that he should accept all his savings, $100, to help equip the volunteers. – The free negroes of Chesterfield have made a similar proposition. Such is the spirit, among bond and free, through the whole of the State.[251]

Shane Anderson wrote for the Abbeville Institute about *Black Southern Support for Secession and War* stating, "*I myself have collected over 1,400 newspaper articles on this subject published between 1861 and 1865. That's a lot of ink spilled over something that some today call a "myth." You will find that these activist historians are not telling you the entire story.*"[252]

The Legislature of Tennessee, that negotiated that State out of the Union, passed, "*An Act authorizing the Governor* (Isham G. Harris) — *"to receive into the military service of the State all male free persons of color, between the ages of 16 and 50."* These Black soldiers were to receive $8 per month, with clothing and rations.[253]

As the war progressed, Abraham Lincoln changed the political war goals of the North from saving the Union to include emancipation by a series of events. Such a goal was political and at first, only effected the Southern states who were fighting the Union. As well, such proposals from the Union government could only be enforced through successful force of arms. Lincoln and his government hoped that the Emancipation Proclamation would deal a devastating blow to the economic interests of the Confederacy as well as causing disruptions on the home front with Black people abandoning their masters' plantations or other strategically vital roles. This meant a sudden dramatic loss of their most valuable asset for White and Black slaveholders. The value of their holdings plummeted overnight, leaving many financially crippled. The Proclamation also raised profound questions about their own social standing, forcing them to confront the contradictions inherent in their dual identities.

Did this proclamation affect free Black support for the war in the Confederacy? The *Nashville Daily Union,* of Tennessee, on the 21st of March 1863, reported, "*Negro rebel Cavalry pickets on the south bank of the Rappahannock below Fredericksburg shows that negroes are ready enough to serve masters on the field, and that the rebels are ready enough to make use of them serve as common soldiers...these negroes are well in the service, as in their sympathy, of the south.*" This piece of evidence indicates no loss towards their determination to serve the South.[254]

Abolitionist Horace Greeley published *The American Conflict* in 1866, and quotes the following wartime newspapers reporting of Black American patriotism in the South as further testament:

- From the *Evening Post* (New York): "*A gentleman from Charleston says that everything there betokens active preparations for fight...negroes busy in building batteries, so far from inclining to insurrection, were grinning from ear to ear at tile prospect of shooting the Yankees.*"

- The *Charleston Mercury* (South Carolina) of January 3 said: "*We learn that 150 able-bodied free colored men of Charleston, yesterday offered their services gratuitously to the Governor, to hasten forward the important work of throwing up redoubts wherever needed along our coast.*"

- The *Memphis Avalanche* (Tennessee) joyously proclaimed that: "*A procession of several hundred stout negro men, members of the "domestic institution," marched through our streets yesterday in military order, under the command of Confederate officers. They were all armed and equipped with shovels, axes, blankets, etc. A merrier set was never seen. They were brimful of patriotism, shouting for Jeff Davis and singing war songs.* "[255]

So why is there so much opposition to the concept of Black support for the Confederacy? Modern authors like Eric Foner, Kevin Levin, Gary Gallagher, and James McPherson count only *federally recognized* soldiers which allows them to dismiss the claims of large numbers of Southern Black soldiers. If cooks, musicians, and those forced into service do not count as actual soldiers, then the Southern and Northern servicemen drafted (white and black) are not actual soldiers. And since the vast majority of soldiers, North and South, were state volunteers, they were not actual soldiers either, according to these authors. They must fight only for the master, the federal government, to be "true" soldiers.

In a 2019 study, historian Kevin M. Levin believed the origin of the myth of Black Confederate soldiers originated in the 1970s after some Confederate heritage groups began to claim that large numbers of Black soldiers fought loyally for the Confederacy. Other historians such as James McPherson, author of *Battle Cry of Freedom*, once state that, *"Confederate heritage groups have been making this claim for years as a way of purging their cause of its association with slavery,"* and Gary Gallagher stated, *"The Black Confederate movement is demented."*[256] These accounts are not given credence by *"Battle Hymer"* historians, as they rely on sources such as postwar individual journals rather than military records.

Historian Bruce Levine wrote:

The whole sorry episode [the mustering of colored troops in Richmond] provides a fitting coda for our examination of modern claims that thousands and thousands of black troops loyally fought in the Confederate armies. This strikingly unsuccessful last-ditch effort constituted the sole exception to the Confederacy's steadfast refusal to employ African American soldiers. As General Ewell's long term aide-de-camp, Major George Campbell Brown, later affirmed, the handful of black soldiers mustered in the southern capital in March of 1865 constituted 'the first and only black troops used on our side.[257]

These historians who believe that *"the Black Confederate movement is demented,"* focus on the fact that there were no organized Black Confederate units and overlook the fact that many Black Confederates served alongside White Confederate troops unlike United States Coloured Troops who were segregated and therefore can be easily accounted. Acording to many present-day statistics, of the 65,000 Black people that toiled in the Southern army as cooks, stable hands and servants, a 'considerable' number must have served as combatants. But just how many is 'considerable'? No one is sure. As the historian William Freehling stated, *"This important subject is now needlessly embroiled in controversy, with politically correct historians of one sort refusing to see the importance (indeed existence) of the minority of slaves who were Black Confederates, and politically correct historians of the opposite sort refusing to see the importance of Black Confederates' limited numbers."*[258]

In his work, *Black Confederates in the Civil War*, Scott K. Williams estimates that over 65,000 Southern blacks were in the Confederate ranks. Over 13,000 of these, "saw the elephant" also known as meeting the enemy in combat. These Black Confederates included both slave and free. The Confederate Congress did not approve blacks to be officially enlisted as soldiers (except as musicians), until late in the war. But in the ranks it was a different story. Many Confederate officers did not obey the mandates of politicians, they frequently enlisted blacks with the simple criteria, "Will you fight?" Historian Ervin Jordan, explains that *"biracial units"* were frequently organized *"by local Confederate and State militia Commanders in response to immediate threats in the form of Union raids...".* Dr. Leonard Haynes, an African-American professor at Southern University, stated, *"When you eliminate the Black Confederate soldier, you've eliminated the history of the South."*[259]

This writer agrees that there were no hundreds of thousands of Blacks that served in the Confederate Army, but how many supported it? No one knows precisely but by drawing on sources written or published during the war, some estimate that between 3,000 and 6,000 served as Confederate soldiers. Another 100,000 or so blacks, mostly slaves, supported the Confederacy as laborers, servants and teamsters. They built roads, batteries and fortifications; manned munitions factories. Many historians will say if this is true, where is the documented evidence. By the end of the war government documents on such was lost due to the Confederate government hurriedly burning many papers just before the fall of Richmond. Also, unlike the muster rolls of the Federal army that indicated US Colored Troop unit designations, Confederate muster rolls do not contain any racial information. While it may be fairly easy to identify Native-American and Hispanic-American names, most Blacks at the time had adopted European names and thus making it hard distinguish Black from White Confederate soldiers. As historians slowly uncover more information, new documents appear giving us tidbits that slowly reveal the past. As more people begin to discover military headstones in local cemeteries, researching family histories, looking a pension records and other documents more and more evidence begins to appear on this intriguing subject.[260]

The end of the Civil War had a disastrous impact on the entirety of the South. The length of the war and the brutality with which it was fought devastated the region in every aspect. The population had been severely reduced from battles and disease with a substantial portion of men of military age in the Confederacy dying in the conflict. Even those who did not fight in the war suffered the material and economic destruction that occurred. The slaveowners and wealthy elites of the South were affected in this devastation as their plantations were untended because of the ravages of war. The death of slavery and the destruction of the war was not unique to the White population as many of the Black denizens suffered alongside them, as slaveowners. The destruction experienced by the Black slaveowners was often greater than their White counterparts, due to their comparatively lesser and more vulnerable social and material capital, and the racial tension that followed. The beginning of Reconstruction did little to alleviate the problems the war caused for these Black former slaveowners.

The closing years of the Civil War led to a rapidly decreasing quality of life for those in the South. The loss of territory and the tightening Federal blockade led to shortages of everything from sugar to medicine. These shortages made it nearly impossible to make largescale profits during the interwar years. No planter was able to make profits similar to their prewar standards and, as the war worsened, as did the little profits they were able to make, and the end of the war did not alleviate these shortages. By the end, the shortages and devastation had caused even the wealthy plantation owners to reach a breaking point. Surrender at Appomattox and the years of Reconstruction which followed (1865-77), did not solve the problems with supply, especially with regards to food production. Crop failures persisted for several years afterwards. **Robert Michael Collins**, a Black rice planter in Georgetown County, South Carolina, experienced this struggle. Following the war and the end of slavery, Collin's rice crop failed every year between 1865 and 1869. This extended to the other former slaveowners in the state as the Freedmen's Bureau noted that most of the rice crops had failed in the previous two seasons and that the planters were on the verge of being unable to pay their workers.[261]

The failure to produce food contributed to the Black slaveowners' inability to regain their prewar wealth as much as their White colleagues. When the Confederacy was formed, the government began printing a currency backed only by credit. When the Confederacy fell, these same bonds and currency became completely worthless. Those who converted their money into this new currency now lost a substantial portion of their prewar finances. Some of the Black slaveowners had invested heavily in the Confederate dollar to show their loyalty (the Ellison brothers invested nearly $10,000 into Confederate investments and lost it all in the end). This loss of funds at the end of the war severely hindered the ability of the Black slaveowners to rebuild after the war's conclusion. As part of an attempt to survive (more than an attempt to reclaim their wealth), former slaveowners were often forced to sell their property. This helped keep them afloat, but also greatly hindered their ability to retain their relative social-fiscal positions. The greatest possession these former slaveowners held was their land. Those who owned plantations suffered the most from this, as the massive tracts of land they once cultivated were gradually sold off, or were left in unproductive manner. For example, at the start of the war, the Ellisons' had cultivated about 900 acres of their lands, but by 1870, only 112 acres were under cultivation. This rapid drop in cultivated land stemmed from the lack of funds available to purchase new seed, and the loss of fiscal value of their slaves significantly damaging slaveowners after the war's conclusion.[262]

The end of the Civil War was as punishing in these respects to the Black former slaveowners as it was for the Whites. In both cases, the late war shortages and crop failures were only exacerbated in the postwar. These wartime struggles worsened as many of the former Black slaveowners now faced destitution. With the loss of much of their wealth and workforce, these former slaveowners were forced to adapt to a new way of life or lose all. The severe losses the Black elite took during the war would make regaining their wealth an exceedingly tiring process. With no funds, the loss of assets in slaves, and shrinking land size, the Black slaveowners now faced an uphill climb they had not experienced since they first gained their freedom.[263]

For these individuals, emancipation presented a unique set of challenges and opportunities. The legal landscape shifted dramatically, rendering their ownership of enslaved people invalid. Social dynamics underwent a profound transformation, as the lines between freedom and bondage blurred, yet experienced simultaneous new configurations, and the concept of race and power experienced redefinitions. The economic implications of emancipation were particularly challenging for those free Black slaveholders who relied on enslaved labour for their plantations or businesses. The loss of free labour and fiscal assets, coupled with the potential for economic instability and the need to adapt to a new labour market, presented significant challenges. Some former Black slaveholders attempted to retain their enslaved workforce by offering them wages, but this often proved ineffective as formerly enslaved individuals sought true autonomy and opportunities for advancement. The shift to a free labour system also affected the broader Southern economy, impacting trade, agriculture, and the overall social fabric.

The Reconstruction era, a period of combined hope and turmoil, presented both opportunities and challenges for free Black slaveholders by creating a period of immense uncertainty. They faced the challenge of navigating a rapidly changing society, one where their status as slaveholders no longer held the same weight and may have well faced negative stigma and/or recriminations as did White American ex-slave owners in the South. The social and political landscape shifted dramatically, leaving many free Black slaveholders questioning their place in the emerging racial order. It also exposed the inherent fragility of their position within the broader community. They were often ostracized by both White and Black communities, seen as a contradiction to the ideals of freedom and equality that were central to the Abolitionist movement. The war's aftermath brought a period of intense introspection, as free Black slaveholders grappled with the moral implications of their actions and the social consequences of their choices.

While they were theoretically afforded equal rights under the law, their social standing and economic prospects remained precarious. Many faced discrimination and prejudice, their efforts to achieve true equality

The Paradox of Freedom

hampered by the deep-seated racism that permeated American society The newly established Freedmen's Bureau, designed to aid formerly enslaved people, offered little support to free Black slaveholders.

Political advancements during Reconstruction, such as the passage of the 14th and 15th Amendments, granted citizenship and voting rights to African Americans. This paved the way for a burgeoning African American political class, with individuals seeking to represent their interests and advocate for equality. Former slave John F. Harris was once such individual who became a State Legislator in 1890 to the House of Representatives. Harris would also support a bill to erect a Confederate monument in Jackson, Mississippi. He arose from his sick bed in Washington county to deliver a speech in support of the monument stating, *"I am sorry any son of a soldier should go on record as opposed to an erection of a monument to the brave dead. I am convinced if he had seen what I saw at Seven Pines and in the seven day's fighting around Richmond, the battlefield covered with the mangled forms of those who had fought for their country and their country's honor, he would not have made that speech."* The speech indicates support for the Confederate cause by a former slave who arose to political prominence.[264]

Holt Collier,
Courtesy of the Public Domain

Another success story was Holt Coller, a former slave born in 1846 on the Hinds Plantation in Washington county, Mississippi. Holt would run away to be with the Hinds after the Civil War began and was wounded in the fight at the Battle of Shiloh while sharpshooting for the Confederate forces. The Hinds family gave him his freedom and he would enlist with Co. I, Ninth

Texas Calvary. After the war he would become a cowboy, lawman, and a famous bear hunter claiming he killed up to 3,000 black bear in Mississippi. His biggest claim to fame was being the guide for President Theodore Roosevelt on his now famous black bear hunt in Sharkey County, Mississippi in 1902 better known as the "Teddy Bear" hunt.[265]

However, the promise of political empowerment was met with widespread resistance and systematic attempts to suppress Black voting. Black slaveholders, already grappling with the economic and social ramifications of emancipation, faced a political landscape rife with challenges and obstacle and as a result, here hope was dashed by the harsh realities of the rise of "Jim Crow Laws" after the Reconstruction period. Many faced hostility from White Southerners who resented the loss of their enslaved labor force. The struggle for equal rights and opportunities became a daily reality, forcing free Black slaveholders to assert their claims to citizenship and equal protection under the law. (Refer to endnote for further information)[266]

Despite the new and significant challenges Black slaveowners encountered in post-slavery America, many were not content to lose their elevated position. Much like their White counterparts, the Black former slaveowners made efforts to retain their prewar status. They utilize the same tactics as their White counterparts to retain their former elite status. Even those who could not, would attempt to utilize the new system to rise to the upper ranks of the African American elite. This struggle to regain their past position of power through the efforts of the planters, merchants, and those who adopted the new system give a different view of Reconstruction from the normal lens of rich Whites or former slaves.

The loss of slaves and most of their wealth caused a reset for most Black former masters. For many, the end of slavery was the end of their way of life and new lives would have to be crafted. For those who refused to accept this new reality, the thought of losing all they had worked for was too much to bear. Following the same path as their White counterparts, these former slaveowners would attempt to force their former slaves to remain reliant on their new employers. The planters had a tough time retaining their former slaves while the urban slaveowners made changes quickly from owner to employer with relative ease and lack of cost which was not readily available to the rural slaveowners. The shortages during the Civil War and the brutal nature of rural slavery made the return to planting difficult. The memory of slavery created a particularly difficult challenge to overcome as many African Americans would rather leave the plantations to find their own path in life. For those who remained, new struggles arose. The former masters attempted to continue planting often going into debt due to the failure of their crops which would harm the workers who remained.

As stated earlier, **Robert Micheal Collins** had experienced such conditions. The struggles from the War Between the States and the failures of his crop in the years following made feeding his family and workers nearly impossible. To alleviate this, Collins' asked the Freedmen's Bureau for help in 1868. The Bureau provided Collins a month's worth of rations for his family and the workers who remained. This was not a gift and came with a bill for $49.53. This debt did not stop him however as Collins was able to pay it entirely back entirely in a year. In terms of his plantation's profits, Collins struggled to regain his former prosperity. The war and poor crop harvests shrunk his plantation's production to a mere fraction of its prewar levels. Collins could not pay his workers and instead, they were paid for their services with food, shelter, and clothing. This system was common following the end of slavery and held many similarities to the now defunct system. The trade of labour for food and shelter remained and was held together by a mutual agreement of needs. The plantation owner needed labour to produce their crops and secure a revenue stream while the workers required a place to live and food for their families. This would not last forever as much like their White counterparts, the Black planters who attempted to regain their wealth would switch from the payment of exchange to a wage-based system by the end of Reconstruction. For Michael Collins, his workers were paid $1,000.00 for their work in 1879. As for Collins himself, he was able to recover most of his prewar wealth at the cost of half his acreage over the 20 years following the Civil War in 1885. This limited how much he could regain in status but did allow him to come close to his prewar production.[267]

Even the cotton producers of the throughout the South suffered a slow and agonizing decline. The vast majority of the Black owned cotton plantations would be unable to recover following the war. This included the largest of the Black cotton producing families, the Ellisons. During the war, the Ellisons were one of the few planters who made a profit during the war. Following the defeat of the Confederacy, all of these profits became defunct. With this loss of money, the vast majority of the slaves who were owned by the Ellisons left and only 12 workers were retained as opposed to the nearly 50 slaves they held at the start of the war. The Ellisons attempted to take part in the system of sharecropping with their White counterparts. With sharecropping, the plantation owners agreed to pay extremely low wages for the labor of the African Americans they hired. These were not ideal conditions for most former slaves who did not like the idea of further control on their lives. The Ellisons made the choice to only hire workers through this method and was the primary reason they lost so many of their former slaves. Due to the low number of workers, the Ellisons were unable to cultivate the same amount of land they had previously. Of the 500 acres they cultivated in 1860, only 118 were still being cultivated by 1870.

Even the old cotton gin shop that built the family fortune under William Ellison could not secure their future. While the destruction of cotton gins in South Carolina by Federal forces would have given the Ellison family a massive competitive advantage, the end of slavery damaged their ability to obtain an adequate labor force to operate the gin. Ironically, the end of slavery gave skilled former slaves the opportunity to start their own businesses. Even though William Ellison's grandson, John Buckner, continued to operate the gin works, the lack of skilled mechanics meant a drop in both quality and quantity of the gins. By 1870, the two sons of William Ellison, who operated the estate, no longer described themselves as planters. Instead marketing themselves as general merchants providing goods for the White planters around them. Despite the decline of their plantation, the Ellisons were able to retain most of their standing with those around them even if their name was no longer widely spread. This luck did not last forever though as the family wealth disintegrated upon the deaths of William Ellison's sons, **Henry and William Jr.** in 1883 and 1904 respectively. Their nephew, John Buckner, moved from Stateburg following a dispute over William Ellison's will. With the deaths and departure of the last remaining members who knew William Ellison, the family no longer had the centralization or strong leadership to continue their businesses, and by 1920 the family held none of its old territory.[268]

As was discussed previously, many of these Black former slaveowners refused to accept the new status of the freedmen. The support that many of them gave to slavery both before and during the war caused them to be fully invested in the system. After the war's conclusion, the South quickly attempted to control the Black population by instituting the first of the Black Codes (or Jim Crow Laws as they would be later known). In these codes, the ability of African Americans to work in a trade was severely limited, due to various laws and regulations mandating the person/s involved obtained an industrial license. These licenses would only be given to those who were able to prove themselves as skilled tradesmen, had good moral character and were able to pay annual sums for said license. This new manner of industry benefited the former slaveowners, who were already known by the White community for their good morality and had the money to pay. In some cases, the Black former slaveowners were able to get the license and fee waived by either the courts, or the local U.S. Army officer, due to their good standing in the community. Using their family's reputation of sound character, the Ellisons were able to run their gin shop and open a general store following the introduction of these codes.[269]

By the end of Reconstruction, White Democrats began to reclaim their state legislatures and rewrite their state constitutions. This led to the rise of Jim Crow and the legal establishment of segregation throughout the South. With the landmark Supreme Court ruling of *Plessy v. Ferguson*, White Democrats in the South began purging their African American members from the party ranks and by 1890, Black Americans had been effectively purged. The few that remained had to prove their loyalty to the party and to their state, in stark contrast to when Black Americans had eagerly participated on both sides of the political arena in the South in an attempt to both assert their newfound civil rights as a group and had even been willing to form partnerships of either toleration, or even outright cooperation, with White, ex-Confederates for the benefit of all in the relevant polity. (Refer to endnote for more information)[270]

During the Gilded Age Period (1870s -1890s) most of the associations between the African American elite and the rest of the African American community changed, mainly because of the deaths of many of the former slave masters. With the deaths of these former masters, the real change and connections between the two communities would begin. While the former masters took many measures to separate themselves from the normal African Americans, their children, even when born prior to the War Between the States, did not continue to hold the same desire to separate themselves from the Black community.

Despite these challenges, many free Black slaveholders rose to the occasion, displaying remarkable resilience and adaptability. Some transitioned into agricultural businesses, diversifying their crops and seeking new markets. Others embraced emerging industries, capitalizing on the opportunities presented by technological advancements while others established themselves in organized sports. Their drive to achieve economic independence was fuelled by a determination to secure their place in a society that had long denied them opportunity. Many of their children would use their education to begin helping the formerly enslaved people. Take for example Anna and Catherine Johnson, daughters of William Johnson, the *Barber of Natchez*.

William and his wife, Ann Battles, recognized that literacy was crucial to their placement within the community and afforded that opportunity to their children by personally teaching them, hiring private tutors, and sending some of the children to schools in New Orleans. While Ann was living, she prepared her children for the future. Education was an essential value that Ann inculcated within her family. Although her mother appears to have been illiterate, Ann Johnson obtained the ability to read and write at some point in her early life. The Johnson children studied reading, writing, mathematics, geography, and literature. Also, the boys learned the barbering trade from their father and Ann instructed her daughters in music as well as domestic skills like sewing. Anna and Catharine utilized this education by eventually becoming schoolteachers. As educators, the Johnson sisters played crucial roles in shaping the educational landscape for Black children after the war. Their commitment to teaching in a time when educational resources were scarce for their community exemplified resilience and dedication.[271]

After their mother's death, the children of William Johnson continued his legacy. She bequeathed to her children William's barbershop, their brick house on State Street, and some rental property, totaling thousands of dollars. Byron became head of the family after his mother's death because William Johnson, Jr. suffered from mental illness, and by 1866 was confined to a New Orleans asylum. After the death of Byron Johnson in 1872, Anna L. Johnson was the most prominent figure in the family. Richard Johnson worked his family's Peachland Plantation (Adams County) in the 1890s. Anna lived at Peachland during the period of 1912 to 1920. Their nephew William R.

Johnston (died 1938) received an undergraduate degree from Wilberforce University in 1897 and earned a medical degree from Howard University. Johnston practiced medicine in Natchez until his death in 1938.[272]

It was the children of the mulatto class former slave masters that was more willing to cross the color line and to bridge the gap between light-skinned and dark-skinned blacks. Also, a large number of the "new" Black leaders in the South came from this class/caste group. The sons and daughters of Black slave masters were educated and resourceful. In the late 1860s, Frances Rollins, the daughter of William Rollins, a Black slave owner of Charleston City, worked as a schoolteacher in Beaufort County. She was educated at the Institution for Colored Youth in Philadelphia and was one of four sisters who worked to uplift the newly freed in South Carolina. Later, she married William James Whipper, a state representative of South Carolina. Thaddeus Sasportas, the son of Joseph A. Sasportas, a mulatto slave owner, went to Orangeburg County to aid the ex-slaves and to work as a teacher, where he taught ex-slaves to read and write.[273]

The Civil War served as a watershed moment, shattering the old order and ushering in a new era of possibilities. The emancipation of enslaved people, enshrined in the 13th Amendment, fundamentally changed the legal and moral landscape, rendering the practice of free Black slaveholding obsolete. The moral debate surrounding the practice, however, did not disappear. The legacy of free Black slaveholding continued to be debated, with some seeing it as a testament to the resilience of free Black communities and others viewing it as a stain on the struggle for racial justice.

The aftermath of the War Between the States saw the emergence of a new generation of African Americans who sought to create a society free from the vestiges of slavery. They championed racial equality, advocated for full citizenship rights, and denounced the legacy of slavery in all its forms. This new generation often viewed the practice of free Black slaveholding as a relic of a bygone era, a practice that was incompatible with their vision of a just and equitable society.

However, understanding the evolution of moral perspectives on Free Black slaveholding requires recognizing the multifaceted nature of history. It is important to acknowledge the complexities of the situation, the challenges faced by free Black populations, and the ways in which their actions were shaped by the historical context of their time. Free Black slaveholders were individuals navigating a system riddled with contradictions, seeking to carve out a space for themselves and their families within a deeply divided and society.

Ultimately, the legacy of Free Black slaveholding is not simply a matter of historical curiosity. It speaks to the enduring complexities of race and power in America. It reminds us that the fight for racial justice is an ongoing struggle, one rooted in a past that continues to shape our present.

Therefore, the path forward lies in embracing the nuances of this history, engaging with its complexities, and challenging ourselves to see the American past with a more holistic, and thereby, accurate lens. This history is not about assigning blame or perpetuating guilt. Nor is it an attempt to suppress indignation or dissuade contemporary readers or historians from imparting a measure of fair and balanced criticism of cruel past practices. It is about attempting to understand and recognize the human dimensions of a complex past in an empathetic and holistic manner and using that understanding to build a better future.

Our journey through this history has been a collective one, a journey that has required us to question our assumptions, confront our biases, and expand our understanding of a crucial but often overlooked aspect of the American experience.

As we move forward, let us remember that history is not simply a collection of facts. It is a living narrative, constantly evolving with each new discovery, each fresh perspective, and each individual's willingness to engage with the past. The legacy of Free Black slaveholding remains a potent reminder of the complexities of history, a testament to the resilience of the human spirit, and a call to action for a more just and equitable future.

Chapter 8:
Conclusion: An Author's View

Free Black slaveholding is a prime example of a hidden history begging to be unearthed. This practice challenges our assumptions about race, power, and freedom in the antebellum South, forcing us to confront the uncomfortable reality that the lines of slavery and liberty were not always as clear-cut as we might imagine. By delving into this previously neglected aspect of American history, we are forced to confront the complex ways in which the institution of slavery permeated every facet of Southern society, and how the lines of race, class, and freedom became entangled in a web of contradictions.

Uncovering these hidden histories allows us to challenge the prevailing narratives that often reduce complex historical events to neat, easily digestible summaries. We are forced to acknowledge that history is not a collection of linear progressions or unwavering moral victories. Instead, it is a messy tapestry woven from threads of triumph and tragedy, of resistance and conformity, of individual agency and systemic oppression.

By shedding light on the experiences of free Black slaveholders, we gain a more nuanced understanding of the complexities of slavery's impact on Black communities and the wider American landscape. These individuals, caught between the oppressive realities of racial discrimination and the opportunities (however limited) presented by the slaveholding system, illuminate the intricate ways in which individuals navigated the moral and social dilemmas of the era. Their stories challenge us to move beyond simplistic interpretations of their motivations, urging us to delve into the complexities of their lives, their choices, and their legacies.

The Paradox of Freedom

The story of free Black slaveholding underscores the enduring influence of slavery on the American social fabric, even as the institution itself was eventually abolished. It highlights the complexities of racial identity and the fluid nature of power in a society deeply divided by race. The very act of free Blacks owning slaves challenged conventional narratives about race and ownership, forcing society to grapple with the uncomfortable truth that the lines of power and privilege were not always as clear-cut as they appeared.

The rise and fall of the Black slaveowners represents a segment of the first formation of Black American elite. These slaveowners set aside the bonds of race that they shared with the slaves and when personal gain was at the core of their decision-making, they chose to side with the White ruling class and establish themselves social and economically. Their use of slaves for profit forced these slaveowners to become steeped in the success of the slave system. Due to being so invested in this system, these individuals contributed to its survival, even going as far as to help stop slave rebellions such as the *Denmark Vesey Conspiracy*. Even when White citizens attacked Black communities, credible evidence reveals that in high numbers, Black slaveowners sided with the White elite over members of their race. The relationship between the Black and White slaveowners was based on how morally upright the Black individual was perceived to be in accordance with White American expectations and allowed some Black slaveowners to earn its trust. With the push for these individuals to join with the White elite came efforts to distance themselves from the Black community. In doing so, the Black elite used the same racial jargon as the White class. Commonly using in tandem the lightness of their skin and the wealth they possessed, the slave owning Black American population of the South sought to create a separation between themselves and other free Black people as a social indicator of their presumed elite status. With the separation from the rest of the Black community and the alliance with the White elites, these Black slaveowners cannot be described in any terms, but as having supported

The Paradox of Freedom

and upheld the system of slavery. This loyalty to slavery led the Black slaveowners to follow it to their destruction just as their White counterparts. Based upon evidentiary scrutiny, Black slaveowners often chose to support the Confederacy, going as far as to supply food and other materials to the Confederate army with some even attempting to enlist and serve. The end of the Civil War was the death nail to the Black slaveowners' way of life. Despite the attempts of these former slaveowners to regain their wealth at the end of the war, the amount that they lost was often too great. Despite this loss, many did not accept their new social status and would attempt to regain their lost position. To make it financially, Black former slaveowners sold off their land to ensure they could feed their families. To regain their wealth and lost position, these former slaveowners again sided with their old allies, even implementing sharecropping to keep their workers tied to the land but with the rise of Jim Crow came the demise of the Black slaveowners. Most of their former allies began to turn against them. Despite how intertwined the Black slaveowners were in the slavery system, their legacy is entirely forgotten. The struggles of the Reconstruction era erased the position that the Black slaveowners once held and forced them into the same group that they had once enslaved.

This last chapter is not merely an end, but a beginning. We have delved into the complexities of free Black slaveholding, a phenomenon that defies easy categorization and challenges the national narrative understanding of American history. It has forced us to confront the unsettling truth that the lines between freedom and enslavement, between victimizer and victimized, were often blurred in Antebellum America. We have encountered individuals, both enslaved and free, whose stories are marked by both agency and constraint, by both resistance and complicity.

The power of storytelling, historical dialogue and the art of collection and interpretation of relevant evidence, no matter what may be revealed, lies at the heart of understanding the past, challenging assumptions, and forging deeper connections with the human experience. By weaving narratives and fostering dialogue, we illuminate the complexities of history, transcending simple narratives and embracing the multifaceted nature of human events. The story of free Black slaveholders in America offers a powerful example of how storytelling and dialogue can bridge the gaps between generations and cultures, fostering a more nuanced and empathetic understanding of our nation's history.

Stories have the power to transport us to different times and places, allowing us to step into the shoes of individuals who lived in the past. They introduce us to real people, their motivations, their struggles, and their triumphs. In the case of free Black slaveholders, their stories challenge our preconceived notions about race, power, and freedom. They reveal the complexities of a system where individuals of color could find themselves in the paradoxical position of holding others in bondage while simultaneously facing their own forms of discrimination and oppression.

Through the power of storytelling and historical dialogue, we can illuminate the past, challenge assumptions, and foster deeper understanding and empathy. The story of free Black slaveholders in America offers a powerful example of how these tools can help us to navigate the complexities of history, to recognize the shared humanity of all individuals, and to strive for a more just and equitable future.

The topic of free Black slaveholding is not simply that of a trivial or minimal historical curiosity; it is a vital thread in the tapestry of American history that demands further exploration and understanding. This book has sought to shed light on a complex and often overlooked chapter in our nation's past, revealing the multifaceted lives of Free Black individuals who navigated the contradictions of freedom and ownership in a society deeply divided by race and power.

As you close this book, I encourage you to consider the significance of this unearthed history and its enduring impact on our present. I invite

The Paradox of Freedom

you to continue the conversation about Free Black slaveholding, not with the intent of casting judgment on individuals who lived in a different time, but to engage with the complexities of their lives and the enduring legacy of their actions.

The stories of free Black slaveholders challenge us to reconsider our understanding of slavery and its impact on both enslaved and free Black communities. They force us to confront the inherent contradictions within the institution of slavery and the ways in which even those who sought to carve out spaces of freedom within the system often found themselves entangled in its web of power and inequality.

The research on free Black slaveholding is ongoing, and new discoveries are constantly emerging. We encourage you to continue exploring this history, engaging with scholarly works, and seeking out primary sources that shed light on the lives and experiences of those involved. By participating in this ongoing conversation, you can contribute to a more inclusive and accurate understanding of the American past and its lasting legacy.

The stories of free Black slaveholding are not simply relegated to the history books; they have a profound relevance to our present-day understanding of race, power, and freedom. They remind us that the struggle for racial justice is a long and ongoing process, shaped by the complexities of history and the enduring need for empathy and understanding.

The pursuit of a more complete and accurate understanding of the American past is essential for building a more just and equitable future. By engaging with the stories of free Black slaveholding, we can contribute to a deeper and more nuanced understanding of our nation's history, recognizing its complexities, its contradictions, and its enduring impact on the lives of all Americans.

Appendix I
An act concerning Servants and Slave – Virginia General Assembly, 1705

I : Any servant brought to the country who is Christian and above nineteen will serve until they reach twenty four.

II: Every indentured servant must be brought to the courts to determine their age and their period of servitude will be dependent on that.

III: If a servant who is being sold claims to have indentures (a legal contract), the master or owner can bring the servant before a justice to verify this claim.

IV: All servants brought into the country, who were not Christians in their home country with a few exceptions will be considered and treated as slaves. Even if they convert to Christianity later, they will still be bought and sold as slaves.

V: If any person imports into the colony and sells as a slave someone who was previously a free person in any Christian country, island, or plantation, the importer or seller will be required to pay double the amount for which the person was sold to the freed individual.

VI: Being in England is not enough to free a slave, they must provide proof of freedom.

VII: Masters of servants are required to provide adequate food, clothing, and lodging. The masters are also prohibited to give excessive punishment to any White Christian servant.

The Paradox of Freedom

VIII: Grants rights to all servants who are not slaves, whether imported or voluntarily becoming servants, or bound by a court or church-wardens. They can present their complaints to a justice of the peace.

IX: States that if a servant is sick, disabled, or otherwise incapable of being sold to cover expenses, the court will order the church-wardens to take care of the servant until their legal time of service is completed, or until they recover to be sold and cover the fees and charges.

X: States that all servants have the right to petition the court for their wages and freedom in cases of mistreatment.

XI: States that no individuals, such as Negroes, mulattos, Indians, Jews, Moors, Muslims, or other non-Christians, will be allowed to purchase Christian servants. If any person from the aforementioned groups purchases a Christian white servant, that servant will automatically become free.

XV: States that no person is allowed to buy, sell, or receive any form of currency or goods from a servant or slave without the permission of their master or owner.

XVI: States that if a person is convicted of dealing with a servant or slave in violation of this act and fails to provide satisfactory security for their good behavior, the court will order the offender to receive specified punishment.

XVII: States that if a female servant has a child out of wedlock with a Negro or mulatto, in addition to completing her designated years of service, she must pay fifteen pounds in current Virginia currency. This is the same case, if a free Christian white woman has a child out of wedlock with a Negro or mulatto. Then the child will serve as a servant until they reach the age of thirty-one.

XIX: States that it is unlawful to intermarry between English or other white individuals and Negroes or mulattos especially if said English is freed.

XX: States that no minister of the Church of England or any other person within the colony and dominion is allowed to knowingly marry a white person with a Negro or mulatto, or vice versa.

XXIII: States that a reward will be given to anyone who successfully captures and returns a runaway servant or slave.

XXIV: States that if a runaway slave, who does not speak English or refuses to disclose their master or owner's name, is captured, the justice of the peace may certify this instead of providing the specific details.

XXV: When a runaway is brought before a justice of the peace, the justice shall issue a warrant to commit the runaway to the next constable.

XXIX: If any constable or sheriff, to whom a runaway servant or slave is entrusted according to this act, allows the escape of such runaway, the constable or sheriff shall be held accountable.

XXXII: Any master, mistress, or overseer of a household shall not knowingly allow any enslaved person who does not belong to them to stay on their plantation for more than four hours without the permission of the enslaved person's master, mistress, or overseer.

XXXIV: If a slave resists their master, owner, or any other person who is authorized by the master or owner to correct them, and as a result, the slave is killed, it shall not be considered a felony. As well as if a negro, mulatto, or Indian, whether enslaved or free, raises a hand in opposition against a non-negro, non-mulatto, or non-Indian individual, they shall receive punishment.

XXXV: No slave shall carry or possess firearms or any other weapons, nor leave the designated plantation or land without a written certificate of permission from their master.

XXXVI: Baptism does not exempt negro, mulatto, or Indians from enslavement

XXXVII: States that slaves often run away and hide in secluded areas, causing harm and damage to the people of the colony. In such cases, if there is information about runaway slaves, two justices of the peace in the relevant county are authorized and required to issue a proclamation.

XXXVIII: For every slave killed, in pursuance of this act, or put to death by law, the master or owner of such slave shall be paid by the public.

XXXIX: To determine the compensation for a slave who has been killed or put to death as mentioned earlier, it is required that the true value of the slave be assessed. The court clerk will then provide a certificate of the assessed value to the assembly along with other public claims.

XL: To ensure the proper enforcement of this act and to prevent any servants or slaves from claiming ignorance of its provisions, the church-wardens of each parish will be responsible for providing a true copy of the act and recording it in the parish register book at the expense of the parish.

XLI: Furthermore, all previous acts, clauses, and articles that pertain to servants, slaves, or any other matter covered by this act are hereby repealed and declared null and void. They shall have no effect or validity as if they had never been enacted.

Appendix II
Chart based upon the Census of 1830

Note: The following facts were extracted from the returns of those who took the census of the United States in 1830. After C. G. Woodson, the editor, had first copied the records of one state to acquaint himself in detail with the information given in these census reports, the statistics were then copied under his direction by three persons. One of them has had the advantage of two years' normal training, after finishing high School and two of whom have finished college courses at Howard University and at the University of Michigan. The matter thus collected was then verified by Mr. Alrutheus A. Taylor, an alumnus of Michigan and a Harvard Master of Arts in History and Economics, now employed as Associate Investigator of the Association for the Study of Negro Life and History. Further verification was made by C. G. Woodson.

These records were copied just as those who took the census returned their findings. The only change made in the case of Negro Owners of slaves was to write the family name first, a rule which these enumerators did not all follow.

Some enumerators made no distinction as to race in recording the names, but merely indicated the status of the head of the family under free persons of color. Other enumerators wrote Negro or Colored or used F. of C. for free person of color, F. M. C. for free man of color, or F. W. C. for free woman of color, directly after the name.

The question mark after a name or a figure or in a column indicates that the record is such that the fact could not be accurately determined.

The column giving the **AGE** does not every time give the age of the head of the family. In some instances the age of the head of the family cannot be actually figured out. The age here given is that of the oldest person in the family of the sex indicated as the head of the family. The record as to sex, moreover, is often confusing. The name of a male is sometimes given as the head of the family while the sex is indicated as female and vice versa. In eighty per cent of the cases which the investigator has tested, however, it can be shown that this is the actual age of the head of the family. "10-24" means between the ages of 10 and 24 and "24-36" means between the ages 24 and 36 etc. The column entitled **SLAVES** gives the number of slaves owned by the head of the family. **TOTAL** means the number of persons in the family together with all of the slaves. This enables the student to figure out for himself whether the slaveholding was an act of exploitation or of benevolence. The small number of slaves, however, does not always signify benevolence on the part of the owner.

The Paradox of Freedom

ALABAMA

Name	Slaves	Total	Age	Name	Slaves	Total	Age
CLARKE COUNTY				Chastang, Basil.........	1	10	55–100
Meggs, James.........	1	2	36–55	Chastang, Bastiste......	1	3	36–55
Harris, P. T...........	24	25	55–100	Chastang, Zane.........	1	3	55–100
Hatcher, William......	2	3	36–55	Chastang, Zeno.........	5	15	36–55
Stapleton, Joseph......	1	2	36–55	Chastang, Louisa.......	14	19	55–100
Monack, David........	27	28	55–100	Nicholas, Jasma........	3	5	24–36
DALLAS COUNTY				*City of Mobile*			
Smith, Tom...........	4	14	36–55	Rutgeron, Frances......	1	2	24–36
				Ferer, Clara...........	4	6	24–36
LAWRENCE COUNTY				Laurendine, Benjamin...	1	7	24–36
Royall, Lewis..........	1	3	55–100	Rozieste, Burnadoz.....	14	32	24–36
				Guile, Mad. O.........	4	10	55–100
MADISON COUNTY				Chastang, Frances......	1	7	55–100
First and Second Ranges of Townships				Gregg, Frances.........	2	8	24–36
				Mary, Mad.............	6	8	36–55
Davis, Betsey..........	1	7	36–55	Rozieste, Peir..........	6	14	24–36
Stewart, James F.......	2	3	36–55	Boshong, Madam.......	16	23	36–55
Third and Fourth Ranges of Townships				**MONROE COUNTY**			
				Sizemore (?), Arthur....	3	8	55–100
Robinson, John........	4	7	24–36	Sizemore (?), Susanna...	2	7	36–55
Blanks, Paschal........	2	4	24–36				
Hunt, Lewis...........	1	4	24–36	**MONTGOMERY COUNTY**			
Hunster, Nancy........	1	8	36–55	Fowler (de), Oxey......	1	3	55–100
Findley, Jenny.........	1	2	24–36	Lanton Joseph (F. of C.)	2	11	55–100
Evans, John...........	1	3	36–55				
Winn, Andrew.........	2	3	55–100	**PERRY COUNTY**			
				Thomas, Frederick V....	1	8	55–100
MOBILE COUNTY							
Minnie................	1	6	36–55	**SHELBY COUNTY**			
Key, Lawrence.........	4	11	24–36	Hadsen, Isah...........	1	12	36–55
Chastang, Theresa......	2	3	100–				
Simore, Felix..........	1	10	55–100	**WASHINGTON COUNTY**			
Colderen, Simore.......	3	8	24–36	Saunsha, John..........	2	3	36–55
Andre, Sylvester.......	2	10	36–55				
Andre, Mademitian.....	6	15	36–55	**WILCOX COUNTY**			
Simore, Jane..........	10	13	36–55	Martin, John...........	1	3	36–55

ARKANSAS TERRITORY

Name	Slaves	Total	Age
LAFAYETTE COUNTY			
Free Bob..............	3	4	36–55

CONNECTICUT

Name	Slaves	Total	Age
FAIRFIELD COUNTY			
Demosat, Amos........	1	6	55–100

DELAWARE

Name	Slaves	Total	Age	Name	Slaves	Total	Age
NEWCASTLE COUNTY				Delahow, Jacob.........	1	6	36–55
Davis, Samuel B.......	3	4	10–24				
Millis, Charles.........	1	3	24–36	**SUSSEX COUNTY**			
Porter, Jessee..........	5	10	24–36	Mosley, Peter..........	6	7	100–
Dale, Hannah..........	1	2	36–55	Sirmon, Caleb..........	1	8	36–55
Tibut, Daniel..........	2	3	36–55	Richards, Robert.......	1	3	36–55

The Paradox of Freedom

DISTRICT OF COLUMBIA

Name	Slaves	Total	Age	Name	Slaves	Total	Age
Washington				Netter, Sarah	2	3	24–36
Fourth Ward				Matthews, Luke	1	2	36–55
Colored, Robinson	3	3	36–55	Baltimore, James	1	2	24–36
" Clark	1	7	24–36	Sewell, Rd.	1	5	36–55
" Hanson, H.	6	7	24–36	Gordon, Wm.	2	5	10–24
" Joice	4	4	24–36	Proctor, Os.	1	7	36–55
" Johnson	4	4	36–55	Glasgow, John	1	3	55–100
" Brown	4	5	24–36	Brooke, Betsy	1	2	55–100
" Dubbon	9	9	36–55	Jenifer, Mary	1	9	36–55
" Tillman	5	5	24–36	Shaw, Simon	6	8	36–55
Bell	1	4	55–100	Curtis, Samuel	6	7	10–24
Dyson	1	6	24–36	Gant, Catharine	3	4	55–100
Colored, Jones, J.	1	3	36–55	Fowler, Mary	1	5	24–36
" Sims, Benj.	3	4	36–55	Eglin, Harry	6	8	24–36
" Brooks, P.	1	6	55–100	Moore, John	2	5	10–24
" Allison, Wm.	1	2	36–55	Ambush, Edward	1	6	36–55
" Hicks, Sandy	1	3	36–55	Bowman, Eliza	1	5	36–55
" McKenzie, J.	1	2	10–24	Lowry, Scilla	1	2	55–100
Simpson, E.	2	7	24–36	Doyne, Benedict	1	6	24–36
Jackson	1	3	10–24	Henderson, Godfrey	2	3	10–24
Reed, J.	1	3	24–36	Myers, Charles	1	2	24–36
Adams, W.	1	7	24–36	Edwards, Griffin	1	2	10–24
Thompson, J.	3	9	36–55	Shorter, Luke	1	4	24–36
Colored, Bonnell, Benj.	1	5	24–36	Bowen, Nancy	1	2	36–55
" Campbell, Wm.	1	2	36–55	Digs, Frank	2	4	10–24
" Allen, N.	1	7	36–55	Diggs, Anthony	1	9	24–36
" Dyer, H.	2	4	36–55	Peters, Nancy	1	5	36–55
" West, P.	1	2	10–24	Patterson, Robert	1	7	36–55
" Leatherberry, L.	1	5	24–36				
" Smiler, M.	1	5	36–55	WASHINGTON COUNTY			
" Butter, J.	1	2	36–55	*East of Rock Creek and*			
" Mann, Ths.	1	2	55–100	*West of 7th Street*			
" Simms, A.	1	4	24–36	*Turnpike*			
Bowen, H.	4	6	24–36	Brooke, Robert	1	9	36–55
Jackson, A.	6	8	55–100	Coats, Nancy	1	2	55–100
Colored, Jenkins, F.	1	2	10–24				
Dexter, S.	1	2	55–100	*Georgetown*			
Colored, Cooper, J.	1	5	24–36	Moore, Mordecai	2	3	36–55
" Brown	4	5	55–100	Murphy, Nathan	2	3	36–55
" Rivers	1	4	36–55	Hawkins, Walter	5	8	36–55
" Liverpool	4	5	36–55	Cole, Horace	1	6	36–55
Gates	1	7	24–36	Brown, David	1	5	24–36
Turner	1	4	55–100	Tolson, Francis	1	7	36–55
Hatton, Ricd.	1	2	36–55	Wilson, Jeffry	1	5	36–55
Neale, S.	3	4	10–24	Freeman, Ignatius	1	2	55–100
Manning, Amelia	5	6	10–24	Dyson, Jno.	1	4	24–36
Sims, Richard	1	3	24–36	Smith, Elizh.	1	3	24–36
Blue, Samuel	4	5	36–55	Bivens, Richd.	1	7	55–100
Smith, John	1	5	24–36	Chew, Saml. (principal)	8	16	24–36
Neale, Kitty	1	3	24–36	Johnson, Fredk	1	5	24–36
Ashley, Martha	4	7	36–55	Littemon, Richd.	2	3	55–100
Dorsey, Kitty	2	6	24–36	Eglan, Saml.	1	2	55–100
Norris, Kitty	1	5	36–55	Chapman, Benjn.	1	2	55–100
Grant, Titus	1	3	36–55	Key, Ann	2	5	24–36
Lewis, James	1	4	24–36	Williams, Susan	1	6	55–100
Mann, Eliza	1	2	24–36	Allen, Nathan	2	3	10–24
Chambers, Ellen	2	4	55–100	Woodward, Lamber	1	5	10–24

The Paradox of Freedom

DISTRICT OF COLUMBIA—Continued

Name	Slaves	Total	Age	Name	Slaves	Total	Age
Georgetown—Cont.				Coffee, Nicholas	1	3	36–55
Chase, Resin	1	3	36–55	Tarey, Andw.	1	3	55–100
Washington, Geo. C.	1	6	10–24				
Mason, Josh	4	6	36–55	ALEXANDRIA COUNTY			
Lancaster, Conky	1	3	55–100	Lawrence, John	3	5	24–36
Butler, Ann	3	4	36–55	Kur & Fitzhugh	1	6	24–36
Washington, Walter	1	2	55–100	Brown, Henry	1	11	36–55
Brown, Isaac	1	6	24–36	Hepburn, Moses	2	5	10–24
Sims, Samuel	1	2	36–55	Myers, Abraham	1	7	36–55
Dines, Peter	1	2	36–55	Bend, Coffie	1	2	36–55
Coffee, Catharin	3	4	24–36	Merrise, Mima	1	2	24–36
Travers, Josh	1	2	24–36	Brown, Grace	1	2	55–100
Lee, Danl	1	3	55–100	Addison, Mary	1	2	36–55
Fenwick, Wm	1	3	10–24	Townsend, James	1	9	36–55
Boswell, Anthy	1	3	55–100	Chinn, Carlus	1	5	24–36
Downes, Susanna	1	7	55–100				

FLORIDA

Name	Slaves	Total	Age	Name	Slaves	Total	Age
ESCAMBIA COUNTY				ST. JOHNS COUNTY			
Fio (or Tio), Joseph M.	3	11	24–36	*St. Augustine*			
Bara, Doretea	3	9	24–36	Pepino, Mary	1	8	55–100
Muertre, Ann	6	11	55–100	Pepino, Valentine	3	8	55–100
Sachet, Gabriel Bertram	1	10	36–55	Clarke, James	3	9	24–36
Hinard, Eufroinne	12	14	55–100	Fish, Clarisa	1	10	36–55
Rouby, Joseph	6	10	36–55	Williams, Sampson	7	11	36–55
Coca, Carmelite	1	5	24–36	Perpall, Gabriel	39	40	55–100
				Sanches, Susan	4	5	36–55
NASSAU COUNTY							
Kingsley, Sophy	2	4	24–36				

GEORGIA

Name	Slaves	Total	Age	Name	Slaves	Total	Age
BURKE COUNTY				Crivillier, Hager	3	6	36–55
Nunes, Charles (colored)	2	6	36–55	Thompson, C.	2	3	10–24
Nunes, Joseph (colored)	6	7	24–36	Craig, Ann	3	12	55–100
Nunes, Janet (colored)	3	6	24–36	Merrillie, Jane	2	3	36–55
				Cruvillier, Justine	6	11	36–55
CAMDEN COUNTY				Jackson, Ragis	2	10	24–36
Brewer, Betsey	1	6	24–36	Gibbons, John	1	4	36–55
				Brown, Rebecca	2	6	24–36
CARROLL COUNTY				Malligo, William	3	6	36–55
Rowe, Arch	9	16	24–36	Whitfield, Sampson	1	5	24–36
Petit, Thomas	7	9	36–55	Harris, F.	1	4	36–55
Cornsilk	3	8	55–100	Luvett, Catherine	1	7	36–55
				Giblory, John	8	12	36–55
CHATHAM COUNTY				Darling, Massa	2	4	36–55
City of Savannah				Grant, Jane	1	2	36–55
Galineau, Rose	1	3	55–100	Wilson, William	3	6	36–55
Cunningham, Harry	7	9	55–100	Greenfield, Allen	6	8	24–36
Woodhouse, Robert	2	7	24–36	Ross, Cudjoe	5	8	36–55
Tenack, Mary	4	14	55–100	Netherclift, Dick	3	4	36–55
Tabeau, Manet	1	9	36–55				
Shomaca, Louisa	1	3	10–24	ELBERT COUNTY			
Ragis, Poline	2	7	36–55	Harper, Grace	1	17	36–55
Teice, M.	2	3	55–100				
Jackson, Susan	6	12	100–	EMANUEL COUNTY			
Neusome, Polly	3	6	36–55	Ruis (Lewis) (?), Polly	1	3	10–24

GEORGIA—Continued

Name	Slaves	Total	Age	Name	Slaves	Total	Age
FAYETTE COUNTY				Bush, Maria	2	4	10–24
Turner, James	2	13	36–55	Cobb, Billy	1	4	36–55
Turner, Silas	1	7	24–36	Monroe, Maria	1	7	24–36
Turner, Moses T	1	10	36–55	Haynes, John	3	4	36–55
				Hicks, Betsey	4	12	55–100
GREENE COUNTY				Brown, Josiah	7	8	24–36
Perry, Betsey	25	26	55–100	Dent, Fred and Jacob	6	12	36–55
				Carns, Lucy	1	8	36–55
MUSCOGEE COUNTY				Smith, Turner	6	15	24–36
Guardian, Phelps	2	3	55–100	Hill, Phillis	4	5	55–100
RANDOLPH COUNTY				**SCREVEN COUNTY**			
Triplett, Jim	2	5	55–100	Nicholson, Thomas	7	8	36–55
Dobbins, Amy	4	8	55–100				
Brown, Milly	3	7	36–55	**WARREN COUNTY**			
				Steth, Dan'l, of Col	1	6	36–55
RICHMOND COUNTY							
City of Augusta				**WILKES COUNTY**			
Moore, Isabella	4	6	24–36	Hoxey, William	1	7	36–55
Kelly, Betsey	2	6	24–36				

ILLINOIS

Name	Slaves	Total	Age	Name	Slaves	Total	Age
UNION COUNTY				**PEORIA AND PUTNAM**			
Robinson, Robert	1	3	55–100	**COUNTIES AND TERRITORY ATTACHED**			
HAMILTON COUNTY							
Shawnee Town				Croaker, Francis	1	4	24–36
Hubbard, Benjamin	3	7	36–55				
Equality Township				**RANDOLPH COUNTY**			
Cheek, Isham	1	12	36–55	Louvier, Margaret	2	5	55–100
Henderson, Louisa	2	6	24–36				
Clark, Gracey	1	7	55–100				

KENTUCKY

Name	Slaves	Total	Age	Name	Slaves	Total	Age
ADAIR COUNTY				**CHRISTIAN COUNTY**			
Burbridge, Sawney	2	2	36–55	*Hopkinsville*			
				Cocke, Michael	3	4	36–55
BARREN COUNTY							
Force, Leander	1	3	55–100	**CLARKE COUNTY**			
				Dudley, John	1	2	55–100
BOURBON COUNTY				Birth, George	1	3	36–55
Allen, Peter	2	4	55–100				
Wallace, Sally	1	2	36–55	**FAYETTE COUNTY**			
Jones, Isaac	1	2	55–100	*Lexington*			
Monday, James	1	3	36–55	Scott, Nancy, Col'd woman	2	3	10–24
Grant, Peter	1	5	36–55				
Gabriel	1	3	36–55	Whiting, Peter, Col'd man	1	2	24–36
Heathman, Allen	3	4	24–36				
Hurley, Edmon	1	5	55–100	Gray, Rob't, Col'd man	4	6	24–36
Brooks, Stephen	2	4	36–55	Lewis, Charlotte, Col'd	1	3	55–100
				Bird, Rich'd, Col'd man	1	2	36–55
BRACKEN COUNTY				Tucker, Wm., Col'd man	1	6	24–36
Thomas, Lethia	1	3	36–55	Smith, Jesse, Col'd man	1	2	36–55
BULLITT COUNTY				Keifer, Nathan, Col'd man	4	6	24–36
Mt. Washington							
Ellison, Isaac	3	5	36–55	Tibbs, Benj'n	1	5	100–
Oldridge, Bash	1	3	55–100	Brittain, Jane	4	8	24–36

KENTUCKY—Continued

Name	Slaves	Total	Age	Name	Slaves	Total	Age
Lexington—Cont.				*City of Louisville*			
Travis, Hannah, Col'd woman	2	4	55–100	Cozzens, Betty	1	2	36–55
Brakenridge, Wittshire, Col'd woman	3	5	36–55	Straws, David	2	4	24–36
Phillips, Harvey	1	2	36–55?	Merriwether, Frank	3	6	36–55
Lee, Frank, and Nich's Black, Col'd men	3	5	55–100	Brigadier, Dan'l	1	2	36–55
				Sally (a Free woman)	1	2	36–55
FAYETTE COUNTY				**JESSAMINE COUNTY**			
Davis, Peter	2	7	55–100	Higenbothan, Judith	1	8	36–55
Martin, Adam B.	1	3	55–100	Anthony of colour	3	5	55–100
Howard, Isaac	2	3	55–100	William a man of color	3	4	36–55
Burk, William	1	4	55–100	**KNOX COUNTY**			
Caulden, Benjamin	4	5	36–55	Goins, Isaiah	7	8	36–55
Francess, Peter	7	8	24–36	**LOGAN COUNTY**			
Williams, Ben	1	3	55–100	*Russellville*			
Shores, Anaka	1	6	36–55	Valentine, Nicholas	2	5	24–36
Allen, Jer'y	9	10	36–55	Buckner, Robert	4	5	55–100
Allen, Alex'dr	2	4	55–100	Jones, Edward	1	5	24–36
Dunlap, Samuel	1	2	36–55	Husketh, Isham	3	16	36–55
Clark, Rhody	1	10	36–55	Barber, William	4	5	36–55
Smith, Robt.	6	7	55–100	**MADISON COUNTY**			
				White, George	4	6	55–100
FLEMING COUNTY							
Eastern Division				**MASON COUNTY**			
Truett, Jacob (A colored man)	3	5	36–55	Bowles, Thomas F.	1	9	24–36
				Glasford, John	1	3	36–55
				Cooper, Edward	1	5	24–36
FRANKLIN COUNTY				Markham, H.	1	6	36–55
North Division				Wann, Roseann	3	4	36–55
Frankfort				More, Charles	6	8	36–55
Mordecai, Harry	4	12	36–55	Baylor, Ann	1	7	55–100
Jones, David	2	4	55–100	Toliver, Edmond	1	4	36–55
Ward, John	1	3	36–55	Diggs, Acam	6	7	36–55
Chiles, Burrel	2	4	55–100				
Goin, John S.	1	12	36–55	*Washington*			
Brown, Samuel	1	4	36–55	*West of Main Street*			
				Miles, Peggy	1	2	55–100
				Lightfoot, John	1	3	55–100
GRAVES COUNTY				Johnson, Isaac	1	3	36–55
Keeling, Alias	3	7	24–36	**MERCER COUNTY**			
				Harrodsburg			
GREENE COUNTY				Harris, Anderson	2	8	36–55
Malone, Thos.	4	5	36–55	Harris, Ben	2	4	36–55
				Easton, Spencer	4	5	24–36
HARRISON COUNTY				Melvin, Fielding	2	4	24–36
West Side of Licking River				Fry, Jemima	1	5	24–36
Berton, Benjamin	3	5	36–55	Jenkins, Hercules	1	4	55–100
				Warman, George	1	3	55–100
HENDERSON COUNTY				Beaty, Adam	1	5	24–36
Pointer, Liverpool	4	5	36–55	Robinson, Sanko	2	6	55–100
JEFFERSON COUNTY				**MONTGOMERY COUNTY**			
Gray, J. T.	4	5	24–36	Lee, Richard	2	3	55–100

KENTUCKY—Continued

Name	Slaves	Total	Age	Name	Slaves	Total	Age
NELSON COUNTY *Bardstown*				*North of the Road from Frankfort to Louisville*			
Smiley, Thomas	3	4	55–100	Henson, Jim	2	3	36–55
Cocke, Joe	1	4	36–55				
Rudd, Thomas	2	3	36–55	**WARREN COUNTY** *Bowling Green*			
Aud, George	5	6	24–36	Palmore, Jane	2	8	24–36
NICHOLAS COUNTY				Russell, Bazzle	2	3	36–55
Mallery, George	1	3	36–55				
ROCKCASTLE COUNTY				**WASHINGTON COUNTY** *South of Main Street, Springfield*			
Cable, David	1	3	36–55	Palmer, Robert C.	2	3	100–
SHELBY COUNTY *South of the Main road from Shelbyville to Louisville and from the Bridge on Clear Creek to the Mt. Eden road thence with Sd. road to Gayaways and down the Bardstown road to the spencer line*				Sandy, Ignatius	2	4	36–55
				WOODFORD COUNTY			
				Miller, Joe	1	3	36–55
				Corbin, Lawrence	1	4	55–100
				Tutt, Betty	7	8	55–100
				Campbell, Billy	8	10	55–100
				Mason, Henry	2	3	55–100
Edwards, John	1	3	36–55	Stratford, Tom	2	5	55–100
Shelbyville North Main Street				Hardy, Ambrose	1	3	55–100
				Harvey, Richard	2	5	36–55
				Cloak, Samuel	3	4	36–55
Short, Peter	1	3	36–55	Twiner, Nathan	4	6	24–36
North of Road from Louisville to Frankfort				Hawkins, Joel	3	8	55–100
				Weaver, Moses	1	8	36–55
Harris, Hannah	3	4	55–100	Ritchie, Jordan	1	4	36–55

LOUISIANA

Name	Slaves	Total	Age	Name	Slaves	Total	Age
ASCENSION PARISH				**BATON ROUGE**			
Jacques	4	8	100–	Benjamin	4	8	10–24
Talmaire, Pommela	4	6	10–24	Tomatiste, Alexandre	1	2	24–36
Trauppe, Jean	1	7	55–100	Lange, Joseph	5	18	36–55
Quezer, François	1	8	36–55				
Grace, Dominique	1	2	24–36	**IBERVILLE**			
				Lacour, Antoine	18	26	55–100
ASSUMPTION				Bory, Augustin	20	26	36–55
Françoise, Mademoiselle	3	4	24–36	De Landre, Georges	46	56	36–55
Julienne, Miss François	2	8	100–	Honoré, Widow Zacharie	21	29	36–55
Poche, Joseph	3	8	36–55	Dubuclet, Madame Antoine	44	52	55–100
François, Jacques	4	6	36–55	Riccard, Madame Ciprien	35	46	36–55
AVOYELLES							
Barzanna, Julien	1	8	36–55	**JEFFERSON**			
				Veraunt, L., f.m.c.	4	10	24–36
CATAHOULA				Martin, J. W., f.w.c.	4	10	55–100
Bowie, James (F.M.C.)	3	11	36–55	Foltz, J. P., f.m.c.	5	9	24–36
CONCORDIA				Pierre, M. J., f.w.c.	3	7	24–36
Victor, Madam	6	9	36–55	Langles, P., f.w.c.	10	19	55–100
				Bowler, J. B., f.m.c.	6	11	36–55
EAST BATON ROUGE				Augustin, J., f.m.c.	6	18	55–100
Marianne	1	9	36–55	Sandors, M., f.m.c.	1	10	55–100
Delande, M. Joseph	4	10	36–55	Dauphin, M. T., f.w.c.	10	25	55–100
Boyd, Robert	7	12	36–55	Bakis, H. (?), f.m.c.	1	8	55–100

The Paradox of Freedom

LOUISIANA—Continued

Name	Slaves	Total	Age	Name	Slaves	Total	Age
JEFFERSON—Cont.				**PLAQUEMINES**			
Drespie, L., f.m.c.	1	3	55–100	Castourling, Jean	3	10	55–100
Rosare, M., f.m.c.	1	9	36–55	Molly	6	10	24–36
Lavand, M., f.m.c.	5	8	55–100	Duplessis, Valery	17	24	36–55
Max, M., f.m.c.	1	3	55–100	Duplessis, Cazimer	3	6	24–36
Brim, C., f.m.c.	1	3	36–55	Duplessis, Honore	4	6	36–55
Rime, F., f.m.c.	4	6	24–36	Duplessis, Michel	5	6	36–55
Dauphin, O., f.m.c.	4	8	24–36	Duplessis, Ciprien	6	9	36–55
Sanlet, T., f.m.c.	12	20	55–100	Troupar, François	1	8	36–55
Cavilier, J., f.m.c.	1	6	36–55	Datty, Anne	2	8	36–55
Packet, J. B., f.m.c.	11	21	55–100	Coutan, Rosette	6	15	24–36
				Barthelemi, François	1	9	36–55
LAFAYETTE				Barthelemi, Paul	4	12	36–55
Mathew, Joseph	2	3	36–55	**POINT COUPEE**			
Darby, Celestin	2	10	24–36	Marimat, Madame	7	8	36–55
				Delhonde, Sophie	38	48	36–55
NATCHITOCHES				Destrehaus fils, Honori	10	11	10–24
Btaue, John Bt.	1	3	10–24	Decuire, Lefroix	59	71	24–36
Cloutier, Augustin	1	8	36–55	Pauche, V.	1	7	24–36
Rachal, Pier	4	11	36–55	Bonfois, Charles	1	6	24–36
Balthasar, Louis	2	4	10–24	Curiel, Joseph	40	44	36–55
Rachal, John Bt.	6	17	36–55	Decuire, Antoine	70	76	36–55
Birt, Asaac	5	11	10–24	Decond, Sostin	10	14	24–36
Ducprie, Phillip	2	5	24–36	Pawk, Jasin	3	4	36–55
Metgier, Naciest	1	6	24–36	Decond, Noré	1	5	55–100
Free, Batteart	1	3	55–100	Severin, Leandre	60	68	36–55
Meytoier, John Bt. Dom.	3	12	24–36	Escoe, Lewis	1	4	36–55
Meytoier, Domnick	25	38	55–100	Perrau, Henriette	1	3	55–100
Meytoier, Joseph	13	21	36–55	Albert, Sallie	1	3	36–55
Meytoier, Fils (?), Francies	2	6	10–24	Duperon, Victor	10	26	55–100
Meytoier, Francies, Sr.	5	9	36–55	De Crosier, Augustin	1	2	36–55
Meytoier Augustin, John Bt.	13	23	24–36	Key, Lucindy	1	4	24–36
Meytoier, Louis	54	66	55–100	**ST. BERNARD**			
Meytoier, Augustin	54	60	55–100	Louis	6	7	36–55
Meytoier, Ogest (?)	13	19	24–36	**ST. CHARLES**			
Meytoier, Susan	20	21	55–100	Fatil, Baptist	3	5	36–55
Meytoier, Agsile	3	8	24–36	Sabatier, Severs	1	7	36–55
Meytoier, Pier, Junior	8	16	55–100	Augustin, Eloise	8	15	36–55
Meytoier, Pier, Sr.	2	5	10–24	D'Arensbourg, Gilbert	1	7	24–36
Lariece, Manieuel	4	11	24–36	Honoré, Gabriel	3	10	24–36
Larcos, Margriet	4	9	55–100	Richoux, Joseph	2	9	36–55
Larvean, Joseph	1	5	10–24	Oldélaide	1	5	55–100
Monett, Louis	1	5	10–24	Molière	10	14	36–55
Rock, Saraham	12	21	24–36				
Samper (?), Jerom	3	9	36–55	**ST. JOHN BAPTISTE**			
Dupas, Ameal	3	8	24–36	Villeré, Vᵉ E., Negˢᵉ Lib.	3	17	55–100
Cottonmie, Atonine	3	7	36–55	Rillieux, Vᵉ Fᵃⁱ (?)	49	62	55–100
Corner, Florentine	16	24	24–36	Deslondes, Victoire	52	77	36–55
Lamote, Louis	4	12	55–100	Ferrand, C., & Sᵗ Sᵗ Dusnan	38	49	36–55
Cemore, Charles	8	15	36–55	Isidor, Auge	1	15	36–55
Grasp, Elijah	3	13	24–36				
Trichel, Joseph L.	1	6	24–36	**ST. LANDRY**			
Trichel, Jocann	2	5	36–55	Frilat, Louis	5	11	36–55
Rochet, Suset	6	14	55–100	Bernard, Victoire	1	5	24–36

LOUISIANA—Continued

Name	Slaves	Total	Age	Name	Slaves	Total	Age
Opelousas				ST. MARTIN			
Baldwin, Manon	1	3	36–55	*St. Martinsville*			
Lange, Leonora	2	7	36–55	Fontenette, Eloise	3	10	24–36
Peignier, Françoise	1	3	55–100	Delahoupage, Isador	3	7	55–100
				Lenormand, Martin	44	54	55–100
Belleview				Chalinette (Osene)	1	9	55–100
Malveau, Laurent	18	26	55–100	Lavillebeune, Charles	1	14	55–100
Malveau, Baptiste	4	13	36–55	Grevernberg, Celestin	2	9	55–100
				Vils, Philip	6	14	24–36
Plaquemine Brulé				Fontenette, Lénon	4	15	36–55
Donatto, Martin	75	87	55–100	Lenormand, Ursin	13	19	36–55
Boulard, Jambe	3	6	24–36	Lenormand, Charte·	14	19	55–100
				Champagne, F.	1	7	24–36
Grand Prairie				Lenormand, Norbert	18	20	36–55
Fontinot, Louis A. B.	4	5	36–55				
George, Baptiste	4	10	24–36	ST. MARY			
				Pinta, Casemir	2	10	24–36
Prairie Maumon?				Frillot, Aimé	3	13	24–36
Fontinot, Augustin B.	7	14	55–100	Boutté, Philipeau	10	15	55–100
Simon, Veuve Louis	8	10	36–55	Verdin, Leon	4	15	24–36
				Verdin, Romain	8	24	36–55
Bayou Mallet				Charlete, Bte., Do.	2	5	36–55
Simeon, François	2	7	24–36	Olivier, Magdelaine	1	11	55–100
				Olivier, Adelaide	4	9	36–55
Coteau of Church Prairie							
Lamelle, François	7	21	36–55	ST. TAMMANY			
Bolan, Veuve George	6	7	36–55	Brasier, Maxilion	1	4	36–55
Paillitte, Antoine	8	16	55–100	Brockston, Phillip	1	4	36–55
Villier, Marie	1	3	55–100	Popelous, Cassimer	1	8	36–55
Thiery, Louis, père	3	5	24 36	Baham, Voltaire	1	3	24–36
				Baham, Pierre	1	5	24–36
Quelquesui				Baham, Seymore	2	4	10–24
Johnson, John	4	8	24–36	Maxon, Roselle	7	11	55–100
Ashworth, Jesse	1	11	36–55	Raby, Antoine	1	3	36–55
Carrillo, Joseph	1	9	55–100	Baham, Mary Ann	6	15	36–55
Bayou Mallet				TERRE BONNE			
Guillory, Jean B.	18	32	55–100	Billeaux, Etienne	5	10	36–55
Donat, Auguste	4	6	24–36				
Simeon, George	1	10	36–55	WASHITA (OUACHITA)			
Charlow, Jacques	5	8	55–100	Watts, Joseph	8	21	36–55
				Jerod, Francis	33	42	24–36
Bayou Teche				WEST BATON ROUGE			
Osanne, Valarien	27	38	36–55	Alsire, Helene	3	8	36–55
Lesassier, Jean	19	27	36–55	Detreant, Mrs. Honoré	2	4	36–55
Balqué, Joseph, père	18	21	36–55	Demonel, Terance	6	15	100–
Balqué, Joseph, fils	1	8	24–36	Hubaut, Charles	1	3	36–55
Muillion, Jean B.	52	57	55–100	Bienville, Julien	6	14	24–36
Lamelle, Narcisse	8	13	10–24	Recard, Saint Luke	16	21	55–100
Lamelle, Marie Jeanne	8	11	55–100	Recard, Widow Mary	11	19	10–24
Gallo, Jean	12	16	24–36	Rapelier, James	9	18	36–55
Lafleur, Baptiste	3	6	55–100	Hubaut, Leopold	1	3	36–55
Valliere, Louis	4	11	24–36	Honoré Fils	30	38	36–55
Papillion, Alexander	1	7	24–36	Polen Verret	69	74	36–55
Cofine, Felicite	3	5	55–100				
Bass, James	5	10	10–24	PARISH OF ST. JAMES			
Sweat, Guilbert	4	5	55–100	—ACADIA			
Fontineau, Juinerice B.	4	6	24–36	Nemorin Rhodanez	3	6	24–36

The Paradox of Freedom

LOUISIANA—Continued

Name	Slaves	Total	Age	Name	Slaves	Total	Age
NEW ORLEANS CITY				Canuel, Julien	1	5	55–100
Inhabitants included between Rampart Street, the new burying ground and the Basin				Rochon, Rosette	2	7	55–100
				Brulée, Similien	5	10	55–100
Labretonnière, M. L.	3	8	36–55	*Between Esplanade St. & Canal Marigny*			
Between the Basin and Bayou Road				Populus Doroté	1	4	24–36
				Françoise, Maria	1	10	55–100
Braquemart, Victoire	1	9	36–55	Fondale	1	6	36–55
Dupré, Celeste	3	6	36–55	Beauguis, F^{cls}	3	11	36–55
Ramos, Philippe	2	6	24–36	Fanchon, F^{cise}	1	5	36–55
Rost, Edouard	1	5	24–36	Jeune, Raimond Gaillard	1	3	55–100
Roy, Usanie	1	3	36–55	Duval, Annette	1	6	36–55
Porté, F^{cls}	1	8	36–55	Marquet, Lewis	1	4	24–36
Forneret, Joseph	3	8	36–55	Beauvais, Marie	1	4	24–36
Coursel, Martil	2	4	24–36	Villard, Marie Louisa	1	6	36–55
Gallo, Widow Noel	1	3	36–55	Dupart, Clerck	7	12	24–36
Caulbet, Widow	1	5	55–100	Moreau, Manuel	3	10	24–36
Montrose, N^{as}	4	17	55–100	Borré, Madeleine	6	8	55–100
				Jounin, Cadet	1	3	24–36
Between Bayou Rd. and the Lake				Gallo, Lewis	2	7	55–100
				Coquillot, Noël	1	3	36–55
Obry, Marguerite	3	9	55–100	Flecheu, Henry	1	4	24–36
Between Bayou Road & l'Amour St.				Jourdan, W^{dow} Celestin	1	7	36–55
				Fouchet, Odele	2	7	55–100
Hazur, Prosper	3	11	36–55	Parilliat, Margueritte	4	8	36–55
Dauphin, W^{dow}	9	15	36–55	Burel, Achille	1	6	36–55
Lavaux, Jarde	3	6	36–55	Taguin, Harnot	3	4	55–100
Cheval, Paul	3	7	55–100	Plaissy, A.	5	12	24–36
Renald, Aug^{te}	4	10	24–36	Lajoncière, Celestine	1	6	24–36
Rebauld	3	5	24–36	Félicié, John Peter	1	6	24–36
Rilieux, Elizié	2	7	24–36	Perrillioto, Joseph	4	5	55–100
Duverlet, F^{cls}	2	9	24–36	Francis	1	3	24–36
Metsinger, Benedique	1	5	36–55	Guenon, Hursin	2	9	36–55
Dolliole, Joseph	5	7	36–55	Macartis, Sophie	4	6	36–55
Azur, Marcelite	4	8	24–36	Thérèse	2	3	36–55
Magnac, Charles	1	7	55–100	St. Amant, Eloise	2	6	24–36
Hurtin, Felicianna	1	3	10–24	Etienne, Louisa	4	10	55–100
Chapdu, Caroline	2	6	24–36	Mariux	1	9	36–55
Duval, Salinette	1	8	36–55	Popotte	3	7	36–55
Enard, Simeon	1	5	24–36	Dautelonne, M. C.	8	14	36–55
Juliette	2	9	10–24	Mercier, Seraphine	2	9	36–55
Decoudwux, Chares	2	7	55–100	Justine	4	11	55–100
Lavarie, Joseph, Son	2	11	10–24	Lambert, Richard	1	6	24–36
Bordier, Petronie	3	7	55–100				
Pernet, Madelaine	2	5	36–55	*Between Canal Marigny & Monderville St.*			
Obry, Zelia	1	7	24–36				
Bellouard, John	3	6	24–36	Simon, Constance	3	5	55–100
Lajoie, Julien	1	9	55–100	Deberque, Constantin	1	8	24–36
Madelaine	2	4	55–100				
Constance	2	9	55–100	*Monderville St. & Faubourg Donois*			
L'amour St. between Esplanade St. & the Canal Marigny				Benjamen, Anthony	2	8	36–55
				Joseph, Bazile	1	3	36–55
Azur, Isidor	1	10	36–55	Maria	3	5	36–55

LOUISIANA—*Continued*

Name	Slaves	Total	Age	Name	Slaves	Total	Age
Monderville St.				Smith, Hellen	1	3	24–36
Fbg. Marigny &				Montgomery, Charles	2	4	55–100
Fbg. Donois				Clement, Richard	1	3	36–55
Aubertine	2	6	24–36	Moore, William	6	12	55–100
Zamor, Madeleine	2	7	55–100	Gravier, Joseph	1	3	36–55
Fouché, Nelson	3	8	24–36	Bonseigneur, Arsene	1	12	10–24
Salbrier, Patry	1	8	24–36	Villemont, Josephine	1	4	55–100
Laurent, W^{dow}	2	4	36–55	Bonseigneur, Nerestan	1	7	24–36
Casimir, W^{dow}	1	3	36–55	Key, Richard	1	2	24–36
Petitgeot, F^{cis}	2	5	36–55	Moise, Justine	6	8	36–55
Lachaise, Catherine	2	9	36–55	Francis, George	1	3	24–36
Doublet, Maurice	1	4	10–24	Cazot, Jean	4	7	36–55
Lacroix	2	4	24–36	Pierre, Elisa	2	4	24–36
Compigny, J. L.	1	6	55–100	Claire, Marie	1	2	55–100
Blouin, Augustin	4	13	36–55	Sepine, F.	2	8	36–55
Denaux, Anne	3	12	36–55	Nicholas, Jenny	1	2	36–55
				Jolibois, Genevieve	3	4	36–55
Upper Suburbs of New				Mathieu, Valmont	1	5	24–36
Orleans				Boyer, Lucy	4	8	36–55
Josspot, J. S.	1	2	24–36	Desvignes, Hellen	1	4	24–36
Diggs, James	2	4	10–24	Patty	6	8	36–55
Smith, Peggy	4	6	36–55	Dupas, Mary	1	3	36–55
Herman	2	4	36–55	Teta, Louis	5	7	36–55
Kelan, Phillip	3	4	36–55	Jenkins, Edward	3	9	55–100
Samba, Marie-louise	4	10	55–100	Hilaire, Rosine	3	4	36–55
Carlon, Etienne	1	5	24–36	Hardy, Jaques	6	8	36–55
Chalambert, M$^{rie.}$ J$^{ne.}$	1	6	55–100	Robert, Louverain	2	10	36–55
Beaulieu, Guilbert	1	9	24–36	Lacöesse, Pierre	1	5	24–36
Hartfield, J$^{h.}$	1	8	24–36	Reymond, Pierre	1	5	24–36
Simmons, Sophia	1	3	10–24	Garcia, Pierre	2	10	36–55
Guyonesse, Baptiste	4	10	36–55	Lawrence, Francis	1	7	36–55
White, Charlotte	2	6	55–100	Botts, Cupids	3	5	36–55
Smith, Henry	2	6	36–55	Escaut, Antoine	1	8	36–55
Elley, John	2	4	24–36	Brown	2	5	36–55
Badon, Rémond	6	8	24–36	Smith, Becky	1	2	24–36
Garaut, Rose	2	16	100–	Degruys, François	1	2	24–36
Smith, Thomas	3	6	55–100	Thomas, Flora	1	3	36–55
Francis, John	2	3	55–100	Hashpy, Nelson	1	2	36–55
Edward, Stephen	1	2	10–24	Bresky, Jacob	2	5	24–36
Smith, Diana	3	9	55–100	Duval, Gaston	1	8	24–36
Jonau, Antoine	8	14	24–36	Monnery, Mrs. A.	1	14	24–36
Dunn, James	2	5	36–55	Barnabé, J$^{n.}$ B$^{te.}$	3	5	36–55
Vembles, Jacob	1	9	36–55	Divivier, Louise	17	18	55–100
Bouté, François P.	1	4	24–36	Manuishon, Jacob	5	10	36–55
Elliot, Maria	2	3	10–24	Dupuis, Mrs.	4	7	36–55
Dauphin, Pelagie	3	11	36–55	Béguin, Agathe	2	4	36–55
Johnson, Anna	2	5	36–55	Tinsley, Nancy	7	11	24–36
Henriette	3	4	36–55	Augustin, Aimee	2	5	24–36
Antoine, Baptiste	1	6	24–36	Asquier, J$^{n.}$ Louis	3	10	55–100
Isidor, Telside	1	2	24–36	Escaut, Louison	4	14	55–100
Woods, George	1	4	36–55	Casson, Pulchérie	2	7	36–55
Johnson, William P.	1	3	24–36	Gaudin, Pelagie	1	3	55–100
Grammont, Jean	1	3	24–36	St. Amant, Louis	1	9	24–36
Boutimé, François	2	8	24–36	Gougis, Leda	2	7	24–36
Keating, Ann B.	1	3	10–24	Cabaret, Marguerite	2	4	24–36
Filié, Pierre	1	7	36–55	Craig, James	1	4	36–55
Champio, Victoire	2	13	55–100	Hamelin, Julien	1	10	36–55

LOUISIANA—Continued

Name	Slaves	Total	Age	Name	Slaves	Total	Age
Upper Suburbs of New Orleans—Cont.				Calvin, Pierre	1	9	100–
				S^t· Toëguo (?), Polenar	4	9	55–100
Laurent, Pierre	3	8	36–55	Chadirac, Miss Fany	2	8	36–55
Porée, Charles, Sen	2	11	55–100	Priet, Henriette	3	14	36–55
Formorette, Pierre	1	5	24–36	Valentin, Fran^s·	1	6	36–55
Dauphin, Catische	5	12	36–55	Girardeau, Bruno	1	5	24–36
Baque, Zelmire	2	5	36–55	Pelerin, Modeste	6	14	36–55
Grandmaison, Sanite	13	16	55–100	Borry, Ursin	1	10	36–55
Lioteau, Pierre	2	4	36–55	Perrauta, Savinien	4	8	36–55
Mallet, Augustin	1	6	55–100	Lathrope, Eulalie	6	14	36–55
Deale, Marie Thereze	3	10	36–55	Faury, Miss Antoinette	4	10	36–55
Miniche, Orphise	1	3	10–24	Populus, Ant	7	11	36–55
Borée, Paul	4	9	55–100	Marias, P^{rre}· Ch^s·	1	8	36–55
Macarty, Jason	4	8	55–100	Lebouh, Marie Victoire	5	8	36–55
Descuirs, Françoise	2	6	36–55	Garridel, Miss Fanny	3	6	24–36
Flemming, Jean	2	5	24–36	Lambert (?), Jean	3	9	24–36
Dimba (?), Phillips	4	7	36–55	Gencau, Rosette	4	6	55–100
Savoie, Françoise	2	12	55–100	St. Ourse, Oursine	3	9	36–55
Sterling, Rose	1	4	24–36	Dalby, Celeste	2	10	36–55
Fortier, Etienne	4	12	36–55	Angnant, Louise S^t·	1	4	36–55
Fleuriau, Mannette	2	5	55–100	Birot, Piron	1	12	36–55
Doriaucourt, Marianne	1	2	55–100	Bourdilles, Ursule	3	7	36–55
Bacchus, Eulalie	2	14	55–100	Cheval, Leandre	1	8	36–55
Percy, Héloise	5	11	55–100	Mortimer, Pepite	1	6	55–100
Apollon, Jaques	1	2	36–55	Borrys, L. A	4	14	36–55
Fabre, Françoise	5	8	36–55	Brion, A	5	15	36–55
Frère, Rosette	4	13	36–55	Savary, M	2	13	36–55
Pierce, George	5	6	36–55	Besson, A	1	9	24–36
Manice, Blaise	1	8	36–55	Bizotte, F^{se}·	1	6	24–36
Nourice, Marie	1	3	36–55	Anoreaux (?), S^{te}·	1	8	55–100
Lewis, Charlotte, Miss	1	3	36–55	Roviaux, Judique	4	13	24–36
S^t· Amand, Mme· Henriette	1	2	10–24	Hardouin, Eugenie	4	13	36–55
				Laroche, Victoire	1	8	36–55
Azur, Philip	3	4	55–100	Davier, Carmelite	6	14	55–100
Dasincourt, Maurice	1	10	36–55	Navard, Modeste	4	10	36–55
Lafitte, Guillaume	1	5	24–36	Purdom, Narcisse	3	12	36–55
Bumchartrean, Melle·H^{tte}·	2	10	36–55	Duforge, Cantrelle	11	18	55–100
Alexandre, Cata	1	4	24–36	Murat, Gaston	7	18	55–100
Ross, Edouard	1	3	36–55	Derbanne, Alcide	3	11	36–55
Victor, Joseph S^t·	2	3	36–55	Silva, François	1	7	36–55
Cavillier, Miss Catherine	5	9	36–55	Bonseigneur, J. B	1	7	24–36
Arnaud, Leandre	1	4	36–55	Pinta, Danatien	1	9	24–36
Bozan, Miss Annette	1	6	55–100	Gabriel, Sanon	4	11	36–55
Raby, Rodolph	4	5	36–55	Maurivez, D	4	12	36–55
Dubranel (Charles)	2	8	36–55	Danache, Ch^s·	5	15	55–100
Jolly, Urbain	1	6	36–55	Rachal, Lucien	5	14	36–55
Campanel, B	3	8	36–55	Auvergne, Philip	5	14	36–55
Legardeur, Charlot	1	10	55–100	Neuville, Ant	2	7	24–36
McCarty, Cécëe	32	38	24–36	Vivier, Ch^s·	4	15	55–100
Borel, Miss Melanie	4	8	36–55	Hopkins, Cicilia	2	6	24–36
Chan, Adolphe	2	5	10–24	Macarty, Brigite	3	5	24–36
Lavinsandier, Charlotte	5	11	36–55	Macoste, Widow Desire	6	17	24–36
Mondelly, Sanon	3	5	36–55	Christophe, Firmin	1	7	24–36
Andre, Mortimer	1	6	36–55	Pierron, Zelime	1	7	24–36
ArtheBuys, Gustave	1	5	55–100	Cavanard, Lolote	4	7	55–100
Guiramond, Barite	1	8	36–55	Perdron, Eloise	3	9	24–36
Mandeville, Judique	1	13	36–55	Ambroises, T. B	2	8	24–36

The Paradox of Freedom

LOUISIANA—Continued

Name	Slaves	Total	Age	Name	Slaves	Total	Age
Upper Suburbs of New Orleans—Cont.				Dubruny, Edouard	1	6	24–36
				Plantevigne, V.	7	15	100–
Ferron, Modeste	2	9	36–55	Macarty, H.	6	8	24–36
Pavis, André	7	17	55–100	Guiramand, R.	3	7	36–55
Toutant, Amelie	1	6	55–100	Seressole, L⁶.	3	12	36–55
Lafoste, Eglé	2	5	24–36	Arnaud, Mimie	3	10	36–55
Barbet, Celeste	3	7	36–55	Berrard, N. B.	3	6	10–24
Rochiblane, Rochebrune	7	10	36–55	Sennette, A.	1	8	36–55
Angelique, Widow	4	7	36–55	Duhart, Ant.	3	6	36–55
Gourge, Poupone	4	9	55–100	Joublotte, Sanite	3	13	36–55
Prauvert, Cephise	7	11	10–24	Laroche, Josephine	1	6	24–36
Barbe, M.	2	6	24–36	Garriques, Louise	2	14	100–
Vermillon (?), Eulalie	2	10	55–100	Maurice, Jeannette	1	5	24–36
Canfran, Misse	10	17	36–55	Anodin, M. B.	2	6	36–55
Dalez, Estelle	1	5	36–55	Joseph, Marie	2	10	36–55
Benite, Michel	3	12	36–55	Volunt, Mimite	10	21	55–100
Lefebre, Eugenie	9	16	36–55	Gayard, Poupone	1	8	36–55
Donaut, Henri	6	9	36–55	Gerard, Rosalie	1	8	36–55
Votaire, Maurice	2	13	36–55	Bertholl, Eugenie	3	9	24–36
Levasseur, Mirabin	4	10	36–55	Arnaud, Gertrude	5	7	55–100
Feron, Marie Dastuge	1	12	55–100	Thomas, Widow R.	5	11	36–55
Liautaud, Elize	4	14	36–55	Cordeviolle, Ignace	2	7	36–55
Claiborne, Augustin	1	9	24–36	Lusignan, Valsin	7	18	55–100
Baulos, Hortaire	4	11	55–100	Zenon, L⁸· A.	2	5	24–36
Montrelle, Mimie	2	6	36–55	Clair, Mar gᵗᵉ· Sᵗ·	3	17	55–100
Ganucheau, Annette	2	13	55–100	Mammes, Helene	1	7	100–
Laborde, Joseph	2	10	36–55	Cezain, Tymothée	1	12	55–100
Dafauchard, Louis	1	8	55–100	Frumence, F.	2	9	36–55
Ursin, Magnola	2	9	24–36	Clement, Cécille	3	11	55–100
Legardeur, Adrien	3	12	55–100	Sosthene, F.	1	2	36–55
Lerond, Henriette	7	16	55–100	Josse, Adelaide	7	17	55–100
Honoré, Elizabeth	1	8	55–100	Dorothe, Agathe	1	8	36–55
Casabon, Widow	3	10	55–100	Séverin, Apauline	2	11	55–100
Garcin, Iris	4	11	55–100	Zacharie, Euphrasie	3	11	55–100
Roche, Athalie	1	6	24–36	Prudent, Zenon	5	9	24–36
Salcas, Fillette	2	6	36–55	Athanase (Desiree)	11	21	55–100
Maurin, Cécé	5	9	36–55	Pascal, Isidore	1	4	24–36
Cornelius, Amelie	3	9	36–55	Urbain, Jeanne	9	20	55–100
Charbonnet, Celeste	3	11	55–100	Hildevert, Philip	1	4	24–36
Caillavette, Aristide	4	14	36–55	Maximin, Germain	4	10	55–100
Legardeur, Arthur	1	7	55–100	Nérée, Petronille	2	5	36–55
Lemoine, Bauvais	5	21	36–55	Silvere, Gervais	2	9	36–55
Torame, Charles	5	13	55–100	Isidore, Prosper	9	16	55–100
Magloiire, Donatien	2	7	55–100	Bajolaire, R. E.	8	19	55–100
Mathurin, Auguste	4	17	55–100	Perdreaux, Clovis	1	6	36–55
Sidney, Louis	1	12	55–100	Fernand, Gérard	1	9	24–36
Anathol, Cyprien	2	11	36–55	Raymond, Adolphe	4	10	24–36
Morrison, Chaˢ·	2	14	55–100	Brodequin, Marie	6	15	55–100
Pontier, Francˢ·	9	19	55–100	Dorfeuelle, Maria	2	6	55–100
Dunand, Chˢ·	4	14	55–100	Schmidt, J. R.	2	9	24–36
Perdreau, Maurice	4	15	55–100	Le Chaste, Aristide	1	5	24–36
Jouacinthe, Ralph	3	12	36–55	Joviolle, Henriette	5	15	36–55
Candide, Théo	1	10	24–36	Duperrier, Daniel	10	21	36–55
Pargon, Barth.	4	13	55–100	Vassant, Celestin	3	15	55–100
Ponponneau, Clara	5	17	36–55	Pavien, Louis	1	10	36–55
Leclair, Jos.	2	7	36–55	Tallarey, Eugenie	5	12	24–36
Gueringer, Ant.	5	16	55–100	Sᵗ· Amand, M. J.	5	10	24–36

LOUISIANA—*Continued*

Name	Slaves	Total	Age	Name	Slaves	Total	Age
Upper Suburbs of New Orleans—Cont.				Lapitto, Marie Rose	4	10	36–55
				Villard, Catiche	5	12	36–55
André, Magdelaine	1	6	36–55	Durand, Pierre	6	13	36–55
Tervallon, F	2	5	24–36	Toussine, Marie	5	14	36–55
Rousseau, Widow P	1	5	36–55	Dufrene, Jean L[s]	5	9	24–36
Dupré, Eulalie	2	5	36–55	Mirbel, Neuris	6	17	55–100
Baudin, Génevieve	2	9	55–100	Merieux, Agathe	3	11	24–36
Dupiton, Widow	3	10	55–100	Mangonna, Virginie	10	20	36–55
Lamotte, Wid	2	6	36–55	Fournier, Camille	5	13	36–55
Duharlet, Rose	4	12	36–55	Roques, Derchal	11	23	55–100
Guirot, Claudine	5	13	36–55	Wilfride, Caliste	4	14	24–36
Fusillier, F	1	4	55–100	Gayac, Anathole	2	9	55–100
Trevigne, Garçon	1	7	10–24	Raphael, Hyacinthe	8	10	24–36
Rouppon, Pierre	13	19	24–36	Maurille, Euphemie	1	4	24–36
Lataure, Severin	6	13	24–36	Rigobert, Geneviève	16	23	36–55
Gabrielle, Ch[a]	2	10	55–100	Gordien, Desire	3	15	55–100
Laire, M. Annette	4	11	55–100	Sabas, Olympe	1	7	24–36
Montreuille, Félicitié	1	3	55–100	Delphin, Ives	5	15	36–55
Roubioux, Rosette	3	15	55–100	Péprin, Aglae	4	12	55–100
Colvis, F	1	4	36–55	Urbain, Jeanne	1	4	36–55
Maurin, Bellone	4	7	55–100	Leufroy, John	6	14	36–55
Tessier, Sanite	8	14	55–100	Paulin, Alexis	1	6	24–36
Dauphin, Marie	7	14	55–100	Aplanas, Meonide	2	7	10–24
Audry, Seraphine	8	15	55–100	Lanoix, Rose	13	23	36–55
Lacroix, Pierre	2	15	55–100	Savary, Emile	8	16	55–100
Alexis, Eglée	1	9	55–100	Dersac, Ignace	4	14	55–100
St. Amand, Sophie	5	13	36–55	Bourgoin, Pierre	2	7	36–55
Dizt, Gustave	2	11	24–36	Lacoste, Pedronille	4	12	24–36
Lancellay, Jerome	1	2	36–55	Macédone, Thérèse	4	12	36–55
Imbert, Eleanore	1	5	36–55	Sévérin, Agathe	1	7	24–36
Dugunge, Amelie	3	10	55–100	Gaudry, Estelle	4	13	55–100
Lafferiere, B	2	9	36–55	Dudley, Alphonse	2	4	36–55
Lahoussey, Simon	3	11	24–36	Mothélose, Gabriel	11	25	55–100
Laborde, Uranie	1	7	36–55	Régio, Antoinette	2	6	24–36
Daw, Camille	1	7	55–100	Pargroux, Zénon	1	9	55–100
Borel, Ch[a]. L[s]	2	15	36–55	Raquet, Antoinette	8	18	55–100
Janvier, Ursin	1	6	24–36	Crosait, Lisida	2	4	24–36
Vivant, Louison	10	23	55–100	Hospineta, Julie	5	10	24–36
White, Palmin	1	4	36–55	Franck, Adelaide	1	2	24–36
Bourjon, André	3	16	55–100	Bronze, Judique	3	9	24–36
Chatelain, Carlos	4	15	36–55	Bajoliere, Edouard	7	14	36–55
Latapie, Poupone	2	10	55–100	Bruno, Edme	1	8	55–100
Magloire, Juliens	2	5	36–55	Roupelin, Osmin	2	7	36–55
Burthe, Benjamin	9	22	55–100	Cabaret, Joseph	9	12	55–100
Casbin, Pierre	3	8	24–36	Parvis, Cécille	7	10	24–36
Latiolet, Magdelaine	4	11	55–100	Lesenne, Adeline	1	3	24–36
Teyoval, Judique	5	9	36–55	Deléandre, Geneviève	3	11	55–100
Montarler, Désirée	9	20	55–100	Foureade, M	1	5	36–55
Blinval, Adolphe	3	6	36–55	Auguste Jé, François	6	12	36–55
Laborde, Eulalie	8	17	55–100	Wiltz, Victoire	1	5	36–55
Purdon, Avelina	1	4	24–36	Bullie, Widow C	3	13	36–55
Rahton (?), Marguerite	1	8	24–36	Ducraix, Marianne	1	5	36–55
Gofte, Adolphe	3	15	55–100	Amoth., Widow	2	6	100–
Espagnette, Marie Charlotte	3	10	36–55	Fromentin, Françoise	1	8	55–100
				Bierra, Rose	5	12	36–55
Baulet, Felicite	1	8	36–55	Guillaume, Toussaint	8	13	24–36
Mandeville, Eulalie	13	17	36–55	Lonny, Luce	2	11	24–36

LOUISIANA—*Continued*

Name	Slaves	Total	Age	Name	Slaves	Total	Age
Upper Suburbs of New Orleans—Cont.				Delille, Felix...........	2	5	24–36
				Séjour, Louis...........	3	10	36–55
Corbet, Julien...........	1	6	36–55	Bordeaux, Jeanne.......	2	8	36–55
Timpêgue, Louis A......	2	9	24–36	Renald, Mimie.........	1	7	55–100
Castillon, Victor........	9	19	55–100	Dubreiulle (?), Marie...	1	2	24–36
Sully (?), C.............	4	13	36–55	Castanette, Suzette.....	1	5	24–36
Lacoste, Constance......	3	12	36–55	Baptiste, Alexandrine....	1	5	55–100
Maurin, Poupone.......	3	11	24–36	Perodin, Wid...........	1	2	36–55
Seradin, Antoinette.....	4	10	24–36	Celestin, Widow........	4	13	55–100
Menas, Stephanie.......	1	2	10–24	Lefevre, Jacques........	3	5	55–100
Etienne, Widow.........	4	15	55–100	Miller, Caroline.........	13	14	24–36
Fortuné, Bonnie........	3	10	36–55	Larday, Fanchette......	5	15	55–100
Dupuy, Mgne·...........	11	15	24–36	Legon, Ariste...........	4	9	24–36
Legian, Fa·.............	1	3	24–36	Noël, Marie............	6	18	55–100
Gouengo, Irene.........	2	4	24–36	Armand, Modeste.......	1	4	24–36
Barbe, Miss............	3	4	10–24	Lagrange, Depit........	2	7	36–55
Rivert, Constce·.........	17	20	55–100	Duperain, M...........	6	15	36–55
D'Emart, Me·..........	2	8	36–55	Ménadier, Rose.........	6	9	24–36
Gayard, Sr·, Rd·.......	6	10	55–100	Gronge, Savarie........	4	14	36–55
DuBois, Eulalie.........	4	10	10–24	Blois, Edmond.........	2	8	24–36
Legoesler, Erasme.......	4	9	36–55	Mercier, Felix..........	2	9	36–55
Bluzeau, Pierre.........	1	5	36–55	Arsene, Désirée........	1	9	36–55
Maurin, Merandine.....	3	4	24–36	Evrard, Omer..........	4	9	36–55
Rosine, M..............	1	10	55–100	Flavien, Noël..........	1	4	24–36
Marcus, Eloise.........	2	12	55–100	Benoist, Ursin.........	4	10	36–55
Reytre, Jeannette.......	1	2	24–36	Bénétaud, Estelle......	4	11	36–55
Barbet, Cloë...........	2	3	10–24	Landrin, Mathieu......	6	20	55–100
Barbet, Delphine.......	1	2	10–24	Néréaud, Benjamin....	2	10	36–55
Borosée, Fred..........	2	4	55–100	Lueguarde, Bazile......	1	7	55–100
Cabaret, Lise..........	2	13	36–55	Martial, A.............	1	4	24–36
Valentin, François.....	4	15	24–36	Castiaux, Bern. (?)....	3	10	36–55
Lanna, Désire.........	1	4	24–36	Daquin, Silvain........	5	10	36–55
Deribon, Widow.......	1	6	36–55	Dalché, Louise.........	1	3	24–36
Tounence, Zizite.......	4	6	24–36	Chery, Chistée........	1	4	36–55
Boutin, Victorine......	3	10	24–36	Linguo, Alexandrine....	1	12	36–55
Guilbaut, Josephine....	1	6	55–100	Camisac, Résinette.....	1	5	24–36
Maurin, Charlotte.....	6	18	36–55	Laurent, Wid. St·.....	3	6	55–100
Montford, Heliopolis...	4	18	36–55	Lange, Florisse........	2	10	36–55
Hilaire, N. A..........	7	15	36–55	Vilmo, Wid. Celeste....	4	6	36–55
Bougère, Rosette......	2	11	36–55	Gautreau, B...........	2	9	55–100
Nicholas, Popote......	1	3	10–24	Caiblet, Ben...........	4	13	55–100
Borbeau, Noel.........	1	5	55–100	Ferraud, Celestin......	2	5	24–36
Forestal, Pauline......	2	6	24–36	Coussin, Marie........	2	8	36–55
Lagrange, Adelle......	3	7	55–100	Cheridan, Emiliana....	3	7	55–100
Foucher, Modeste.....	1	12	36–55	Jerreau, Théodule.....	6	14	36–55
Pradex, Rosiette......	2	9	36–55	Daboval, Jules.........	1	5	36–55
Duehemin, Aimée.....	2	4	36–55	Bernard, Guillme·.....	5	6	36–55
Cambre, Thérèse......	1	3	36–55	Saramon, Henriette....	1	7	100–
Montreuille, Monon....	3	7	36–55	Labruyère, Désirée....	1	13	55–100
Leon, Thos............	2	7	24–36	André, Judice.........	2	5	36–55
Mayero, Toussine.....	2	5	36–55	Poinset, Thémire......	5	13	36–55
Bertheno, Laïsse.......	2	8	24–36	Duchesne, Ferd........	1	3	24–36
D'Arneville, Pelagie....	4	16	100–	Montamar, V. A.......	1	5	55–100
Talhand, Pierre........	2	10	24–36	Piron, Emélie.........	2	8	36–55
Aubert, Elizabeth......	3	10	55–100	Cobet, Caliste.........	1	8	24–36
Gentilles, Lsc·.........	1	4	24–36	Bienaimee, B..........	1	7	36–55
Durel, Justine.........	1	6	36–55	Duraine, Jean.........	5	16	55–100

LOUISIANA—Continued

Name	Slaves	Total	Age	Name	Slaves	Total	Age
Upper Suburbs of New Orleans—Cont.				Jupiton, Manette	2	11	36–55
				Brunette, Betzi	2	11	36–55
Laroque, Ed	2	10	36–55	Romain, P	2	6	24–36
St. Amand, Pierre	17	23	24–36	Emillien, Fred	1	6	36–55
Torrès, Marie	1	7	24–36	Riviere, Celeste	1	10	24–36
Teo., Théodule	1	5	24–36	Chery, Ernest	2	11	36–55
Pouleau, Maurice	5	16	36–55	Jolly, Henriette	5	13	24–36
Sabin, Lolote	5	15	55–100	Benjouin, Charles	3	14	36–55
Spallino, Vallery	3	14	55–100	Sherburne, Maurice	6	10	24–36
Cuvillier, Barth	4	16	36–55	Cinet, Etienne	1	11	36–55
Bertholin, Paul	4	10	36–55	Rousseau, T	6	16	55–100
Brunette, Carmelite	2	10	55–100	Dupuy, Adelaide	10	12	24–36
Rebaudy, Ant	1	9	55–100	Boucher, A. G	6	17	55–100
Bertrand, Rosalie	6	13	55–100	Trevigne, Auguste	5	15	24–36
Populus, Maurice	2	8	55–100	Laignel, Jean	3	11	36–55
Morange, Silvie	3	14	55–100	Brunel, Philip	15	30	55–100
Jolivet, Poupone	5	13	36–55	Courcelle, Mirtille	8	15	36–55
Damien, Alfred	1	11	36–55	Delerry, A	3	12	55–100
Raboul, Ant	2	5	10–24	Boisseau, Manon	8	16	55–100
Macarty, Silvanie	4	13	36–55	Dalon, Auguste	3	10	36–55
Montanno, Albert	3	12	10–24	Donet, Ernest	6	14	36–55
Sacriste, Juliette	9	21	36–55	Snaer, Ambroise	1	7	36–55
Toussaint, Lse	1	5	24–36	Saulet, Jacques	7	17	55–100
Druillet, A	2	10	36–55	Joubert, Mathilde	3	9	55–100
Berger, Théodule	2	12	24–36	Jolly, Ant	3	6	36–55
Montassa, Emille	3	5	36–55	Marie, St. Jean	1	5	36–55
Guéringer, Ernestine	2	9	55–100	Roviaux, Gaston	1	6	24–36
Pioreau, Laurt	13	24	55–100	Beaurpeau, Noël	1	5	36–55
Mauret, Louis	2	8	24–36	Beaurocher, Fredk	5	11	24–36
Carrière, Noël	2	4	36–55	Cheval, Louise P	8	14	55–100
Lacroix, Pierre	1	8	24–36	Cheval, Léandre P	1	8	36–55
Girardy, Wid	4	11	36–55	Abejan, Jos	1	6	36–55
Lébastien, Jean	3	8	24–36	Blanche, Lse. Mia	2	7	36–55
Philistin, Wid	1	10	55–100	Bondellie, Bonne	2	7	24–36
Monnet, Pierre	4	9	24–36	Allegre, Rosiette	1	6	55–100
Despres, Manette	9	20	36–55	Almazor, Mary	3	12	55–100
Henry, Marie R	1	7	55–100	Noël Bel., Ant	3	8	36–55
Renaud, Jacques	4	13	36–55	Bellotte, Pognone	3	10	36–55
Perrin, Rosette	3	14	55–100	Constantin, H	2	4	55–100
Bouny, Marie	4	11	36–55	Dupain, Miss C	1	5	24–36
Gambal, Ant	6	16	36–55	Passement, A. B	2	11	55–100
Legouvée, Marie Lse	1	10	55–100	Poyroux, Miss Ména	2	4	10–24
Barjon (?), D	8	17	55–100	Prieur, Sanite	1	7	36–55
Duvallon, Wid	10	19	55–100	Raphael, Wid	3	4	36–55
Lacoste, Catiche	1	4	24–36	Simon, L	2	7	24–36
Many, Marie	1	5	10–24	Thomassin, B	5	8	55–100
Leroy, Malthilde	1	14	55–100	Pinta, C. B	4	7	24–36
Mayet, Henriette	4	14	36–55	Pilon, Fs	1	7	24–36
Seraphin, Aglaë	1	2	10–24	Baquet, Fs	1	4	24–36
Thiot, Zelie	8	12	36–55	Leroux, Wid	1	8	55–100
Danoranero, D. V	5	17	55–100	Ternien, Miss	1	8	24–36
Boutin, Leon	5	12	24–36	Cornier, L	4	5	24–36
Gautreaux, Geneviève	4	14	36–55	Joublotte, Sanite	2	5	24–36
Noffre, Helene	4	17	55–100	Peyproux, Aug	1	9	55–100
Morcau, Cecile	10	20	36–55	Larien (?), J	9	16	36–55
Conand, Amede	1	4	36–55	Chanal, Martin	2	11	36–55
Durneville, André	2	10	24–36	Belisaire, Severin	5	11	55–100
Lafitte, Siméon	1	9	36–55				

MAINE

Name	Slaves	Total	Age	Name	Slaves	Total	Age
KENNEBEC COUNTY							
Albion							
Tolbut, Abram	1	2	55-100				

MARYLAND

Name	Slaves	Total	Age	Name	Slaves	Total	Age
ALLEGANY COUNTY				Keys, Moses	1	3	10-24
Peney, Bazle	5	6	55-100	Lee, Sarah	1	17	36-55
Isaac, Black	1	3	36-55	Pully, Jenny	2	3	36-55
				Robinson, George	3	4	55-100
ANNE ARUNDEL COUNTY				Stewart, Ellick	1	3	55-100
Barnett, Richard	3	7	36-55				
Gambrill, Orang	2	7	55-100	*City of Annapolis*			
Hoxton, Rd.	1	6	24-36	Tidd, James	1	3	36-55
Scosey, Ann	2	6	36-55	Thomas, Rose	1	5	36-55
Holland, Sophy	2	4	24-36	Williams, Valentine	1	2	55-100
Johnson, Stephen	1	4	36-55	Watkins, Stephen	1	6	36-55
Harwood of Thos., Richd.	39	42	36-55				
Jacobs, Geo.	3	7	36-55	**CITY OF BALTIMORE**			
Dorsey, Nichs.	2	4	24-36	*First Ward*			
Anderson, Saml.	1	3	24-36	Smith, James	1	5	36-55
Dorsey, Vacheal	1	5	24-36	Sims, Henry	2	3	55-100
Meed, M.	17	18	100-	Anderson, Saml.	3	4	24-36
Peach, Joseph	1	11	24-36	Barnett, Stephen	1	5	24-36
Wells, George	5	6	10-24	Thomas, Seth	1	6	24-36
Waters, Wilson	3	4	36-55	Banks, Benjamin	1	5	55-100
Chase, Richard	15	23	55-100	Burk, Thos.	1	3	36-55
Manidier, Henry	17	25	55-100	*Second Ward*			
Wells, George	5	7	55-100	Talbot, Benjamin	1	6	36-55
Barnes, Henry	3	8	36-55	Robinson, Christena	1	4	24-36
Bryan, Peter	1	8	36-55	Johnston, Nicholas	2	5	36-55
Fleetwood, Jane	1	3	24-36	Robinson, Zachariah	1	4	24-36
Gray, Ephraim	2	6	24-36	Buly, Cirus	6	8	36-55
Johnson, Thomas	2	7	36-55	Phillips, Charles	8	9	24-36
Lee, Charles	2	5	36-55	Elliott, David	1	6	24-36
Leichlightner, Philips	11	16	24-36	Clark, James	1	5	36-55
Mann, Pero	1	7	55-100	Cain, Elenor	1	3	55-100
Purdy, Alice	2	3	36-55				
Ringgold, Edward	3	4	36-55	*Third Ward*			
Richardson, James	4	5	36-55	Wallace, Charles	1	11	55-100
Ringgold, Jacob	3	7	36-55	Harden, James	1	3	24-36
Stephens, Sophia	1	5	36-55	Cooper, Thomas	2	5	36-55
Tunks, John	1	12	55-100	Smallwood, Richard	2	7	24-36
Wilson, Richard	1	8	24-36	Ridgley, Charlotte	1	4	55-100
Young, Walter	1	2	24-36	Fleetwood, Thomas	1	3	36-55
Talable, Adam	2	4	55-100	Green, Peter	1	5	36-55
Williams, Abraham	2	3	36-55	Smith, Rebecca	1	6	24-36
Giles, Rachel	1	3	36-55	Nelson, Sarah	1	2	36-55
Dorsey, Jemima	3	4	55-100	Harriss, Cecelia	1	3	55-100
Sim, Robert	2	4	24-36	Cooper, Benjamin	1	3	24-36
Wells, Daniel	1	4	55-100	Fisher, Levin	3	4	24-36
Brashears, Gilbert	1	4	24-36	Smith, Perry	1	3	24-36
Brown, Joseph	1	2	55-100	Dixson, Perry	1	3	36-55
Folks, Charity	3	13	55-100				
Franklin, York	3	4	36-55	*Fourth Ward*			
Gantt, Jenny	1	5	55-100	Williams, Nathaniel	1	8	36-55
Harris, Thomas	1	5	55-100	Castle, William	1	5	10-24
Ireland, Mary	5	7	55-100	Grason, Elizabeth	1	7	55-100

MARYLAND—Continued

Name	Slaves	Total	Age	Name	Slaves	Total	Age
Fourth Ward—Cont.				Johnson, Job	2	4	36–55
Strupping, Priscilla	1	3	55–100	Parker, Jas.	2	7	36–55
Blake, Vincent	1	9	36–55	Tile, Hannah	1	4	55–100
Presco, James	1	8	55–100	Johnson, Richard	1	4	36–55
Hollowday, Ann	1	4	55–100	Carrol, Peter	1	4	55–100
Hollowday, James	2	9	55–100	Smith, Perry	1	6	24–36
				Gamble, Peter	2	5	24–36
Fifth Ward				Wilson, Wm.	1	2	24–36
Allen, William	1	3	24–36	Calhoon, Peter	1	3	24–36
Henson, Emory	1	5	24–36	Anderson, James	1	6	55–100
				Howard, James	2	3	24–36
Sixth Ward				Hains, Thomas	1	3	24–36
Lewis, John	5	8	24–36	Mitchel, Ann E.	2	3	55–100
				Steward, Stephen	2	3	36–55
Seventh Ward				Fuller, Clm.	1	2	36–55
Gage, Dina	1	2	55–100	Primrose, Geo.	1	4	36–55
Robinson, Sarah	1	3	36–55				
Ridgely, Loyed	4	5	24–36	*First Collection District*			
Sprigg, Margaret	1	5	36–55	Morris, John B.	2	3	55–100
Pinkney, William	1	4	24–36	Smith, Andrew	2	10	24–36
				Hall, Ephraim	1	16	55–100
Ninth Ward				Bishop, John	1	4	55–100
Griffin, Maria	1	8	36–55	Whiper, Luke	1	7	36–55
Sherrick, John F.	1	2	55–100	Wallace, Bazil	1	2	55–100
Scott, Margaret	1	2	55–100	Williams, Hannah	1	7	36–55
Thomson, Lewis	1	11	55–100				
Hicks, Emanuel	1	6	55–100	*Second Collection District*			
Butler, Basil	1	6	55–100	Smith, Lindy	1	3	24–36
Clark, Nancy	1	8	24–36	Smith, Joseph	1	3	24–36
Askins, Christ.	1	9	36–55	Hooper, Samuel	1	4	55–100
Kill, David	1	4	24–36	Wicks, Jacob	2	11	36–55
West, Charles	5	8	36–55	Saddler, Perry	1	2	36–55
Howard, Edward	1	6	24–36	Jones, Flora	5	6	55–100
Dailey, Richard	1	4	24–36	Hicks, Rosetta	1	2	36–55
Gilles, Ann	1	7	36–55	Bently, Amey	1	5	36–55
Curtis, Henrey	1	9	24–36	Dorsey, Harry	1	4	55–100
Limas, Brudame	1	4	55–100	Brown, Lucy Ann	1	2	55–100
McCay, Robert	1	4	36–55	Preston, Pompey	11	12	24–36
Smith, Edward	1	4	24–36	Brown, Abraham	2	7	36–55
Miller, Henrey	3	6	24–36	Procter, Charlotte	4	6	36–55
Shivers, Widow	1	3	55–100				
Noal, John	1	8	24–36	*Third Collection District*			
Johnston, Charles	4	7	24–36	Jackson, Jeremiah	1	4	36–55
Young, Benj.	1	4	36–55	Clark, James	1	7	36–55
Hall, Peter	1	4	36–55				
Ridgeley, Pompey	6	9	36–55	*Fourth Collection District*			
Scott, Charlotte	1	3	24–36	Johnson, Henry	2	3	10–24
Gray, David	3	5	36–55	Carey, John	5	8	36–55
Griffin, Alexander	9	10	55–100	Brooks, Edward	2	5	36–55
Victoire, Mary A.	1	3	36–55	Matthews, Alexander	1	3	24–36
Gibson, Jacob	1	4	24–36	Cook, Henry	3	4	36–55
Boston, John	1	2	24–36	Walker, Hannah	4	9	24–36
Bradley, Samuel	3	6	36–55	Brown, G.	2	12	36–55
Johnston, Gustus	1	3	24–36	Mickle, Anthony	1	3	10–24
Williams, Dinah	2	8	24–36	Neibours, Elizabeth	6	9	24–36
Johnson, Robert	5	6	24–36	Owings, Sarah	1	4	55–100
Stephens, Littleton	1	6	36–55	Brown, Isaac	1	6	36–55
Snowden, Peter	2	5	24–36	Jackson, Tobias	2	3	24–36

MARYLAND—Continued

Name	Slaves	Total	Age	Name	Slaves	Total	Age
Sixth Collection District				Butler, Tom............	1	3	55-100
Govens, Jane (Coled) ...	1	4	55-100	Parker, Jno............	2	4	24-36
Fenton, James (Coled) ..	1	9	36-55	Gordan, Rebecca........	1	4	36-55
				Thomas, Mikeal.........	1	6	24-36
Seventh Collection District				Holler, James...........	1	5	55-100
Patterson, William......	9	10	36-55	Hawkins, James.........	2	5	24-36
Price, Robert...........	2	4	10-24	Johnston, Abram........	1	10	36-55
				Glover, Joseph..........	2	8	36-55
CALVERT COUNTY				Jonas, Spencer..........	1	14	55-100
Hardesty, Samuel.......	3	6	36-55	Share, Moses...........	3	4	36-55
Skinner, Sarah..........	13	16	36-55	Johnston, James........	3	5	55-100
Denton, Susan..........	1	3	100-	Shields, George.........	1	5	36-55
Jones, Mathew..........	2	4	24-36	Collins, Henry..........	3	4	24-36
Cooper, Henson.........	3	4	24-36	Brown, Robt...........	1	7	24-36
Quill, Benjamin.........	1	4	10-24	Ferl, John.............	1	6	100-
Evans, Sarah...........	1	6	36-55				
				CHARLES COUNTY			
CAROLINE COUNTY				*Durham District*			
Upper District No. 1				Washington, Ignatius....	7	11	36-55
Flamer, William.........	2	9	24-36	Greer, James...........	3	5	55-100
Downs, Benjamin........	1	4	36-55	Skinner, Clement.......	5	10	36-55
Kennady, David.........	2	5	24-36	Queen, Charles.........	2	10	36-55
Fritchett, Samuel........	2	7	24-36	Butler, Hezekiah........	3	9	24-36
Green, Christopher......	5	6	55-100	Bond, Jane............	1	2	36-55
Dawson, Saml..........	2	5	24-36	Ray, Abednago.........	1	4	36-55
				Johnson, Samuel........	3	4	36-55
Middle District No. 2				Carnel, Benjamin.......	1	3	55-100
Baynard, Clarricy, Negro	1	5	36-55				
Turner, Aaron, Negro...	2	3	24-36	*Allens Fresh District*			
Clarke, Edward, Negro..	1	3	24-36	Butler, Henry (?).......	1	10	10-24 ?
Boon, Jacob, Negro.....	1	3	24-36	Collins, William........	1	5	10-24 ?
Red, Stephen, Negro....	4	5	55-100	Hill, Elizabeth.........	3	5	10-24
Holland, William, Negro.	1	4	10-24	Shurborn, Judy.........	2	4	10-24
Murry, Amy, Negro.....	2	8	36-55	Hall, Betsey...........	1	13	55-100
Sutton, Reason, Negro ..	3	4	24-36	Hungerford, John.......	29	30	36-55
Rich, Daniel, Negro.....	2	8	36-55	Butler, Charles.........	6	16	24-36
Register, Peter, Negro...	3	6	55-100	Hawkins, Ignatius......	1	4	55-100
Blake, James, Negro....	2	3	10-24	Smith, William.........	7	8	55-100
Lockerman, Jno.........	1	4	24-36	Dodson, Elizabeth......	1	7	36-55
Green, Levi, Negro......	1	5	24-36	Moore, John...........	7	8	24-36
Rotter, Cidney, Negro...	1	5	36-55	Day, Henry............	3	4	55-100
Hollyday, Richard.......	1	2	24-36	Butler, Ignatius.........	2	3	36-55
Jacobs, Mooder, Negro..	1	3	55-100	Procter, Thomas........	1	3	24-36
Hubbard, Daniel, Negro .	4	5	24-36	Morrison, Mary.........	1	5	55-100
Bachus, John, Negro....	2	4	55-100				
Willgon, Francis, Negro .	1	4	24-36	DORCHESTER COUNTY			
Chase, Hannah, Negro...	1	4	24-36	*Election District No. 1*			
Stokley, Peter, Negro...	8	9	36-55	Callender, Patrick......	1	4	55-100
Haskins, Edward, Negro.	3	5	55-100	Robinson, Rachel.......	1	2	55-100
Bowdle, Jacob, Negro...	3	5	36-55				
West, Jeremiah, Negro..	2	5	36-55	*Election District No. 2*			
				New Market			
CECIL COUNTY				Cornish, Peter..........	6	8	36-55
First Election District				Chamberlain, Esther....	4	6	36-55
Anderson, Ben..........	1	6	36-55	Hubbard, Peter.........	1	6	36-55
Gans, Clem............	1	4	24-36	Murray, Prince.........	1	3	24-36
Mercer, George.........	1	3	36-55	Washington, John.......	3	7	24-36

MARYLAND—Continued

Name	Slaves	Total	Age	Name	Slaves	Total	Age
New Market—Cont.				Cephas, Ibby	3	6	55-100
Dye, Mary	2	3	24-36	Woolford, Nelly	6	7	24-36
Woolford, Adam	1	3	36-55	Young, James, sen.	1	3	55-100
Dennis, Casidy	1	9	55-100	Pinder, Stephen	3	6	10-24
Lloyd, Barthenia	3	4	36-55	Cephas, Joseph	1	4	55-100
Smith, Richard	1	4	55-100	Kennard, Nathan	4	5	?
Standley, Jeffrey	2	3	24-36	Smallwood, William	5	7	24-36
Dickerson, Richard	1	7	24-36	Roberts, Edmond	6	7	55-100
Johnson, Abram	1	2	36-55	Scye, Tom	3	4	55-100
Mathews, Diana	1	2	36-55	Quinton, Jacob	1	5	55-100
Warfield, Thomas	4	5	36-55	Johnson of Knot, George	2	7	55-100
Atkinson, Joe	2	4	24-36	Holiday, Thomas	3	6	55-100
Hardcastle, Simon	7	8	36-55	Thompson, Daniel	1	6	24-36
Jenkins, Rosanne	1	3	55-100	Coleman, Daniel	1	5	55-100
Green, Leah	3	7	55-100	Sampson, James	2	7	24-36
Thompson, Jim	6	7	55-100				
Moor, Richard	1	3	24-36	*Election District No. 4*			
Thompson, Eliza	4	5	55-100	Travers, Thomas	3	4	55-100
Smallwood, Ezekiel	5	6	55-100	Gainby, Jacob	3	7	24-36
Kier, Joshua	4	5	36-55	Stanley, James	1	3	36-55
Dockins, Peter	4	5	36-55	Ellis, Thomas	3	6	36-55
Henry, Mahala	1	3	10-24	Saunders, Rose	1	3	10-24
Banks, William	1	4	55-100	Dickson, Jacob	5	9	55-100
Coleman, George	3	4	24-36	Keene, Phebe	3	4	24-36
Cornish, Joshua	1	7	36-55	Woodland, Cilas	1	3	36-55
Darby, John	1	4	55-100	Manokin, Charles	2	10	36-55
Johnson, William	1	2	55-100	Bright, Fountain	3	6	24-36
Horsman, Eliza	1	6	36-55	Keene, Draper	1	8	36-55
Dillen, Lucy	1	4	36-55	Slater, Robert	2	4	55-100
Beard, Charles	3	6	36-55	Colson, Drew	1	3	55-100
Standley, Robert	1	8	55-100	Thomas, Elizabeth	3	9	24-36
Young, Adam	3	5	36-55	Henry, James	1	2	24-36
Neal, Thomas	1	2	100-	Keene, Lydia	2	9	55-100
Sullivan, Minty	2	4	55-100	Bright, Moses	1	7	24-36
Parker, George	4	6	36-55	Travers, Francis	1	11	36-55
Pearce, Nancy	4	5	55-100	Barnes, Henry	1	3	36-55
Hall, Joseph	1	5	55-100	Brohawn, Rhoda	1	11	36-55
Nace, Jesse	2	4	24-36	Cornish, Any	1	6	24-36
Smart, Richard	1	3	55-100	Pattison, Samuel	5	10	36-55
Fisher, Isaac	1	5	24-36	Willson, Jacob	5	6	36-55
Pharrow, Sarah	1	2	24-36	Edwards, Charles	2	7	55-100
Mitchell, Ralph	7	8	36-55	Travers, Dinah	1	7	36-55
Brooks, Dennis	1	6	55-100				
Cephas, Sophia	1	5	36-55	*Election District No. 5*			
Tilghman, James	1	4	36-55	Dier, Margaret	5	7	36-55
Woolford, Jeffrey	1	6	55-100				
Waters, John	4	6	24-36	*Election District No. 6*			
Lee, Harry	1	11	55-100	Ross, Henry	3	6	36-55
Crier, James	1	6	36-55				
Jolly, David	1	4	24-36	*Election District No. 7*			
Atkinson, Tom	4	12	36-55	Addison, Jacob	6	7	36-55
Parker, Isaac	1	2	36-55	Woolford, Ezekiel	1	3	55-100
Knotter, Hewit	1	2	36-55				
Camper, Charles	1	3	55-100	*Election District No. 8*			
Nicols, James	2	10	36-55	Brooks, Curtis	2	6	24-36
Banup, Ansy	5	6	24-36	Macer, Jacob	3	4	36-55
Lockerman, Prissa	1	2	36-55	Pendleton, Lovey	1	5	36-55

MARYLAND—Continued

Name	Slaves	Total	Age	Name	Slaves	Total	Age
Elec. Dist. No. 8—Cont.				*District No. 2*			
Bennet, Manuel	2	15	36–55	*Frederick Town*			
Lee, David	1	3	36–55	Hillman, Aaron	1	3	36–55
Bird, Toby	5	7	36–55	Mitchell, Casandra	2	4	24–36
Blake, Nancy	7	9	36–55	Boone, David	3	6	55–100
Quash, Alsy	3	6	55–100	Hawkins, Aaron	2	3	55–100
Johns, Sarah	3	4	55–100	Gaines, William	2	3	24–36
Smith, Allen	4	8	55–100	Gray, Joseph	1	2	36–55
Brown, John	1	12	55–100	Harper, Alley	1	3	24–36
Macer, Henry	5	6	55–100	Hammond, Samuel	1	7	36–55
Lee, Levin	3	10	55–100	Pratt, Solomon	2	7	55–100
Lee, Nero	1	3	55–100	Carr, Isaac	1	7	55–100
Nutter, Nancy	1	3	24–36	Gordon, Thomas	1	4	36–55
Johnson, Charles	2	4	36–55	Dorsey, Harriet	1	4	36–55
Hooper, John	1	9	55–100	Davis, Francis	2	3	24–36
Green, Allen	9	10	36–55	Schneevilly, Edward	8	12	36–55
Ross, Priscilla	8	9	36–55	Devan, William	1	4	10–24
Cook, Robert	1	8	36–55	Hill, Anthony	1	2	55–100
Nicols, Moses	3	6	36–55	Leake, Peter	1	5	55–100
Stanley, Nathan	3	4	36–55	Roberson, Esther	2	3	55–100
Nunum, John	6	9	36–55	Noland, Elisabeth	1	5	24–36
Kennedy, Jeremiah	1	3	10–24				
Stanley, Charles	2	4	10–24	*District No. 4*			
Blake, James	4	12	36–55	Groce, Sampson	1	2	55–100
Cromwell, Shadrack	2	9	24–36				
Bruffit, Aaron	4	5	55–100	*Lewiston*			
Griffith, Sophia	1	5	24–36	McKinney, Patsy	2	8	55–100
Barnes, Scippio	2	7	55–100				
				District No. 8			
FREDERICK COUNTY				*Woodsboro*			
District No. 1				Wicks, Jane	1	3	55–100
Green, Ceaser	2	7	55–100	Key, Sarah	1	5	24–36
Ingland, Arch	1	4	24–36	Murdok, Aaron	1	6	24–36
Rollings, Henry	1	6	24–36	Roberts, Mary	3	7	55–100
Caleb, Joseph	1	8	36–55	Todd, Upton	2	3	24–36
Waters, Jacob	2	3	55–100	Jackson, John	1	3	36–55
Duffin, Bassil	2	4	10–24				
Berrit, William	1	5	36–55	*Uniontown*			
Combs, Jenne	1	3	36–55	Moales, Lloyd	1	2	36–55
Norriss, Thos.	2	8	24–36	Stoner, John, Jnr.	2	13	24–36
Ford, Nathan	1	8	10–24				
Dawkins, Henry	1	2	36–55	HARFORD COUNTY			
Armstrong, John	1	7	55–100	Hipkins, Charles G.	2	6	36–55
Carroll, Polly	3	6	36–55	Carlile, Washington	3	7	36–55
Rollings, Mary	1	4	24–36	More, Samuel	3	5	36–55
				Hendley, John D.	8	9	36–55
District No. 9				Smith, Samuel W.	6	12	10–24
Stuart, Nathan	1	9	36–55	Hall, William B.	17	22	36–55
Proctor, Michael	1	8	36–55	Banks, James	5	6	36–55
Coats, George	2	3	55–100	Amos, Henry	1	3	55–100
Thorn, Frederick	1	6	24–36	Scott, Susan	1	2	36–55
Davis, Eli	2	5	36–55	Amos, Thomas	4	5	55–100
Valentine, Amos	3	5	36–55	Witmore, Abraham	1	8	36–55
Ogle, Samuel	1	5	24–36				
				KENT COUNTY			
District No. 3				Ward, Letty	3	4	55–100
Caywood, Abraham	1	6	36–55	Anderson, John B. H.	6	7	10–24

MARYLAND—*Continued*

Name	Slaves	Total	Age	Name	Slaves	Total	Age
Kent County—*Cont.*				**Talbot County**			
Byram, Edward	1	2	55–100	Scott, Philomon	1	3	36–55
Tilghman, Susan	3	4	36–55	Dorrell, Wm.	5	7	24–36
Nicols, Moses	1	3	55–100	Tilghman, Ann	6	11	55–100
Fountain, Joe	1	6	36–55	Cornish, Tilly	2	6	36–55
Bordley, Lisbon	2	4	55–100	Stokely, Ezekiel	1	3	36–55
Warner, Harry	3	7	36–55	Kelly, Joseph	4	5	100–
Warren, David	1	3	55–100	Hall, Ara (?)	2	4	24–36
Wickes, Peter	2	10	55–100	Banning, Jerry	2	6	100–
Hollyday, William	6	7	36–55	Tripp, Dick	4	11	24–36
Cuff, Thomas	3	6	55–100	Dove, James	2	3	55–100
Rogers, Eliza	1	4	24–36	Mackey, Susan	1	3	36–55
Boyer, Lucy	10	16	36–55	Tripp, Bill	1	5	36–55
Boyer, Philip	2	5	36–55	Potter, Grace	1	11	55–100
Hynson, Joseph	1	6	36–55	Goldsborough, Jane	2	5	100–
Forman, Ezekiel	1	3	24–36	Sinclair, Joe	3	4	24–36
Woodland, Emory	3	4	10–24	Hawkins, Tom	1	2	55–100
Thomas, Moses	1	4	10–24	Nelson, Parris	1	7	36–55
Anderson, Henry	1	11	55–100	Thomas, James	1	2	55–100
Richardson, Moses	1	6	55–100	Brown, Sarah	1	3	55–100
Leger, Philis	2	5	55–100	Hopkins, Violett	3	6	24–36
Jones, James	1	4	24–36	Calloway, Philip	1	6	55–100
Pearce, Maria	1	4	55–100	Madden, Crecy	2	5	36–55
Rogers, Samuel	2	5	55–100	Brion, Aron	3	6	55–100
Smith, Elijah	4	5	24–36	Williams, Isaac	1	4	24–36
Mechanick, James	1	7	24–36	Potter, Nero	3	4	36–55
Constable, John	13	14	10–24	Pipes, Peter	1	5	55–100
Palmer, Priscilla	1	6	36–55	Bantom, Joe	1	3	55–100
Hynson, Charles	2	7	36–55	Cuff, Horris	5	6	24–36
Anderson, Thomas	3	4	36–55	Jone (June ?)	1	2	36–55
Philips, George	1	7	24–36	Tender, Dembey	3	7	24–36
Taylor, Stepney	1	3	36–55	Warner, Cain	1	2	24–36
Rasin, William	1	6	36–55	Donsbuary, Scipio	2	3	24–36
Lamb, Rachel	1	5	55–100	Tillison, Henry	1	2	24–36
Massey, James Taes (?)	1	3	36–55	Summers, Henry	1	4	55–100
Dudley, Perigrine	6	7	36–55	Porter, John	4	5	24–36
Simmons, Stephen	1	4	36–55	Harriss, James	2	3	55–100
Mason, Isaac	2	5	36–55	Cox, Jenny	1	6	100–
Anderson, Richard	5	6	55–100	Hill, Sarah Fox	4	5	36–55
Mason, William	1	7	36–55	Mackey, Ross	2	5	36–55
Mann, Abraham	2	7	55–100	Caulk, James	3	5	36–55
Chambers, William	1	6	55–100	Banning, Ned	2	5	36–55
Graves, Milky	1	3	24–36	Bantom, Henry	7	8	36–55
Black, Jacob	1	5	55–100	Benson, Solomon	4	13	10–24
Harding, Stephen	2	8	36–55	Homes, Henry	4	6	24–36
Wilson, William	1	2	36–55	Murry, Samuel	4	5	36–55
Doman, Daniel, Jr.	2	9	24–36	Harriss, Leven	4	5	36–55
Jones, Thomas	1	2	55–100	Bantom, Lilly	2	5	36–55
Hollingsworth, Benjamin	4	5	55–100	Mobry, Jacob	3	5	10–24
Bassle, William	7	8	24–36	Brooks, George	3	6	36–55
Harris, Jacob	4	10	55–100	Cuff, Sally	2	3	55–100
Moffett, Samuel	2	5	55–100	Brooks, George	5	6	36–55
Hackett, Clem	2	4	36–55	Downes, Edward	5	7	36–55
Wilson, William	2	3	55–100	Brooks, David	7	8	55–100
Williams, Sarah	1	2	55–100	Clash, Wrighton	1	2	?
Grey, Susan	1	3	24–36	Thomas, Thomas	3	4	24–36
Wilson, Trump	1	2	36–55	Williams, Charles	1	5	10–24

MARYLAND—Continued

Name	Slaves	Total	Age	Name	Slaves	Total	Age
Talbot County—*Cont.*				Sturges, William	1	10	55-100
King, Daniel	2	6	36-55	Purnell, Nimrod	5	11	36-55
Barrott, Samuel	2	4	55-100	Turpin, Elijah	4	5	55-100
Commons, Stephen	1	3	10-24	Robins, Rhoda	1	5	36-55
Nicols, Philip	2	10	24-36	Messick, Draper	2	3	55-100
Burley, Richard	2	6	36-55	Townsend, Sophia	4	5	55-100
				Stevenson, Arthur	1	4	55-100
Washington County				Collins, Levin	1	2	24-36
Long, Catherine	4	7	55-100	Hammond, Jacob	3	5	55-100
Rideout, Charles	3	7	24-36	Hammond, Isaac	3	8	55-100
Harris, Jno	1	5	24-36	Norris, Hessy	1	8	55-100
Howard, Lewis	1	6	36-55	Purnell, Josiah	3	4	36-55
Negro Phil	1	3	36-55	Morris, Minty	1	9	10-24
Cranford, James	3	6	24-36	Purnell, Amos	1	3	55-100
McHenry Neg (Negro?)	2	4	36-55	Bowen, William	1	4	36-55
				Marshall, Caleb	6	11	36-55
Worcester County				Miller, Ann	5	7	36-55
Mills, Robert	1	9	36-55	Rackliffe, Draper	1	6	55-100
Parks, Henry	1	2	55-100	Stevenson, Jacob	2	4	55-100
Dennis, Rose	8	10	55-100	Johnson, Peter	3	4	36-55
Riggin, Joseph	3	6	36-55	Massy, Hannah	1	2	36-55
Long, Lydia	2	4	55-100	Rockliffe, Jesse	2	3	55-100
Layfield, Henry	1	8	36-55	Brevard, Isaac	4	5	24-36
Bayly, York	5	7	24-36	Massy, Peter	1	5	24-36
Long, Stephen	1	7	36-55	Pitts, Lydia	1	2	55-100
Mills, James	1	7	36-55	Gray, Luke	7	9	55-100
Purnell, Levin	1	5	36-55	Holland, Sarah	1	4	24-36
Tarpin, Titus	5	6	55-100	Pitts, Milby	1	3	55-100
Ross, Robert	1	4	10-24	Selby, James	1	3	55-100
White, Jasper	1	6	36-55	Whittington, Ephraim	2	3	36-55
Jenkins, Isaac	1	5	55-100	Handy, Richard	1	5	36-55
Purnell, Minadab	5	7	36-55	Johnson, Daniel	1	3	36-55
Purnell, Lucretia	2	4	36-55	Johnson, Rachel	2	4	55-100
Purnell, Peter	8	10	55-100	Dashiell, Jacob	1	6	36-55
Purnell, Sacker	5	8	36-55	Sturges, Jessee	3	4	55-100
Purnell, Peter	8	9	24-36	Fookes, Easther	2	5	36-55

MISSISSIPPI

Name	Slaves	Total	Age	Name	Slaves	Total	Age
				Martin, Samuel	1	7	36-55
Adams County				Simpson, Gloster	2	5	36-55
Winn, George	16	17	55-100	Harris, Hardy	1	6	55-100
City of Natchez				Holly, Christopher	3	5	55-100
Carey, Robert M	2	4	10-24	Moore, David	5	6	24-36
Miller, Jas	5	12	24-36				
Battles, Harriet	1	3	24-36	**Hancock County**			
Gilson, Sam	5	6	10-24	Asmard, Charles, Senior	3	4	100-
				Benoit, Benard, Senior	6	8	55-100
Claiborne County				Perkins, William P	17	18	10-24
Willis, Mary	1	5	36-55				
Bell, Henry	4	5	55-100	**Warren County**			
Butler, Hanibal	1	5	36-55	Miller, Elisha	1	3	24-36

MISSOURI

Name	Slaves	Total	Age	Name	Slaves	Total	Age
Franklin County				**St. Charles County**			
Rogers, Lewis	1	8	36-55	Buet, Louise	1	7	36-55

MISSOURI—Continued

Name	Slaves	Total	Age	Name	Slaves	Total	Age
PERRY COUNTY				NEW MADRID COUNTY			
Dickson, Joseph	3	4	36–55	Scarret, Sally	1	1	36–55

NEW HAMPSHIRE

Name	Slaves	Total	Age	Name	Slaves	Total	Age
ROCKINGHAM COUNTY				Cutler, Rufus	1	5	55–100
Portsmouth				Cutler, Rufus T.	1	5	24–36
Whipple, Joshua	1	2	24–36				

NEW JERSEY

Name	Slaves	Total	Age	Name	Slaves	Total	Age
BERGEN COUNTY				MONMOUTH COUNTY			
Pompton Township				*Middletown*			
Green, Sizar	1	7	24–36	Holmes, Hercules	1	3	36–55
				Holmes, Isaac	1	4	36–55
ESSEX COUNTY				*Freehold*			
Elizabeth Township				Wolley, Nean	3	5	24–36
Stout, Silas	2	8	24–36				
Van Horn, Richard	1	4	24–36	MORRIS COUNTY			
Dunn, John	1	3	36–55	*Township of Morris*			
Messalier, Henry	1	6	24–36	Cutler, Jacob	2	4	36–55
Township of Acquackonconk				*Jefferson Township Chatham*			
Sip, Thomas	1	2	36–55	Linn, Cato	1	3	36–55
BURLINGTON COUNTY				HUNTERDON COUNTY			
Township of Nottingham				*Trenton*			
Morris, Thomas	2	5	24–36	Hulicks, Jas	1	3	36–55
				Hutchins, Perry	2	3	36–55
Township of Springfield				*Laurence*			
Bowan, Robert	1	3	24–36	Duncan, Phillis	1	4	24–36

NEW YORK

Name	Slaves	Total	Age	Name	Slaves	Total	Age
MONTGOMERY COUNTY				*Thompson Street*			
Minden				Jones, John	2	5	55–100
Wilson, Thomas	3	4	24–36	Walker, Benjamin	1	2	24–36
Jackson, Abraham	1	2	10–24	Scott, John	3	6	55–100
				Kip, Sara	1	2	24–36
Canajoharie Village				Thomas, Charles	4	7	24–36
Cockburn, Elizabeth	1	2	10–24	Oatfield, Andrew	4	6	10–24
Hawn, William	1	4	36–55	Low, Abraham	1	3	36–55
Livingston, Dian	2	6	55–100				
Lando, Henry	4	5	24–36	PUTNAM COUNTY			
Clady, Robert	3	5	24–36	*Patterson*			
Day, William	3	4	36–55	Townsend, Joseph	2	3	55–100
Florida				TIOGA COUNTY			
Freeman, Joseph	1	3	24–36	*Catharine*			
				Rice, Tobias, Col.	1	2	10–24
				Hall, James, Col.	1	3	10–24
NEW YORK CITY							
King Street				WASHINGTON COUNTY			
Ritchinson, William	1	2	10–24	*Cambridge*			
				Hoase, Sunn	1	3	55–100

NORTH CAROLINA

Name	Slaves	Total	Age	Name	Slaves	Total	Age
ANSON COUNTY				Hornablow, Marey	2	6	36-55
Jones, Thomas	3	12	36-55	Iredell, Jeffrey	1	7	100-
				How, Lucey	3	4	55-100
BEAUFORT COUNTY				Littlejohn, John	1	4	24-36
Washington				Johnson, Gustavus A.	4	12	36-55
Anderson, Hull (?)	4	8	36-55	Bozman, James	1	2	36-55
Bonner, Jos	2	3	36-55				
Brown, Edme	1	2	36-55	**CRAVEN COUNTY**			
Walker, Betsy	3	7	10-24	Stanly, James G.	10	11	55-100
Moore, Church	2	4	24-36	Green, James Y.	4	8	36-55
Brown, John	2	4	36-55	Hollister, Thomas	1	7	36-55
Newton, Clarrissa	4	9	24-36	Street, Delia	2	3	55-100
Allen, Abram M.	1	7	24-36				
Moore, Eli	3	7	24-36	*Town of Newbern*			
Rose, Easter (?)	1	3	36-55	Mumford, Donum	10	27	55-100
				Austin, Anne	1	2	36-55
North Creek Town				Warrick, Brister	8	9	36-55
Walker, Thos.	2	4	55-100	Green, John R.	6	10	36-55
Bowen, Thos.	2	4	36-55	Lisbon, Matilda	2	4	10-24
				Warrick, Brister	1	6	55-100
BERTIE COUNTY				Garrett, Jane	1	4	55-100
James, Mary	1	3	36-55	Stanly, John S.	18	22	24-36
James, Sally	1	2	36-55	Stanly, John C.	14	26	55-100
Hill, Penelope	3	6	55-100				
Ash, Jane	5	6	55-100	**CUMBERLAND COUNTY**			
Tutle, Willie	1	2	55-100	*(The Division West Side Cape Fear)*			
BLADEN COUNTY				*Bones Creek Dist.*			
Bowen, Gooden E.	44	45	36-55				
Spendlove, Eliza	1	6	36-55	MacIver, Wining (?)	1	5	36-55
Spendlove, Molsy	3	5	24-36	Jackson, Polly	1	2	36-55
Blanks, Michael	1	2	24-36				
Allen, Samuel	4	5	24-36	*East Side of Cape Fear*			
Spendlove, Ann	1	9	24-36	Hadley, Bella	1	2	55-100
Smith, Catharine	1	11	24-36	Artis, Lucretia	1	2	36-55
				Tutte (Tutle), William	1	4	55-100
BRUNSWICK COUNTY				Jordan, Judy	1	2	55-100
Potter, John A.	4	8	24-36	Alvis, Esther	3	4	36-55
McKenzie, Jimboy (?)	2	4	55-100	Munroe, Daniel	1	2	10-24
				Wood, John	4	8	24-36
CAMDEN COUNTY				Freeman, Sally	1	2	10-24
Griffin, Samuel	1	5	100-				
Spelmon, Thomas	4	5	24-36	*Town of Fayetteville*			
Spelmon, Owen	2	5	36-55	Grimes, Thomas	1	4	36-55
				Hammonds, Elsey	5	9	55-100
CASWELL COUNTY				Dennis, Phillis	4	5	36-55
Day, Thomas	2	6	24-36	Revels, Margaret	2	9	55-100
Jones, Mary	1	2	24-36	Mallett, Betty	1	5	36-55
Wilson, John (Free Col'd)	4	11	24-36	Dunn, James	3	4	36-55
Caswell, Allen	3	4	36-55	Ragland, George W.	1	7	36-55
Worsham, James	1	4	55-100	Mallett, Charles	36	37	10-24
				Chester, Lott	2	7	24-36
CHATHAM COUNTY							
Town of Pittsboro				**DAVIDSON COUNTY**			
Anderson, Jerry	1	3	55-100	Hatcher, Tabitha	1	5	55-100
				Cain, Jesse	1	5	24-36
CHOWAN COUNTY				David, Sarah	1	3	36-55
Town of Edenton							
Grean, Ritchard M.	4	8	24-36				

The Paradox of Freedom

NORTH CAROLINA—Continued

Name	Slaves	Total	Age	Name	Slaves	Total	Age
EDGECOMB COUNTY				Jones, Pompey.........	2	3	55–100
District No. 1				Hammons, Olive.......	1	7	36–55
Tarborough							
Scott, Elizabeth........	3	4	24–36	HERTFORD COUNTY			
Thompson, William.....	5	6	24–36	Melton, Meede.........	2	8	55–100
				Mandley, Penelope.....	1	7	36–55
District No. 15				Renalds, Jeston........	2	3	24–36
Morgan, Henry.........	1	5	24–36	Jordan, Lewis.........	3	4	10–24
				Roberts, David........	2	6	36–55
FRANKLIN COUNTY				Renalds, Jeston........	1	3	24–36
Louisburg—Perrie's Dist.				Boon, David..........	1	5	55–100
Armstrong, John.......	1	2	36–55				
Williams, Jeremiah.....	3	4	24–36	LENOIR COUNTY			
				Dutton, Nellie.........	1	3	55–100
Pearce's Dist.							
Tucker, Robert.........	2	6	36–55	MARTIN COUNTY			
				Crichlon, John.........	24	25	36–55
Bledsoe's Dist.				James, Larry..........	1	5	24–36
Charles, Thomas'es.....	6	7	36–55	James, Martha........	1	3	55–100
Foster's Dist.				NASH COUNTY			
Mitchel, John..........	3	6	36–55	Revill, Humphrey......	14	18	36–55
Edward's Dist.				NORTHAMPTON COUNTY			
Blacknel, Thomas......	7	15	36–55	Wheeler, Anthony.....	2	3	36–55
Hicks, Benjamin.......	4	5	24–36	Boone, Ruthy.........	1	2	55–100
Alford's Dist.				NEW HANOVER COUNTY			
Mitchel, Milbry........	2	6	36–55	Ware, George.........	1	8	36–55
				Mosely, Wanely (?)....	1	6	36–55
Dunn's Dist.				Cruise (?), Mary.......	3	8	36–55
Evans, Rosetta........	2	7	24–36	Larington, Simon......	1	1	36–55
				Bazadeir, Phillis.......	1	5	36–55
GATES COUNTY				Buffo, William.........	1	2	10–24
Martin, Jottro (?)......	1	6	36–55	Pajay, Lewis..........	4	5	10–24
Cuff, Nisom...........	1	2	36–55	Walker, John..........	44	45	36–55
Hansford, Thomas.....	1	4	55–100	Hazell, Roger.........	5	9	10–24
				Campbell, James.......	2	4	24–36
GRANVILLE COUNTY				Sampson, Henry	5	9	36–55
(*North Regiment*)							
Fain, Jacob...........	1	8	55–100	ONSLOW COUNTY			
Cousins, Nelson........	1	8	36–55	Loomiss, Caesar.......	2	3	55–100
				Jarmen, Benjamin.....	5	7	55–100
HALIFAX COUNTY				Tatom, Sally..........	1	12	36–55
Jourdan, John.........	1	6	24–36				
Richardson, Absalom...	1	11	36–55	ORANGE COUNTY			
				(*North Dist.*)			
District of North Carolina				Hartgrove, Fed........	3	4	36–55
2nd Regiment District				Peters, Lucy..........	1	2	55–100
Howard, Miles.........	2	9	24–36				
Jones, Tabitha.........	1	2	24–36	PASQUOTANK COUNTY			
Mills, Wesley..........	2	3	24–36	Morris, Will., Senr. (of			
Worrel, Lucy..........	1	3	10–24	Colr................	2	10	10–24
Taylor, Sally..........	1	4	55–100	Price, Aaron (of Colr.)...	1	13	24–36
Johnson, Amy.........	3	5	24–36	Harvey, Alfred (of Colr.)	1	2	24–36
Taylor, Peggy.........	1	9	55–100				
Cain, Malissa..........	1	3	24–36	PERQUIMANS			
Curtis, Ann...........	3	8	36–55	Bogue, Dorothy (of Colr.)	1	5	36–55

NORTH CAROLINA—Continued

Name	Slaves	Total	Age	Name	Slaves	Total	Age
PERQUIMANS—Cont.				WAKE COUNTY			
Randol, Charlotte (of Colr.)	1	9	36–55	Jones, Allen	6	10	24–36
				Burwell, Pope	1	2	36–55
Winslow, Mills (of Colr.)	7	8	36–55	Jones, Charles	3	4	55–100
Robins, Jacobs (of Colr.)	1	6	36–55	Malon, John (Colored)	3	5	36–55
Overton, Judith (of Colr.)	1	3	10–24	Green, Samuel	7	10	36–55
Nixon, Charlotte (of Colr.)	2	3	55–100	Scott, John D	4	6	55–100
Wadkins, James (of Colr.)	4	6	55–100	*St. Maries District*			
Wadkins, Nathaniel (of Colr.)	4	5	36–55	Wilson, Marsh	1	3	24–36
				Simms, Nancy	1	2	100–
Overton, Winney (of Colr.)	1	4	36–55	Evins, Abigail	4	8	10–24
				Smith, William	2	7	10–24
Modlin, Nancy (of Colr.)	1	6	55–100	Dunn, John	5	6	10–24
Overton, Penny (of Colr.)	2	5	36–55	Snellings, Silvans	2	21	36–55
Overton, Levina (of Colr.)	1	5	24–36	Taylor, Prudy	1	2	36–55
Overton, Theny (of Colr.)	1	5	10–24	Holmes, William	3	8	36–55
Overton, Nelly (of Colr.)	1	3	10–24	Seawell, Phil	5	6	36–55
Winslow, Rose (of Colr.)	3	4	55–100	Woodward, Sally	1	2	24–36
White, Luke (of Colr.)	5	6	36–55	Maxwell, Polly	4	11	24–36
Lawrence, Sampson (of Colr.)	7	9	55–100	WARREN COUNTY			
				Cosey, William	1	8	55–100
PITT COUNTY				Day, John	1	3	55–100
Brown, Med	3	4	24–36	Holmes, Stephen	1	4	55–100
				Burt, Jacob	1	5	55–100
RICHMOND COUNTY				Evans, Isaac	1	7	24–36
Mask, Pleasant M	8	9	10–24	Evans, Tabby	1	6	55–100
				Evans, Matthew	5	7	55–100
ROBESON COUNTY				Green, Thomas	1	7	55–100
Lowrie, James	5	14	55–100	WASHINGTON COUNTY			
				Boston, Nancy	1	3	55–100
SAMPSON COUNTY							
Pope, West	1	8	10–24	WAYNE COUNTY			
				Burnet, Joel	3	7	24–36
STOKES COUNTY							
Shepperd, William	1	5	55–100	WILKES COUNTY			
Mason, Ralph	1	3	55–100	Anthony, Negro	1	4	36–55

OHIO

Name	Slaves	Total	Age				
WARREN COUNTY							
Wayne Township							
Ferguson, Charles, Col	6	9	24–36				

PENNSYLVANIA

Name	Slaves	Total	Age	Name	Slaves	Total	Age
ALLEGHENY COUNTY				Cary, William	2	6	36–55
Borough of Allegheny Town				Lewis, Gideon	3	6	36–55
				Merrit, Prince	4	5	10–24
Jackson, Powell	1	2	24–36	Riley, Jacob	5	6	10–24
				Campbell, Samuel	3	5	24–36
BUCKS COUNTY				Campbell, Jesse	1	3	10–24
Paxson, Jos	2	6	24–36				
Lambert, William	4	7	24–36	CHESTER COUNTY			
Moort, Jane	3	5	24–36	*East Nottingham Township*			
Barry, Robert	3	6	24–36				
Harris, Robert	3	6	24–36	Green, Stacey	3	5	55–100
Brown, Peter	2	6	100–				

PENNSYLVANIA—Continued

Name	Slaves	Total	Age	Name	Slaves	Total	Age
DELAWARE COUNTY				*Philadelphia*			
Aston				Gallaway, Isaac........	1	3	10–24
Gibson, Charles.......	1	6	24–36				
				YORK COUNTY			
FRANKLIN COUNTY				*York Borough*			
Montgomery Township				Goodridge, William.....	1	9	10–24
Maxwell, William.......	1	5	10–24	Hartman, Charles.......	2	5	55–100
Cuff, Sampson.........	1	7	24–36				
Blackburn, John........	1	5	24–36	*Spring Garden Township*			
				Johnston, John.........	1	5	10–24
LANCASTER COUNTY							
Conestoga Township							
Robison, Solomon......	2	6	55–100				

RHODE ISLAND

	Slaves	Total	Age		Slaves	Total	Age
Providence				Ray, John.............	1	3	55–100
Treadwell, Philip.......	1	5	10–24	Hamlin, Wyllys........	1	2	24–36

SOUTH CAROLINA

Name	Slaves	Total	Age	Name	Slaves	Total	Age
ABBEVILLE COUNTY				*Christ Church*			
Davis, Ezekiel.........	1	3	36–55	Legare, John D........	12	17	?
Payne, Jerry...........	2	3	24–36	Venning, Robert.......	30	32	10–24
				Venning, Nicholas, Junr..	7	9	24–36
BEAUFORT COUNTY							
Brown, Alexander......	15	17	55–100	**ST. JAMES SANTEE**			
Houston, Ann..........	1	9	36–55	Aiken, Thomas........	7	15	55–100
St. Luke's Parish				*City of Charleston*			
Bing, Gordon..........	1	8	24–36	*Ward No. 1*			
Cuthbert, Sarah........	3	4	55–100	Parsons, Emmey.......	2	5	24–36
				Veree, Christiana......	1	4	24–36
St. Peter's Parish				James, Henry..........	4	7	24–36
Powers, Mack..........	1	3	36–55	Cain, John............	6	14	55–100
				Spencer, Amey........	1	5	24–36
BERKELEY				Wilkinson, Scipio......	2	10	100–
St. John's				Duncan, Rebecca......	3	17	24–36
Eady, Daniel...........	7	8	100–	Leach (Seach?), Sarah...	7	29	36–55
				Fell, Eleanor..........	3	6	24–36
				Walker, Samuel........	24	25	36–55
St. Stephen's				Ward, Fortune........	8	9	36–55
Blute, Hester..........	1	5	55–100	Best, Amaretta........	12	13	10–24
Davis, Samuel.........	1	4	55–100	Holman, Susan........	1	8	24–36
Freeman, Jacob........	4	8	55–100	Huger, Sarah..........	1	3	55–100
Wilson, Jenny.........	16	21	55–100	Vanderhorst, Ebenezer..	1	2	10–24
				Morrison, Pollidore.....	14	15	24–36
St. Thomas & St. Dennis				Brown, Moses.........	2	4	10–24
Collins, Robert........	11	20	55–100	Mitchell, Jane.........	15	25	24–36
Collins, Jonathan......	3	6	55–100	See, Edward..........	2	12	24–36
Collins, William.......	1	4	24–36	Mitchell, Abigail.......	1	6	55–100
Capers, Thomas F......	47	48	36–55	Ricard, Sally..........	1	2	24–36
Cumbo, Susan.........	6	9	36–55	Inglis, Eleanor........	1	5	10–24
Fowler, Stanhope......	5	13	36–55	Gardner, Jack.........	4	8	36–55
Givins, Abraham.......	1	3	55–100	Wilson, George........	3	9	24–36
Smith, Robert.........	8	9	55–100	Prereze, François......	6	7	24–36
Waring, Daniel J.......	41	42	55–100	Rogers, Mary..........	1	5	55–100
Warren, Juba..........	8	9	55–100	Monies, Jane..........	1	6	36–55

SOUTH CAROLINA—*Continued*

Name	Slaves	Total	Age	Name	Slaves	Total	Age
Ward No. 2				Creighton, Grace	8	14	36–55
Ingles, Thomas	11	17	36–55	Roteraux, Mary Ann	1	2	10–24
Douglass, Margaret	7	8	24–36	Fenwick, Mary	11	14	10–24
Cotton, Eleanor	12	13	24–36	Harper, Jack	3	4	55–100
Bush, Adam	7	9	36–55	Ferguson, Sarah	8	9	55–100
Chisolm, William	1	6	10–24	Pere, Emele	8	11	24–36
Sommers, Rosetta	3	4	24–36	Mills, Sally	5	10	24–36
Elliott, Daphne	2	3	24–36	Wilson, Dolly	5	6	55–100
Holmes, Sarah	12	17	24–36	Allen, Martha	12	13	24–36
Brown, Peter	3	12	24–36	Martin, Elizabeth	8	10	55–100
Savage, Silvey	4	14	55–100	Crawley, Frank	13	15	55–100
Lloyd, Dina	6	10	24–36	White, Betsy	1	2	24–36
Sorie, François	1	4	10–24	Lindsay, Eliza	2	3	10–24
Brown, John	3	6	24–36	Evans, Charlotte	3	6	10–24
May, Ann	3	8	24–36	Bremar, Rebecca	3	8	10–24
Cooper, William	2	10	36–55	Cooper, Cecelia	3	6	24–36
Keeter, Mary	6	7	10–24	Simmons, Affey	6	7	10–24
Graves, Mindas (?)	5	6	24–36	Cochran, Eliza	1	3	36–55
Townsend, Effey	1	9	24–36	Simpson, Smart (?)	8	19	55–100
Middleton, Sally	16	22	55–100	Brisbane, Flora	1	3	24–36
Flagg, Diana	8	13	55–100	Burnie, Lydia	41	75	55–100
Whaley, Rose	1	4	55–100	Salarey, Mary St.	2	4	36–55
Mushington (?), William	1	7	36–55	Holton, Elizabeth	8	14	24–36
Hannahan, Hetty	4	12	24–36	Jackson, Rachel	1	2	24–36
Williamson, Maria	1	4	55–100	Gardner, Mary	1	2	10–24
Huger, Benjamin T.	8	22	36–55	Barquet, Barbara	9	22	24–36
Duprat, Hannah	2	7	36–55	Brown, Darcus	1	5	55–100
Mathews, George	13	18	55–100	Cookson, Josephine	2	8	55–100
Watson, Lydia	3	5	55–100	Gibson, Rachel	2	9	55–100
Gordon, James	2	11	36–55	Belanto, Philette	2	4	55–100
Irving, Moses	4	6	36–55	Creighton, Maria	1	5	55–100
Wright, Casar	14	15	10–24	Weston, Lydia	1	3	24–36
See, John	22	28	24–36	Jenkins, Patty	1	7	36–55
Wale, Gilbert	2	5	10–24	Drayton, Jane	17	18	55–100
Dwight, Eliza	3	5	10–24	Whitehart, Peggy	10	11	55–100
Johnston, Camilla	16	21	24–36	Hinson, Elizabeth	15	25	10–24
Smith, Eleanor	1	2	10–24	Hinson, Mary	1	2	10–24
Dubois, Rose	2	4	55–100	LaFayette, Naselye	5	6	36–55
Carado, Mary	1	4	55–100	Florin, Ann	1	6	24–36
Nelson, Peggy	1	2	24–36	LaPorte, Ellen	1	6	24–36
Cooper, Thomas J.	2	5	10–24	Turner, Sarah	1	3	10–24
McBeath, John	3	7	10–24	Johnston, Catherine	2	9	55–100
Pennington, Martha	3	5	10–24	Lockwood, Henrietta	1	5	24–36
Seymour, William W.	1	7	24–36	DeSage, Mary	2	5	55–100
				Duncan, Phillis	4	10	36–55
Ward No. 3				Richards, Mary	2	7	24–36
Batemen, Edward	12	14	36–55	Lloyd, Emma	4	5	24–36
DeSiesseline, Kitty	9	14	36–55	Smith, Mary	2	6	36–55
Cliss (?), Sarah	1	2	24–36	Wells, Rachel	3	4	55–100
Smith, Linda	5	8	36–55	Newton, Betsey	5	11	24–36
Brown, Jane	8	14	10–24	Brown, Malcolm	5	10	24–36
Campbell, Samuel	1	2	10–24	Lewis, Polly	1	3	24–36
LeCombe, Joseph	5	6	10–24	Jenkins, Harriot	1	7	36–55
French, Hester	2	3	10–24	Fuller, Rosetta	5	11	36–55
Ball, Sylvia	1	4	24–36	Careu, Jenny	1	2	55–100
Jackson, Ellen	3	8	24–36	Eason, James	3	14	36–55
Buckle, Maria	2	13	55–100	Levy, Affey	6	13	55–100

SOUTH CAROLINA—*Continued*

Name	Slaves	Total	Age	Name	Slaves	Total	Age
Ward No. 3—Cont.				King, Crecia	3	4	36–55
Johnson, Sophia	9	10	55–100	Freeman, Mary	3	11	24–36
McKenzie, Patience	1	10	55–100	Groning, Simons	9	14	10–24
Brown, Molly	7	9	55–100	Townsend, Tenah	2	3	55–100
Cornwell, Emele L.	3	9	55–100	Smith, Cyrus	2	7	10–24
Legare, Doily	14	15	24–36	Garden, Martha	2	8	24–36
Bourneau, Adel	2	5	55–100	North, Priscilla	3	4	10–24
Trenne, E.	2	6	55–100	Lord, Maria	1	9	36–55
Gregorie, Adam	6	9	24–36	Taylor, Martha	3	8	10–24
Le Marr, Charles	5	8	36–55	Harrison, John	4	8	24–36
Simmons, William	2	3	36–55	Cole, Hagar	1	13	36–55
Armou, Louisa	3	6	55–100	Jones, Jehu, Jr.	1	11	55–100
Bemar, Mary	5	6	55–100	Mitchell, Ann	6	16	55–100
Watts, Mary	10	11	55–100	Savage, Henrietta	1	2	10–24
Singleton, Michl.	1	2	55–100	Hollowell, Richard	8	19	55–100
Smith, Carlos	4	12	24–36	Blanchard, Charlotte	1	7	24–36
Wilson, Susan	1	3	24–36	Harrison, James	1	4	24–36
Cox, Julia	3	10	24–36	Hannahan, Hetty	2	7	24–36
Ward, Rose	5	11	55–100	Liston, Henry	2	5	24–36
Mathews, John B.	6	17	24–36	McCall, Samuel	10	13	24–36
Stevenson, Lydia	1	10	55–100	Lesessue, Betsey	4	5	10–24
Aiken, Bella	4	9	36–55	Maxwell, James	2	6	24–36
Magwood, Sandy	12	19	24–36	Veree, Elizabeth	2	4	24–36
Simons, Mary	1	5	24–36	White, Zanza	7	8	24–36
Mathews, Peter	1	7	24–36	Roberts, Venus	2	3	36–55
Jacobs, Catherine	8	33	55–100	Smith, John	3	4	24–36
Thorn, Rebecca	3	9	36–55	Jones, Benjamin	1	4	24–36
				Johnston, Sarah	1	6	24–36
Ward No. 4				Simonds, Clarissa	6	8	55–100
Barquet, Barbara	9	22	24–36	Lawrence, Benjamin	8	18	10–24
Miller, Sylvia	1	6	24–36	Lee, Grace	3	7	55–100
Langlois, Antonet	1	6	55–100	Peronneau, Datey	6	15	55–100
Francis, John	5	12	24–36	Rivers, Stephen	5	7	24–36
Johnston, James D.	6	14	24–36	Barron, Mary	1	5	36–55
Walker, Betsey	1	4	36–55	Houlton, Mary	4	11	10–24
Boyce, Rachel	6	7	10–24	Mathews, Henry B.	4	7	24–36
Lee, Elsey	2	3	24–36	De Soures, Harriot	1	4	36–55
Canter, Julietta	14	16	36–55	Ezzart, Julia	2	5	24–36
Weston, Samuel	1	5	24–36	Shaw, Sarah	6	10	24–36
Humphreys, Joseph	3	18	36–55	Cameron, Rose	4	6	36–55
Mathews, Mary	8	15	10–24	Esuard, Jane	2	4	36–55
Roberts, Cater (?)	2	3	55–100	Lewis, John	2	12	36–55
Manuel, Nancy	2	4	36–55	Beale, Sally	7	15	24–36
Brown, Ann	4	5	36–55	Cummings, James	1	5	24–36
Cole, Hagar	2	13	10–24	Berry, Mary Ann	5	6	55–100
McCall, Eliza	2	3	24–36	Philips, Ann	1	2	24–36
Ives, Sophia	1	7	36–55	White, Mary	1	3	24–36
LeSessene, F.	1	4	55–100	Badger, Portia	1	2	24–36
Smith, Angeline	12	14	36–55	Legg, William	3	7	24–36
Holmes, Maria	5	6	55–100	Turner, Philide	5	8	55–100
Barelle, Joseph	1	3	10–24	James, Emma	6	11	55–100
Pinckney, E.	7	10	36–55	Duverse, Priscilla	7	13	36–55
Drayton, Susan	2	6	55–100	Downes, Jane	4	8	10–24
Wilson, Nancy	1	4	36–55	Bridgewood, Catherine	6	15	55–100
Mitchell, Ann	10	15	55–100	Cochran, Thomas	11	14	10–24
Small, Thomas	3	8	24–36	Dart, Bella	2	6	24–36
Ross, F.	7	8	55–100	Anderson, Catherine	12	16	24–36

The Paradox of Freedom

SOUTH CAROLINA—Continued

Name	Slaves	Total	Age	Name	Slaves	Total	Age
Ward No. 4—Cont.				Smith, Simon	5	9	10–24
Kinloch, Richmond	2	6	36–55	North, Mary Ann	6	9	10–24
Francis, John	3	15	55–100	Michel, Assent	4	13	55–100
Lawrence, George	9	10	55–100	Wilson, Sylvia	10	16	36–55
Burseir, C. E.	7	8	24–36	Belmore, Ann	10	14	36–55
Yeadon, Mary	11	14	24–36	Pope, Mary Ann	10	15	36–55
Tucker, Samuel	6	10	36–55	Payne, Mary	10	15	55–100
Shaw, Sarah	10	14	24–36	Cripps, Peggy	10	11	36–55
Izard, Isabella	1	5	24–36	Simons, Amelia	3	6	55–100
Ashe, Abraham	4	13	55–100	Filbin, Flora	11	17	55–100
Shaw, Margaret	3	4	55–100	Wilkinson, Lucy	3	11	55–100
Moultrie, Roxana	1	7	24–36	Creighton, Diana	11	14	55–100
Young, C.	1	3	36–55	Keith, Henry	7	17	24–36
Cypress, Susan	5	9	36–55	Busby, Mary	10	15	24–36
				Pogson, Mary	9	14	24–36
CHARLESTON NECK				Buckmyer, Isaac	3	8	24–36
Vesey, Susan	10	13	36–55	Holmes, Cato	6	15	55–100
Robinson, Betty	10	13	36–55	Talley, Jane	11	16	55–100
Righton, Mary	12	15	36–55	Furman, Mary	1	8	36–55
Johnston, Sophia	6	12	55–100	Service, James	2	6	55–100
Deas, Mary	12	13	24–36	Edward, Jacob	10	16	36–55
Brown, Polly	10	14	24–36	Dewees, Sarah	1	5	55–100
Connor, Daffney	1	13	55–100	Weston, John	1	11	36–55
Inglesby, Betty	11	12	36–55	De Reif, Richard	5	16	36–55
Ball, Nat	7	14	55–100	Brown, James	5	13	36–55
Dill, Antony	13	14	55–100	Drayton, Hector	5	16	24–36
Jervey, John	14	16	36–55	Dereif, Susan A.	5	10	24–36
Bell, James	11	15	55–100	Jamieson, John	2	6	36–55
Jackson, Martha	11	15	55–100	Cross, Phoebe	11	13	55–100
Johnston, Hager	11	15	55–100	Pohl, Joe	12	15	24–36
Franklin, Eliza	10	15	55–100	Edwards, Henry	3	6	55–100
Stiemetz, Baron	1	6	55–100	Lee, Elizabeth	12	14	10–24
Cordes, Rebecca	10	13	36–55	Harleston, Nancy	4	9	36–55
Mott, Jacob	1	15	36–55	Holmes, Hagar	5	11	55–100
Clarke, James R.	12	15	24–36	Mickey, Nelly	1	7	36–55
Wilson, Mary	5	14	36–55	Edwards, James	10	13	36–55
McIntosh, Betsey	10	16	55–100	Camer, Susan	4	14	24–36
Williams, Ann	11	15	36–55	Bateman, Isaac	5	7	55–100
Delancy, Nancy	2	5	24–36	Gregory, Mary	6	11	36–55
Baxter, Amos	1	7	36–55	Pillotte, Mary C.	14	17	55–100
Syllable, Castille	6	7	36–55	Kelly, Margaret	8	10	24–36
Solomon, Hannah	20	26	24–36	Langlois, Antonet	2	7	36–55
Turpin, Jane	1	12	24–36	Plumet, Juliet	3	4	36–55
Sasportes, Catherine	5	13	24–36	Gregory, Eleanor	2	6	36–55
Glen, Rachel	12	14	10–24	Mitchell, Crissy	4	7	36–55
Parsons, Hannah	6	7	24–36	Gowan, Thomas	10	12	55–100
Gilchrist, Martha	11	14	(?)	Crummell, Margaret	1	11	55–100
Cochran, Samuel	6	14	36–55	Antonie, Belser	4	8	36–55
Jones, Jeremiah	10	14	36–55	Legare, Susan	10	15	36–55
Mathews, Henry	6	12	36–55	Henry, Charles	2	7	24–36
McCleod, Cato	2	12	55–100	Mayrant, Diana	8	9	10–24
Mathews, Jane	14	17	36–55	Strobel, Thomas	13	15	55–100
Bercier, Charles	10	14	36–55	Wilson, Ann	13	16	24–36
Bolard, Eliza	5	15	24–36	Wall, Peter	13	18	24–36
Liles, Maria	5	7	24–36	McCready, Mary	12	17	36–55
Gilberry, Catherine	4	14	36–55	Fair, Pleasant	7	13	55–100
McKinney, William	4	15	55–100	Moore, Richard	3	16	24–36

SOUTH CAROLINA—*Continued*

Name	Slaves	Total	Age	Name	Slaves	Total	Age
CHARLESTON NECK—*Cont.*				*St. Bartholomews Parish*			
Brown, Mary	6	11	24–36	Horry, L., Mistress	84	93	10–24
Jones, Cuffey	8	18	36–55	Seabrook, Ephraim	44	53	36–55
Bishop, George	4	8	36–55	Stock, Margaret	46	47	24–36
Tucker, Nancy	11	16	55–100				
Alston, Cuffey	13	23	55–100	*St. Paul's Parish*			
Pryor, Will	11	20	24–36	Logan, Jane	16	17	55–100
Rosenberg, Betty	12	17	36–55	Johnson, Henry (Esta.)	3	7	36–55
Small, Reuben	11	13	24–36	Martin, George (Esta.)	3	8	36–55
Dallas, Benjamin	13	14	10–24	Dalton, Frances	1	4	55–100
Cleaveland, Paul	8	14	36–55	Postell, Daniel	11	18	24–36
Guest, William	7	10	24–36				
Watson, D.	7	14	55–100	*St. Georges Parish*			
Sayward, James	6	11	36–55	Stevens, Lamb	7	9	55–100
Parlar, Peter	10	15	36–55				
Parker, Hager	9	15	55–100	EDGEFIELD COUNTY			
Lee, Elizabeth	3	6	36–55	Moore, Marey	3	10	24–36
Mitchell, Ann	2	5	36–55				
Wigfall, Mary	3	5	36–55	KERSHAW COUNTY			
Deport, Louisa	2	10	24–36	Harris, George	1	12	55–100
Mishaw, John	8	21	36–55	Richard, (Chestnut)	2	3	36–55
Lamford, Jos.	3	5	36–55	Spikes, Ceiley	1	8	55–100
Tardiff, William	4	12	36–55	Scott, David	4	6	55–100
Johnston, Mary L.	4	8	10–24	Taylor, Theresa	1	2	55–100
Shilon (?), Mary	3	4	36–55				
Marchant, Peter	1	10	36–55	NEWBERRY COUNTY			
Friday, William	2	17	24–36	Brown, Charles	4	6	55–100
Johnson, Louisa	3	10	24–36	Felker, Nancy	1	2	55–100
Capers, Frank	2	9	55–100	Heller, Moses	2	3	55–100
Lyon, Thomas	3	5	24–36	Glouster, Jesse	4	5	36–55
Garden, John	10	18	36–55	Thompson, Jane	2	5	10–24
Smith, Albert	1	5	24–36	Dennis, Lucy	3	5	55–100
Foster, A. W.	14	15	24–36	Bugg, Hannah	1	5	24–36
Maverick, Samuel	6	12	36–55	Leonard, Martha	1	5	36–55
Oliver, Nelly	4	9	55–100				
				RICHLAND COUNTY			
CHESTERFIELD COUNTY				*Columbia*			
Shade, Michell	8	7	36–55	Patterson, Jim	3	7	36–55
Revells, Jno.	4	5	24–36	Bostick, Susan	4	8	24–36
				Moore, Sally	2	3	55–100
COLLETON COUNTY				Green, Peter	4	8	10–24
St. Johns				Mote, Rebecca	1	2	24–36
Angel, Justus	84	88	55–100	Jackson, Mary	2	4	24–36
				Shavers, Mary	1	3	24–36
St. James Goose Creek							
Brown, S.	2	3	36–55	SUMTER COUNTY			
Russel, Richard	2	3	24–36	Elison, William	4	12	36–55
Tennant, Charles	38	42	55–100				
Holmes, Henry	12	18	24–36	WILLIAMSBURGH COUNTY			
Bell, John	12	18	36–55	Cockfield, Hesekiah	2	3	10–24
Simons, James	5	12	36–55				
Simons, John	2	7	55–100	YORK COUNTY			
Simons, E. J.	4	7	24–36	Michum, Cassy	1	9	36–55

TENNESSEE

Name	Slaves	Total	Age	Name	Slaves	Total	Age
BEDFORD COUNTY				Ede..................	1	1	24–36
Bass, John.............	1	10	55–100	Campbell, Philip........	1	2	55–100
				Williams, Moses........	2	4	36–55
DAVIDSON COUNTY				Reagan, Milly..........	2	3	55–100
Sherod, Bryant.........	4	20	36–55				
Young, Harriet.........	1	3	10–24	**LINCOLN COUNTY**			
Taylor, Jacob...........	1	2	24–36	Batey, Landon.........	5	6	55–100
				Smith, William.........	5	6	24–36
Nashville							
Bell, Buck..............	2	3	10–24	*Town of Fayetteville*			
Butcher, Ann...........	1	2	24–36	Kennedy, Allen.........	1	7	36–55
Childress, Dilcy........	1	4	36–55	Goodlow, James........	2	5	55–100
Cook, Hubbard.........	1	10	55–100				
Call, Joseph............	3	8	36–55	**MADISON COUNTY**			
Graham, R. P...........	1	5	36–55	Lane, Isaac............	2	4	55–100
Hart, Samuel...........	1	2	55–100				
Hudson, Harry.........	3	6	36–55	**MAURY COUNTY**			
Jefferson, Thomas......	4	5	24–36	Woodson, Cuffee.......	4	11	55–100
Lytle, Stephen..........	3	7	36–55				
Lockhart, Jefferson.....	1	6	24–36	**MONROE COUNTY**			
Myres, Trim............	1	4	36–55	*98th Regiment*			
Martin, Albert..........	1	2	24–36	Crusoe, John...........	1	6	36–55
Mandley, Williams......	1	4	24–36				
Rankin, James..........	1	3	36–55	**MONTGOMERY COUNTY**			
Shanklin, Johnston......	2	3	24–36	Barrett, Sampson.......	4	7	36–55
Staggs, James...........	1	3	24–36	Casey, Willis...........	2	3	24–36
Thomas, John..........	3	6	24–36	Hunt, Herod...........	1	3	55–100
Woods, Claricy.........	1	7	24–36	Mayo, Quaminy........	1	2	36–55
Wamack, Patience......	4	6	55–100	Moore, Benjn..........	6	8	55–100
DICKSON COUNTY				*Clarksville*			
Dyre, Polly.............	1	9	10–24	Brown, Ned............	1	4	55–100
				Dandridge, Agatha......	5	6	55–100
GIBSON COUNTY							
Feggins, Peter..........	3	4	36–55	**OVERTON COUNTY**			
				Coop, Alexander........	1	2	36–55
GILES COUNTY							
Henderson, Mary.......	1	2	24–36	**SHELBY COUNTY**			
				Kinkead, W............	1	7	55–100
GREENE COUNTY				Loiselle, A.............	3	8	10–24
Davis, Thos............	1	4	55–100	Brocar, C..............	7	9	55–100
				Blackwell, J............	5	6	10–24
HUMPHREYS COUNTY				Dickens, J.............	1	10	36–55
Bunch, Winny..........	1	4	55–100	Smith, J...............	1	8	24–36
JEFFERSON COUNTY				**SUMNER COUNTY**			
Elias—free.............	4	5	36–55	Jones, Priscilla.........	1	2	36–55
James and Wife (Slaves).	2	2	55–100	Hodge, Caesar.........	1	4	36–55
Milly—free.............	1	3	55–100				
Levina—free...........	1	2	24–36	**WHITE COUNTY**			
				Wilson, Thomas........	1	5	36–55
KNOX COUNTY							
Knoxville				**WILLIAMSON COUNTY**			
Emmett, Reuben........	1	6	36–55	Brooks, Gamble........	11	12	36–55
Smith, Solomon.........	1	6	24–36				
Judy...................	1	1	55–100	**WILSON COUNTY**			
Phoebe.................	1	1	55–100	George, Polly..........	2	9	55–100
Beauman, Ailey.........	1	3	24–36	Stewart, Joseph........	9	14	100–

The Paradox of Freedom

VIRGINIA

Name	Slaves	Total	Age	Name	Slaves	Total	Age
ACCOMAC COUNTY				Ligon, Else............	1	9	36–55
St. Georges Parish				Hughes, Samuel........	2	5	36–55
Ames, Bridget..........	1	2	36–55	Hilton, Will...........	2	6	55–100
Bevans, Sheppard.......	1	6	24–36	Hughes, Edith.........	1	2	36–55
Bird, Levin............	1	4	55–100	Osborne, Nancy........	1	6	10–24
Custis, Littleton........	1	3	55–100	Bragg, Joseph..........	23	25	24–36
Chandler, Tamer........	1	6	55–100	Harriss, Nancy S.......	1	3	55–100
Chandler, Southey.....	2	4	36–55				
Drummond, Charles.....	3	9	36–55	**AUGUSTA COUNTY**			
Dennis, Solomon........	3	5	55–100	Norris, Humphrey......	3	4	24–36
Elliott, Esther..........	1	2	36–55	Stepney, Peter.........	7	9	36–55
Ker, Milly.............	1	2	36–55	White, Peter...........	5	6	55–100
Ker, Caleb.............	1	3	36–55				
Ker, Priscilla...........	1	4	36–55	*Staunton*			
Leatherbury, James.....	2	7	55–100	Ware, Daniel...........	1	6	36–55
Moses, Hannah.........	1	2	36–55				
Pitts, George..........	2	4	24–36	**BATH COUNTY**			
Parker, Appy..........	1	3	55–100	Clark, Milly...........	1	3	36–55
Poulson, Shadrack......	1	3	36–55				
Parker, Simon..........	2	3	55–100	**BEDFORD**			
Poulson, William.......	2	3	10–24	Jackson, Nicy..........	2	8	55–100
Stokely, Betsey.........	1	3	55–100	Arthur, George.........	1	3	55–100
Teague, Marshall.......	1	5	36–55	Hughes, John..........	3	9	55–100
				Lewis, Bosan..........	2	5	55–100
Accomack Parish							
Blake, Polly............	1	5	36–55	**BERKELEY COUNTY**			
Conquest, Thomas......	2	6	55–100	Anderson, Samuel......	2	9	24–36
Carter, Benjamine.....	1	2	55–100	Compton, Solomon.....	1	3	55–100
Crippen, James........	2	4	55–100	Coalston, Randle.......	3	4	?
Carter, Benjamin.....	1	2	55–100	Furlong, Henry........	6	8	100–
Duncan, Sarah.........	7	9	55–100	Logan, William........	4	5	36–55
Dix, Sally.............	6	7	24–36	Parrot, Elenor.........	2	3	36–55
Feedaman, Eli..........	4	9	36–55	Sands, Hannah.........	2	3	55–100
Fields, Elizabeth........	3	5	55–100				
Harman, Walter........	1	5	24–36	**BUCKINGHAM COUNTY**			
Henderson, Levin.......	1	5	55–100	Nicholas, Lucy.........	1	2	36–55
Outten, Selby (on farm).	4	5	10–24	Hughes, Molley (?)....	5	5	?
Purnell, William........	4	8	55–100				
Piper, Henry...........	4	5	36–55	**CAMPBELL COUNTY**			
Selby, Meshack.........	1	4	55–100	Bartlett, Chls..........	1	2	36–55
Tunnell, Sarah, or Sml.				Jackson, Daniel.........	2	3	36–55
Westerhouse.........	1	4	36–55	Lucas, Samuel.........	1	2	55–100
Rew, John (on farm)	2	3	55–100	Powell, Lucy..........	2	6	36–55
				Turner, James.........	2	4	24–36
ALBEMARLE COUNTY				Tupence, Ann..........	1	4	24–36
Battles, Braskin (?).....	1	8	36–55	Thomas, Sally.........	1	9	36–55
Battles, Robert.........	1	4	55–100	Watts, Betsey.........	1	6	24–36
Farrar, Reuben........	3	7	55–100	Howe, Isaac...........	2	5	36–55
Fosset, Joseph..........	5	6	36–55	Fields, Sally...........	2	7	55–100
Farsley, Daniel.........	1	2	55–100	Jackson, John.........	2	6	24–36
Harris, Charles.........	2	11	36–55	Jones, Richard.........	2	4	55–100
Kenny, Betsy..........	4	5	10–24	Jennings, Sally.........	1	2	36–55
Middlebrooke, William..	2	8	24–36				
Scott, Jesse.............	1	7	36–55	**CAROLINE COUNTY**			
				Braxton, George........	1	6	36–55
AMELIA COUNTY				Courtney, John........	1	8	24–36
Hamm, Sally..........	2	6	24–36				

VIRGINIA

Name	Slaves	Total	Age	Name	Slaves	Total	Age
CHARLES CITY COUNTY				Duzard, Ann	1	9	36–55
Bailey, Robert	1	3	36–55	Chavers, Milly	1	5	36–55
Cole, Elizabeth	5	6	36–55	Pegram, Thos	4	5	55–100
Brown, William T	4	8	24–36	Ellis, Wyat	1	2	24–36
Christian, Mourning	1	2	36–55	Newney, John	1	2	36–55
				Eppes, Peterson	3	6	24–36
CHARLOTTE COUNTY				Elliot, Thos	1	7	55–100
Rawlins, Julius	1	3	55–100	Scott, Patsey	1	3	24–36
Jackson, Preston	1	5	24–36	Burnet, Robert	1	9	24–36
Minnis, Carroll	1	5	36–55	Crook, Betty	2	3	55–100
Ealand, John (& W. E.)	7	8	36–55	Walker, Lud	1	7	55–100
Chavis, John	1	8	55–100	Crook, Robert	2	11	36–55
Chavis, Mack	1	3	10–24	Monday, Thomas	2	6	55–100
Byrd, William	3	7	55–100	Walker, Eliza	1	4	24–36
Jackson, William	1	5	24–36	Lee, Polly	2	3	36–55
				Green, Patty	1	2	36–55
CHESTERFIELD COUNTY				Brown, Samuel	1	3	10–24
Smith, Robert	3	5	55–100	Scott, Aggy	1	3	55–100
Clarke, Nancy	1	4	24–36	Russel, Honoria	1	6	55–100
Cunningham, Nancy G.	1	9	36–55	Jackson, Daniel	7	9	55–100
Fields, Ned	5	6	36–55	Jeffers, Sylvia	2	7	36–55
McCreddy, Betsy	4	7	24–36	Wahron, John	1	5	24–36
Cunningham, Alexander	1	4	10–24	Smith, Patsey	1	2	24–36
Patterson, Sigh	1	4	36–55	Thomas, Susan	1	9	36–55
Morris, Elijah	3	5	36–55	Harris, Jos	1	10	10–24
Batts, Nancy	8	10	36–55	Bailey, Aquil	6	7	36–55
Gillum, Eady	1	8	36–55	Shields, Edward	4	5	24–36
Brown, Rebecker	2	3	55–100	Butler, Peggy	1	3	55–100
Perry, Lucy	1	2	55–100	Booker, Jack	2	3	24–36
Logain, Watthall	1	7	55–100	Gilliam, Eady	1	10	55–100
Gates, James R	1	2	36–55	Galleo, Frances	2	4	55–100
				Eppes, James	4	7	24–36
CUMBERLAND COUNTY				Corn, Henry	2	3	24–36
Booker, Billy	2	4	55–100	Harris, Jackey	2	6	24–36
Drew, Jack	2	4	55–100	Coupland, Rachel	2	5	36–55
Daniel, William	32	33	36–55	Robinson, Diana	1	11	36–55
Ellison, Chloe	2	6	55–100	Robinson, Lavina	1	3	10–24
Edwards, George	2	3	55–100	Stuart, Peggy	1	9	36–55
Freeman, York	2	4	36–55	Graves, Eliza	1	2	24–36
Higginbotham, Sophia	1	6	24–36	Ellerson, Sarah	3	7	24–36
Kidd, Pleasant	1	6	24–36	Galle, Eliza	5	6	24–36
Logan, Chastaine	1	3	24–36	Galle, Amelia	2	6	36–55
Mayo, Nancy	1	6	24–36	Quarles, Jane	2	5	36–55
Martin, Nancy	1	4	10–24	Molson, William	1	7	10–24
Mayo, Robert	1	3	36–55	Anter, Polly	5	7	36–55
Mayo, William	4	11	55–100	Overton, Rebecca	2	4	24–36
Reynolds, Lewis	1	3	24–36	Walker, William	3	11	36–55
Turpin, Strato	1	3	55–100	Bonner, Rebecca	2	3	24–36
				Stuart, John	1	8	24–36
DINWIDDIE COUNTY				Jones, Mary	2	14	55–100
Petersburg				Smith, Esther	2	11	55–100
Lawson, Booker	1	7	24–36	Kennon, Eliza	1	2	36–55
Turner, Milly	1	11	55–100	Wilson, Saml	1	2	24–36
Freeman, Lenn A	1	5	55–100	White, Susan	1	3	36–55
King, Hannah	1	3	55–100	Biggins, Mary	1	5	24–36
Scott, Daniel	2	8	36–55	Martin, James	1	7	36–55
Matthews, Bailey	1	5	24–36	Thomas, Isaac	1	7	36–55
Brander, Shedr	2	10	36–55				

VIRGINIA—*Continued*

Name	Slaves	Total	Age	Name	Slaves	Total	Age
Petersburg—Cont.				Tabb, Nancy	1	4	36–55
Thomson, Ann	1	5	24–36	Bridget, Thomas	2	3	24–36
King, Anna	1	7	24–36	Allen, Samuel	3	4	55–100
Bailey, Precilla	1	4	55–100	Hopson, James	1	10	36–55
Bailey, Eliza	1	9	36–55	Hampton, Bray	1	2	55–100
Brown, John	1	2	36–55	Evans, James	1	3	24–36
Ferrell, Polly	1	2	36–55	Essex County			
Webster, Abby	1	3	24–36	Nelson, Bunday	1	11	36–55
Lewis, Peyton	3	4	36–55	Anky, Cole	1	2	55–100
Eaves, Martin B.	5	11	24–36	McDowney, Mildred	1	9	55–100
Donaldson, Susan	1	2	55–100	McDowney, Peter	1	6	24–36
Dunn, Lewis	1	4	24–36	Richardson, Austin	6	8	55–100
Hamilton, Richard	3	5	24–36	Rich, William	1	3	24–36
Booker, Jack	4	13	55–100	Fairfax County			
Carter, Moses	1	8	55–100	Hathaway, James (fb)	3	10	24–36
Jones, Fedr.	1	2	55–100	Simms, Lee (fbk)	1	5	36–55
Minor, Jane	5	6	36–55	William, Lee (fbk)	1	2	55–100
Edwards, George S.	2	7	24–36	Hopkins, Keziah	1	8	36–55
Eppes, William	1	2	36–55	Lee, William L. (fbk)	3	6	36–55
Valentine, John	2	3	?	Stuart, James (Negro)	9	9	55–100
Bolling, Eliza	2	5	?	Harriss, Edmond (fb)	2	7	36–55
Wright, Frank	2	3	24–36	Cromer, Dennis (fb)	1	4	36–55
Gilliam, Eady	1	7	36–55	Honesty, John (fbk)	1	7	36–55
Lewis, Charles	1	4	36–55	Lyles, William (fb)	1	2	24–36
Williams, Betsy	1	11	55–100	Fluvanna County			
Majors, Thos.	2	6	55–100	Norris, Jesse	3	5	36–55
Campbell, Jack	1	4	36–55	Couzens, John	3	14	36–55
Elliot, Sally	1	4	36–55	Couzens, Jordon	3	4	36–55
Wilson, Joseph	1	2	36–55	Gypson, Moses	1	4	55–100
Perry, Lucy	1	2	36–55	Barnet, Charles	1	9	36–55
Brown, James	2	4	55–100	Peyton, Samuel	4	7	55–100
Allen, Lucy	1	3	24–36	Wood, Jeremiah	1	4	36–55
Banks, Hannah	1	4	24–36	Wood, Nelly	2	3	55–100
Wilcox, Thos.	1	2	55–100	Quarles, Nelly	1	2	55–100
Bailey, Judy	2	4	24–36	Franklin County			
Angus, George	2	7	24–36	Boyd, Samuel	1	4	55–100
White, Milly	1	2	24–36	Callaway, Squire	1	5	55–100
Holcomb, Benjamin	1	2	55–100	Early, Elizabeth	4	7	36–55
Jackson, Nancy	1	4	36–55	Green, Nelly	1	11	36–55
Minor, Jincey	8	9	36–55	Frederick County Eastern District			
Taylor, Sarah	3	5	10–24	Adams, Sylva	1	7	24–36
Angus, Judy	1	7	55–100	Brady, Henry	6	7	24–36
Fagan, Bridget	1	5	55–100	Caeser, Julius	1	4	55–100
Coupland, Rachel	2	5	55–100	Folks, Mima	1	7	55–100
Dinwiddie County				Whiting, Thomas	5	8	55–100
Jones, Benson	4	5	24–36	Gloucester County			
Freeman, Lewis	1	3	55–100	Annaka	1	4	55–100
Clanton, Hartwell	2	3	36–55	Bowles, Jefferson	2	7	24–36
Berry, Thomas	6	10	36–55	Chavis, Becky	1	4	24–36
Elizabeth City County				Chevis, Kitty	1	6	36–55
Pane, Jack	1	3	55–100	Dennis, Peggy	1	4	24–36
Robbins, Daniel	3	4	24–36				
Johnson, Matthew	1	2	36–55				
Allen, Stephen	3	6	24–36				
Reid, Jeffres	4	6	24–36				
Brown, Champion	2	3	10–24				

The Paradox of Freedom

VIRGINIA—Continued

Name	Slaves	Total	Age	Name	Slaves	Total	Age
GLOUCESTER CO.—Cont.				Scott, Aaron	2	5	36–55
Fox, James	1	5	55–100	Spencer, Gabriel	5	6	24–36
Gregory, James	13	15	55–100	Wood, Wislon	4	6	24–36
Hearn, Ephraim	9	11	55–100	Whitlock, Phebe	1	4	55–100
Lemon, John H.	1	6	24–36	Liggon, Sally	1	2	55–100
Lemon, Eliza	1	6	24–36	Smith, Peyton	1	4	24–36
Rowe, Fanny	1	4	55–100	Housling, Edith	1	2	36–55
Rilee, Frank	1	2	36–55	Harris, Alice	1	5	55–100
Southerland, James	3	4	24–36	Ellis, Milly	4	5	36–55
Southerland, Jeremiah	1	4	36–55	Rutherford, Thomas	5	7	36–55
West, John	1	4	24–36	Harris, Thomas	1	2	10–24
Ward, Jane	1	2	55–100	King, Billy	2	3	36–55
Wilmore, Peggy	1	6	24–36	Coleman, Elizabeth	2	6	55–100
				Bluefoot, Lucey	1	6	55–100
GOOCHLAND COUNTY				Owen, Sally	1	3	55–100
Cooper, Roger	1	7	55–100	Cross, Moses	2	5	36–55
Sampson, Jacob	2	10	24–36	Cousins, Barbara	1	6	55–100
Turner, Milly	1	3	24–36	Adams, Harry	1	10	36–55
				Crenshaw, Edmund (of Hanover)	9	10	24–36
(Eastern District)							
James, Eady	1	4	24–36	Carter, Betsy	4	7	36–55
Pearce, Milly	1	9	55–100	Harvie, J. B.	2	4	36–55
Shelton, James	1	7	24–36	Laurence, Cesar	1	3	36–55
Cousins, Henry	1	11	36–55	Price, Becky	2	4	24–36
Pearce, John	18	27	36–55	Russel, Archer	2	4	36–55
Frazier, Wat	1	3	55–100	Jones, Agness	1	2	36–55
Lynch, John	8	9	55–100	Carter, Henry	1	4	36–55
Mayo, Dinor	1	3	36–55	Hill, Robert	1	8	36–55
				Banks, Peters	2	3	24–36
GREENSVILLE COUNTY				Whistler, Betty	1	5	24–36
Hunt, Goodwin	2	16	55–100	Cowles, Thomas	2	4	24–36
Day, John	2	8	10–24	Reynolds, Dinah	2	3	55–100
Wadkins, David	11	33	36–55	Waddill, Kitty	1	8	36–55
Wadkins, Daniel	6	14	36–55	Hewlett, Michael	1	3	55–100
Jones, Eliza	1	12	36–55	Picot, Cyles	5	6	10–24
Mason, Mildred	2	3	55–100	Harris, Polly	2	3	36–55
Watkins, Robert	1	10	36–55	Selden, Cary	2	3	36–55
				Little-page, Lettitia	1	2	24–36
HANOVER COUNTY				Bailey, Betsy	2	4	36–55
Stone, Matthew, F.N.	1	3	36–55	Moore, Maria	1	4	36–55
Smart, Thomas	1	5	36–55	Ruffin's, Betsy, Estate	3	8	36–55
Burnett, Richard	3	4	55–100	Blaky's, George, Estate	1	3	24–36
Brockenbrough, William	46	47	36–55	Sprigs, Robert	3	7	36–55
Gist, Lucy, F.N.	1	4	36–55				
				City of Richmond			
HENRICO COUNTY				Anderson, Samuel	2	3	36–55
Foster, Henry (of Richmond)	2	4	24–36	Bell, Kitter	1	3	36–55
				Brooks, Mike	1	6	24–36
Lablong, Eleoner	1	3	24–36	Bowler, Miller	2	6	24–36
Murray, Polly	1	2	36–55	Bingley, Martha	1	2	100–
Crouch, Jaspar	2	6	36–55	Baker, Betsy	1	2	55–100
Peters, Isabella	1	6	36–55	Bohannan, Rachael	1	2	24–36
Weeks, Bristo	1	3	55–100	Brown, Nancy	1	5	55–100
Macon, Marshal	1	7	36–55	Baker, Hannah	1	2	10–24
Anderson, John	1	7	10–24	Cowlin, Isaac	1	2	24–36
Langley, Eveline	2	7	24–36	Carter, Clara	2	5	24–36
Dugard, Sally	2	5	36–55	Cole, Polly	1	2	36–55

The Paradox of Freedom

VIRGINIA—Continued

Name	Slaves	Total	Age	Name	Slaves	Total	Age
City of Richmond—Cont.				*Madison Ward*			
Carter, Patsy	3	5	24–36	Armistead, Lewis	3	9	36–55
Carter, Curtis	22	25	10–24	Amos, Mahala	1	8	24–36
Deane, Charlotte	1	2	24–36	Brown, Celia	1	6	24–36
Dickson, Patsy	1	2	10–24	Billbrough, Aggy	2	4	55–100
Elson, John	1	2	36–55	Braxton, Sukey	1	2	36–55
Gilliam, Sarah	1	2	10–24	Butler, Hope	5	6	36–55
Galt, Elizabeth	2	5	24–36	Cooly, Sarah	1	9	55–100
Granger, Joseph	1	2	24–36	Courtney, Martha	1	2	55–100
Goodwyn, Moses	4	5	55–100	Cross, Fanny	1	3	24–36
Greenhow, James	1	5	36–55	Cox, Jane	1	2	36–55
Hunt, Gilbert	1	2	36–55	Cosby, James	1	6	55–100
Harris, George	3	4	36–55	Chain, Cold	2	3	55–100
Hill, Minnis	2	9	24–36	Ellet, Mary	1	2	24–36
Hawkins, Mary	1	7	24–36	Friend, Caroline	4	7	10–24
Harris, Eliza	1	3	55–100	Graves, Elizabeth P	3	5	55–100
Harris, Milly	1	8	36–55	Harris, Rebecca	1	3	10–24
Henry, Joanna	1	5	36–55	Haxall, Philip	18	19	55–100
Harler, Jinny	1	4	24–36	Harrison, Rachel A	1	5	24–36
Harris, Maria	1	2	10–24	Jones, Matilda	1	2	24–36
Jones, Eve	1	3	55–100	Jackson, Mary	1	2	24–36
Johnson, Nelly	1	6	36–55	Morton, Rueben	3	15	36–55
Judah, Benjn	2	6	24–36	Madden, Walter	1	4	10–24
Jackson, John	3	4	55–100	Page, Penelope	1	4	24–36
Jackson, Ann	1	3	24–36	Page, George	2	4	55–100
Jackson, Lewis	2	5	55–100	Reynolds, Isaac	4	5	36–55
Jordan, Isham	1	4	36–55	Robertson, Henry	4	6	36–55
King, Rhody	1	3	55–100	Roney, Frederick	1	6	36–55
Loney, James	4	5	36–55	Smith, Ann	3	4	24–36
Lee, Richard	1	5	24–36	Smith, Elizabeth	1	2	10–24
McEnery, Nancy	1	2	10–24	Slow, Milly	1	3	55–100
Muse, William	4	6	36–55	Scott, China	1	3	36–55
Mitchell, Lucy	1	9	10–24	Webb, Nancy	2	3	55–100
Mayo, Nelly	1	2	100–	Williams, Milly	1	2	24–36
Marshall, Davy	1	2	36–55	Yancey, Celinda	1	6	24–36
Mitchell, Elizabeth	2	3	10–24				
Patterson, Joe	1	3	24–36	*Jefferson Ward*			
Pendleton, Nellie	1	2	55–100	Anderson, Nancy	2	3	36–55
Pleasants, Milton	6	9	36–55	Anderson, Eliza	2	5	24–36
Ross, George W	2	9	24–36	Burke, Emmy	3	4	24–36
Randolph, Harriet	1	4	24–36	Barnett, Polly	1	5	36–55
Robertson, Philip	1	2	24–36	Brown, Hannah	1	3	55–100
Smith, Betsy	2	3	24–36	Ball, Henry	1	2	24–36
Scott, Patience	1	8	24–36	Byrd, Nancy	1	4	55–100
Swann, William	5	9	55–100	Binford, Keziah	4	7	55–100
Sampson, David	5	7	36–55	Bowson, Judy	1	2	55–100
Smith, Nancy	1	3	55–100	Carter, Charles	2	3	24–36
Selden, Winny	1	2	36–55	Cooper, Maria	3	5	24–36
Smith, Charlotte	1	3	55–100	Crump, Edward	1	4	24–36
Tinsley, Betsy	1	2	24–36	Carter, Elvira	1	3	24–36
Tillman, Luby	2	3	55–100	Cokely, Milly	1	6	24–36
Tuppence, Becky	1	3	36–55	Calbert, Martha	1	2	24–36
Vaughan, Richard	5	6	36–55	Carey, Lucy	1	4	36–55
Wilkerson, Polly	1	2	36–55	Dalney, Julia	1	2	24–36
Wales, Elizabeth	2	5	24–36	Deane, Julia	2	4	36–55
Williams, Nancy	1	2	55–100	Dickson, Patty	6	7	36–55
Yates, Sylvia	2	4	55–100	Ellis, Isham	1	8	24–36

VIRGINIA—Continued

Name	Slaves	Total	Age	Name	Slaves	Total	Age
Jefferson Ward—Cont.				Flud, John, fre	2	3	24-36
Eppes, Milly	1	3	24-36	Wilson, Henry, fre	2	3	24-36
Ellis, Fleming	3	4	36-55	Hollaway, Dilson, fre	1	7	36-55
Fagan, Ann	1	6	36-55	Purdie, Eliza, fre	3	4	36-55
Ferguson, John	2	4	10-24	Partrick, Judia, fre	2	6	55-100
Graves, Richmond	1	5	36-55	Hawkins, Nathl., fre	10	11	36-55
George, Polly	1	2	10-24	Wyzell, Isham, fre			
Hall, Billy	1	2	55-100	(Uzzell?)	3	4	36-55
Henderson, James	2	13	24-36	Johnes, John, fre	1	4	36-55
Hendley, Wilson	3	5	36-55	Jordan, Henry, fre	1	2	24-36
Johnson, John J	3	5	36-55	Tynes, Fanny, fre	1	3	10-24
Johnson, Moses	1	3	36-55	Tynes, Jenny, of Clo (?)			
Lewis, John	3	9	36-55	fre	1	3	55-100
Lewis, John	1	2	55-100	Tynes, Nancy, fre	1	8	36-55
Lightfoot, Armistead	3	4	24-36	Tynes, Rebecca, fre	2	14	55-100
Maxwell, Julia	2	3	10-24	Pool, James, fre	1	2	36-55
Morris, Wilson	1	5	24-36	Hollaway, Sampson, fr	1	8	24-36
Morris, Reuben	3	4	24-36	Wilson, Edy, fre	1	9	36-55
Miller, Polly	1	2	36-55				
Munford, Patty	1	7	55-100	JAMES CITY COUNTY			
Oliver, Ann	1	2	24-36	Tyler, George	1	9	36-55
Price, Isham	1	2	36-55				
Ricks, Cyrus	1	4	24-36	JEFFERSON COUNTY			
Robertson, Taylor	3	4	24-36	(*Western District*)			
Rix, Jesse	1	3	24-36	Richardson, Cyrus	3	13	55-100
Scott, Mary	1	2	10-24	Gust, John	5	7	36-55
Stewart, Billy	6	7	24-36				
Smith, Eliza	1	4	24-36	KING & QUEEN COUNTY			
Thomas, Betsy	1	3	24-36	Deleaver, William	2	4	36-55
Tillman, Luby	3	4	55-100	Gilmour, Ben	1	10	36-55
Taylor, Nathl	3	4	10-24	Ham, Shadrick	3	4	24-36
Vines, Isaac	3	4	55-100	Hill, Lucy	7	8	55-100
Wallace, Nathan	2	5	24-36	Harris, Ransom	5	9	36-55
Woodson, Jim	1	2	36-55	Dungy, Polly	1	5	36-55
				Carter, Caty	1	10	36-55
ISLE OF WIGHT COUNTY				Gilmour, Fanny	1	8	36-55
(*Eastern District*)				Hill, Hetty	2	5	24-36
Short, Sam, fre	1	3	24-36	Chapman, Lewis	1	7	24-36
Green, John, fre	1	7	36-55	Gilmour, Elliott	4	5	24-36
Crocker, Agga, fre	1	3	10-24	Goulman, Willis	5	7	55-100
Christain, Ben, fre	3	5	55-100	Harris, Grace	1	12	55-100
Jordan, Biner, fre	1	3	55-100	Kidd, Hannah	1	4	55-100
Newby, Milly, fr	1	9	36-55	Cole, Betsy	1	4	55-100
Ash, Charles, fre	1	5	36-55				
Hill, Betty, fre	1	3	36-55	KING GEORGE COUNTY			
Barlow, Abraham, fre	1	15	36-55	Kendall, Elzey	1	4	36-55
Baker, Belinda, fre	1	5	55-100	Pestridge, William Henry	6	8	24-36
Tynes, Nancy, fre	2	13	36-55	Scott, Polly	1	9	36-55
Johnson, Scotland, fre	2	6	55-100	Tolson, Dennis	1	3	55-100
Crump, John C. (Surry)	11	12	36-55	Taylor, Benjamin O	71	78	10-24
Callvert, Abba, fre	4	5	55-100				
Floyd, Violet, fre	2	3	55-100	KING WILLIAM COUNTY			
Hollaway, Sally, fre	1	8	24-36	Anderson, James	1	4	55-100
Wills, Jesse, fre	3	6	55-100	Bradby, Jesse	1	6	36-55
Hollaway, Dinah, fre	1	9	36-55	Sweat, Joanna	2	6	36-55
Hollaway, Betty, fre	2	3	24-36				

The Paradox of Freedom

VIRGINIA—Continued

Name	Slaves	Total	Age	Name	Slaves	Total	Age
LANCASTER COUNTY				**NANSEMOND COUNTY**			
Adams, Daniel........	2	3	55–100	Amelia of Sawyer......	1	5	24–36
Fauntelroy, Duke......	1	3	55–100	Jacob of Holt..........	3	6	36–55
Weaver, Moses........	3	10	36–55	Jacob of Read & white			
Hurst, John...........	2	6	24–36	wife................	2	9	36–55
				Jack of Hawksey......	1	4	36–55
LOUDON COUNTY				Anthony of Pugh......	3	10	55–100
Cameron Parish				Sally of Pearce........	1	6	24–36
Clemmon, H., F.N.....	2	5	24–36	Oxford of Brewer......	3	7	100–
Robison, Cupit, F.N....	1	3	55–100	Nancy of Hare........	2	4	24–36
				Thomas of Bowsar.....	1	7	55–100
Shelburn Parish				Hetty of Walker.......	2	6	10–24
Hull, John, F.N........	1	10	55–100	Arrenia of Cowling & C..	1	5	55–100
Selva, Esther, F.N......	4	8	36–55	Gibson of Burket......	2	3	24–36
Gale, Dugless, F.N.....	2	4	36–55	Geo. of Walker........	2	3	24–36
Corben, Milly, F.N.....	5	7	55–100	Absalum of Whillock...	3	5	55–100
Doe, William, F.N.....	1	4	55–100	Jack of Brown.........	1	4	10–24
Jackson, Jesse, F.N.....	1	6	10–24	Joseph of Walker......	1	4	24–36
Mitchell, James, F.N....	5	8	24–36	John of Walker (Senr.)..	1	8	55–100
Ellzey, James, F.N.....	1	4	55–100	Jack of Atkins.........	2	12	55–100
Cross, Stephen, F.N....	2	3	55–100	Betty of Campbell.....	4	6	24–36
				Polly of Manly........	1	3	55–100
LOUISA COUNTY				Jim of Elliot..........	1	8	24–36
Mosby, Pleasant, F.N...	3	8	36–55	Wilson of Teamer......	1	5	24–36
Mosby, Samuel, F.N....	6	7	24–36	London of White......	4	8	36–55
Wilkerson, Peggy......	4	11	24–36	Peggy of Jordan.......	1	4	36–55
Poindexter, Daniel, F.N.	2	16	36–55	Sally of Cowling.......	1	4	36–55
Moore, Hezekiah, F.N...	1	4	36–55	Bob of Scott..........	3	4	36–55
Kinney, William, F.N...	1	11	55–100	Watson of Bowsar.....	1	5	36–55
Edwards, Dicy, Jr., F.N.	1	4	24–36	Elvy of Ash...........	5	6	36–55
Joen, Anny, F.N.......	3	4	55–100	Jim of Bowsar Sen.....	1	7	55–100
				John of Norfleet.......	1	4	55–100
LUNENBURG COUNTY				Holliway of Copeland...	3	6	36–55
Epes, Edward (F.N.)...	4	10	36–55	Bill of Griffin.........	1	2	36–55
Evans, Thomas (F.N.)..	3	6	55–100	Syphe of Matthews &			
Hitchins, Nancy (F.N.).	1	6	55–100	white wife..........	1	2	24–36
Archer, James (F.N.)...	4	5	36–55	Jerry of Johnson.......	1	4	24–36
				Amia of Holland.......	3	4	55–100
MATHEWS COUNTY				Edith of Crocker.......	1	5	55–100
Callis, Sally...........	2	6	55–100	Rachel of Shepherd....	1	7	24–36
				Saml of Hacket........	2	9	36–55
MECKLENBURG COUNTY				Dempsy of Stallings			
Ivy, Prissilla..........	5	13	55–100	(Slave).............	6	8	36–55
				David of Holland (Jr.)...	2	5	36–55
MIDDLESEX COUNTY				Charles of Crews......	2	3	55–100
Cassity, James........	1	3	36–55	Peggy of West........	3	4	36–55
Cole, Penny...........	2	6	36–55	Bridget of Godwin.....	3	4	55–100
Gowin, Nancy.........	1	2	55–100	Nancy of Shepherd....	1	4	24–36
Hord, Benjamin.......	8	9	10–24	Mourning of Wilkins...	1	4	55–100
Rylee, Charles.........	1	2	55–100	Rebecka of Catchen (?)..	1	8	55–100
Thomas, Lancaster.....	1	7	36–55	Lieucy of Winslow.....	1	4	36–55
West, Daphny.........	4	5	55–100	Jerry of Whitfield......	1	4	24–36
West, Priscilla.........	6	7	100–				
Peters, Betsy..........	1	3	55–100				
				NELSON COUNTY			
MONTGOMERY COUNTY				Arnold, Robert........	1	10	55–100
Langhorn, William.....	7	10	10–24				

VIRGINIA—*Continued*

Name	Slaves	Total	Age	Name	Slaves	Total	Age
NEW KENT COUNTY				Miller, Willm.	2	4	55–100
Dungee, Jesse (F.c.p.)	1	5	36–55	Joseph, Lilly	3	6	36–55
Fox, Sally (F.c.p.)	2	5	55–100	Allen, Stephen	2	5	24–36
Fox, Sukey (F.c.p.)	1	5	36–55	Baucher, Desebri	4	6	24–36
Fox, Thomas (F.c.p.)	1	5	24–36	Wiles, James	2	6	24–36
Johnson, Ned (F.c.p.)	3	5	55–100	Eastwood, Jupiter	3	8	24–36
Lewis, Roger (F.c.p.)	4	6	36–55	Gibbs, Toney	1	4	24–36
Meekins, Peggy (F.c.p.)	1	2	55–100	Herbert, Sally	2	2	36–55
Ozborne, Squire (F.c.p.)	1	8	55–100	Williams, James	3	4	24–36
Pearman, Michael (F.c.p.)	5	15	36–55	Delaware, Amy	4	5	24–36
Pearman, Thomas (F.c.p.)	2	11	36–55	Shuster, Hannah	1	2	36–55
				Hunter, Sarah	1	3	55–100
Parke, Hannah (F.c.p.)	3	5	55–100	Ivey, Nelly	1	3	36–55
NORFOLK COUNTY				Smith, Peggy	2	3	55–100
				Naylor, Ann	1	2	36–55
Bressie, Lucy	4	7	24–36	Rogers, Adrian	1	5	55–100
Halstead, Israel	3	6	24–36	Caucey, Nancy	1	8	100–
Watts, Jesse	1	4	10–24	Banks, Phillis	1	2	36–55
Elliot, Bill	1	4	36–55	Magnieu, Lovey	1	2	36–55
Shepherd, Nancy	1	9	36–55	Hancock, Arthur	3	8	24–36
Billey, Samuel	1	2	55–100	Hunter, Nancy	3	10	55–100
Pitt, Nancy	1	4	24–36	Hancock, Priscilla	5	8	55–100
Cornick, Peggy	1	2	36–55	English, Priscilla	1	5	24–36
Laverence, Juan Pedre	1	3	24–36	Miller, Robert	2	3	24–36
Nash, Aggy	1	3	10–24	Fuller, William	1	9	36–55
Bressie, Reitta	1	3	36–55	Smith, Hannah	2	5	55–100
Jones, William	3	4	36–55	Clayton, Moses	4	6	10–24
Godwin, Benjamin	1	7	36–55	Singleton, Jim	3	4	55–100
Scott, Mary	1	3	36–55	Lewis, Sam	2	5	36–55
Cooper, Charles	4	5	24–36	Ruffin, Evelina	2	6	36–55
Dixon, Mingo	2	3	24–36	Fentress, David	1	6	36–55
Sample, Nanny	1	4	55–100	Randall, Moses	1	2	36–55
Smith, Fanny	1	4	24–36	Rae, Betty	2	6	36–55
Hoggard, Thummer	15	21	36–55	Nimmo, Paul	4	9	24–36
Wilkinson, Jesse	4	5	55–100	Saunders, Allsey Ann	1	4	55–100
Africa, Wright	1	3	36–55	Ball, Sarah	1	3	55–100
				Roundtree, Anthony	2	4	24–36
NORFOLK BORO, NORFOLK COUNTY				Dixon, Thomas	1	6	24–36
				Voyart, John	2	6	36–55
Lucy	1	2	55–100	Berry, Jane	1	3	10–24
Haines, Cuffey	1	3	55–100	Bligh, John	3	7	36–55
White, Patience	1	8	55–100	Nicholson, Katy	3	5	36–55
Cooper, George	3	4	55–100	Reed, Luke	1	5	24–36
Johnson, Lamb	4	5	55–100	Shepherd, Frank	1	5	36–55
Walke, Arthur	1	2	55–100	Carr, Patsey	1	4	55–100
Travers, Peggy	1	4	55–100	Sawyer, Mary	7	8	55–100
Ingram, Billy	1	3	55–100	Boucher, Agnes	1	2	24–36
Walker, America	1	6	55–100	Collins, Racheal	4	5	55–100
Landford, Soloman	1	5	36–55	Robertson, Joe	2	4	36–55
Green, Hurt	3	5	24–36	Taylor, John	1	4	24–36
Hodges, Matt	2	5	36–55	West, Beverly	2	8	36–55
Jasper, Lucy	2	9	?	Gilmore, Henry	2	13	36–55
Spencer, John	2	4	36–55	Vickery, Ned	6	4	36–55
Suckey, Aunt	5	6	24–36	Nancy & Lydia	1	4	55–100
Bailey, Joe	2	6	36–55	Bligh, James	2	5	36–55
Slaughter, Stephen	4	5	55–100	Jordan, Moses	4	10	36–55
Bobee, Felix	4	6	24–36	Carey, Daniel	1	5	36–55

VIRGINIA—Continued

Name	Slaves	Total	Age	Name	Slaves	Total	Age
NORFOLK BORO, NORFOLK COUNTY—Cont.				Market Square			
Newby, Jacob	2	4	36-55	Lee, Judy	2	3	36-55
Williams, Maria	1	3	36-55	ORANGE COUNTY			
Henly, Charlotte	5	12	24-36	Long, Betsy	1	7	36-55
Richardson, Lucinda	1	4	36-55	Rolls, William	5	8	36-55
Cuthbert, Matilda	2	4	24-36				
Harman, Hannah	3	5	36-55	PITTSYLVANIA COUNTY			
Singleton, Frank	3	8	10-24	Robertson, Faith	1	7	36-55
Camp, Jacob	2	3	36-55	Booker, Jessee	1	3	36-55
Tines, Patience	1	7	36-55	Wimbish, Chas	1	3	55-100
Boush, Nancy	5	7	55-100	Wisdom, George	1	2	55-100
Bonney, Aunt	1	6	55-100				
Wright, Amy	3	7	24-36	POWHATAN COUNTY			
Robertson, James	9	10	55-100	Ellis, Nancy	2	9	55-100
Ashley, Jenny	2	6	55-100				
Copelan, Seny (?)	2	4	24-36	PRINCE EDWARD COUNTY			
Jasper, Elizabeth	1	6	24-36	Homes, Lucy	1	9	36-55
Thomas, Molly	1	3	55-100	White, Toney	1	2	55-100
Newsum, Basset	1	4	36-55	White, Sam	1	17	55-100
Scott, Louisa	1	6	24-36	Epperson, Rody	2	3	55-100
Baker, Parish	2	4	24-36	Morton, Thomas A. (Cumberland)	45	49	24-36
Jackson, Manuel	1	3	55-100				
Banks, Mary	1	2	36-55				
Gibson, Ottway	2	11	24-36	PRINCE GEORGE COUNTY			
Seaman, Tamer	1	6	36-55	Walthal, John B	2	5	55-100
White, Anthony	1	2	10-24	Gilliam, Mary Ann	1	5	24-36
Howard, Frank	2	3	24-36	Davis, Julia	4	6	24-36
Boucher, Lewis	2	4	55-100	Eppes, Eliza	3	10	24-36
Curtis, Lavina	1	13	36-55	Smith, John	1	4	36-55
Hays, William	1	6	36-55	Smith, Drury	2	5	36-55
Locust, Katy	1	4	24-36	Batte, Fanny	2	6	55-100
				Damsel, Samuel	3	4	36-55
Queen Street				Chance, James	1	5	55-100
Boyd, Nancy	1	3	36-55	Sykes, World	1	5	55-100
				Lee, Richard	3	2	36-55
Charlotte & Bute Streets							
Connor, Susan	2	4	24-36	PRINCESS ANNE COUNTY			
Jones, Cyrus	1	6	24-36	Owens, Tait	1	6	55-100
				Sparrow, Corinna	1	3	24-36
Free Mason Street				White, Sonnon (?)	1	6	36-55
Keeling, Ned	5	14	24-36	Barnes, Tom	1	9	24-36
				Fentress, Nanny	1	3	100-
Little Water Street & Vicinity				Woodhouse, George	6	7	36-55
Palmer, John	4	5	36-55	Anderson, Jack	2	3	36-55
Smith, Daniel	2	3	36-55	Smith, Jane	1	3	24-36
Commerce Street				PRINCE WILLIAM COUNTY			
Byrd, Sally	4	5	55-100	Carr, Daniel	2	4	55-100
Mandeville, John C	3	8	55-100	Kendall, Thornton	4	10	36-55
Cocke, Joseph	3	10	24-36				
				RICHMOND COUNTY			
Main Street				Hall, Peter	1	2	55-100
Williams, Jane	1	4	36-55	Newman, Louisa	1	3	55-100
Robertson, James	2	10	36-55	Lancaster, Nancy	1	3	55-100
Knight, Thomas	1	8	55-100	Bragg, Keziah	2	3	55-100
Slaughter, Betsey	1	5	24-36	Barnes, Simon	3	4	55-100

The Paradox of Freedom

VIRGINIA—*Continued*

Name	Slaves	Total	Age	Name	Slaves	Total	Age
RICHMOND CO.—*Cont.*				**SURRY COUNTY**			
Allen, Frank............	5	8	36–55	Scott, Nicholas G.......	1	11	36–55
Saws, Chris.............	1	2	55–100	Browne, Mariah........	1	6	24–36
Veney, Jessee...........	1	5	24–36	Hardy, Simus..........	5	6	36–55
				Jonathan, Molly........	1	2	55–100
ROCKBRIDGE COUNTY				Cocke, Ceasar..........	7	8	36–55
Henry, John............	2	3	36–55	Banks, Benjamin.......	4	12	55–100
Sims, John.............	4	7	36–55	Tines, James...........	1	4	36–55
Rachael................	3	3	36–55	Pritlow, William........	2	12	36–55
Henry, William.........	4	6	36–55	Cornwell, Tom.........	1	7	24–36
Jackson, Reuben........	1	3	24–36	Deborix, Anny.........	1	5	36–55
SHENANDOAH COUNTY				**SUSSEX COUNTY**			
Woodstock, County seat				Canada, John..........	1	5	55–100
Edwards, Prince........	1	6	24–36	Hill, Frederick.........	4	7	36–55
				Parkam, Jesse..........	3	4	24–36
1st Batts. of 13 7 97				Turner, Olive..........	1	8	55–100
Regtms.				Hill, Charles...........	3	6	36–55
Spencer, Edward........	5	6	36–55				
Tasker, Eward..........	1	3	36–55	**WESTMORELAND COUNTY**			
				Asten (?), Jerry	1	4	24–36
2nd B. 13 Rt.				Bradley, Arthur........	1	4	55–100
Bailey, James...........	1	2	36–55	Bradley, Lucy..........	1	3	10–24
				Bundy, William........	1	5	10–24
SOUTHAMPTON COUNTY				Bailey, Fanny..........	1	8	24–36
Turner, Edith..........	1	5	55–100	Jackson, Cupid.........	3	5	55–100
Taylor, Perry...........	1	3	55–100	Wright, Isaac..........	1	9	36–55
SPOTTSYLVANIA COUNTY				**WYTHE COUNTY**			
Anderson, Catharine....	3	9	36–55	Pool, Nelly............	1	4	36–55
Garnett, Caesar........	1	5	24–36				
Johnson, Alsey.........	1	9	36–55	**YORK COUNTY**			
Simmons, Sthresley (?)..	1	9	24–36	Johnson, William.......	3	4	55–100
Brown, Maria..........	1	6	55–100	Foredice, Patsey........	2	3	36–55
Brooke, Lucy...........	1	4	36–55	Bassett, William........	3	4	55–100
Catlet, Jane............	1	3	36–55	Dipper, John...........	4	6	36–55
Debaptist, Nancy.......	7	12	36–55	Debrix, Mary..........	2	9	36–55
Harrison, Suckey.......	1	4	55–100	Porter, Richard........	2	6	24–36
Miller, Armstead.......	2	3	36–55	Williams, Godfrey......	1	9	55–100
Wilkins, James.........	2	7	55–100	Deavenport, Anthony...	3	9	36–55
Waning, William........	3	8	24–36	Yates, William C.......	6	8	36–55
White, Robert..........	4	8	10–24	White, Benjamin.......	1	2	55–100
STAFFORD COUNTY				China, Ceaser..........	3	5	55–100
Bossy (?), Nancy.......	3	4	36–55	Barber, James..........	6	10	36–55
Guin, Tom.............	1	5	55–100	Minor, John...........	6	8	55–100
Froggett, John.........	2	3	55–100	Williams, Henry........	1	5	36–55
Howard, Abra:.........	11	21	24–36	Waller, Littleton.......	28	29	55–100
Walker, Alexr..........	7	8	10–24	Jarvis, Thomas.........	6	7	24–36
Jones, Chars...........	1	4	55–100	Jarvis, John...........	3	7	10–24
Butler, Seth............	1	5	24–36	Jarvis, Susan..........	1	2	55–100
Arnold, Lewis..........	2	3	36–55	Morris, George.........	6	9	36–55

Endnotes

Chapter 1

[1] Austin, Andre, "The Dirty South: Blacks Owned Blacks too in the USA," *Academia,* retrieved December 16, 2024, https://www.academia.edu/33021954/THE_DIRTY_SOUTH_Blacks_owned_Blacks_too_in_the_USA

[2] Adams, Colton, "A Peculiar Institution Within the Peculiar Institution: An Examination of Affluent Free Black Slave Owners in the Third Caste," *Journal of Interdisciplinary Undergraduate Research*, Vol. 8, Article 5, 2016, 1.

[3] Wilson, Calvin D., "Negros Who Owned Slaves," *Popular Science Monthly*, Vol. 81, November 1912.

[4] Wilson, Calvin D., "Black Masters, A Side-Light on Slavery," *The North American Review,* Vol. 181, No. 588 (November 1905), 685-698.

[5] Ibid, 689.

[6] "Black Slave Owners," Encyclopedia.com, visited on May 10, 2024; Schweninger, Loren, "Prosperous Blacks in the South, 1790-1880," *The American Historical Review* 95, no. 1 (1990): 31–56. https://doi.org/10.2307/2162953.

[7] Abzug, Robert H., *Passionate Liberator. Theodore Dwight Weld and the Dilemma of Reform*, (Oxford University Press, 1980), 87.

[8] Loren Schweninger. "Prosperous Blacks in the South, 1790-1880." American Historical Review. Vol. 95, no. iii (Feb. 1990). 36.

[9] Fleming, Walter L., *Civil War and Reconstruction in Alabama,* (New York: Columbia University Press, 1905); Thompson, C. Mildred, *Reconstruction in Georgia: Economic, Social, Political: 1865-1872,*

(New York, 1915); Hamilton, J.G. De Roulhac, *Reconstruction in North Carolina*, (New York, 1914); Garner, James W., *Reconstruction in Mississippi*, (New York, 1901); Dunning, William A., *Reconstruction, Political and Economic, 1865-1877*, (New York, 1907); Woodson, Carter G., *Free Negro Owners of Slaves in the United States in 1830; Together with Absentee Ownership of Slaves in the United States in 1830*, (Washington, D.C., 1924), 60; Woodson, Carter G. and Lindsay, Arnett G., eds.; *The Negro as a Businessman*, (Washington, D.C., 1929); Harris, Abram L., *The Negro as a Capitalist: A Study of Banking and Business Among American Negros*, (Philadelphia: 1936); Stuart, Merah S., *An Economic Detour: A History of Insurance in the Lives of American Negros*, (Philadelphia: 1936); Jackson, Luther Porter, *Free Negro Labor and Property Owning in Virginia, 1830-1860*, (New York, 1942); "The Free Negro Farmer and Property Owner, 1830-1860," *Journal of Negro History*, 24 (October 1939), 390-489; Franklin, John Hope, *The Free Negro in North Carolina, 1760-1860*, (Chapel Hill: NC, 1943); "The Free Negro in Economic Life in Antebellum North Carolina," *North Carolina Historical Review*, 19 (July and October 1942), 239-259, 359-375; Wharton, Vernon Lane, *The Negro in Mississippi, 1860-1890*, (Chapel Hill: NC, 1947).

[10] Levine, Lawrence W., *Black Culture and Black Consciousness: Afro-American Folk Thought from Slavery to Freedom*, (New York: Oxford University Press, 1977); Gutman, Herbert, *The Black Family in Slavery and Freedom, 1750-1925*, (New York: Oxford University Press, 1976); Rawick, George P., *From Sundown to Sunup: The Making of the Black Community*, (Westport, Conn.: Greenwood Publishing Company, 1972); Blassingame, John W., *The Slave Community: Plantation Life in the Antebellum South*, (New York: Oxford University Press, 1971); Roll, Eugene Genovese and Roll, Jordan, *The World the Slaves Made* (New York: Oxford University Press, 1974); Taylor, Arnold, *Travail and Triumph: Black Life and Culture in the South since the Civil War*, (Westport, Conn.: Greenwood Publishing Company, 1976); Vincent, Charles, *Black Legislators in Louisiana during Reconstruction*, (Baton Rouge, La.: Louisiana State University Press, 1976); Holt, Thomas, *Black over White: Negro Political Leadership in South Carolina during*

Reconstruction, (Urbana, Ill.: University of Illinois Press, 1977); Rankin, David, "The Origins of Black Leadership in New Orleans during Reconstruction," *Journal of Southern History*, 40 (August 1974): 417- 440. This has also been true for recent economic historians who have paid only slight attention to property ownership and have said virtually nothing about prosperous blacks. See Higgs, Robert, *Competition and Coercion: Blacks in the American Economy, 1865-1914,* (Cambridge, Mass.: Cambridge University Press, 1977); DeCanio, Stephen J., *Agriculture in the Postbellum South: The Economics of Production and Supply*, (Cambridge, Mass.: MIT Press, 1974); Shlomowitz, Ralph, "Planter Combinations and Black Labour in the American South, 1865-1880," *Slavery and Abolition: A Journal of Comparative Studies,* 9 (May 1988): 72-84; Wiener, Jonathan, *Social Origins of the New South: Alabama, 1860-1885*, (Baton Rouge, La.: Louisiana State University Press, 1978); Madle, Jay R., *The Roots of Black Poverty: The Southern Plantation Economy after the Civil War,* (Durham, N.C.: Duke University Press, 1978); Jaynes, Gerald David, *Branches without Roots: Genesis of the Black Working Class in the American South, 1862-1882*, (New York: Oxford University Press, 1986); Ransom, Roger L. and Sutch, Richard, *One Kind of Freedom: The Economic Consequences of Emancipation*, (New York: Cambridge University Press, 1977); Woodman, Harold, "Sequel to Slavery: The New History Views the Postbellum South," *Journal of Southern History*, 43 (November 1977): 523-54. Although characteristic of a slightly later time, one exception to these trends was Weare, Walter, *Black Business in the New South: A Social History of the North Carolina Mutual Life Insurance Company*, (Urbana, Ill.: University of Illinois Press, 1973).

[11] Woodson, "Free Negro Owners of Slaves in the United States in 1830," *Journal of Negro History*, 9:1, 60.

[12] Franklin, John Hope, *From Slavery to Freedom: A History of Negro Americans,* (New York: Alfred A. Knopf, 1974), 173.

[13] Mathews, Lipton, "A Brief History of Nonwhite Slave Owners in America," *MISES.ORG,* (November 11, 2020), www.mises.org/

mises-wire/brief-history-nonwhite-slave-owners-america (Site visit May 30, 2025)

[14] Ibid.

[15] Ibid.

[16] Olmsted, Frederick Law, *The Cotton Kingdom: A Traveler's Observations on Cotton and Slavery in the American Slave States*, Volume 1, (New York: Mason Brothers, 1861), 246-247.

[17] Holloway, Joseph, "Black Slaveowners," *The Slave Rebellion Website*, SlaveRebellion.org. Visited on May 30, 2025.

[18] Halliburton, "Free Black Owners of Slaves: A Reprisal of the Woodson Thesis," 129; "Negros Who Owned Slaves," *Popular Science Monthly*, LXXXI (November 1912), 484; Russell, John H., "Colored Freedmen as Slave Owners in Virginia, 1619-1865," *Journal of Negro History*, Vol. 1, (The University of Chicago Press, July 1916), 235.

[19] Frazier, Edward Franklin, *The Free Negro Family, (New York, 1932)*, 1-2; Seybert, Tony, *Slavery and Native Americans in British North America and the United States: 1600 to 1865*, web.archive.org/web/20040804001522/ http://www.slaveryin america.org/history/hs_es_indians_slavery.htm, retrieved November 29, 2024.

[20] Ibid.

[21] Finkleman, Paul, ed., *Encyclopedia of African American History, 1619–1895: From the Colonial Period to the Age of Frederick Douglass*, (Oxford University Press, 2006), www.oxfordreference.com May 8, 2024; Foner, Eric, *Give Me Liberty: An American History*, (New York: W. W. Norton & Company, 2012), 18; Gates, Henry Louis, "Did Black People Own Slaves?", *The Root Magazine*, March 4, 2023, www.africanamerica.org/ topic/did-black-people-own-slaves.;

Halliburton, "Free Black Owners of Slaves: A Reprisal of the Woodsen Thesis; *"The South Carolina Historical Magazine,* Vol. 76: 3, (Charleston, SC: The South Carolina Historical Society, July 1975), 129; Seligman, Edwin R. A., ed., *Encyclopaedia of the Social Sciences,* 15 vols., transcribed by Andrew Chrucky, March 23, 2004, (New York: The Macmillan Company, 1930-1935, Reissued 1937), www.ditext.com/ moral/slavery.html May 8, 2024

[22] Rohrs, Richard C., "State v. Edmund, a Slave (1833): Perceptions of the Legal Status of Slaves and Free Blacks in Antebellum North Carolina," The *North Carolina Historical Review,* 95:1, (North Carolina Office of Archives and History, 2018), 29-46.

[23] Koger, Larry, *Black slaveowners: free black slave masters in South Carolina, 1790-1860,* (North Carolina: Mc Farland, 1995), 88.

[24] Ibid.

[25] Ibid, 31; Johnston, James Hugo, *Race Relations in Virginia and Miscegenation in the South, 1776-1860,* (Amherst, Mass., 1970).

[26] Niven, Steven J., A Cane River Tale: From Slave to Free Woman to Slave Owner, *The Root,* (March 10, 2015. theroot.com/ a-cane-river-tale-from-slave-to-free-woman-to-slave-ow-1790859045 site visit on January 7, 2025.

[27] Woodson, "Free Negro Owners of Slaves in the United States in 1830," *Journal of Negro History,* 9:1, 41.

[28] "Black Slave Owners," *Encyclopedia.com*; Guild, June Percell, *Black laws of Virginia;: A summary of the legislative acts of Virginia concerning Negroes from earliest times to the present,* (Negro Universities Press, 1936), 72. The 1806, Chapter 63 law stated that if a slave, emancipated after May 1, 1806, remained in the Commonwealth for more than a year, his freedom would be forfeited by law and he would be sold by the Overseer of the Poor for the benefit of the parish [Beckford Parish in Shenandoah County].

[29] Gates, "Did Black People Own Slaves?," *The Root Magazine*; Adams, "A Peculiar Institution Within the Peculiar Institution: An Examination of Affluent Free Black Slave Owners in the Third Caste," 3-4.

[30] Ibid, 3-4.

[31] Halliburton, "Free Black Owners of Slaves: A Reappraisal of the Woodson Thesis," 129, Woodson, "Free Negro Owners of Slaves in the United States in 1830," *Journal of Negro History*, 9:1, 159, 161.

[32] Ibid, 3-4; "Black Slave Owners," *Encyclopedia.com*.

[33] Rankin, David, "The Impact of the Civil War on the Free Colored Community of New Orleans," *Perspectives in American History*, 11 (1977-78): 379-418; Mills, Gary B., *The Forgotten People: Cane River's Creoles of Color*, (Baton Rouge, La.: Louisiana State University Press, 1977); Whitten, David O., *Andrew Durnford: A Black Sugar Planter in Antebellum Louisiana,* (Natchitoches, La.: Northwestern State University Press, 1981)

[34] Adams, "A Peculiar Institution Within the Peculiar Institution: An Examination of Affluent Free Black Slave Owners in the Third Caste," 3-4.

[35] Koger, *Black slaveowners: free black slave masters in South Carolina, 1790-1860*, 101.

[36] Franklin, *From Slavery to Freedom: A History of Negro Americans*, 155-156.

[37] Cohen, Irving S., and Logan, Raford, *The American Negro; Old World Background and New World Experience,* (New York: Houghton and Mifflin, 1970), 72.

[38] Mills, Gary, *The Forgotten People: Cane River's Creoles of Color*, (Baton Rouge, 1977), Johnson, Michael P., and Roak, James L., *Black Masters: A Free Family of Color in the Old South*, (New York:

Norton, 1986), 128; Soltow, Lee, *Male Inheritance Expectations in the United States in 1870*, (New Haven, 1975), 85.

[39] Ibid; Johnson, Michael and James L. Roark, *Black Masters: A Free Family of Color in the Old South*, 23; Kranz, Rachel, *African-American Business Leaders and Entrepreneurs*, (Infobase Publishing, 2004), 72.

[40] Gates, "Did Black People Own Slaves?," *The Root Magazine;* Breen, T. H., *"Myne Owne Ground": Race and Freedom on Virginia's Eastern Shore, 1640-1676,* (New York: Oxford University Press, 2004), 13–15

[41] Schweninger, "Prosperous Blacks in the South, 1790-1880," 40; Extracted from Federal Census data and figures from R. Halliburton Jr., Larry Koger, and Carter G. Woodson; Admittedly, this average can be skewed in some ways.

[42] Berlin, Ira, *Slaves Without Masters: The Free Negro in the Antebellum South,* (New York, 1974); Cohen, David W. and Greene, Jack P. eds., *Neither Slave Nor Free: The Freedmen of African Descent in the Slave Societies of the New World* (Baltimore, 1972); Patterson, Orlando, *Slavery and Social Death: A Comparative Study,* (Cambridge, Mass., 1982); Woodson, *Free Negro Owners of Slaves*; Jackson, *Free Negro Labor and Property*, pp. 200-229; Russell, John H., *"The Free Negro in Virginia, 1619-1865,"* Johns Hopkins University Studies in Historical and Political Science, ser. XXXI, no. 3 (Baltimore, 1913); Writers' Program in Virginia, *"The Negro in Virginia",* (New York, 1940), 122-23; Chesterfield, Fairfax, Princess Anne, and Spotsylvania Counties Personal Property Taxes, 1790, 1800, 1810, 1820, and 1830; Hanover and Northampton Counties Personal Property Taxes, 1830 and] 860; Fredericksburg Personal Property Taxes, 1790, 1800, 1810, 1820, and 1830; Petersburg Personal Property Taxes, 1795, 1800, 1810,] 820, and 1830; Richmond Personal Property Taxes, 1791, 1801, 1811, 1821, and 1830. (Decennial years could not always be used because of gaps in records.) Using these records, it can be determined that more free black Virginians owned chattel in 1810, 1820, and 1830 than in any

preceding decennial year-that is, 1790 and 1800. The new law of 1832 guaranteed a decline in ownership thereafter.

[43] Berlin, Ira, *Generations of Captivity: A History of African-American Slaves,* (Harvard University Press, 2003), 9.

[44] Degler, Carl N., "Remaking American History, " *Journal of American History,* LXVII (1980-81), 20; Woodson, "Free Negro Owners of Slaves in the United States in 1830," 41-43.

[45] Berlin, *Slaves Without Masters: The Free Negro in the Antebellum South.* 29, 92, 102, 138, 140-142, 145; Mark V. Tushnet, *The American Law of Slavery, 1810-1860: Considerations of Humanity and Interest* (Princeton: Princeton University Press, 1981), 193. (South Carolina, Georgia, Alabama, Mississippi, and Louisiana allowed slaves to be emancipated in 1830, only by special resolutions.)

[46] 1835 Constitution of the State of Tennessee, Article I, Section XXVI; and Article IV, Section I.

[47] U.S. Department of Commerce and Labor, Bureau of the Census, Eight Federal Census of the United States, Taken in 1860.

[48] Ibid.

[49] Ibid.

Chapter 2
[50] Cobb, Thomas R. R., *An Inquiry into the Law of Negro Slavery in the United States of America,* (University of Georgia Press, 1999) (1858), reprinted in Paul Finkleman, The Law of Freedom and Bondage: A Casebook 21 (1986).

[51] Ruffin, Edmund, "Two great evils of Virginia, and their common remedy," found in "Political Pamphlets," vol. xii, Library of Virginia, 5. As noted by John H. Russell in "Origin of the Free Negro Class." *The Free Negro in Virginia, 1619-1865.*

[52] *"African Americans in St. Augustine 1565-1821"*, National Park Service Pamphlet; Lauber, Almon Wheeler, *"Enslavement by the Indians Themselves," Indian Slavery in Colonial Times Within the Present Limits of the United States,* Studies in history, economics and public law, 53:3, (Columbia University, 1913), 25–48; Rivers, Larry E., *Slavery in Florida: territorial days to emancipation,* (Gainesville: University Press of Florida, 2000), 2.

[53] *Louisiana's Territorial Period, 1803-1812,* LSU Libraries, 2021, www.ib.lsu.edu/sites/all/files/sc/fpoc/history.html

[54] McCoy, Kelli, "John Rolfe's Letter to Sir Edwin Sandys, *Milestone Documents in African American History, Volume 4,* (Salem Press, October 2017), 1; Deetz, Kelley Fanto, "400 years ago, enslaved Africans first arrived in Virginia", *National Geographic* (August 13, 2019). Retrieved December 30, 2024; Waxman, Olivia B., "Where the Landing of the First Africans in English North America Really Fits in the History of Slavery", *Time* (August 20, 2019), Retrieved December 30, 2019; Finley, Ben, "Virginia marks pivotal moment when African slaves arrived", *Associated Press.* (August 22, 2019), Retrieved December 30, 2024; Indentured Servants In The U.S., www.pbs.org/opb/historydetectives/ feature/indentured-servants- in-the-us/; Austin, Beth, *1619: Virginia's First Africans (Report),* Hampton History Museum (December 2019), 12, 17–20; Sainsbury, W. Noel, ed., "America and West Indies: September 1672", *Calendar of State Papers Colonial, America and West Indies: Volume 7, 1669-1674,* (London: Her Majesty's Stationery Office, 1889) 404–417. www.british-history.ac.uk/cal-state-papers/colonial/america-west-indies/vol7/pp 404-417, Retrieved December 30, 2024.

[55] Foner, Philip S., *History of Black Americans: From Africa to the Emergence of the Cotton Kingdom,* (Oxford University Press, 1980).

[56] Botzer, Tally, "Myths and Misunderstandings: Slavery in the United States," The American Civil War Museum, August 15, 2017. Accessed on December 20, 2024. https://acwm.org/blog /myths-and-misunderstandings-slavery-united-states/

[57] Wood, Betty, *Origins of American Slavery, 1619-1776,* Rowman & (Littlefield Publishers, 2005), 64-65.

[58] "Massachusetts Constitution and the Abolition of Slavery," www.mass.gov/guides/massachusetts-constitution-and-the-abolition-of-slavery. Visited on June 10, 2025.

[59] Greene, Evarts B. and Harrington, Virginia, D., *American Populations before the Federal Census of 1790*, (New York, 1932), 4.

[60] There is no general census of New England available for any one of the years. These numbers are a composite taken over a five year period. Williams, Samuel, E.B., LL. D., *History of Vermont,* (Walpole, 1794), 425; *Connecticut Colonial Records, 1636-1776,* (Hartford, 1850-1890), XIV, 485-491; Lincoln, William, ed., *Journals of the Massachusetts Provisional Congress,* (Boston, 1838), 755; Bartlett, John Russell, ed., *Records of the Colony of Rhode Island and Providence Plantations, 1736-1792,* (Providence Press, 1856-1865), VII, 253; Greene, Evarts B. and Harrington, Virginia, D, *Records of the State of Vermont,* (Montpelier, 1873), I, 403.

[61] McManus, Edgar J., *Black Bondage in the North,* (Syracuse University Press, 1973), 17; Klein, Herbert S., *The Atlantic Slave Trade*, (Cambridge University Press, 1999), 46.

[62] Brooks, Rebecca Beatrice, "Slavery in Massachusetts," *History of Massachusetts Blog.* www.historyofmassachusetts.org/slavery-in-massachusetts/

[63] Wiecek, William M., "the Statutory Law of Slavery and Race in the Thirteen Mainland Colonies of British America", *The William and Mary Quarterly*, 34 (2): 261; *1641: Massachusetts Body of Liberties*, www.mass.gov/ info-details/massachusetts-body-of-liberties, visited January 8, 2025.

[64] Brooks, "Slavery in Massachusetts," *History of Massachusetts Blog. www.historyofmassachusetts.org/slavery-in-massachusetts/*

[65] O'Callaghan, E.B. and Fernow, Berthold, eds., *Documents Relative to the Colonial History of the State of New York,* (Albany: Weed, Parsons and Company, 1856-87).

[66] Klein, *The Atlantic Slave Trade,* 76-77.

[67] *Board of Audit of the West India Company,* May 27, 1647.

[68] McManus, Edgar J., *A History of Negro Slavery in New York,* Syracuse University Press, 1966), 7.

[69] Ibid, 23.

[70] McManus, *Black Bondage in the North,,* 20.

[71] Ibid, 41-42.

[72] For Seward, see Goodwin, Doris Kearns, *Team of Rivals,* (Simon & Schuster, 2005), 30-31. For Lincoln: "RUN away on the 13th of *September* last from Abraham Lincoln of Springfield in the County of Chester, a Negro Man named Jack, about 30 Years of Age, low Stature, speaks little or no *English,* has a Scar by the Corner of one Eye, in the Form of a V, his Teeth notched, and the Top of one of his Fore Teeth broke; He had on when he went away an old Hat, a grey Jacket partly like a Sailor's Jacket. Whoever secures the said Negro and brings him to his Master, or to *Mordecai Lincoln* ... shall have *Twenty Shillings* Reward and reasonable Charges", *Pennsylvania Gazette,* Oct. 15, 1730. Mordecai Lincoln (1686-1736) was great-great-grandfather of President Lincoln.

[73] "African Burial Ground Proves Northern Slavery," *The City Sun,* Feb. 24, 1993.

[74] Main, Jackson Turner, *Society and Economy in Colonial Connecticut,* (Princeton University Press, 1983), 177; Greene, Lorenzo Johnston, *The Negro in Colonial New England, 1620-1776,* (N.Y.: Columbia University Press, 1942), 74-75.

[75] *1641: Massachusetts Body of Liberties*, www.mass.gov/ info-details/massachusetts-body-of-liberties.

[76] "Massachusetts Constitution and the Abolition of Slavery," Official Website of the Commonwealth of Massachusetts. www.Mass.gov, retrieved on December 11, 2024.

[77] Ibid.

[78] Foner, *History of Black Americans: From Africa to the Emergence of the Cotton Kingdom.*

[79] Wood, Betty; et al. "Slavery in Colonial Georgia". *New Georgia Encyclopedia*, Retrieved December 30, 2024.

[80] Foner, *History of Black Americans: From Africa to the Emergence of the Cotton Kingdom.*

[81] Horton, James Oliver and Lois E. Horton, *Hard Road to Freedom: The Story of African America*, (Rutgers University Press, 2002), 2, 26; Breen and Innes, *"Myne Own Ground" Race and Freedom on Virginia's Eastern Shore*, 4; Indentured Servants In The U.S., pbs.org. Accessed March 9, 2023.

[82] Breen and Innes, *"Myne Own Ground" Race and Freedom on Virginia's Eastern Shore*, 10; Rodriguez, Junius, *Slavery in the United States: A Social, Political, and Historical Encyclopedia, Volume 2*, (ABC-CLIO, 2007), 453.

[83] Walker, Juliet, *The History of Black Business in America: Capitalism, Race, Entrepreneurship, Volume 1*, (University of North Carolina Press, 2009), 49; Sweet, Frank W., *Legal History of the Color Line: The Rise and Triumph of the One-Drop Rule*, (Backintyme Publishing, 2005), 117.

[84] *Original MS, Records of the County Court of Northampton, Orders, Deeds and Wills, 1651-1654*, 10.

[85] Federal Writers' Project, *Virginia: A Guide to the Old Dominion*, (US History Publishers, 1954),*76;* Danver, Steven, *Popular Controversies in World History,* (ABC-CLIO, *2010), 322;* Kozlowski, Darrell, *Colonialism: Key Concepts in American History,* (Infobase Publishing, 2010*), 78;* Conway, John, *A Look at the Thirteenth and Fourteenth Amendments: Slavery Abolished, Equal Protection Established,* (Enslow Publishers, 2008), *5;* Toppin, Edgar, *The Black American in United States History,* (Allyn & Bacon, 2010), 46.

[86] Finkleman, Paul, *Slavery in the Courtroom: An Annotated Bibliography of American Cases*, (Library of Congress, 1985).

[87] There is dispute as to when the first individual was deemed an indefinite servant, and to whom. However, it is not within this writers scope to argue the exact instant when slavery was legally legitimized within the American Colonies. Consequently, the Anthony Johnson case is considered "one of the first," as it is one of the earliest records of such existence; *U.S. Department of Commerce and Labor, Bureau of the Census, First Federal Census of the United State, Taken in the Year 1790.*

[88] Ibid.

[89] Ibid.

[90] Heinegg, Paul, *Free African Americans of North Carolina, Virginia, And South Carolina from the Colonial Period to About 1820 (2 Volumes),* 5th edition, (Clearfield Co, 2007).

[91] Ibid.

[92] Ibid.

[93] Bush, Jonathan A., "The British Constitution and the Creation of American Slavery", *Finkelman, Paul (ed.), Slavery & the Law,* (Rowman & Littlefield, 2002), *392;* Ibram X. Kendi, *Stamped from the Beginning: The Definitive History of Racist Ideas in America,* (Nation Books, 2016), 53-54, 67-68; Eric Foner, *Give Me Liberty!:*

An American History, (W.W. Norton & Company, 2009), 100; "Hening's Statutes at Large", *Encyclopedia Virginia,* Volume 3, 459; "African American Heritage and Ethnography", *National Park Service Pamphlet*, (U.S. Department of Interior), www.nps.gov.

[94] "Massachusetts Constitution and the Abolition of Slavery," Official Website of the Commonwealth of Massachusetts. www.Mass.gov, retrieved on December 11, 2024.

[95] Dworkin, Shari L., "Race, Sexuality, and the 'One Drop Rule': More Thoughts about Interracial Couples and Marriage", *The Society Pages*. Retrieved 27 February 2015; Sharfstein, Daniel J., "Crossing the Color Line: Racial Migration and the One-Drop Rule, 1600-1860", (*Minnesota Law Review*, 2007), 627.

[96] Gruber, Kate Egner, "Slavery in Colonial America", *The American Battlefield Trust*, retrieved December 11, 2024. www.battlefields.org/learn/articles/slavery-colonial-america

[97] "Goyen Family Tree," www.goyengoinggowengoyneandgone.com/1630-mihil-gowen-black-servant-given-freedom-in-1657/; Heinegg, Paul, "Freedom in the Archives: Free African Americans in Colonial America," *Common Place, the Journal of Early American Life*, Issue 5., (October 2004). Retrieved December 12, 2024. www.commonplace.online/article/ freedom-in-the-archives/; "The Cumbo Family: Tracing one of the First African descended families in America," *The Cumbo Family Website*, (October 22, 2020). https://cumbofamily.com/ ?p=879

[98] Heinegg, "Freedom in the Archives: Free African Americans in Colonial America," *Common Place, the Journal of Early American Life*, Issue 5., (October 2004).

[99] Hening, William Waller, *The Statutes at Large; Being a Collection of All the Laws of Virginia from the First Session of the Legislature in the Year 1619*, (New York: R. & W. & G. Bartow, 1823), 4:132.

[100] Heinegg, "Freedom in the Archives: Free African Americans in Colonial America," *Common Place, the Journal of Early American Life*, Issue 5., (October 2004).

[101] Ibid; "African American Heritage and Ethnography", *National Park Service Pamphlet*, (U.S. Department of Interior), www.nps.gov.

[102] Ibid.

[103] Wolfe, Brendan, "Free Blacks in Colonial Virginia," In *Encyclopedia Virginia*. https://encyclopediavirginia.org/entries/free-blacks-in-colonial-virginia.

[104] Gruber, Kate Egner, "Slavery in Colonial America", *The American Battlefield Trust*, retrieved December 11, 2024. www.battlefields.org/learn/articles/slavery-colonial-america

[105] Hening, *The Statutes at Large; Being a Collection of All the Laws of Virginia from the First Session of the Legislature in the Year 1619*, 2:280.

[106] MS. Deeds of Henrico County, Number 4, 692.

[107] Hening, ed., *Statutes at Large,* XI, 39-40; Russell, *Free Negroes of Virginia*, 42-59.

[108] Heinegg, *Free African Americans of North Carolina, Virginia, and South Carolina*, 695-696; Koger, *Black Slaveowners*, 13-14, 108-110.

[109] E. Louise, *Elizabeth Cleveland Hardcastle 1714-1808*, (South Carolina Phoenix Publishers, 2001), 57-104.

[110] Koger, *Black Slaveowners*, 209-210, 78, 97, 24, 166.

[111] *The End of Colonial Dominion*, https://www.floridamuseum.ufl.edu/staugustine/timeline/the-end-of-colonial-dominion/

[112] Landers, Jane, "Ana Gallum, Freed Slave and Property Owner," *Women in Colonial Latin America*, ed. Nora E. Jaffary and Jane E. Mangan, (Indianapolis/Cambridge: Hackett Publishing Company, Inc., 2018); Landers, Jane, "Founding Mothers: Female Rebels in Colonial New Granada and Spanish Florida," *Journal of African American History* 98, no. 1 (2013).

[113] Ibid.

[114] Koger, *Black Slaveowners*, 29.

[115] The amount of land varied with rank, ranging from 100 acres for privates and noncommissioned officers to 500 acres for colonels and 1,100 acres for major generals. After the Revolution, the federal government reserved several million acres in Ohio for the settlement of Veterans who earned a bounty land warrant. www.department.va.gov/history/100-objects/object-2-bounty-land-warrant/#:~:text=The%2amount%20of%20land%20varied,earned%20a%20bounty%20land%20warrant.

[116] "Documenting a Slave's Birth, Parentage, and Origins (Marie Thérèse Coincoin, 1742–1816): A Test of "Oral History"", *National Genealogical Society Quarterly*, 96: 245–266.

[117] Historic American Buildings Survey (HABS), in cooperation with Cane River National Heritage Area et al., "Coincoin-Prudhomme House (Maison de Marie Therese)", HABS No. LA1295, *National Park Service*, 1; Klier, Betje Black, *Pavie in the Borderlands,* (Baton Rouge: Louisiana State University Press, 2000), 15; For a detailed delineation of Coincoin's three separate land acquisitions, see Elizabeth Shown Mills, "Demythicizing History: Marie Thérèse Coincoin, Tourism, and the National Historical Landmarks Program." *Louisiana History* 53 (Fall 2012): 402–37.

[118] Allured, Janet and Gentry, Judith F., "Marie Thérèse Coincoin (1742–1816): Slave, Slave Owner, and Paradox", *Louisiana Women: Their Lives and Times Series,* (University of Georgia Press, 2009); Louis Metoyer Private Land Claim Certificate B1953 (sections 17 and

94, Township 7 North, Range 6 West), Record Group 49, *General Land Office, National Archives*; Louis Mettoyer claim for 883.60 acres, OPEL: May 1796, File B1953, Louis Metoyer, Opelousas Notarial Records, Louisiana State Land Office, Baton Rouge; *Boissier et al. v. Metayer*, 5 Mart. (O.S.), 678 (1818).

[119] Ibid.

[120] Holloway, Joseph, "Black Slaveowners," *The Slave Rebellion Website,* SlaveRebellion.org. Visited on May 30, 2025.

Chapter 3
[121] Olmsted, Frederick Law, *The Cotton Kingdom: A Traveller's Observations on Cotton and Slavery in the American Slave States*, (New York: Knopf, 1953), 262.
[122] Woodson, *Free Negroes Owners of Slaves*, v.

[123] Reeves, John, "Unraveling Ulysses S. Grant's Complex Relationship With Slavery," *Smithsonian Magazine* (December 5, 2023), www.smithsonianmag.com/history/unraveling-ulysses-s-grants-complex-relationship-with-slavery-180983360/ (Visited on July 24, 2025); Johnson, Kevin Orlin, *The Lincolns in the White House*, (Pangaeus Press, 2023); Fate, Michael, "Jehu Jones, Sr., 1769-1833," *Black Past*, Retained December 31, 2024, www.blackpast.org/african-american-history/jones-jehu-sr-1769-1833/; "Jehu Jones", *South Carolina Encyclopedia*, www.scencyclopedia.org/sce/entries/jehu-jones/.

[124] Fate, "Jehu Jones, Sr., 1769-1833," *Black Past*, "Jehu Jones", *South Carolina Encyclopedia*.

[125] Ibid.

[126] Ibid.

[127] Ibid.

[128] Ibid; Court Petition #11382705, Charleston District/Parish, South Carolina. filing started November 6, 1827.

[129] Fate, "Jehu Jones, Sr., 1769-1833," *Black Past*.

[130] Fitchett, E. Horace, "The Origin and Growth of the Free Negro Population of Charleston, South Carolina," *Journal of Negro History*, 26 (October 1941): 425-26; Foner, Laura, "The Free People of Color in Louisiana and St. Domingue: A Comparative Portrait of Two Three-Caste Slave Societies," *Journal of Social History*, 3 (Summer 1970): 408-11; Robertson, James, ed., *Louisiana under the Rule of Spain, France, and the United States, 1785-1807; Social, Economic, and Political Conditions of the Territory represented in the Louisiana Purchase*, 2 vols. (Cleveland, Ohio, 1910-11, rpt. edn., Freeport, N.Y., 1969), 1: 218-19; Jordan, Winthrop, *White over Black: American Attitudes toward the Negro, 1550-1812*, (Chapel Hill, N.C., 1968), 77-81.

[131] Ibid.

[132] United States Congress, *"Transactions in the Floridas,"* American State Papers: Documents, Legislative and Executive, of the Congress of the United States, (Washington, D.C.: Gales and Seaton, 1834); Clinton, Catherine and Gillespie, Michele, *The Devil's Lane: Sex and Race in the Early South*, (Oxford, England: Oxford University Press, 1997), 238–239.

[133] Ibid.

[134] Fitchett, E. Horace, "Traditions of the Free Negro in Charleston, South Carolina," *Journal of Negro History*, 25:2 (April 1940), 141; Harris, Robert L., "Charleston's Free Afro-American Elite," *The South Carolina Historical Magazine*, (South Carolina Historical Society, October 1981), 82:4, 308; Koger, *Black Slaveowners*, 10-14, 23, 135, 165; Legislative Records, [Petition of John Holman] to the South Carolina General Assembly, October 3, 1791, South Carolina Department of Archives and History, Columbia, S.C.; ibid., Memorial of Thomas Cole, Peter Bassnett Mathews, and Mathew Webb to the

South Carolina General Assembly, January 13, 1791, no. 181, SCDAH; ibid., Petition of John L. Wilson Jehu Jones's guardian] to the South Carolina General Assembly, December 6, 1823, SCDAH; Records of the County Probate Court [hereafter, RCPC], Charleston Co., S.C., Miscellaneous Land Records, pt. 87, bks. R6-S6 (February 16, 1795), 161-62, in Museum of Early Southern Decorative Arts, Winston-Salem, N.C. [hereafter, MESDA]; ibid., pt. 88, bks. T6-U6 (October 11-12, 1794), 520-22, in MESDA; Brent H. Holcomb, ed., "1786 Tax Returns," South Carolina Magazine of Ancestral Research, 9 (Spring 1981): 73; Philip D. Morgan, "Black Life in Eighteenth-Century Charleston," in Perspectives in American History, n.s., 1 (1984): 191, 193, 205, 216, 222; Extract of the Will of Philip Stanislas Noisette, ca. 1830, in Noisette Family Papers, South Carolinian Library, Columbia, S.C.; RCPC, Effingham Co., Ga., Deeds, bk. G (January 1, 1806), 445-46, in Charles Odingsells Papers, Georgia Historical Society, Savannah, Ga.; Thomas, David, "The Free Negro in Florida before 1865," South Atlantic Review, 10 (October 1911): 336; Homes, Jack D. L., "The Roles of Blacks in Spanish Alabama: The Mobile District, 1780-1813," *Alabama Historical Quarterly*, 37 (Spring 1975): 10-11; Legislative Records, Petition of L. Rowan, John Smith, et al. [concerning the Barland family], to the Mississippi General Assembly, ca. 1830, Record Group 47, box 19, Mississippi Department of Archives and History, Jackson, Miss.; General Index of All Successions, Opened in the Parish of Orleans, From the Year 1805, to the Year 1846, comp. P. M. Bertin (New Orleans, 1849), passim; Records of the Parish Probate Court [hereafter, RPPC], Pointe Coupe Parish, La., Successions, no. 176, April 5, 1839; Deed of Emancipation for Jean Meullion, February 21, 1776, in Meullion Family Papers.

[135] Oakes, James, The Ruling Race, *A History of American Slaveholders*, (New York: Alfred A. Knopf, 1982), 47-49.

[136] Berry, Thomas S., *Western Prices before 1861*, (Cambridge, Mass: 1843), 186; *The Holloway Family Papers*, (College of Charleston, Charleston, SC); Catterall, Helen, ed., *Judicial Cases Concerning Slavery and the American Negro*, 5 vols.,

(March 22, 1830), 32-33; Sterkx, Herbert, *The Free Negro in Antebellum Louisiana*, (Rutherford, N.J., 1972), 204-207.

[137] Woodson, "Free Negro Owners of Slaves in the United States in 1830," *Journal of Negro History*, 9 (January 1924), 41-85.

[138] "Louise Pecquet du Bellet", *Some Prominent Virginia Families Vol. 4*, (Lynchburg, VA: J.P. Bell Company Inc. 1907), 188-189; Frangos, Steve, "First Greek Couple of North America: Andrea Dimitry and Marianne Celeste Dragon", *The National Herald, (June 12, 2018).*

[139] Thompson, Shirley Elizabeth, *Exiles at Home The Struggle to Become American in Creole New Orleans*, (Cambridge, MA: Harvard University Press, 2009), 39; "Gwendolyn Hall", *Afro Louisiana History and Genealogy 1719-1820*, The University of North Carolina at Chapel Hill, www.ibiblio.org/laslave/fields.php

[140] *"Portrait of Marianne Celeste Dragon Dimitry"*, Smithsonian National Portrait Gallery. www.si.edu/object/ npe_5750. Retrieved May 31, 2025.

[141] *Louisiana's Territorial Period, 1803-1812*, LSU Libraries, 2021, www.ib.lsu.edu/sites/all/files/sc/fpoc/history.html

[142] "Louise Pecquet du Bellet", *Some Prominent Virginia Families Vol. 4*, 188-189; *Louisiana's Territorial Period, 1803-1812*, LSU Libraries, 2021, www.ib.lsu.edu/sites/all/ files/sc/fpoc/history.html

[143] Whitten, David O., *Andrew Durnford: A Black Sugar Planter in Antebellum Louisiana*, (Natchitoches, La.: Northwestern State University Press, 1981), 57-67.

[144] Whitten, *Andrew Durnford: A Black Sugar Planter in Antebellum Louisiana*, 3-11, 68-69.

[145] Ibid, 57-67.

[146] Ibid.

[147] Schweninger, Loren, "John Carruthers Stanly and the Anomaly of Black Slaveholding," *The North Carolina Historical Review* (April 1990), **67** (2): 159–192; Garrett, Crystal, "Family Ties: Those Wild and Crazy Stanlys," *Sun Journal* (New Bern, North Carolina, March 9, 2015); Sullivan, Elizabeth, "Blacks' Journey to Cleveland Laid Groundwork for Success, " *Cleveland.com,* (January 12, 2019).

[148] Ibid.

[149] Ibid.

[150] Ibid.

[151] "The Blurred Racial Lines of Famous Families," www.pbs.org/wgbh/pages/frontline/shows/secret/famous/pendarvis.html, visited on June 10, 2025.

[152] EbonyRose, "Did Black People Own Slaves?" *African American.org,* Retrieved June 10, 2025; "The Black Code of Louisiana, 1806," *The Law Library of Louisiana,* www.lasc.libguides.com/history-of-the-codes-of-Louisiana, June 10, 2025;.Northup, Solomon, *Twelve Years a Slave Narrative of Solomon Northup, a Citizen of New-York, Kidnapped in Washington City in 1841, and Rescued in 1853, from a Cotton Plantation near the Red River in Louisiana,* (London: Sampson Low, Son and Company, 1853), 194.

[153] Johnson and Roark, *Black Masters. A Free Family of Color in the Old South,* 14-15; "Ellison Family Graveyard" and "William Ellison", photos and transcriptions, bio of William Ellison, 2009, *Rootsweb,* accessed June 10, 2025;; Koger, *Black Slaveowners: Free Black Slave Masters in South Carolina, 1790-1860,* 53-63, 145, 144–145.

Chapter 4
[154] Whitten, *Andrew Durnford: A Black Sugar Planter in Antebellum Louisiana,* 57-67.

[155] Conlin, *The American Past: A Survey of American History*, 370; Stampp, Kenneth, *The Peculiar Institution: Slavery in the Antebellum South*, (New York: Vintage Books, 1956), 194; Oakes, *The Ruling Race, A History of American Slaveholders*, 47-48.

[156] Woodson, "Free Negro Owners of Slaves in the United States in 1830," *Journal of Negro History*, 9 (January 1924), 41-85.

[157] Ibid, 41-42.

[158] Ibid, 42-43.

[159] Ibid.

[160] "Stepping," *Encyclopedia Brittanica,* www.britannica.com/art/stepping (Visited on July 24, 2025); "African American Gospel," *The Library of Congress,* www.loc.gov/collections/songs-of-america/articles-and-essays/musical-styles/ritual-and-worship/african-american-gospel (Visited on July 25, 2025)

[161] *Hutchinson's Code of Mississippi*, 1798-1848, pp. 524-525, 533; Mississippi's laws required every person of free status to appear before the local court to give evidence of his or her freedom. When the court was provided satisfactory proof, the applicants received certificates of free status, or freedom papers, as the certificates became commonly known. The certificate indicated the bearer's name, color, physical stature, and any distinguishing features, such as scars. The certificate had to be renewed every three years at a fee of $1, the equivalent of $25 today, and increased to $3 in 1831.

As a result of these laws, free Black people in Mississippi placed themselves at great risk if they failed to have in their possession a certificate of registration. They ran the risk of seizure and even jail. If Blacks were unable to establish their free status within a specified period of time, they could, as allowed by law, be sold into slavery at public auction. For free people, the certificates of registration were their single most important source of documentation.

[162] "Narrative of the Seizure and Recovery of Solomon Northrup," *New York Times*, Documenting the American South, January 20, 1853.

[163] Woodson, "Free Negro Owners of Slaves in the United States in 1830," *Journal of Negro History*, 41-85.

[164] Ibid.

[165] Ibid; Court Petition #11382705, Charleston District/Parish, South Carolina. filing started November 6, 1827.

[166] Koger, *Black Slaveowners: Free Black Slave Masters in South Carolina, 1790-1860*, 154-155.

[167] Ibid.

[168] Kissner, James, "Who is Justus Angel?", Home.org. h-o-m-e.org/who-is-justus-angel/, visited on June 5, 2025.

[169] Davis, Edwin Adams and William Ransom Hogan, *The Barber of Natchez*, (LSU, 1954, 1973), 8; Cornelius, Janet Duitsman, *When I Can Read My Title Clear: Literacy, Slavery, and Religion in the Antebellum South*, (Columbia, South Carolina: University of South Carolina Press, 1991).

[170] Ibid, 2, 19.

[171] Ribianszky, Nik, "Generations of Freedom: The Natchez Database of Free People of Color, 1779-1865," *Journal of Slavery and Data Preservation4*, no. 1 (2023): 11- 23. Site visited on June 9, 2025. https://doi.org/10.25971/9k0y-s795

[172] Ibid.

[173] Davis and Hogan, *The Barber of Natchez,* 227, 232, 260.

[174] *Diary of William Johnson Free Black Businessman Natchez, Mississippi Diary Selections from Jan. 1, 1838 – Jan. 1, 1844*, National Humanities Center Resource Toolbox, The Making of African American Identity: Vol. I, 1500-1865, www.National humanitiescenter.org/pds/maai/identity/text4/williamjohnsondiary.pdf; Ribianszky, "Generations of Freedom: The Natchez Database of Free People of Color, 1779-1865," *Journal of Slavery and Data Preservation4,* no. 1 (2023): 11-23.

Chapter 5

[175] Schweninger, "Prosperous Blacks in the South, 1790-1880," *The American Historical Review* 95 (February 1990): 31-56.

[176] Master of Equity, Bills of Complaint 1847, Record Number 52 (Charleston County), "Wills of Elias Collins."

[177] Johnson, Michael P., and Roak, James L., *Black Masters: A Free Family of Color in the Old South*, (New York: Norton, 1986), 136.

[178] *American Colonization Society Papers,* "William Kellogg to William McLain", 6 October 1852, (Library of Congress), 90; Berlin, *Slaves without Masters*, 279.

[179] Schweninger, Loren, "Prosperous Blacks in the South, 1790-1880," *The American Historical Review*, 95, no. 1 (1990): 37; Wikramanayake, Marina, *A World in Shadow: The Free Black in Antebellum South Carolina*, (Columbia, SC: University of South Carolina Press, 1973), 81.

[180] Bartlett, Sarah, "Brown Fellowship Society (1790-1945)," *Black Past* (14 September 2010). www.blackpast.org/african-american-history/brown-fellowship-society-1790-1945/ (Visited June 14, 2025)

[181] Robert L. Harris Jr, "Charleston's Free Afro-American Elite: The Brown Fellowship Society and the Humane Brotherhood," The South Carolina Historical Magazine 82, no. 4 (October 1981): 297-298.

[182] Bartlett, "Brown Fellowship Society (1790-1945)," *Black Past* (14 September 2010); Harris, "Charleston's Free Afro-American Elite: The Brown Fellowship Society and the Humane Brotherhood," *The South Carolina Historical Magazine*, 289-310; Fitchett, E. Horrace, "The Negro in Charleston, South Carolina," PH.D. dissertation, University of Chicago, 1950, 1-2, 163.

[183] Ibid.

[184] Koger, *Black Slaveowners*, 107; Johnston and Roark, *Black Masters*, 134.

[185] *Charleston Courier*, December 8, 1835.

[186] Johnston and Roark, *Black Masters*, 123, 128.

[187] Ibid, 143.

[188] William Ellison to Henry Ellison, March 26,1857, Ellison Family Papers, South Carolina Library, University of South Carolina, Columbia, South Carolina.

[189] Span, Christopher M., "Learning in Spite of Opposition: African Americans and their History of Educational Exclusion in Antebellum America," The Politics of Curricular Change: Race, Hegemony, and Power in Education, vol. 31, (Peter Lang Publishing Group, 2005), 26-53

[190] Winch, Julie, *A Gentleman of Color: The Life of James Forten*, (New York: Oxford University Press, 2002), 16; Zielinski, Adam E., "James Forten, Revolutionary: Forgotten No More," *Journal of the American Revolution, (23 June 2023)*; Wright, Robert E., "Bank Ownership and Lending Patterns in New York and Pennsylvania, 1781-1831," *The Business History Review*, vol. 73, no. 1, 1999, 55, footnote 54.

Chapter 6

[191] Hayes, Amy, "Antebellum South: What Was the Identity of the Old South?" *thecollector.com* (September 15, 2022). Retrieved June 17, 2025; "The Antebellum South In America, a story", *aaregistry.org*, Retrieved June 17, 2025.

[192] Van Cleave, Timothy, "The Barber of Natchez", *National Park Service*; Hogan, William and Edwin Davis, eds., *The Barber of Natchez*, (Baton Rouge: Louisiana State University Press, 1972), 15-16, 28-29, 45-46, 58-59, 75; Shoenbaum, Eric, "A Precious Balance: The Free Blacks of Natchez," 3-7, an unpublished paper.

[193] The original news clipping resides at the Department of Archives and History. This copy was taken from *Mississippi History Now*, May 2000. Visited the site on June 29, 2025. www.Mshistorynow.mdah.ms.gov/issue/a-contested-presence-free-blacks-in-antebellum-mississippi-18201860.

[194] Berry, Thomas S., *Western Prices before 1861*, (Cambridge, Mass., 1943), 186; "Last Will and Testament of Richard Holloway, October 19, 1842," *Holloway Family Papers*, College of Charleston, Charleston, S.C.; Catterall, Helen, ed., *Judicial Cases Concerning American Slavery and the Negro*, 5 vols., (Washington, D.C., 1932), 3: 292, 589, 611-12; Sterkx, Herbert, *The Free Negro in Antebellum Louisiana*, (Rutherford, NJ, 1972), 204-07.

[195] Ibid; Record of Wills vol. 22 1786-1793 (Charleston County), 194-196 (Department of Archives & History, Columbia, South Carolina); Inventories vol. B 1787-1793 (Charleston County), 15 (Department of Archives & History, Columbia, South Carolina).

[196] Koger, *Black Slaveowners*, 38-39, 154-155, 168, 177.

[197] Schweninger, "Prosperous Blacks in the South, 1790-1880," *The American Historical Review* 95 (February 1990): 36.

[198] Ibid.

[199] Whitten, *Andrew Durnford: A Black Sugar Planter in Antebellum Louisiana*, 3-11, 68-69.

[200] Koger, *Black Slaveowners*, 110-113; Rogers, Jr., George C. and David R. Chestnutt, eds.,, *The Papers of Henry Laurens* vol. 7, (Columbia, Published for the South Carolina Historical Society by the University of South Carolina Press, 1968), 344.

[201] Koger, *Black Slaveowners*, 113-114

[202] Legislative Records, Petition of John Holman to the South Carolina General Assembly, October 3, 1791, SCDAH; Koger, Black Slaveowners, 110, 119, 254; Spraggins, Tinsley L., "The History of the Negro in Business prior to 1860," (M.A. thesis, Howard University, 1935), 33.

[203] Koger, *Black Slaveowners*, 113-121.

[204] Ibid, 144–145; Johnson and Roark, *Black Masters*, 15, 26.

[205] Bush, Jonathan A., "Free to Enslave: The Foundations of Colonial American Slave Law," *Yale Journal of Law & the Humanities*, Vol. 5: 417, (1993). Bush continues this discussion in his endnotes as follows: For nineteenth-century opinion, see Thomas R.R. Cobb, *An Inquiry into the Law of Negro Slavery in the United States of America* § 83, at 82 (photo. reprint 1968) (1858); William Goodwell, *The American Slave Code in Theory and Practice*, 258-65 (photo. reprint 1968) (1853); *Miller v. McQuerry,* 17 F. Cas. 335, 336 (C.C.D. Ohio 1853) (No. 9583) (McLean, J.). Bush also includes in the endnote the views of historians as follows: see Wesley F. Craven, *The Southern Colonies in the Seventeenth Century 1607-1689*, 217 (1949); Wesley Craven, *White, Red, and Black: The Seventeenth Century Virginian*, 75 (1971); David D. Davis, *The Problem of Slavery in the Age of Revolution,1770-1823*, 473-74 (1975); *English Historical Documents: Vol. IX, American Colonial Documents To 1776*, 491 (Merrill Jensen ed., 1955); Paul Finkelman, *The Law of Freedom and Bondage: A Casebook*, 1, 10 (1986); Winthrop D. Jordan, *White Over Black: American Attitudes Toward the Negro, 1550-1812*, 72, 81

(1968); Kenneth M. Stampp, *The Peculiar Institution*, 21, 22 (1956); Alan Watson, *Slave Law in the Americas*, 11-12, 64 (1989); Whittington B. Johnson, *The Origin and Nature of African Slavery in Seventeenth Century [sic] Maryland*, 73; William M. Wiecek, *Somerset: Lord Mansfield and the Legitimacy of Slavery in the Anglo American World*, 86, 127 (1974) (citing prescription, parliamentary act, custom, and local legislative fiat as bases for slavery), The Maryland act is cited in James Oakes, *Slavery and Freedom*, 68 (1990) and Jonathan L. Alpert, *The Origin of Slavery in the United States-The Maryland Precedent*, 189-90 (1970) (dating act to 1639).

[206] "Slave Codes," Britannica. www.britannica.com/topic/slave-code Visited on July 2, 2025; "United States Slavery Laws and Restrictions," *Pure History*, November 18, 2011. www.purehistory.org/united-states-slavery-laws-and-restrictions/. Visited on July 2, 2025.

[207] Smith, Henry A. M., "Goose Creek," *South Carolina Historical & Genealogical Magazine,* vol. 23 (1928), 179-180; *Seventh Census of the United States:* Schedule I, St. James & Goose Creek Parish, Charleston County, South Carolina, 427; Ibid., Schedule II, 407; Ibid., Schedule IV, 353-354; Koger, *Black Slaveowners*, 39.

[208] Brophy, Alfred L., "The Nat Turner Trials", *North Carolina Law Review* (June 2013), volume 91: 1817–80; White, Deborah Gray, *Freedom on My Mind: A History of African Americans*, (New York Bedford/St. Martin's, 2013), 225.

[209] McPherson, James M., *Battle Cry of Freedom*, (New York: Oxford University Press, 1988), 207–208.

[210] Bryant, Christopher J., "Without Representation, No Taxation: Free Blacks, Taxes, and Tax Exemptions Between the Revolutionary and Civil Wars," *Michigan Journal of Race and Law*, 91 (2015); Butler, Nic, Ph.D. , *South Carolina's Capitation Tax on Free People of Color, 1756–1864,* Charleston County Public Library, January 28, 2022; Goodson, Noreen J. and Donna Tyler Hollie, *Through the Tax*

Assessor's Eyes: Enslaved People, Free Blacks and Slaveholders in Early Nineteenth Century Baltimore, (Clearfield, 2017).

[211] ***Hinds v. Brazealle*** (1838) was a freedom suit decided by the Supreme Court of Mississippi, which denied the legality in Mississippi of deeds of manumission executed by Elisha Brazealle, a Mississippi resident, in Ohio to free a slave woman and their son. Hinds ruled that Brazealle was trying to evade Mississippi law against manumissions except when authorized by the state legislature, and the actions were invalid. Both the mother and son were declared legally still slaves in Mississippi, and the son was prohibited from inheriting his father's estate, as Brazealle had left it all to him. This case would prevent free blacks who were descendants of slave owners from inheriting property from their parents unless they followed state laws of manumissions. As a result this process began to restrict in many cases the right of manumissions; ***Dred Scott v. Sandford***, 60 U.S. (19 How.) 393 (1857), was a landmark decision of the United States Supreme Court that held the U.S. Constitution did not extend American citizenship to people of black African descent, and therefore they could not enjoy the rights and privileges the Constitution conferred upon American citizens thus limiting the rights of free Blacks thus allowing states to pass laws that could restrain or even strip Black slave masters of their rights to own slaves and reserve that right for only whites if so desired to prevent a threat of Black masters from freeing their slaves. Of course this ruling's main purpose would be used to determine the legal status of Dred Scott's freedom but the ruling was used as a precedent to restrain rights of free Blacks as well.

[212] Marriage Book, St. Phillip's Church, Charleston, S.C., in Fitchett, "Origin and Growth," 431-32; Records of Charleston Probate Court, Charleston, S.C., Estates, no. 229-6, December 30, 1874; Hogan, William and Edwin Davis, eds., *William Johnson's Natchez: The Antebellum Diary of a Free Negro*, (Baton Rouge, La., 1951), 11, 43, 334, 399; Legislative Records, *Petition of Andrew Barland to the Senate and House of Representatives of Mississippi*, ca. 1824, Record Group 47, boxes 16-17, Mississippi Department of Archives and History; *"A Contract of Marriage between JOSEPH METOYER and MARIE*

LODOISKA LLORENS, " January 28, 1840, Cane River Collection, Historic New Orleans Collection, New Orleans, La.; Records of Parish Probate Court, Pointe Coupee Parish, La., Marriage Contract, February 26, 1835; U.S. Manuscript Population Census, St. Landry Parish, La., 1860; Records of Parish Probate Court, St. Landry Parish, La., Marriage Certificate, March 25, 1796, Meullion Family Papers; Records of Parish Probate Court, Natchitoches Parish, La., *Successions,* no. 344, September 7, 1838; Records of Parish Probate Court , Plaquemines Parish, La., *Successions,* no. 167, May 12, 1840; Records of Parish Probate Court, East Baton Rouge Parish, La., *Successions,* no. 640, August 14, 1855; Records of Parish Probate Court, West Baton Rouge Parish, La., *Successions,* no. 176, July 18, 1829.

[213] *Hutchinson's Code of Mississippi,* 1798-1848, 524-525, 533.

[214] Davis, Dernoral, "A Contested Presence: Free Black People in Antebellum Mississippi, 1820–1860," *Mississippi History Now,* May 2000. Visited the site on June 29, 2025. www.mshistorynow.mdah.ms.gov/issue/a-contested-presence-free-blacks-in-antebellum-mississippi-18201860.

[215] Franklin, *From Slavery to Freedom: A History of Negro Americans,* 214-222; Klebaner, Benjamin Joseph, "American Manumission Laws and the Responsibility for Supporting Slaves," *The Virginia Magazine of History and Biography,* 63:4 (Oct. 1955), 443-453.

[216] Whitten, *Andrew Durnford: A Black Sugar Planter in Antebellum Louisiana,* 57-67; *Diary of William Johnson Free Black Businessman Natchez, Mississippi Diary Selections from Jan. 1, 1838 – Jan. 1, 1844*; Ribianszky, "Generations of Freedom: The Natchez Database of Free People of Color, 1779-1865," *Journal of Slavery and Data Preservation4,* no. 1 (2023): 11- 23.

[217] Olmsted, Frederick Law, *The Cotton Kingdom: A Traveller's Observations on Cotton and Slavery in the American Slave States,* (New York: Knopf, 1953), 262.

[218] *King James Bible*, (Harper-Collins Christian Publishing, Inc, 2017), Genesis IX, verses 18–27.

[219] Ibid, Ephesians, VI, verses 5-7.

[220] Ibid, Colossians III, verse 22.

[221] Ibid, Galatians III, verse 28.

[222] Johnston and Roark, *Black Masters*, 123, 128.

[223] Douglas, Frederick, *Narrative of the life of Frederick Douglass, an American slave*, (Boston: Published at the Anti-slavery Office, 1847), 2.

Chapter 7
[224] *St. Louis Republic*, August 16, 1891

[225] Smith, Jeb, "African Americans who Supported the Confederacy in the U.S. Civil War," *American History Now Magazine,* December 5, 2024. Site visited on July 6, 2025, www.historyisnow magazine.com/blog/2024/12/5/african-americans-who-supported-the-confederacy-in-the-us-civil-war.

[226] Washington, Booker T., *Up From Slavery,* (New York: Doubleday & Company, Inc., 1901), 12-13.

[227] Hammond, John Craig, "President, Planter, Politician: James Monroe, the Missouri Crisis, and the Politics of Slavery," *Journal of American History,* (March 2019*)*, 105 (4): 843–867; Clay, Henry, "Remarks on the Compromise of 1850 Resolutions," *Milestone Documents*; "Compromise of 1850," *National Archives*, Retrieved July 4, 2025; Smith, Elbert B., *The Presidencies of Zachary Taylor & Millard Fillmore*, (University Press of Kansas, 1988), 136-142; Remini, Robert V., *Daniel Webster: The Man and His Time*, (W.W. Norton & Company, 1997), 695–696; Dangerfield, George, *The Awakening of American Nationalism: 1815–1828,* (New York: Harper & Row, 1966), 125; Wilentz, Sean, *The Politicians &*

the Egalitarians: The Hidden History of American Politics, (New York: W.W. Norton & Company, 2004), 382.

[228] Sutton, Robert K, *"The Wealthy Activist Who Helped Turn 'Bleeding Kansas' Free,"* Smithsonian. Archived from the original on March 27, 2019, *Retrieved July 4, 2025;* Sumner, Charles, *Speech of the Honorable Charles Sumner of Massachusetts, In the Senate of the United States, May 19, 1856,* (Temple University Library, Digital Collections), www.digital.library.temple.edu/digital/collection/p160 02coll5/id/7881, *Retrieved July 4, 2025;* Nicole Etcheson, *Bleeding Kansas: Contested Liberty in the Civil War Era,* (University Press of Kansas, 2006), ch 1.

[229] "The senators who were expelled after refusing to accept Lincoln's election," *The Washington Post,* January 5, 2021; "In Washington D.C., the second South Carolina senator, James Henry Hammond, resigns his seat," *House Divided, The Civil War Research Engine at Dickenson College,* site visited on July 4, 2025, www.hd.house divided.dickinson.edu/node/34503

[230] The United States Senate, www.senate.gov/artandhistory/history/minute/ Civil_War_Begins.htm, site visited on July 4, 2025.

[231] Ibid, www.senate.gov/artandhistory/history/minute/Jefferson_ Davis_Farewell.htm, visited on July 4, 2025.

[232] Ibid, www.senate.gov/about/powers-procedures/expulsion/Civil War_Expulsion.htm, visited on July 5, 2025.

[233] Ibid, senate.gov/artandhistory/history/minute/Civil_War_Begins. Htm, visited on July 5, 2025.

[234] Conlin, *The American Past: A Survey of American History*, Cengage Learning, 370.

[235] *Douglass Monthly*, September 1861.

[236] Greeley, Horace, *The American Conflict: A History of the Great Rebellion in the United States of America*, vol. 2, (Hartford: O.D. Case and Company, 1866), 521.

[237] Steiner, Lewis H., *Report of Lewis H. Steiner, inspector of the Sanitary Commission : containing a diary kept during the rebel occupation of Frederick, Md., and an account of the operations of the U.S. Sanitary Commission during the campaign in Maryland, September 1862*, (New York : Anson D.F. Randolph, 1862), 19-20.

[238] Levine, Bruce, *Confederate Emancipation Southern Plans to Free and Arm Slaves during the Civil War*, (Oxford University Press, 2005), 16-18, 39, 40-45, 75-77.

[239] Smith, "African Americans who Supported the Confederacy in the U.S. Civil War," *American History Now Magazine*.

[240] Ibid.

[241] The A.R.T. of Human Rights—a collaboration between the American Repertory Theater & Carr Center for Human Rights Policy at Harvard University—presents the conversation *Fighting for Freedom: The Civil War and Its Legacies* livestreaming on the global, commons-based peer produced HowlRound TV network at howlround.tv, Sunday, February 8, 2015.

[242] Smith, "African Americans who Supported the Confederacy in the U.S. Civil War," *American History Now Magazine*.

[243] Ibid.

[244] Jackson, Joelle, "CSA 1st Louisiana Native Guard (1861-1862)," *BlackPast.org, June 23, 2011*, www.blackpast.org/african-american-history/1st-louisiana-native-guard-csa-1861-1862/, visited on July 5, 2025.

[245] *Richmond Daily Dispatch*, April 19, 1861.

²⁴⁶ Jordan, Ervin, *Black Confederates and Afro-Yankees in Civil War Virginia (A Nation Divided: Studies in the Civil War Era)*, (University of Virginia Press, January 29, 1995), 59.

²⁴⁷ Ibid.

²⁴⁸ Ibid.

²⁴⁹ Koger, *Black Slaveowners,* 190; Sumter, Thomas S., *Stateburg and Its People,* (Sumter: 1922), 11–12.

²⁵⁰ Smith, "African Americans who Supported the Confederacy in the U.S. Civil War," *American History Now Magazine.*

²⁵¹ *The Daily Dispatch, April 25, 1861.*

²⁵² Smith, "African Americans who Supported the Confederacy in the U.S. Civil War," *American History Now Magazine.*

²⁵³ Greeley, *The American Conflict: A History of the Great Rebellion in the United States of America*, vol. 2, 521.

²⁵⁴ *The Nashville Daily Union* (Nashville, Tennessee), March 21, 1863.

²⁵⁵ Greeley, *The American Conflict*, 521-522.

²⁵⁶ James McPherson's comments on Black Confederates, *Washington Post*, October 19, 2010. Retrieved on August 10, 2025;; Gallagher, Gary, "Black Confederate Movement 'Demented'," *YouTube*, Mar 13, 2014

²⁵⁷ Levin, Kevin M., *Searching for Black Confederates: The Civil War's Most Persistent Myth,* (University of North Carolina Press, 2019); Levin, Kevin, "The Myth of the Black Confederate Soldier", *The Daily Beast,* (August 8, 2015) , Retrieved August 19, 2025; Marshall, Josh, "In Search of the Black Confederate Unicorn", *Talking Points Memo*, (January 2, 2018), Retrieved August 19, 2025.

[258] Stauffer, John, "Yes, There Were Black Confederates. Here's Why," *The Root Magazine* (January 20, 2015), www.theroot.com/yes-there-were-black-confederates-here-s-why-1790858546, Visited on August 19, 2025.

[259] Williams, Scott K., *Black Confederates in the Civil War*, 2. www.scribd. com/document/157772219/Black-Confederates, Visited on August 20, 2025.

[260] Williams, *Black Confederates in the Civil War*, 7-8.

[261] Johnston and Roark, *Black Masters*, 303; Koger, *Black Slaveowners*, 193; *Letters Sent to Georgetown, South Carolina 1867-1868*, "Wesley Markwood to Major E.L. Dean, 14 March 1867," Freemen Bureau, Record Group 105 (National Archives, Washington D.C.).

[262] Johnston and Roark, Black Masters, 305, 316.

[263] Please note, because of the conditions that former Black Slaveholders faced after the War Between the States, it is not the intentions or desire to manufacture sorrow over the loss of the slave system, but to simply present a historical examination of the financial consequences that occurred because of the Civil War.

[264] Black Mississippi State Legislator John F. Harris's speech as recorded in the *Clarion-Ledger*, February 23, 1890.

[265] Buchanan, Minor Ferris, *Holt Collier: His Life, His Roosevelt Hunts, and the Origin of the Teddy Bear,* (Centennial Press of Mississippi, 2002).

[266] Many former Confederate Generals became advocates of Black Suffrage such as General P.G.T. Beauregard who helped establish a new political party in Louisiana called the Reform Party. With Beauregard as the cornerstone, the Reform Party consisted of conservative businessmen that advocated economical state government and recognition of the civil and political rights of Black

Americans; New Orleans *Times*, May 29, 1872; General James Longstreet became a supporter of black civil rights during Reconstruction; Wert, Jeffrey D., *General James Longstreet: The Confederacy's Most Controversial Soldier, A Biography,* (Simmon and Schuster, 1993), 411; Wade Hampton and Martin Delany attempting to foment some kind of new race relations in politics in 1870s South Carolina, albeit quite imperfectly. Delany would endorse Democrat candidate Hampton for Governor in October 1876. Hampton would go on to win the election and usher in the "Redeemer" government and end Reconstruction in the state, Poole, W. Scott, "Religion, gender, and the lost cause in South Carolina's 1876 governor's race: 'Hampton or Hell!'," *Journal of Southern History* 68.3 (2002): 573-598; General John B. Gordon's speech he gave running for Governor of Georgia contains extremely racist language and ideas, it also reflects a recognition by white Democrats in the South that unless they could pull off a small portion of African American voters, the Republicans would enjoy a permanent electoral majority in both South Carolina, where Gordon spoke, and in Mississippi. A report on the same speech by the *Charleston Daily News*, published on Sep 12, 1868, leads me to believe that most of those listening to Gordon were white Democrats. There were African Americans present as well, and their negative reaction to Gordon led to their chastisement by another speaker, Judge Campbell.

[267] Randall, J.G. and David Herbert Donald, *The Civil War and Reconstruction,* (Lexington: D.C. Health and Company, 1969), 576-577. 145; Koger, *Black Slaveowners*, 193-195; Genovese, Eugene D., *Roll, Jordan, Roll: The World the Slaves Made,* (New York: Pantheon Books, 1974), 3-10.

[268] Johnston and Roark, *Black Masters*, 316-317; 331-338.

[269] *An Act To Establish and Regulate the Domestic Relations Of Persons of Color, and to Amend the Law in Relation to Paupers and Vagrancy (1865),* in The Statutes at Large of South Carolina (Columbia, S.C.: Republican Printing Company, 1875), 13: 279. 158. Such acts as this was seen in almost every Southern state as Black Codes and Jim Crow Laws were being establish throughout the South

during and after Reconstruction; Johnston and Roark, *Black Masters*, 318.

[270] Jonathan C. Gibbs, African American Secretary of State for Florida, was on such person. Gibbs was an unwavering advocate for Black suffrage and equal political representation. He fought to ensure that African American men, who had just won the right to vote, were able to exercise that right without interference. He also supported land ownership for freedmen, recognizing that economic independence was essential for true freedom. Despite his dedication, Gibbs faced constant opposition from white supremacists and the growing influence of organizations like the Ku Klux Klan. The Reconstruction era was a volatile time in Florida, as it was in the rest of the South, and Gibbs' policies were met with hostility from the former Confederate elites who were determined to regain control of the state; *Jonathan C. Gibbs, Letter to Charles Barrett, Grafton, Vt., Tallahassee, Fla.,* (June 7, 1869). Rauner Special Collections Library, Dartmouth College, Hanover, New Hampshire; Foner, Eric, *Reconstruction: America's Unfinished Revolution, 1863–1877,* (New York: Perennial Classics, 1988), 354; *Florida Constitution,* (1868). Article VIII, Sec. 9; Wade Hampton and Martin Delany attempting to foment some kind of new race relations in politics in 1870s South Carolina, albeit quite imperfectly. Delany would endorse Democrat candidate Hampton for Governor in October 1876. Hampton would go on to win the election and usher in the "Redeemer" government and end Reconstruction in the state, Poole, W. Scott, "Religion, gender, and the lost cause in South Carolina's 1876 governor's race: 'Hampton or Hell!'," *Journal of Southern History* 68.3 (2002): 573-598; Confederate General John B. Gordon's speech in Tennessee to Black voters reflects a recognition by white Democrats in the South that unless they could pull off a small portion of African American voters, the Republicans would enjoy a permanent electoral majority in both South Carolina, where Gordon spoke, and in Mississippi; *Daily Phoenix,* Sep 23, 1868, Columbia, SC, 4: 2.

[271] Ibid.

[272] "William T. Johnson and family papers, 1793-1951 (bulk 1830-1870)," *ArchiveGrid*, site visited on July 6, 2025. www.Researchworks.oclc.org/archivegrid/data/262551773#:~:text=William%20married%20a%20former%20slave%2C%20Ann%20Battles%20%281815%3F-1866%29%3B,1846%29%2C%20Josephine%20%28born%201849%29%2C%20and%20Clarence%20%28born%201851%29.

Chapter 8
[273] Holloway, "Black Slaveowners." *The Slave Rebellion Website.* SlaveRebellion.org.

Bibliography

Primary Materials

Books

Berry, Thomas S. *Western Prices before 1861*. Cambridge, Mass: 1843.

Catterall, Helen, ed. *Judicial Cases Concerning Slavery and the American Negro*, 5 vols. March 22, 1830.

Clay, Henry. "Remarks on the Compromise of 1850 Resolutions." *Milestone Documents*. 1850.

Cobb, Thomas R. R. *An Inquiry into the Law of Negro Slavery in the United States of America.* University of Georgia Press, 1999) (1858), reprinted in Paul Finkleman, The Law of Freedom and Bondage: A Casebook 21 (1986).

Davis, Edwin Adams and William Ransom Hogan. *The Barber of Natchez.* LSU, 1954, 1973.

Douglas, Frederick. *Narrative of the life of Frederick Douglass, an American slave*. Boston: Published at the Anti-slavery Office, 1847.

Dunning, William A. *Reconstruction, Political and Economic, 1865-1877.* New York, 1907.

Fleming, Walter L. *Civil War and Reconstruction in Alabama.* New York: Columbia University Press, 1905.

Garner, James W. *Reconstruction in Mississippi*. New York, 1901.

Greeley, Horace. *The American Conflict: A History of the Great Rebellion in the United States of America*, vol. 2. Hartford: O.D. Case and Company, 1866.

Guild, June Percell. *Black laws of Virginia: A summary of the legislative acts of Virginia concerning Negroes from earliest times to the present*. Negro Universities Press, 1936.

Hamilton, J.G. De Roulhac. *Reconstruction in North Carolina.* New York, 1914.

Harris, Abram L. *The Negro as a Capitalist: A Study of Banking and Business Among American Negros.* Philadelphia: 1936.

Heinegg, Paul. *Free African Americans of North Carolina, Virginia, Virginia, And South Carolina from the Colonial Period to About*

1820 (2 Volumes), 5th edition. Clearfield Co, 2007.

Hogan, William and Edwin Davis, eds. *William Johnson's Natchez: The Ante-bellum Diary of a Free Negro*. Baton Rouge, La., 1951.

Jackson, Mary Ann. *Life and letters of General Thomas J. Jackson (Stonewall Jackson)*. New York: Harper and Brothers, Franklin Square, 1892.

King James Bible. Harper-Collins Christian Publishing, Inc, 2017.

Lauber, Almon Wheeler. *"Enslavement by the Indians Themselves." Indian Slavery in Colonial Times Within the Present Limits of the United States. Studies in history, economics and public law. 53:3.* Columbia University, 1913.

McCoy, Kelli. "John Rolfe's Letter to Sir Edwin Sandys, *Milestone Documents in African American History, Volume 4,* Salem Press, October 2017.

Northup, Solomon. *Twelve Years a Slave Narrative of Solomon Northup, a Citizen of New-York, Kidnapped in Washington City in 1841, and Rescued in 1853, from a Cotton Plantation near the Red River in Louisiana*. London: Sampson Low, Son and Company, 1853.

Olmsted, Frederick Law. *The Cotton Kingdom: A Traveler's Observations on Cotton and Slavery in the American Slave States*. 2 Volumes. New York: Mason Brothers, 1861.

Robertson, James, ed. *Louisiana under the Rule of Spain, France, and the United States, 1785-1807; Social, Economic, and Political Conditions of the Territory represented in the Louisiana Purchase*, 2 vols. Cleveland, Ohio, 1910-11, rpt. edn., Freeport, N.Y., 1969.

Rogers, Jr., George C. and David R. Chestnutt, eds. *The Papers of Henry Laurens* vol. 7. Columbia, Published for the South Carolina Historical Society by the University of South Carolina Press, 1968.

Stuart, Merah S. *An Economic Detour: A History of Insurance in the Lives of American Negros*. Philadelphia:1936.

Thompson, C. Mildred, *Reconstruction in Georgia: Economic, Social, Political: 1865-1872*. New York, 1915.

Washington, Booker T. *Up From Slavery*. New York: Doubleday & Company, Inc., 1901.

Whitten, David O. *Andrew Durnford, A Black Sugar Planter in the Antebellum South.* Transaction Publishers, 1995.

Williams, Samuel, E.B., LL. D. *History of Vermont.* Walpole, 1794.

Wilson, Calvin D. "Negros Who Owned Slaves," *Popular Science Monthly,* Vol. 81, November 1912.

Woodson, Carter G. *Free Negro Owners of Slaves in the United States in 1830; Together with Absentee Ownership of Slaves in the United States in 1830.* Washington, D.C., 1924.

_____ and Lindsay, Arnnett G., eds. *The Negro as a Businessman.* Washington, D.C., 1929.

Government Documents

"African American Heritage and Ethnography." *National Park Service Pamphlet.* U.S. Department of Interior.

An Act To Establish and Regulate the Domestic Relations Of Persons of Color, and to Amend the Law in Relation to Paupers and Vagrancy (1865), in The Statutes at Large of South Carolina. Columbia, S.C.: Republican Printing Company, 1875.

"A Contract of Marriage between JOSEPH METOYER and MARIE LODOISKA LLORENS," January 28, 1840. Cane River Collection, Historic New Orleans Collection, New Orleans, La.

Bartlett, John Russell, ed. *Records of the Colony of Rhode Island and Providence Plantations, 1736-1792.* Providence Press, 1856-1865, 10 volumes.

Boissier et al. v. *Metayer,* 5 Mart. (O.S.), *1835 Constitution of the State of Tennessee,* Article I, Section XXVI; and Article IV, Section I.

Board of Audit of the West India Company, May 27, 1647.

Butler, Nic, Ph.D. *South Carolina's Capitation Tax on Free People of Color, 1756–1864.* Charleston County Public Library, January 28, 2022.

"Compromise of 1850." *National Archives.*

Connecticut Colonial Records, 1636-1776. Hartford, 1850-1890, 15 Volumes.

Court Petition #11382705, Charleston District/Parish, South Carolina. filing started November 6, 1827.

Deed of Emancipation for Jean Meullion. February 21, 1776, in Meullion Family Papers.

Florida Constitution, (1868). Article VIII, Sec. 9.

General Index of All Successions. Opened in the Parish of Orleans. From the Year 1805 to the Year 1846, comp. P. M. Berlin (New Orleans, 1849).

Goodson, Noreen J. and Donna Tyler Hollie. *Through the Tax Assessor's Eyes: Enslaved People, Free Blacks and Slaveholders in Early Nineteenth Century Baltimore.* Clearfield, 2017.

Greene, Evarts B. and Harrington, Virginia, D. *Records of the State of Vermont.* Montpelier, 1873.

Hening, William Waller. *The Statutes at Large; Being a Collection of All the Laws of Virginia from the First Session of the Legislature in the Year 1619.* New York: R. & W. & G. Bartow, 1823.

Hutchinson's Code of Mississippi, 1798-1848.

Inventories vol. B 1787-1793 (Charleston County). Department of Archives & History, Columbia, South Carolina.

General Land Office, National Archives.

Legislative Records. *Petition of Andrew Barland to the Senate and House of Representatives of Mississippi*, ca. 1824. Record Group 47, boxes 16-17, Mississippi Department of Archives and History.

Legislative Records. *Petition of John Holman to the South Carolina General Assembly, October 3, 1791.* South Carolina Department of Archives and History, Columbia, S.C.

_____. Memorial of Thomas Cole, Peter Basnett Mathews, and Mathew Webb to the South Carolina General Assembly, January 13, 1791, no. 181. South Carolina Department of Archives and History, Columbia, S.C.

_____. Petition of John L. Wilson [Jehu Jones's guardian] to the South Carolina General Assembly, December 6, 1823. Department of Archives and History, Columbia, S.C.

Lincoln, William, ed. *Journals of the Massachusetts Provisional Congress.* Boston, 1838.

Master of Equity, Bills of Complaint 1847, Record Number 52 (Charleston County), "Wills of Elias Collins."

MS. Deeds of Henrico County, Number 4.

1641: Massachusetts Body of Liberties. The Online Library of Liberty. Oll.libertyfund.org

Opelousas Notarial Records, Louisiana State Land Office, Baton Rouge.

Records of Charleston Probate Court, Charleston, S.C., Estates, no.

229-6, December 30, 1874.
Records of Parish Probate Court. Pointe Coupee Parish, La., *Marriage Contract*, February 26, 1835
_____. Natchitoches Parish, La., *Successions*, no. 344, September 7, 1838.
_____. Plaquemines Parish, La., *Successions*, no. 167, May 12, 1840.
_____. East Baton Rouge Parish, La., *Successions*, no. 640, August 14, 1855.
_____. West Baton Rouge Parish, La., *Successions*, no. 176, July 18, 1829.
Record of Wills vol. 22 1786-1793 (Charleston County). Department of Archives & History, Columbia, South Carolina.
U.S. Manuscript Population Census, St. Landry Parish, La., 1860.
U.S. Department of Commerce and Labor, Bureau of the Census, *First Federal Census of the United State, Taken in the Year 1790.*
U.S. Department of Commerce and Labor, Bureau of the Census, *Eight Federal Census of the United States*, Taken in 1860.
Object 2: Bounty land warrant. department.va.gov/history/100-objects/object-2-bounty-land-warrant/#:~:text=The%20amount%20of%20land%20varied,earned%20a%20bounty%20land%20warrant.
O'Callaghan, E.B. and Fernow, Berthold, eds. *Documents Relative to the Colonial History of the State of New York.* Albany: Weed, Parsons and Company, 1856-87.
Petition of L. Rowan, John Smith, et al. [concerning the Barland family], to the Mississippi General Assembly, ca. 1830. Record Group 47, box 19, Mississippi Department of Archives and History, Jackson, MS.
Records of the County Probate Court, Charleston Co., S.C. Miscellaneous Land Records, pt. 87, bks. R6-S6 (February 16, 1795), in Museum of Early Southern Decorative Arts, Winston-Salem, N.C.
_____. pt. 88, bks. T6-U6 (October 11-12, 1794), 520-22, in Museum of Early Southern Decorative Arts, Winston-Salem, N.C.
_____. Effingham Co., Ga., Deeds, bk. G (January 1, 1806).
Records of the Parish Probate Court. St. Landry Parish, La., Marriage Certificate, March 25, 1796. *Meullion Family Papers.*

Records of the Parish Probate Court. Pointe Coupe Parish, La. Successions, no. 176, April 5, 1839.

Seventh Census of the United States: Schedule I, II, IV, St. James & Goose Creek Parish, Charleston County, South Carolina.

Steiner, Lewis H. *Report of Lewis H. Steiner, inspector of the Sanitary Commission : containing a diary kept during the rebel occupation of Frederick, Md., and an account of the operations of the U.S. Sanitary Commission during the campaign in Maryland, September 1862.* New York : Anson D.F. Randolph, 1862.

United States Congress. "Transactions in the Floridas." *American State Papers: Documents, Legislative and Executive, of the Congress of the United States*. Washington, D.C.: Gales and Seaton, 1834.

Historical Papers, and Unpublished Letters

Adams, Colton. "A Peculiar Institution Within the Peculiar Institution: An Examination of Affluent Free Black Slave Owners in the Third Caste." *Journal of Interdisciplinary Undergraduate Research*. Vol. 8, Article 5.

Allured, Janet and Gentry, Judith F., "Marie Thérèse Coincoin (1742–1816): Slave, Slave Owner, and Paradox", *Louisiana Women: Their Lives and Times Series,* (University of Georgia Press, 2009)

American Colonization Society Papers. "William Kellogg to William McLain", 6 October 1852. Library of Congress.

Charles Odingsells Papers. Georgia Historical Society, Savanah, GA.

Extract of the Will of Philip Stanislas Noisette, ca. 1830, in *Noisette Family Papers*. South Carolinian Library, Columbia, SC.

Halliburton, R. Jr. *Free Black Owners of Slaves: A Reappraisal of the Woodson Thesis*. The South Carolina Historical Magazine. 76:3 (July 1975).

Ellison Family Papers. William Ellison to Henry Ellison, March 26, 1857. South Carolina Library, University of South Carolina, Columbia, South Carolina.

Jonathan C. Gibbs, Letter to Charles Barrett, Grafton, Vt., Tallahassee, Fla., (June 7, 1869). Rauner Special Collections Library, Dartmouth College, Hanover, New Hampshire;

"Last Will and Testament of Richard Holloway, October 19, 1842," *Holloway Family Papers*, College of Charleston, Charleston, S.C.

Letters Sent to Georgetown, South Carolina 1867-1868, "Wesley Markwood to Major E.L. Dean, 14 March 1867," Freemen Bureau, Record Group 105 (National Archives, Washington D.C.).

"Negros Who Owned Slaves." *Popular Science Monthly.* LXXXI (November 1912).

Rankin, David. "The Origins of Black Leadership in New Orleans during Reconstruction." *Journal of Southern History, 40 (August 1974).*

_____. "The Impact of the Civil War on the Free Colored Community of New Orleans." *Perspectives in American History,* 11 (1977-78).

Rohrs, Richard C. "State v. Edmund, a Slave (1833): Perceptions of the Legal Status of Slaves and Free Blacks in Antebellum North Carolina." *The North Carolina Historical Review,* 95:1. North Carolina Office of Archives and History, 2018.

Russell, John H., "The Free Negro in Virginia, 1619- 1865," *Johns Hopkins University Studies in Historical and Political Science,* ser. XXXI, no. 3, Baltimore, 1913.

_____. "Colored Freedmen as Slave Owners in Virginia, 1619-1865." *Journal of Negro History*, Vol. 1, The University of Chicago Press, July 1916.

Schweninger, Loren. "Prosperous Blacks in the South, 1790-1880." *The American Historical Review,* 95, no. 1.

Shlomowitz, Ralph. "Planter Combinations and Black Labour in the American South, 1865-1880." *Slavery and Abolition: A Journal of Comparative Studies.* 9 (May 1988).

"The Free Negro Farmer and Property Owner, 1830-1860." *Journal of Negro History.* 24 (October 1939).

"The Free Negro in Economic Life in Antebellum North Carolina." *North Carolina Historical Review.* 19 (July and October 1942).

The Holloway Family Papers, (College of Charleston, Charleston, SC.

Wiecek, William M. "the Statutory Law of Slavery and Race in the Thirteen Mainland Colonies of British America." *The William and Mary Quarterly.* 34 (2): 261.

Woodman, Harold. "Sequel to Slavery: The New History Views the Postbellum South." *Journal of Southern History.* 43 (November 1977).

Woodson, Carter G. "Free Negro Owners of Slaves in the United States in 1830." *Journal of Negro History.* 9:1.

Writers' Program in Virginia. *"The Negro in Virginia."* New York, 1940.

Newspapers

Charleston Courier, December 8, 1835.
Charleston Daily News, September 12, 1868
Clarion-Ledger, February 23, 1890.
Daily Dispatch, April 25, 1861.
Daily Phoenix, Sep 23, 1868, Columbia, SC.
Douglass Monthly, September 1861.
"Narrative of the Seizure and Recovery of Solomon Northrup." *New York Times*, Documenting the American South. January 20, 1853.
New Orleans *Times*, May 29, 1872
Nashville Daily Union (Nashville, Tennessee), March 21, 1863.
Pennsylvania Gazette, Oct. 15, 1730.
Richmond Daily Dispatch, April 19, 1861.
St. Louis Republic, August 16, 1891.

Online Primary Sources

"The Black Code of Louisiana, 1806." The Law Library of Louisiana. www.lasc.libguides.com/history-of-the-codes-of-Louisiana.

Sumner, Charles. *Speech of the Honorable Charles Sumner of Massachusetts, In the Senate of the United States, May 19, 1856.* Temple University Library, Digital Collections. *www.digital.library.temple.edu/digital/collection/p16002coll5/id/7881*

Davis, Dernoral, "A Contested Presence: Free Black People in Antebellum Mississippi, 1820–1860," *Mississippi History Now*, May 2000. www.mshistorynow.mdah.ms.gov/issue/a-contested-presence-free-blacks-in-antebellum-mississippi-18201860.

Diary of William Johnson Free Black Businessman Natchez, Mississippi Diary Selections from Jan. 1, 1838–Jan. 1, 1844. National Humanities Center Resource Toolbox. The Making of African American Identity: Vol. I, 1500-1865. www.nationalhumanitiescenter.org/pds/maai/identity/text4/williamjohnson

diary. pdf
Ribianszky, Nik. "Generations of Freedom: The Natchez Database of Free People of Color, 1779-1865." *Journal of Slavery and Data Preservation*, no. 1 (2023): 11- 23. https://doi.org/10.25971/9k0y-s795
The United States Senate. senate.gov/artandhistory/history/minute/Civil_War_Begins.htm.
"William T. Johnson and family papers, 1793-1951 (bulk 1830-1870)." *ArchiveGrid*. www.Researchworks.oclc.org/archivegrid/data/262551773#:~:text=William%20married%20a%20former%20slave%2C%20Ann%20Battles%20%281815%3F-1866%29%3B,1846%29%20%20Josephine%20%28born%201849%29%2C%20and%20Clarence%20%28born%201851%29.

Secondary Materials
Books
Abzug, Robert H. *Passionate Liberator. Theodore Dwight Weld and the Dilemma of Reform*. Oxford University Press, 1980.

Berlin, Ira. *Slaves Without Masters: The Free Negro in the Antebellum South*. New York, 1974.

_____. *Generations of Captivity: A History of African-American Slaves*. Harvard University Press, 2003.

Berry, Thomas S. *Western Prices before 1861*. Cambridge, Mass., 1943.

Billingsley, Andrew. *Yearning to Breathe Free: Robert Smalls of South Carolina and His Families*. The University of South Carolina Press, 2007.

Blassingame, John W. *The Slave Community: Plantation Life in the Antebellum South*. New York: Oxford University Press, 1971.

Breen, T. H. *"Myne Owne Ground": Race and Freedom on Virginia's Eastern Shore, 1640-1676*. New York: Oxford University Press, 2004.

Buchanan, Minor Ferris. *Holt Collier: His Life, His Roosevelt Hunts, and the Origin of the Teddy Bear*. Centennial Press of Mississippi, 2002.

Catterall, Helen, ed. *Judicial Cases Concerning American Slavery and the Negro*, 5 vols. Washington, D.C., 1932.

Clinton, Catherine; Gillespie, Michele. *The Devil's Lane: Sex and

Race in the Early South. Oxford, England: Oxford University Press, 1997.

Cohen, David W. and Greene, Jack P. eds. *Neither Slave Nor Free: The Freedmen of African Descent in the Slave Societies of the New World*. Baltimore, 1972.

Cohen, Irving S. and Logan, Raford. *The American Negro; Old World Background and New World Experience*. New York: Houghton and Mifflin, 1970.

Conlin, Joseph. *The American Past: A Survey of American History*. Cengage Learning, 2011.

Conway, John. *A Look at the Thirteenth and Fourteenth Amendments: Slavery Abolished, Equal Protection Established*. Enslow Publishers, 2008.

Cornelius, Janet Duitsman, *When I Can Read My Title Clear: Literacy, Slavery, and Religion in the Antebellum South*. Columbia, South Carolina: University of South Carolina Press, 1991.

Dangerfield, George. *The Awakening of American Nationalism: 1815–1828*. New York: Harper & Row, 1966.

Danver, Steven. *Popular Controversies in World History*. ABC-CLIO, 2010.

DeCanio, Stephen J. *Agriculture in the Postbellum South: The Economics of Production and Supply*. Cambridge, Mass.: MIT Press, 1974.

Finkleman, Paul, *Slavery in the Courtroom: An Annotated Bibliography of American Cases*, (Library of Congress, 1985).

Foner, Eric. *Give Me Liberty: An American History*. New York: W. W. Norton & Company, 2012.

_____. *Reconstruction: America's Unfinished Revolution, 1863–1877*. New York: Perennial Classics, 1988.

Foner, Philip S. *History of Black Americans: From Africa to the Emergence of the Cotton Kingdom*. Oxford University Press, 1980.

Franklin, John Hope. *The Free Negro in North Carolina, 1760-1860*. Chapel Hill: NC, 1943.

_____. *From Slavery to Freedom: A History of Negro Americans*. New York: Alfred A. Knopf, 1974.

Genovese, Eugene D. *Roll, Jordan, Roll: The World the Slaves Made*.

New York: Pantheon Books, 1974.
Goodwin, Doris Kearns. *Team of Rivals*. Simon & Schuster, 2005.
Greene, Lorenzo Johnston. *The Negro in Colonial New England, 1620-1776*. N.Y.: Columbia University Press, 1942.
Greene, Evarts B. and Harrington, Virginia, D. *American Populations before the Federal Census of 1790*. New York, 1932.
Gutman, Herbert. *The Black Family in Slavery and Freedom, 1750-1925*. New York: Oxford University Press, 1976.
Higgs, Robert. *Competition and Coercion: Blacks in the American Economy, 1865-1914*. Cambridge, Mass.: Cambridge University Press, 1977
Holt, Thomas. *Black over White: Negro Political Leadership in South Carolina during Reconstruction*. Urbana, Ill.: University of Illinois Press, 1977.
Horton, James Oliver and Lois E. Horton. *Hard Road to Freedom: The Story of African America*. Rutgers University Press, 2002.
Jackson, Luther Porter. *Free Negro Labor and Property Owning in Virginia, 1830-1860*. New York, 1942.
Jaynes, Gerald David. *Branches without Roots: Genesis of the Black Working Class in the American South, 1862-1882*. New York: Oxford University Press, 1986.
Johnson, Kevin Orlin. *The Lincolns in the White House*. Pangaeus Press, 2023.
Johnson, Michael P. and Roark, James L. *Black Masters: A Free Family of Color in the Old South*. New York: Norton, 1986.
Johnston, James Hugo. *Race Relations in Virginia and Miscegenation in the South, 1776-1860*. Amherst, Mass., 1970.
Jordan, Ervin. *Black Confederates and Afro-Yankees in Civil War Virginia (A Nation Divided: Studies in the Civil War Era)*. University of Virginia Press, January 29, 1995.
Jordan, Winthrop. *White over Black: American Attitudes toward the Negro, 1550-1812*. Chapel Hill, N.C., 1968.
Klein, Herbert S. *The Atlantic Slave Trade*. Cambridge University Press, 1999.
Koger, Larry. *Black slaveowners: free black slave masters in South Carolina, 1790-1860*. North Carolina: Mc Farland, 1995.
Kozlowski, Darrell. *Colonialism: Key Concepts in American*

History. Infobase Publishing, 2010.

Kranz, Rachel. *African-American Business Leaders and Entrepreneurs.* Infobase Publishing, 2004.

Landers, Jane. "Ana Gallum, Freed Slave and Property Owner." *Women in Colonial Latin America.* ed. Nora E. Jaffary and Jane E. Mangan. Indianapolis/Cambridge: Hackett Publishing Co., Inc., 2018.

Levine, Bruce. *Confederate Emancipation Southern Plans to Free and Arm Slaves during the Civil War.* Oxford University Press, 2005.

Levin, Kevin M. *Searching for Black Confederates: The Civil War's Most Persistent Myth.* University of North Carolina Press, 2019.

Levine, Lawrence W. *Black Culture and Black Consciousness: Afro-American Folk Thought from Slavery to Freedom.* New York: Oxford University Press, 1977.

Louise, E., *Elizabeth Clevland Hardcastle 1714-1808: A Lady of Color in the South Carolina Low Country.* South Carolina: Phoenix Publishers, 2001.

Madle, Jay R. *The Roots of Black Poverty: The Southern Plantation Economy after the Civil War.* Durham, N.C.: Duke University Press, 1978.

Main, Jackson Turner. *Society and Economy in Colonial Connecticut.* Princeton University Press, 1983.

McManus, Edgar J. *A History of Negro Slavery in New York.* Syracuse University Press, 1966.

_____. , *Black Bondage in the North.* Syracuse University Press, 1973.

McPherson, James M. *Battle Cry of Freedom.* New York: Oxford University Press, 1988.

Mills, Gary B. *The Forgotten People: Cane River's Creoles of Color.* Baton Rouge, La.: Louisiana State University Press, 1977.

Nicole Etcheson. *Bleeding Kansas: Contested Liberty in the Civil War Era.* University Press of Kansas, 2006.

Oakes, James. *The Ruling Race, A History of American Slaveholders.* New York: Alfred A. Knopf, 1982.

Patterson, Orlando. *Slavery and Social Death: A Comparative Study.* Cambridge, Mass., 1982.

Randall, J.G. and David Herbert Donald. *The Civil War and*

Reconstruction. Lexington: D.C. Health and Company, 1969.
Ransom, Roger L. and Sutch, Richard. *One Kind of Freedom: The Economic Consequences of Emancipation.* New York: Cambridge University Press, 1977.
Rawick, George P. *From Sundown to Sunup: The Making of the Black Community.* Westport, Conn.: Greenwood Publishing Company, 1972.
Remini, Robert V. *Daniel Webster: The Man and His Time.* W.W. Norton & Company, 1997.
Rivers, Larry E. *Slavery in Florida: territorial days to emancipation. Gainesville: University Press of Florida, 2000.*
Roll, Eugene Genovese and Roll, Jordan. *The World the Slaves Made.* New York: Oxford University Press, 1974.
Smith, Elbert B. *The Presidencies of Zachary Taylor & Millard Fillmore.* University Press of Kansas, 1988.
Soltow, Lee. *Male Inheritance Expectations in the United States in 1870.* New Haven, 1975.
Stampp, Kenneth. *The Peculiar Institution: Slavery in the Antebellum South.* New York: Vintage Books, 1956.
Sumter, Thomas S. *Stateburg and Its People.* Sumter: 1922.
Sterkx, Herbert. *The Free Negro in Antebellum Louisiana.* Rutherford, N.J., 1972.
Sutton, Robert K, *"The Wealthy Activist Who Helped Turn 'Bleeding Kansas' Free,"* Smithsonian. Archived from the original on March 27, 2019.
Sweet, Frank W. *Legal History of the Color Line: The Rise and Triumph of the One-Drop Rule.* Backintyme Publishing, 2005.
Taylor, Arnold. *Travail and Triumph: Black Life and Culture in the South since the Civil War.* Westport, Conn.: Greenwood Publishing Company, 1976.
Toppin, Edgar. *The Black American in United States History.* Allyn & Bacon, 2010.
Tushnet, Mark V., *The American Law of Slavery, 1810-1860: Considerations of Humanity and Interest,* (Princeton University Press, 1981).
Vincent, Charles. *Black Legislators in Louisiana during Reconstruction.* Baton Rouge, LA: LSU Press, 1976.
Weare, Walter. *Black Business in the New South: A Social History*

of the North Carolina Mutual Life Insurance Company. Urbana, Ill.: University of Illinois Press, 1973.

Wharton, Vernon Lane. *The Negro in Mississippi, 1860-1890.* Chapel Hill: NC, 1947.

White, Deborah Gray. *Freedom on My Mind: A History of African Americans.* New York Bedford/St. Martin's, 2013.

Whitten, David O. *Andrew Durnford: A Black Sugar Planter in Antebellum Louisiana.* Natchitoches, La.: Northwestern State University Press, 1981.

Wiener, Jonathan. *Social Origins of the New South: Alabama, 1860-1885.* Baton Rouge, La.: LSU Press, 1978.

Wikramanayake, Marina. *A World in Shadow: The Free Black in Antebellum South Carolina.* Columbia, SC: University of South Carolina Press, 1973.

Wilentz, Sean. *The Politicians & the Egalitarians: The Hidden History of American Politics.* New York: W.W. Norton & Company, 2004.

Winch, Julie. *A Gentleman of Color: The Life of James Forten.* New York: Oxford University Press, 2002.

Wood, Betty. *Slavery in Colonial America, 1619-1776.* Rowman & Littlefield Publishers, 2005.

Websites

"African American Gospel," *The Library of Congress,* www.loc.gov/collections/songs-of-america/articles-and-essays/musical-styles/ritual-and-worship/african-american-gospel

Austin, Andre. "The Dirty South: Blacks Owned Blacks too in the USA." *Academia.* www.academia.edu/33021954/THE_DIRTY_SOUTH_Blacks_owned_Blacks_too_in_the_USA

Bartlett, Sarah. "Brown Fellowship Society (1790-1945)." *Black Past* (14 September 2010). www.blackpast.org/african-american-history/brown-fellowship-society-1790-1945/

"Black Slave Owners." Encyclopedia.com.

"The Blurred Racial Lines of Famous Families." www.pbs.org/wgbh/pages/frontline/shows/secret/famous/pendarvis.html

Brooks, Rebecca Beatrice. "Slavery in Massachusetts." *History of Massachusetts Blog.* www.historyofmassachusetts.org/slavery-in-massachusetts/

Dworkin, Shari L., "Race, Sexuality, and the 'One Drop Rule': More Thoughts about Interracial Couples and Marriage." *The Society Pages*. Thesocietypages.org

"Ellison Family Graveyard" and "William Ellison", photos and transcriptions, bio of William Ellison, 2009, Rootsweb, www.sites.rootsweb.com/~scsumter/cemeteries/ ellison.html

Fate, Michael. "Jehu Jones, Sr., 1769-1833," *Black Past*. www.blackpast.org/african-american-history/jones-jehu-sr-1769-1833/

Finkleman, Paul, ed. *Encyclopedia of African American History, 1619–1895: From the Colonial Period to the Age of Frederick Douglass*. Oxford University Press, 2006. www.oxfordreference.com

Gallagher, Gary, "Black Confederate Movement 'Demented'," *YouTube*.

Gates, Henry Louis. "Did Black People Own Slaves?" *The Root Magazine,* March 4, 2023. www.africanamerica.org/topic/did-black-people-own-slaves

Gruber, Kate Egner. "Slavery in Colonial America." *The American Battlefield Trust*. www.battlefields.org/learn/articles/slavery-colonial-america

Hayes, Amy. "Antebellum South: What Was the Identity of the Old South?". *thecollector.com*. September 15, 2022.

Heinegg, Paul. "Freedom in the Archives: Free African Americans in Colonial America." *Common Place, the Journal of Early American Life*, Issue 5 (October, 2004). www.commonplace.online/article/ freedom-in-the-archives/

Holloway, Joseph. "Black Slaveowners." *The Slave Rebellion Website*. SlaveRebellion.org.

"In Washington D.C., the second South Carolina senator, James Henry Hammond, resigns his seat," *House Divided, The Civil War Research Engine at Dickenson College,* www.hd.housedivided.dickinson.edu/node/34503

Indentured Servants In The U.S., pbs.org.

"Jehu Jones", *South Carolina Encyclopedia*. www.scencyclopedia.org/sce/entries/jehu-jones/.

Jackson, Joelle. "CSA 1st Louisiana Native Guard (1861-1862)." *BlackPast.org, June 23, 2011*. www.blackpast.org/african-american-history/1st-louisiana-native-guard-csa-1861-1862/

Kissner, James. *"Who is Justus Angel?"* Home.org.h-o-m-e.org/who-is-justus-angel/

"Massachusetts Constitution and the Abolition of Slavery," Official Website of the Commonwealth of Massachusetts. www.Mass.gov.

Mathews, Lipton, "A Brief History of Nonwhite Slave Owners in America," *MISES.ORG,* (November 11, 2020). www.mises.org/mises-wire/brief-history-nonwhite-slave-owners-america

Niven, Steven J. A. "Cane River Tale: From Slave to Free Woman to Slave Owner". *The Root,* (March 10, 2015). www.theroot.com/a-cane-river-tale-from-slave-to-free-woman-to-slave-ow-1790859045

Pender, Alicia. "Catholics who care about US Black history must read 'Four Hundred Souls'." *National Catholic Reporter.* www.ncronline.org/authors/alicia-pender-stanley

Reeves, John. "Unraveling Ulysses S. Grant's Complex Relationship With Slavery." *Smithsonian Magazine* (December 5, 2023), www.smithsonianmag.com/history/unraveling-ulysses-s-grants-complex-relationship-with-slavery-180983360/

Ribianszky, Nik. "Ann Battles Johnson," *People's of the Historical Slave Trade.* visited on July 6, 2025. www.enslaved.org/fullStory/16-23-126896/

Seligman, Edwin R. A., ed. *Encyclopaedia of the Social Sciences.* 15 vols., transcribed by Andrew Chrucky, March 23, 2004. New York: The Macmillan Company, 1930-1935. www.ditext.com/moral/slavery.html

"Slave Codes." *Britannica.* www.britannica.com/topic/slave-code

"Stepping," *Encyclopedia Brittanica,* www.britannica.com/art/stepping

Stauffer, John. "Yes, There Were Black Confederates. Here's Why," *The Root Magazine* (January 20, 2015). www.theroot.com/yes-there-were-black-confederates-here-s-why-1790858546

"The Antebellum South In America, a story." *aaregistry.org.*

The End of Colonial Dominion, https://www.floridamuseum.ufl.edu/staugustine/timeline/the-end-of-colonial-dominion/

"United States Slavery Laws and Restrictions." *Pure History.* November 18, 2011. www.purehistory.org/united-states-slavery-laws-and-restrictions/.

The A.R.T. of Human Rights—a collaboration between the American Repertory Theater & Carr Center for Human Rights Policy at Harvard University—presents the conversation *Fighting for Freedom: The Civil War and Its Legacies* livestreaming on the global, commons-based peer produced HowlRound TV network at howlround.tv, Sunday, February 8, 2015.

Williams, Scott K. *Black Confederates in the Civil War.* www.scribd.com/document/157772219/Black-Confederates.

Wolfe, Brendan. "Free Blacks in Colonial Virginia." *In Encyclopedia Virginia.* https://encyclopediavirginia.org/entries/free-blacks-in-colonial-virginia.

Newspapers, Magazines, Historical Society Papers, Thesis Papers, and National Park Service Pamphelets

"African Burial Ground Proves Northern Slavery," *The City Sun* (Feb. 24, 1993).

Austin, Beth. *1619: Virginia's First Africans (Report).* Hampton History Museum (December 2019).

Botzer, Tally, *"Myths and Misunderstandings: Slavery in the United States."* The American Civil War Museum (August 15, 2017). https://acwm.org/blog/myths-and-misunderstandings-slavery-united-states/

Brophy, Alfred L. "The Nat Turner Trials", *North Carolina Law Review* (June 2013). volume 91: 1817–80.

Bryant, Christopher J. "Without Representation, No Taxation: Free Blacks, Taxes, and Tax Exemptions Between the Revolutionary and Civil Wars." *Michigan Journal of Race and Law*, 91 (2015).

Bush, Jonathan A. "Free to Enslave: The Foundations of Colonial American Slave Law." *Yale Journal of Law & the Humanities*, Vol. 5: 417, (1993).

Deetz, Kelley Fanto. *"400 years ago, enslaved Africans first arrived in Virginia." National Geographic. Archived from the original on August 13, 2019.*

Degler, Carl N. "Remaking American History, " *Journal of American History.* LXVII, 1980-81.

"Documenting a Slave's Birth, Parentage, and Origins (Marie Thérèse Coincoin, 1742–1816): A Test of "Oral History".

National Genealogical Society Quarterly, 96: 245–266.
Federal Writers' Project. *Virginia: A Guide to the Old Dominion.* US History Publishers, 1954.
Finley, Ben. "Virginia marks pivotal moment when African slaves arrived". *Associated Press* (August 22, 2019).
Fitchett, E. Horace. "The Traditions of the Free Negro in Charleston, South Carolina." *Journal of Negro History*, 25:2 (April 1940).
_____. "The Origin and Growth of the Free Negro Population of Charleston, South Carolina." *Journal of Negro History, 26* (October 1941).
_____. "The Negro in Charleston, South Carolina." PH.D. dissertation, University of Chicago, 1950.
Foner, Laura. "The Free People of Color in Louisiana and St. Domingue: A Comparative Portrait of Two Three-Caste Slave Societies." *Journal of Social History,* 3 (Summer 1970).
Garrett, Crystal. "Family Ties: Those Wild and Crazy Stanlys." *Sun Journal* (New Bern, North Carolina, March 9, 2015).
Hammond, John Craig. "President, Planter, Politician: James Monroe, the Missouri Crisis, and the Politics of Slavery," *Journal of American History,* March 2019.
Harris, Jr., Robert L. "Charleston's Free Afro-American Elite: The Brown Fellowship Society and the Humane Brotherhood." *The South Carolina Historical Magazine*. Vol. 82, No. 4 (Oct., 1981).
Holcomb, Brent E., ed. "1786 Tax Returns," *South Carolina Magazine of Ancestral Research*, 9 (Spring 1981).
Homes, Jack D. L. "The Roles of Blacks in Spanish Alabama: The Mobile District, 1780-1813." *Alabama Historical Quarterly, 37* (Spring 1975)
Landers, Jane. "Founding Mothers: Female Rebels in Colonial Hew Granada and Spanish Florida." *Journal of African American History* 98, no. 1 (2013).
Levin, Kevin. "The Myth of the Black Confederate Soldier". *The Daily Beast,* (August 8, 2015).
Marshall, Josh. "In Search of the Black Confederate Unicorn". *Talking Points Memo,* (January 2, 2018).
Morgan, Philip D. "Black Life in Eighteenth-Century Charleston." *Perspectives in American History*, n.s., 1, 1984.
O'Neil Spady, James. "Power and Confession: On the Credibility of

the Earliest Reports of the Denmark Vesey Slave Conspiracy." *William and Mary Quarterly*, (April 2011) 68 (2): 287–304.

Poole, W. Scott, "Religion, gender, and the lost cause in South Carolina's 1876 governor's race: 'Hampton or Hell!'," *Journal of Southern History* 68.3 (2002): 573-598.

Rodriguez, Junius. *Slavery in the United States: A Social, Political, and Historical Encyclopedia, Volume 2*. ABC-CLIO, 2007.

Sainsbury, W. Noel, ed. "America and West Indies: September 1672". *Calendar of State Papers Colonial, America and West Indies: Volume 7, 1669-1674*. London: Her Majesty's Stationary Office, 1889. www.british-history.ac.uk/cal-state-papers/ colonial/ america-west-indies/ vol7/pp404-417

Schweninger, Loren. "Prosperous Blacks in the South, 1790-1880." *American Historical Review*. 95:3 (Feb. 1990).

_____. "John Carruthers Stanly and the Anomaly of Black Slaveholding," *The North Carolina Historical Review (April 1990)*.

Sharfstein, Daniel J. "Crossing the Color Line: Racial Migration and the One-Drop Rule, 1600-1860." *Minnesota Law Review*, 2007.

Shoenbaum, Eric, *"A Precious Balance: The Free Blacks of Natchez,"* 3-7, an unpublished paper.

Smith, Henry A. M. "Goose Creek." *South Carolina Historical & Genealogical Magazine*, vol. 23, (1928).

Sullivan, Elizabeth. "Blacks' Journey to Cleveland Laid Groundwork for Success." *Cleveland.com*, (January 12, 2019).

Thomas, David. "The Free Negro in Florida before 1865." *South Atlantic Review*, 10 (October 1911).

Spraggins, Tinsley L., "The History of the Negro in Business prior to 1860," M.A. thesis, Howard University, 1935.

Van Cleave, Timothy. "The Barber of Natchez". *National Park Service*.

Walker, Juliet. *The History of Black Business in America: Capitalism, Race, Entrepreneurship, Volume 1*. University of North Carolina Press, 2009.

Washington Post, October 19, 2010.

Washington Post, January 5, 2021.

Waxman, Olivia B. "Where the Landing of the First Africans in

English North America Really Fits in the History of Slavery." *Time.* August 20, 2019.

Wilson, Calvin D. "Black Masters, A Side-Light on Slavery," *The North American Review,* Vol. 181, No. 588 (November 1905).

Wood, Betty; et al. "Slavery in Colonial Georgia." *New Georgia Encyclopedia,* (September 19, 2002).

Wright, Robert E. "Bank Ownership and Lending Patterns in New York and Pennsylvania, 1781-1831." *The Business History Review,* vol. 73, no. 1, 1999.

Zielinski, Adam E. "James Forten, Revolutionary: Forgotten No More." *Journal of the American Revolution.* 23 June 2023.

Index

A

Adams, Colton, 14, 15, 124, 130, 148, 189
Alabama, 20, 23, 26, 77, 151
American Revolutionary War, 5, 33, 82
An Act to Prevent Disorder in the Night, 46
Angel, Justus, 107
Anti-Slavery Movement, 108
Abolitionism, 152
Arkansas, 20, 22, 134

B

Battles, Ann, 111, 189
Bailey, Anne, 98, 102
Barber of Natchez, 110, **See also William Johnson**
Barland, John, 146
Black slaveholders, vi, ix, 4, 9, 11, 15, 16, 18, 19, 20, 22, 23, 24, 25, 26, 58, 59, 61, 64, 65, 66, 68, 70, 71, 75, 78, 80, 81, 82, 90, 91, 93, 95, 98, 99, 100, 101, 102, 103, 104, 105, 108, 109, 110, 115, 116, 117, 120, 121, 122, 124, 125, 126, 127, 128, 135, 137, 138, 139, 140, 142, 146, 152, 154, 158, 172, 183, 184, 191, 196, 197
Body of Liberties, 45

C

Carolinas, 20, 57, 71, 96, 98, 103, 104, 105, 107, 108
Casor, John, 50, 51
Castilian Code of Law, 29
Catholic Church, 30
Census of 1850, 16
Charleston, South Carolina, 12, 18, 61, 62, 71, 72, 73, 74, 75, 77, 88, 91, 92, 105, 106, 118, 119, 121, 133, 134, 136, 146, 167, 176
Civil War, v, viii, ix, 10, 15, 26, 43, 88, 90, 94, 112, 121, 152, 153, 162, 188, 190
Cobb, Thomas R.R., 28
Coincoin, 13, 67, 68
Collier, Holt, 183, 184

Collins, Elias, 77, 116
Collins, Robert Micheal, 180, 185, 186
Committee of Thirteen, 166
Compromise of 1850, 162, 164
Confederacy, 20, 90, 170, 171, 172, 174, 186
Connecticut, 19, 34, 38, 41, 42, 43, 44
Creole, 70, 77, 82, 83, 155, 172

D
Deas, Ann, 71, 105, 106, 133
Denmark Vesey Conspiracy, 74
Douglas, Frederick, 157, 160, 168
Dragon, Marianne Celeste, 82
Dunford, Andrew, 15, 84, 85, 91
Dubuclet, Antoine, 8, 18, 146
Duke of York, 41

E
Ellison, William, 7, 15, 77, 88, 89, 97, 100, 116, 118, 122, 123, 124, 138, 158
Emancipation Proclamation, 2, 152
Ephesians VI:5-7 (KJV), 157
Epistle to the Colossians, 157

F
1st Louisiana Native Guard, 172
Florida, 12, 20, 30, 33, 48, 63, 74, 77, 106
Foner, Eric, 171, 177
Franklin, Benjamin, 43
Franklin, John Hope, 6, 14, 16, 17, 115
Free Black slaveholders, *See Black Slaveholders*
Free People of Color, 1, 10, 15, 76, 77, 84, 89, 101, 112, 132
Free Person of Color, *See Free People of Color*
Free to Enslave, The Foundation of Colonial American Slave Law, 140
Free Women of Color, 76, *See also Free People of Color*
French Code Noir, 30

G

Galatians 3:28 (KJV), 157, 158
Gallum, Ana, 62
Genesis IX:18-27 (KJV), 156
Georgia, 20, 23, 26, 48, 77, 89, 136
Grant, Ulysses S., 71
Greeley, Horace, 168, 176
Griffin, Charles, 148, 149

H

Halliburton Jr, R., 14
Hancock, John, 43
Harris, John F., 183
Holman, Jr, John, 77, 135, 136, 137
Holloway, Joseph, 8

I

indentured servants, 9, 19, 25, 28, 31, 33, 36, 40, 47, 49, 51, 60, 100

J

Jamestown, 30
Johnson, Anthony, 19, 48, 49, 50, 51, 100
Johnson, William, 73, 110, 112, 113, 114, 130, 131, 189
Jones, Abigail, 73, 74, 105
Jones Hotel, 73, 75, 106
Jones, Sr., Jehu, 72, 74, 105, 106

K

Kansas-Negraska Act, 164
King James Bible, 156
Koger, Larry, 6, 12, 15, 18

L

Lee, Elizabeth Seymore, 106, 133
Levin, Kevin, 171, 177
Lincoln, Abraham, 2, 43, 71

Louisiana, 5, 8, 15, 18, 20, 23, 30, 58, 67, 68, 75, 76, 77, 79, 82, 83, 84, 85, 91, 93, 99, 116, 132, 134, 146, 172

M
Main, Jackson Turner, 44
Mansion House Hotel, 71, 75, 106
manumission, 3, 9, 11, 12, 13, 22, 24, 55, 56, 57, 60, 78, 80, 92, 100, 101, 113
Manus, Edgar, 35
Maryland, 11, 19, 20, 22, 25, 32, 38, 47, 53, 91, 93, 96, 97, 101, 102, 103, 109, 140, 174
Massachusetts, 31, 33, 34, 36, 37, 38, 42, 43, 44, 45, 46, 54, 141
Meachum, John Barry, 93
Melrose Plantation, 68
Metoyer, Marie Thérèse, 67, *See also* **Coincoin**
Mexican War, 163
Mississippi, 20, 23, 26, 33, 77, 93, 98, 110, 112, 113, 130, 146, 148
Missouri Compromise (or Compromise of 1820), 162
mulatto, 15, 17, 19, 61, 73, 75, 83, 85, 112, 136, 146

N
Natchez, Mississippi, 110, 111, 112, 114, 130, 131, 146, 148, 190
Negro, 1, 6, 7, 10, 13, 14, 16, 17, 19, 21, 28, 44, 46, 49, 50, 53, 55, 56, 60, 61, 93, 94, 110, 115, 119, 140, 162
Nell, William C., 127
New England colonies, 34
New Jersey, 38, 46
New Netherland, 35, 38, 39, 40, 41
New Orleans, Louisiana, 3, 15, 17, 67, 82, 83, 84, 91, 112, 134, 135, 172, 189
New York, 38, 39, 41, 42, 43, 46, 74, 106, 127, 176
North Carolina, 8, 11, 14, 17, 23, 47, 53, 58, 86, 87, 117
North Carolina v. Edmund, a slave, 11

O
Odingsells, Anthony, 77
Olmstead, Fredrick Law, 8

one-drop rule, 55

P
peculiar institution, 1, 5, 150
Pendarvis Family, 61, 62, 87, 88
Pendarvis, Joseph, 61, 87
Pennsylvania, 35, 38, 42, 43, 45
Peter Stuyvesant, 41
pigmentocracy, 16
placage, 75
Plessy v. Ferguson, 186
Prosperous Blacks in the South, 134
Punch, John, 51

R
Raper, William, 133
Reconstruction, 6, 115, 152, 183
Rhode Island, 34, 38, 41, 42, 43, 44, 140
Russell, John H., 29
Russworm, John, 127

S
Schweninger, Loren, 115, 134
1625 Census, 31
South Carolina, 6, 12, 15, 18, 20, 23, 45, 47, 54, 57, 58, 61, 62, 72, 73, 74, 75, 77, 88, 89, 91, 92, 93, 105, 106, 107, 116, 118, 133, 134, 136, 137, 140, 141, 146
Stanly, John Carruthers, 86
Stiener, Lewis H., 169

T
Tariff Bill, 166
Tennessee, 20, 23
Tennessee Constitution of 1835, 23
Texas, 20
The Act of 1820, 90
The Brown Fellowship Society, 73, 119
The Invention of Free Labor, 43

The Negro in Colonial New England, 44
The Virginia Muster, 49
13th Amendment, 166
Turner, Nat, 25, 155

U
U.S. Census of 1860, 17, 18

V
Virginia, 11, 13, 19, 20, 21, 25, 30, 31, 32, 45, 47, 49, 50, 51, 53, 54, 55, 56, 57, 58, 60, 85, 91, 92, 93, 96, 97, 98, 99, 100, 101, 108, 109, 112, 138, 158, 174, 175
Virginia Slave Codes, 54

W
Washington, Booker T., 2, 162
West India Company, 38, 39, 40
White Lion, 31
Wilson, Calvin, 7
Woodson, Carter G., 1, 6, 7, 8, 13, 14, 79, 92, 93, 115, 134, 203

About the Author

Larry Allen McCluney, Jr. is the son of the late Larry Allen McCluney, Sr., and Mary Kathyren McCluney. He has been a member of the Sons of Confederate Veterans for over twenty-nine years and was the organization's Seventy-Sixth Commander-in-Chief (2020- 2022); a past Chairman of the Combined Boards of the nonprofit that oversees Beauvoir, the Last Home of President Jefferson Davis; a former member of the Golden Triangle Civil War Roundtable; and a Civil War Reenactor/Living historian.

McCluney received his master's and bachelor's degrees in history from Mississippi State University (1993 and 1988 respectively) and has taught history on the high school level in the public school system for 31 years and has been an instructor of history at Mississippi Delta Community College for twenty-two years. He was the 2014 US History Teacher for the state of Mississippi chosen by the Daughters of the American Revolution and has won numerous awards from the

United Daughters of the Confederacy; the Sons of Confederate Veterans; and has been placed on the Who's Who of America's Top Teachers on numerous occasions. He previously published The *Yazoo Pass Expedition: A Union Thrust into the Delta* (2017), *On to Vicksburg! The North Mississippi Central Railroad Campaign* (2019), *In General Beauregard's Defense* (2022), and *Gunboats, Rivers, Bayous, and Railroads* (2024). All four books won the General William D. McCain Publication award from the Mississippi Division, Sons of Confederate Veterans. Larry currently lives in Greenwood, Mississippi with his wife of 32 years, Julia Annette.

The Paradox of Freedom

www.ingramcontent.com/pod-product-compliance
Lightning Source LLC
Chambersburg PA
CBHW070128080526
44586CB00015B/1599